"Dr. Alice Bar Nes' book, Psychoanalysis, Mysticism and the Problem of Epistemology: Defining the Indefinable, is an impressive work that brings the reader into an area of psychoanalytic thinking that has been much-maligned over the years - the question of mysticism. The author offers an integrative perspective that recognizes 'the mystical at the heart of the analytic project.' Dr. Bar Nes' book is a tour de force that reveals an underlying mystical element in psychoanalysis that is implicit in Freud's early thinking, Ferenczi's thoughts about mysticism, Winnicott's transitional space, Bion's notion of a 'messianic idea,' and the work of other well-known analysts. These concepts are impressively woven together and subsequently integrated with the work of philosophers, especially the contributions of William James and Martin Buber. This book is recommended for students and practitioners of psychoanalysis interested in the broader scope of psychoanalytic thinking."

Lawrence J Brown, PhD, *is the author of* Intersubjective Processes and the Unconscious: Freudian, Kleinian and Bionian Perspectives *and* Transformational Processes in Clinical Psychoanalysis: Dreaming, Emotions and the Present Moment

"O, what a powerful book! Alice Bar Nes takes the reader on a journey to the unexplainable domains of patient-therapis tinteractions. Her book sheds new light on the mystical ingredients of psychoanalysis, the possibilities of which clinicians are only just beginning to appreciate. William James, Wilfred Bion, Donald Winnicott, Christopher Bollas, and Michael Eigen, together with thinkers such as Saint-Exupery and Martin Buber, serve as Bar Nes' fellow guides along the magical, and, at times, sacred path of the psychoanalytic therapeutic relationship. Masterfully combining the inexpressible with the practical, the enigmatic with the down-to-earth, Bar Nes invites us to explore new intrapsychic and intersubjective territories; to explore her own faith journey; and to re-discover the area of faith in ourselves."

Amit Fachler, PhD, *Clinical Psychologist and author of* Too Much in the Son: Fatherless Fathers' Accounts of Love, Guilt, and Reparation *(Hebrew)*

"This book is a work of a true lover of psychoanalytic theories, with exquisite knowledge, depth and wisdom – on faith in the power of the human contact to act as the clinical core.

The meeting of psychoanalysis and mysticism, through the vibrating presence of Alice Bar-Nes, is structured as 'the meaning of being human', as she puts it; in her person and writing, psychoanalytic foci that touch upon the mystical - transform into emotionally-felt and communicated experiences.

The book is a serious contribution and guide for those engaged in psychoanalytic treatment on how to navigate in the realm of the spiritual and theoretical via the subjective, the intersubjective and the practical, and enlightenment for those interested in mysticism."

Nitza Yarom, PhD, *Clinical psychologist and psychoanalyst; the author of* Psychic Threats and Somatic Shelters and Matrix of Hysteria

"Alice Bar Nes' book is a welcome contribution to understanding and broadening the deep connection between mysticism and psychoanalysis. She penetrates, analyzes and connects philosophical thinking and clinical understanding in a highly original way.

I was especially impressed by her extraordinary ability to present indefinable concepts in a crystal clear way and to engage the reader in the flow of her text. Her proposed definition of mysticism is elegant, clear and succeeds in shedding new light on the contribution of influential writers in the psychoanalytic field, through that unique prism. Most significantly, she succeeds in making the mystical a concept that resonates with the experiences of every human being."

Ilana Laor, PhD, *Clinical psychologist and group analyst; head of the Israeli chapter of the IARPP*

Psychoanalysis, Mysticism and the Problem of Epistemology

This book presents key psychoanalytic theories from a fresh perspective: that of the mystical element.

The author explores the depth-structure of central assumptions in psychoanalytic theory to uncover the mystical core of conventional analytic thinking. Exploring authors from Freud and Ferenczi, through Bion and Winnicott, to contemporary voices such as Ogden, Bollas and Eigen, the book shows that psychoanalysis has always operated on the assumption of psychic overlap, a "soul-to-soul" contact, between patient and analyst. Surprisingly, the book shows how this "magical" facet goes hand in hand with a pragmatic worldview that explores the epistemological complexities of psychoanalysis in search of a way to join the subjective, even the mystical, with the practical aim of serving as a validated mental health discipline. This is accomplished through an interdisciplinary and intertextual encounter between psychoanalysis and the innovative pairing of William James' pragmatic philosophy and Martin Buber's dialogic thought. The author's paradoxical stance surrounding the nature and role of psychoanalysis and its mystical facet resonate the great challenge embedded in Winnicott's insistence on tolerating paradox and Bion's demand to respect all parts of the (psychoanalytic) truth, in this case, the practical and mundane alongside the mystical and magical.

The book's broad, interdisciplinary outlook will captivate both psychoanalysts and psychoanalytic therapists as well as scholars of philosophy.

Alice Bar Nes, Ph.D., is a clinical psychologist with a private practice; faculty member and a supervisor at the Temurot school of psychotherapy and group supervisor at the continuing medical education psychiatry program at Tel Aviv University's Sackler Faculty of Medicine.

Psyche and Soul: Psychoanalysis, Spirituality and Religion In Dialogue Book Series

Jill Salberg & Melanie Suchet
Series Editors

The *Psyche and Soul: Psychoanalysis, Spirituality and Religion in Dialogue* series explores the intersection of psychoanalysis, spirituality and religion. By promoting dialogue, this series provides a platform for the vast and expanding interconnections, mutual influences and points of divergence amongst these disciplines. Extending beyond western religions of Judaism, Christianity and Islam, the series includes Eastern religions, contemplative studies, mysticism and philosophy. By bridging gaps, opening the vistas and responding to increasing societal yearnings for more spirituality in psychoanalysis, *Psyche and Soul* aims to cross these disciplines, fostering a more fluid interpenetration of ideas.

For a full list of titles in this series, please visit the Routledge website: https://www.routledge.com/Psyche-and-Soul/book-series/PSYSOUL

Psychoanalysis, Mysticism and the Problem of Epistemology

Defining the Indefinable

Alice Bar Nes

Routledge
Taylor & Francis Group

LONDON AND NEW YORK

First published 2022
by Routledge
2 Park Square, Milton Park, Abingdon, Oxon OX14 4RN

and by Routledge
605 Third Avenue, New York, NY 10158

Routledge is an imprint of the Taylor & Francis Group, an informa business

British Library Cataloguing-in-Publication Data
A catalogue record for this book is available from the British Library

Library of Congress Cataloging-in-Publication Data
Names: Bar Nes, Alice, 1978- author.
Title: Psychoanalysis, mysticism and the problem of epistemology : defining
the indefinable / Alice Bar Nes.
Description: Abingdon, Oxon ; New York, NY : Routledge, 2022. |
Includes bibliographical references and index.
Identifiers: LCCN 2021011969 (print) | LCCN 2021011970 (ebook) |
ISBN 9781032061184 (hardback) | ISBN 9781032056852 (paperback) |
ISBN 9781003200796 (ebook)
Subjects: LCSH: Psychoanalysis and religion. | Mysticism--Psychology.
Classification: LCC BF175.4.R44 B355 2022 (print) | LCC BF175.4.R44
(ebook) | DDC 150.19/5--dc23
LC record available at https://lccn.loc.gov/2021011969
LC ebook record available at https://lccn.loc.gov/2021011970

ISBN: 978-1-032-06118-4 (hbk)
ISBN: 978-1-032-05685-2 (pbk)
ISBN: 978-1-003-20079-6 (ebk)

DOI: 10.4324/9781003200796

Typeset in Times New Roman
by MPS Limited, Dehradun

To my grandmother, Risa Resnick.

Contents

This book is based on a doctoral dissertation submitted to The Program for Hermeneutics and Cultural Studies at Bar Ilan University, under the supervision of Prof. Avi Sagi and Dr. Dorit Lemberger.

Alice Bar Nes, Ph.D., is a clinical psychologist with a private practice. She is a faculty member and a supervisor at the Temurot school of psychotherapy and group supervisor at the continuing medical education psychiatry program at Tel Aviv University's Sackler Faculty of Medicine. She has published various papers in both journals and edited volumes. These include: "Sense and Sensibility: The psychoanalytic mystic and the interpretive word" (in Feeling the Elephant: The Blind Spots of Psycho-analytic Psychotherapists [Hebrew]) and "Thinking about the Psycho-analytic Encounter: Theory and psychoanalytic mysticism" (in The soul Beetle: Interdisciplinary Perspectives in Psychanalysis [Hebrew]).
Orcid id: https://orcid.org/0000-0002-5549-7486

Acknowledgments

I am very grateful to the editors of the "Psyche and Soul" series, Dr. Melanie Suchet and Dr. Jill Salberg, for their professionalism and kindness, for believing in this book, for offering good advice, and showing me the path to turn a doctoral thesis into a book.

I am also grateful

To Amir Atsmon, who helped revise and prepare the manuscript, whose rich knowledge of the English language, dedication, and meticulous and erudite work helped the text become a better version of itself.

To Dr. Dorit Lemberger, a true teacher, an inspiration and a guide, who supervised the doctoral thesis on which this book is based.

To Dr. Ilan Berant, for providing the kind of mentoring and support I needed to make this book happen; for reading, giving good advice, directing me towards more thoughts, more materials, and my own strength. Thank you for your faith in me.

To my dear friend, Asaf Ravitz, for giving me courage and for helping me, both with his thoughts about writing and with his deep friendship.

To my dear friend, Dr. Amit Fachler, who was the first to give my written voice a place to be heard, for being an inspiration, a source of support, and a true friend.

To Edith Barak Melamed, for kindly agreeing to read and comment on chapter 8 with her expert knowledge of the middle school.

To Avner Gershon, for being with me and guiding me through the ineffable and the painful.

Finally, to my one-of-a-kind husband, who has always shown me his love by encouraging my growth – even in difficult times – for always being there.

Introduction

I love psychoanalytic texts. For me, they make sense of and give meaning to being human, to having a psyche. I can barely imagine handling my own without them. When I was studying and later interning in clinical psychology, as I read more and more theoreticians and tried to assimilate their ideas, it began to dawn on me that there was a common, unspoken thread, that ran through many theories, however different. They all assumed some kind of connection between therapist and patient that was unexplainable. It was not only about what was said or about what was left unsaid but conveyed through nonverbal means such as facial expressions, posture, tone of voice, or silence. I felt that many concepts, like projective identification, assumed some kind of "telepathic" contact; in this case, of a primitive, possessive, unintentional kind. But no author I had read back then talked about it explicitly. So I kept my ideas to myself, not wanting to be the "weird" one. Still, I kept wondering, whenever I encountered this hidden assumption in the way supervisors spoke about using countertransference to understand the patient, in the way I used my own intuition in the consulting room, in reports by colleagues of "weird" sensations that turned out to be intimately connected to the transference and, of course, in analytic texts. Kohut's notion of empathy, Ogden's analytic third, Winnicott's theory … Was I the only one seeing this?

Then, during the third year of my internship, I happened to come across a folder of papers left on the desk of the room I was sharing, by one of the supervising psychologists at my clinic. Among these papers was Ghent's "Masochism, Submission and Surrender:

DOI: 10.4324/9781003200796-101

Masochism as perversion of Surrender." The title seemed interesting to me; a "juicy" subject. Little did I know that it was about to change my life in a much deeper way. Upon reading it, I was excited and moved in a way that no other professional text had ever made me feel before. I could only compare it to the feeling of being a teenager and reading *Jonathan Livingston Seagull*, which seemed – at least at the time – like a revelation: something completely new and profoundly important in my young life.

Ghent's texts made me feel that something had finally happened: I was not alone. Someone has seen the deep connection between "spiritual" experiences and core psychoanalytic concerns (like the development of object-relations) and related it to clinical issues in an innovative, beautifully written way. This was the path for me, the road I wanted to tread, though I still did not know how. In that same folder, I later found Eigen's paper, "The Area of Faith in Winnicott, Lacan and Bion," and fell deeply in love with this author. Now I knew that I was *certainly* not alone. Eigen brought to light that hidden thread of meaning in three leading theoreticians. He showed that it was there, only waiting for a reader with a certain sensitivity. But for me, it was not just about these three authors and Eigen was not the only "psychoanalytic mystic." I wanted to find a way to uncover the mystical undercurrent of psychoanalysis as a whole.

However, I also had another master to serve alongside what I later came to understand as my fascination with the magical facet of life, namely, my adoration for the scientific or, more accurately, for reason. I wanted to talk about mysticism in a way that would make sense to nonmystics, to unveil its omnipresence in human relations while showing that such explorations did not mean one had to give up systematic examination and academic discourse.

It was the "Psychoanalysis and Hermeneutics" PhD program at Bar Ilan University that gave me the how. It encouraged philosophical readings of psychoanalysis and expected students to produce original ways to integrate the two disciplines. The tenuous position of psychoanalysis in the field of knowledge – questions such as what we know and how we know it, whether psychoanalysis was a science or a hermeneutic discipline – was thoroughly discussed, especially in Dr. Aner Govrin's course. Still, I felt that some "third way" was being overlooked. Being in psychotherapy is certainly not like being in a chemistry lab, but it is not like reading a poem, either. I felt that psychoanalysis was different from both the empirical sciences and the humanities, though it shared certain qualities with both.

Quite unexpectedly, these seemingly unrelated, even opposite concerns – uncovering the mystical element in psychoanalysis while maintaining some "scientific" rigor – came together with yet another "meeting" with a text, that of philosopher William James. I was already familiar with James' *The Varieties of Religious Experience.* Having read it many years ago, it not only provided me with joy and information but it also caused some internal "click," by presenting a way to talk about religion and mysticism in an inquisitive and academic, yet deeply interested, respectful, and nonreductionistic manner. James treated religion as a phenomenon in its own right, but not necessarily on its own terms. Meeting his texts again, in Dr. Dorit Lemberger's course on pragmatism, made me realize that this approach to religion can be generalized and applied to other fields and that *there was* a place where scientific culture and spirituality can truly meet.

James' theory suggested a remarkably common-sensical, yet deep and integrative worldview explaining how to rationally discuss and pragmatically examine the fundamentally nonrational. This did not mean "rationalizing" mystical experience or explaining it by either the materialistic or the religious worldviews. James proclaimed loud and clear that thinking in a critical way does not necessitate giving up on what feels intuitively important, including mystical experience. It is by asking about the implications of this experience, about what it means to have such an experience in the tangible world, that one engages in a pragmatically meaningful discussion. Dr. Lemberger's most memorable advice to me showed the spirit of pragmatic thinking: if there is a mystical element in psychoanalysis, how does it show itself? How does this unspoken (perhaps unspeakable) element leave its mark on the overt text? Show it!

This love for James and his practical yet reverent approach to subjective experience was also the "place" where Dr. Lemberger and I met and she became my PhD supervisor. I felt that I had found, in James' pragmatism, the theoretical container for what I saw as the whimsical "place" of psychoanalysis in the field of knowledge, and that I also found a supervisor that could contain and further inspire my own peculiar project, my deep need for both clarity and mystery, logical conclusions, and intuitive leaps.

After Dr. Lemberger, I found more partners for this dialogue, who enriched it and gave me the courage to turn it into this book. Some were colleagues, some were mentors, and some were patients. It is in the consulting room that "psychoanalytic mysticism" though never overtly discussed, becomes a living reality. Following Bollas and Eigen, I see psychoanalytic psychotherapy as one of the culminations of the human potential for encounter, which for me is the most potent transformative force. It is between two human beings who truly strive to meet each other that the mystical takes place. It does not have to be an encounter with God. It might be an encounter with the divine in the human, the creative force of two minds thinking and dreaming together, thus creating each other anew.

Even more surprisingly, it can happen with a text. For me, psychoanalytic theory is a transformative object (Bollas, 1987) that, like real-life encounters with inspiring supervisors (which I was fortunate to have) opened me up to the human-to-human mystical experience. They helped me not only to think it but also to feel and to *know* it in the deepest sense, as well as to have the courage to meet the challenge of being a therapist: coping with psychic death, over-demanding, feeling too close, or too detached. I came to realize that all of these challenges can be weathered better if we have faith in the immense potential of the human encounter – the mystical effect of what I call "psychic overlap," an intimate "touch" connecting the souls of therapist and patient, which is the path to real "knowledge" (an almost firsthand experience of the patient) and change.

This book is the result of the most formative encounters I have had with psychoanalytic texts and with some philosophical ones (mainly those of James and Buber). It unfolds the fertile dialogue I believe these two disciplines and myriad authors can have about mysticism, knowledge, faith, and how all of this ultimately relates to what happens in the consulting room.

The first three chapters of this book are of a methodological nature. They unfold my main thesis about the mystical element in psychoanalysis, about what I call the "epistemology of faith" and how this is balanced with pragmatism, resulting in the paradoxical stance of pragmatic epistemology of faith. The other six chapters discuss psychoanalytic theoreticians, whose thinking significantly impacted the evolution of the mystical element. Since, in my view, a great many thinkers participated (whether knowingly or unknowingly) in this collective theoretical effort, I was obliged to limit my focus to those authors who are the most central, who greatly influenced not only the mystical element but psychoanalytic discourse as a whole. This choice is in line with my argument that the mystical is not some marginal topic or curiosity, but an organic part and a core assumption (though often a hidden one) in psychoanalysis. Since even these influential analysts prove too many for the scope of this work, I chose to discuss those who touched me personally – my own transformational objects, to whom I am indebted for my personal development. Since these are renowned authors, I believe many share my feelings, and may join me on my journey to understanding their thinking in a new light – that of the mystical element.

The first chapter is dedicated to the definition of the mystical and to the question of whether and how this term, derived from the field of religious studies, can be relevant to psychoanalysis. This chapter presents some classical definitions of the term and focuses on James' definition of the mystical and Buber's philosophy of encounter in order to arrive at a definition of the mystical in psychoanalysis.

The second chapter offers a short review of the history of the mystical element in psychoanalysis: its birth alongside the psychoanalytic unconscious, its repression as a threat, the various forms in which it reappeared and important milestones in its development (some of these are further elaborated in subsequent chapters). This chapter summarizes the historical narrative put forward by this book: the mystical element as omnipresent and constantly changing, taking on different forms in different theories and evolving from the "oceanic feeling" to a full "I-Thou encounter" in the thinking of Winnicott and his successors.

The third chapter focuses on epistemology, presenting James' pragmatic theory as the possible source of a new epistemological underpinning for psychoanalysis. The concept of faith as knowledge is discussed from the perspective of a novel integration of the notions of James and Buber and Winnicott's idea of transitional reality. This integration leads me to suggest a new concept – the epistemology of faith – as a working assumption of how we know things in psychoanalysis. The epistemology of faith is balanced by pragmatic criteria, creating a model of validity that is specifically tailored for psychoanalysis, as a field that both deals with highly subjective, unique, even mystical occurrences and functions as a discipline that aspires to academic relevance and practical applicability.

The model developed in these three chapters is implemented in the subsequent chapters, each of which is dedicated to a single theoretician, with the exception of Chapter 4, that discusses the Freud-Ferenczi rift. Each of these chapters stands on its own right, as an exploration of a particular psychoanalytic theory's mystical facet, Its epistemological assumptions and their pragmatic implications.

Chapter 4 discusses Freud's stance toward the mystical, analyzing his ambivalence as it appears in his texts, mostly those on telepathy. His position is contrasted with that of Ferenczi, whose painful conflict – unfolded throughout his *Clinical Diary* – ended in adopting a metaphysical position for which he payed dearly. The rift between the two and the shockwaves it sent throughout psychoanalytic history is discussed.

Chapter 5 is devoted to Bion's thinking and especially to two of his later texts: *Attention and Interpretation* and *Caesura*. I discuss Bion's explicit mystical element and offer my understanding of his much-debated concept of O, the implications of the radical abstractness of his concepts and a new model suggested in *Caesura*.

Chapter 6 is dedicated to Winnicott, arguing that his thinking represents a paradigm shift in psychoanalysis, both in terms of the mystical element and in terms of his notion of reality and knowledge. The chapter discusses how his innovative concept of transitional space contains both revolutions and how his writings are imbued with a sense of the magical, as manifest in various forms throughout different developmental stages.

Chapter 7 analyzes Ogden's theory of the analytic third. It argues that the notion of the third is the culmination of a long-standing psychoanalytic intuition about patient-analyst overlap as manifest in a non-oceanic concept of mystical relatedness. Though Ogden himself rejected the theoretical relevance of the term "mystical," "the third" is shown to be a perfect example of it and its clinical application. Ogden's elegant theoretical constructions and his empowering of the analyst's intuition are explored as powerful pragmatic tools.

Chapter 8 is devoted to Bollas' rich yet complex notion of the esthetic and to the argument that this notion contains an esthetic manifestation of the mystical. The chapter offers an analysis of Bollas' early and late periods, stressing the difference between their respective iterations of the mystical element and the tensions between different notions of the analytic encounter in his second period.

Chapter 9 traces the thinking of Eigen, the "psychoanalytic mystic." It is argued that his inspiring frankness about his mysticism and colorful descriptions thereof breath new life into the concept, while his informal style leaves it in comparative obscurity. I offer a threefold analysis of Eigen's use of the term "mystical" and discuss his many unique contributions to its understanding. I then discuss his paradoxical ontological and epistemological theory and his potential revolutionary impact on psychoanalysis, by offering a new integration of Bion's and Winnicott's thinking and bringing to fruition the Winnicottian revolution through Eigen's acute aliveness. The book concludes with Eigen's mystical, yet pragmatic vision.

Chapter 1

Defining the ineffable: What is the mystical?

"Mystical" is a provocative word to place at the center of an academic text. The term carries with it many emotional overtones: for some, it is appealing and curious; for others, it is off putting. The latter would tend to automatically dismiss any possible connection between mysticism and psychoanalysis. In both cases, however, these emotional reactions have little to do with the actual use of the term in the academic literature that focuses on mysticism as its field of study. This repugnance is very much the result of the positivistic legacy of 19th century science, which has strongly influenced western academic culture in general and psychoanalysis in particular. Following the revolution that resulted in academic reverence for materialism, empiricism, and formal logic, the analytic philosophers of the late 19th and early to mid-20th centuries considered mysticism as part of "metaphysics": a set of leftover terms from an old, religious way of thought that is full of inaccurate, nebulous concepts. They wished to cleanse our language from such misleading words and render it immaculately "accurate" and fit for scientific use.

This cleansing mission, however, was only partially successful because "metaphysics" continued to be of interest to certain philosophers and, later on, to some psychoanalysts as well. I wish to argue that the mystical, in its broad, nonreligious definition, is closely related to key aspects of the psychoanalytic endeavor. Its exploration, therefore, ought to be a major psychoanalytic concern. The mystical element in psychoanalysis carries with it much deeper implications for theory, meta-theory and practice, than its current, relatively marginal position in psychoanalytic discourse may suggest.

DOI: 10.4324/9781003200796-1

This chapter serves as a methodological introduction, reviewing some of the leading definitions of the mystical, from the classical works of Rudolf Otto and William James to the mysticism of meeting developed by Martin Buber. Following these classical definitions, a brief presentation of the views of Michael Eigen will serve to illustrate the use of the term in psychoanalysis and present the theoretical questions raised by such use. Eigen discerns the mystical in openness to experience and in the encounter with Otherness. The discussion will aim at answering the question of whether such broad use of the term is justified and whether the term mystical can indeed apply to the human encounter in general and the psychoanalytic encounter in particular.

The notion of nonreligious mysticism, immanent to deep human intimacy, will be developed through William James and Martin Buber's notion of a spectrum of mystical phenomena and "this world" mysticism. At the end of the chapter, the ideas of these two thinkers will be combined in order to formulate a definition of the specific meaning of the mystical in psychoanalysis and, hopefully, enable a more scholarly, focused, and less prejudiced discussion thereof.

Classical definitions

Two classical books are often quoted when discussing mystical and religious experience: Rudolf Otto's *The Idea of the Holy* and William James' *The Varieties of Religious Experience*. Both these fundamental works focus on the features of *experience* rather than religious history or sociological structure. Both are thus committed to analyzing something deeply personal. As such, they may help elucidate not only what "mysticism" means in scholarly contexts (as these authors can be viewed as the founders of such discourse) but also its potential meaning in a psychoanalytic context, as a phenomenon of consciousness and possibly a form of connection.

Both thinkers viewed mystical experience as a unique phenomenon in its own right and rejected any reductionistic view of it. Both characterized it in similar terms. But whereas Otto still saw it only as meaningful in the religious context, expressing perhaps the more familiar stance toward mysticism, James' view was both more neutral and more inclusive, bringing us closer to the sought-after definition of the mystical in psychoanalysis.

Rudolf Otto was a protestant theologian and philosopher influenced by Kant and the phenomenological tradition. He put forth a thesis that integrated Kant's ideas about *a priori* categories of thought, such as time and space – which Kant believed to be preexisting structures of mind that shape and predate our perceptions – and his own (Otto's) Christian belief. He suggested that there is a mental category that is designed to perceive the "Noumenon" – hidden, divine reality. Otto (1917/1950) also makes an important distinction between rational thought and the ostensibly "raw" experience of the holy. To him, religious emotion arises primarily from the latter. He writes:

> whoever makes use of the word 'non-rational' today ought to say what he actually means [...] we began by the rational in the idea of God and the divine meaning by the term that in it which is clearly to be grasped by our power of conceiving, and enters the domain of familiar and definable conceptions. We went on to maintain that beneath this sphere of clarity and lucidity lies a hidden depth, inaccessible to our conceptual thought, which we in so far call the 'non- rational.' (p. 58)

In Otto's terms, "rational" does not resemble the common meaning of the phrase "rational explanation" – a statement that is both logical and adheres to a materialistic worldview. Rather, he referred to everything that can be formulated in concepts and discussed – including ideas about the nature of God. Otto considered such theological concepts essential for a "mature" religion, which must integrate experience and rational conceptions for the sake of achieving moral goals. For him, the moral element was particularly important and he held protestant Christianity to be the perfect model for such mature religiosity.

Nevertheless, for Otto, theological concepts are nothing more than "ideograms" that can only point toward something nonrational, that lies beyond the reach of discursive thought. In one of the opening paragraphs of his book, Otto gives a provocative warning: those who have not experienced what he is talking about at first hand, who have never had a "deeply felt religious experience" (p. 8), might as well stop reading. They would not understand his book. This statement is a strong expression of the paradoxical mission Otto felt he had undertaken – to talk about that which cannot be put into words.

According to Otto, not only is the religious feeling nonrational, it belongs to an essentially different emotional category. Though it has "neighboring" emotions, most notably the esthetic feeling – which Otto saw as the most adjacent to the religious feeling and as potentially facilitating the evocation of the Numinous, the Numinous is an independent, *a-priori* category of thought, and the only thing that can trigger this unique emotional experience is contact with the Noumenon.

This contact may be experienced in different ways because, according to Otto, the Noumenon has many facets or "moments," which he sought to catalogue. The *mysterium tremendum*, for example, is the experience of awe-inspiring mystery that arises from encountering the total Otherness of the Numinous. According to Otto, the mystical experience brings the mystic closer to God, but the feeling of otherness, both terrific and beatific, is never wholly overcome. Contact with the deity can also inspire a feeling of "fascination" – an energetic, passionate aliveness. This "moment" is responsible for the deep happiness reported by mystics who feel that they have been granted living contact with God. Otto, however, stresses the element of awe and, after describing this passionate encounter, mentions the *augustum* – a feeling of holiness and moral perfection which gives rise to the moral facet of religion. By delineating these different "moments," which parse the ineffable into distinct emotional hues, Otto is attempting to bridge between the rational thinking required for discursive communication about religion and the nonrational feeling experienced in a true encounter with the Noumenon – to which no words could ever do justice.

Several years prior to Otto's efforts, another thinker also sought to develop a systematic approach to religious experience. This was philosopher and pioneer psychologist William James, one of the two fathers of pragmatic philosophy. In *The Varieties of Religious Experience* (1902/1987), he tried to capture the essence of what he called "personal religion," as opposed to the institutionalized facet of religious life. He sought to establish a new science of religion, one based on actual religious experiences and their myriad varieties. To that end, he collected many reports of mystical and religious experiences from around the world. As a pragmatist, the potential implications of religious experiences for the lives and surroundings of those who have had them were of the outmost importance to him. The effects on the person's quality of life and psychological health, and the effects these people, in turn, exert on those around them, are what allows the investigator to capture the value and impact of a given phenomenon. According to James' pragmatic approach, anything that cannot be understood in terms of its implications is meaningless – both scientifically and morally. The meaning of the mystical experience is thus derived from the fact that it can be life changing. In this context, James claimed that the mystical experience may generate an inner transformation that later coalesces into a way of life; thus, it is the source of both personal religion and the phenomenon of conversion.

James offers a definition of mystical states with the ambitious goal of making it universally applicable to any religion, as well as to nonreligious mystics. For him, mysticism was an alternative state of consciousness with several definable characteristics that can be observed across different cultures and historical eras. This notion of the universality of mystical experience is shared by many later scholars of religion, including Otto.

There is, however, an important difference between the views of James and those of Otto, that may help elucidate the question of nonreligious "profane mysticism" (Ben-Shlomo, 2012). For Otto, "mature religion" must derive a set of rational conceptions from the mystical experience. In his view, the pure experience of the Numinous is essential, but it is only a starting point – perhaps like when a baby meets the world for the first time, still unable to name or understand the things it encounters. In contrast, James holds that the interpretations people give their mystical experience are neither "derived" from it nor essential to it. Rather, they are rooted in a person's cultural background and affected by their level of intelligence. They might be sophisticated or simplistic and infantile. Either way, such interpretations are subsequent constructs and are theoretically secondary to the moment of pure experience. In a way, both thinkers distinguish between mystical experience and the religious "meaning" often attached to it. Their main disagreement concerns the value of, so to speak, naked experiencing, unclothed by dogma.

In defining this unique experience, James – much like Otto and other thinkers who preceded him – begins with a negative characteristic: the experience is felt to be *ineffable*. Those who have not had such an experience stand in relation to it as those who have never loved are in relation to love; as those who lack musical hearing are in relation to music. In fact, James views openness to this kind of state of consciousness as a sort of talent, much like musical or mathematical ability. Second, the mystical experience has a *Noetic quality*. Though it is more akin to a state of feeling than to intellectual knowledge, one feels as though one has been gifted with deeply meaningful knowledge: a truth that lies beyond the reach of regular discursive thought, beyond the intellect. While these two characteristics are sufficient for James in defining an experience as mystical, he nevertheless adds two more which, although not essential, are very common: first, the mystical experience is usually transient and short-lived; second, the experience is markedly passive. The mystical experience is felt to be received, sometimes even forced, from the outside. A person may seek out a mystical experience and try to prompt its occurrence, through practices such as meditation, but they cannot compel or will it to happen.

James thus resembles Otto in viewing the mystical experience as essentially nonrational, in Otto's terms. He would probably understand Otto's grave, though moving appeal that his book be read only by those who can grasp its meaning. But, where Otto greatly stresses the elements of strangeness and of overwhelming, awe-inspiring holiness, James' definition does not commit itself to any specific emotional content. On the contrary, He shows that mystical experiences have many shapes and colors. James' case studies seem to suggest that he leans more toward the "charming" aspect of the Noumenon, but this is a subtle preference. Importantly, this difference between the two thinkers in terms of dominant "mood" seems to derive from Otto's commitment to his protestant belief. His description of strangeness and awe clearly assumes the transcendence of the Noumenon. While this view is typical to western religions, it is less dominant in eastern ones, which stress unity and the immanent presence of the divine in the human. Loyal to the "variety" of his chosen title, James recorded the testimonies of Christians who believed Jesus had found and saved their ailing soul, as well as those of eastern mystics and even those recounting nonreligious mystical experiences of unity with the natural world, who tended toward a pantheistic interpretation. His resulting model of a powerful, non-verbal Noetic feeling of "illumination [and] revelation, full of significance and importance" (James, 1902/1987, p. 343) is therefore more elegant and concise, as well as more inclusive and universal.

Importantly, James does not take any definite position regarding the ontological reality of the mystical experience (although, as will be discussed, he does have a certain hypothesis) be it theistic, pantheistic or reductionist (such as explaining it away as an illusion resulting, perhaps, from neurological abnormality). In general, he rejects any essentialist view – unlike Otto, who speaks of contact with the Numinous. The only commitment James makes is to the experience itself, in all its richness. For him, the experiences of "spiritual" life are neither less nor more valid than other feelings or perceptions. They are simply part of the wide range of human experience and, given their particular importance to and influence on those who have them, they deserve the attention of the psychologist and the philosopher. His parsimonious approach respects experience yet steers clear of any theological agenda or other preimposed answers, such as those offered by the positivistic view. Thus, it serves as a good lens for observing this field of human experience, which has previously been used (and sometimes abused) by so many biased or interested parties such as the church, contemporary scientific hegemony or its counterpart – modern "new age" culture.

The mystical as a meeting – Michael Eigen

I will now take a short detour into psychoanalysis in order to offer a taste of the potential meaning of "mystical" in that context and to present a glimpse of the relevant discourse and the questions it leaves open. To that end, I will briefly present the view of a thinker for whom the relation between psychoanalysis and mysticism presents no mystery: Michael Eigen. Eigen stands out among contemporary psychoanalytic thinkers for his preoccupation with "mysticism" as a central topic, and in resisting reduction to other theoretical constructs, such as viewing mystical experience as an illusion to be explained by certain needs within the object-relations framework (Black, 2006). In blatantly bringing the mystical phenomenon to the center of academic attention, Eigen is, in psychoanalysis, the counterpart of Otto and James in the field of philosophy. Like Otto, Eigen views the mystical feeling as possessing an autonomous quality, even though it is intimately related to and intertwined with many other aspects of life. In contrast with Otto and James' systematic philosophical effort, however, Eigen does not aspire to offer any definition of the mystical.

Eigen states that he would not attempt to define the mystical and would be unable to do so. Instead, he hopes that "if I speak around it, or from it, well enough, something of value will be communicated to the reader and myself. Discussions of mystical awareness tend to undo themselves because of the paradoxical nature of the experience involved" (Eigen, 1998, p. 31). Accordingly, Eigen attempts to convey to his readers this paradoxical nature of the mystical experience. He does this by openly discussing his associations about psychoanalytic theories or about the bible, by mentioning Jewish and Buddhist mystical notions, by relying on literature and by means of intimate delves into his own experiences and those of his patients. This "free style" is connected to Eigen's view of the nature of the subject at hand: undefinable, yet extremely rich; essential to life and imbued with all the variety of human experience. Eigen stresses the paradoxical nature of the mystical by returning time and again to the idea of irreducible tensions: the mystical experience is (or can be) both wonderful and terrible; it is a state of fullness, but it can be a state of emptiness too. In fact, for Eigen, fullness and emptiness are interdependent. The mystical experience is essential to the growth of the self, but it can also serve pathology and result in the withdrawal and even withering away of the personality. Sometimes, it serves both purposes. It is special, powerful, mysterious – a Numinous experience. At the same time, it is immanent in daily life, interwoven with everything that gives life meaning. It is about knowing oneself and knowing what is beyond the self. Most importantly, for Eigen, *meeting* is at the very core of the mystical experience.

To appreciate that point, it is important to understand that for Eigen, mystical moments are characterized by a fluctuation between different dimensions of experience and between self and Other. A meeting of two subjects can be particularly "charged" with mystical feeling. Accordingly, Eigen embraces Martin Buber's saying that "all real living is meeting" (Buber in Eigen, 1998, p. 13). The mystical is a facet of the human soul which allows contact with different parts of experience, with parts of the self that are mysterious and Other, and with the mystery of the self's true meeting with other minds. The confusion between such a general ability and a particular kind of experience will be explored in Chapter 9. Here, it is important to note that for Eigen, the Numinous lives in interpersonal connections and, in particular, in the powerful analytic relationship. It is not necessarily a result of an encounter with the divine, though such an encounter is one of the important presentations of the mystical (Eigen 1993, 1998).

For Eigen, the mystical experience arises from a profound stance of faith in what might be called the sacred place of experience. The true Eigenian mystic believes that every experience, every experiential truth – be it wonderful or horrifying – is worth recognizing, even if it threatens one's sanity. Sensitivity itself, with all it can bring, is life's precious spring. The mystical, therefore, is true openness to experience. Could it be as simple as that? And is openness to experience not the very essence and aim of psychoanalysis? Interestingly, the characteristics of the mystical in Eigen's writings bear some resemblance to Otto's Noumenon: potentially awe-inspiring (in Eigen's words, a potential threat to sanity) but charming; distant and unreachable, yet imprinted in the very structure of the human mind. In lieu of Otto's protestant perspective, however, the reader can easily pick up the distinctive scent of modern psychanalytic values: a deep respect for human experience in all its variety alongside a definite idea of what constitutes a healthy personality and a commitment to its growth.

Eigen is a central voice in understanding the applicability of the mystical element in psychoanalysis. But, while Eigen's writing is rich and evocative, his notion of the mystical is somewhat confusing: it seems to be both "structure" (the capacity to tolerate experience) and content (certain experiences), both intra-psychic and inter-psychic. Above all, he does not systematically defend the claim that the term "mystical" can really stretch itself to suit the whole spectrum to which he applies it: to widespread psychic phenomena, even to the very capacity for experiencing, and to sharing a therapeutic encounter.

Consequently, he posits the mystical at the center of psychoanalytic thought. Can such application be justified?

Beyond the definition: A fuller portrait of James's mystical experience

To answer this question, it is best to leave psychoanalysis for a while and turn back to an interdisciplinary position and, first of all, to James. Although the lion's share of *The Variety of the Religious Experience* is strictly devoted to methodically gathering descriptive information and extracting generalizations, at the end of the book James nevertheless offers certain overarching conclusions and even personal opinions. In this part, James comes closer to Eigen's broad and free use of the term "mystical."

James endeavors to give some account of what he hitherto carefully avoided: the ontological basis of religion, the "underlying truth." The truth he offers is alluring, as it is both psychological and transcends psychology. James claims that the subconscious self, "nowadays a well accredited psychological entity," is a bridge between the religious feeling of contact with something beyond ourselves and scientifically verifiable reality: "I believe that in it we have exactly the mediating term required. Apart from all religious considerations, there is actually and literally more life in our total soul than we are at any time aware of" (James, 1902/1987, p. 457). When taking this into account, says James, the mystic's experience of being in contact with something beyond what is usually felt as the "self" is literally true. Moreover, he suggests that this "bridge" might actually be connected with realms that are usually inaccessible to the conscious human mind:

> Let me then propose, as an hypothesis, that whatever it may be on the *further* side, the 'more' with which in the religious experience we feel ourselves connected is on its *hither* side the subconscious continuation of our conscious life [...] this doorway into the subject seems to me the best one for a science of religion, for it mediates between a number of different points of view. (ibid, pp. 457–458)

James admits to a personal belief in this "more" – in wider spheres of existence than those intimated by our daily lives. Still, for James, even our everyday experience clearly points to the fact that there are multiple states of consciousness. This wider range reveals itself in all kinds of phenomena, from slips of tongue and dreams through telepathy, to genius leaps of thought or religious revelations. As we know, Freud, used a similar array of phenomena to corroborate the existence of the unconscious. James would agree, but he makes a wider claim: for him, these phenomena indicate that some of us have a broader or more flexible range of consciousness, even if the question of any ontological counterpart for these special states must remain unsettled.

Unlike Eigen, who makes meeting and communication a key element of his inferred characterization of the mystical, James leaves it out of his concise, four-fold definition of the mystical experience. Nevertheless, it is clear that the assumption of communication is there, even before James offers his hypothesis regarding the bridge between "further" and "hither." In fact, James' definition presupposes the existence of communication. This can clearly be extrapolated from the element of passivity and, more importantly, from the Noetic element. The mystical experience feels as if immensely valuable knowledge, an ineffable revelation, has been received, granted by something beyond the individual's normal range of experience. This contact with "something beyond" causes the self to change, to transcend its previous state.

In fact, James claims that communication with the divine, as well as the change it affects, is the core of any "living" personal religion. Though such communication usually occurs through prayer, James does not mean any formal, canonical prayer, but any form of personal communication with God:

> The religious phenomenon, studied as an inner fact and apart from ecclesiastical and theological complications, has shown itself to consist everywhere, and in all its stages, in the consciousness which individuals have of an intercourse between themselves and higher powers with which they feel themselves to be related. This intercourse is realized at the time as being both active and mutual. If it be not affective; if it be not a give and take relation; if nothing

be really transacted while it lasts; if the world is no whit different
[...] then prayer, taken in this wide meaning of a sense that
something is transacted, is of course a feeling of what is illusory,
and religion must on the whole be classed not simply as containing
elements of delusion, – these undoubtedly everywhere exist, but as
being rooted in delusion altogether. (ibid, pp. 416–417)

There are two important claims here. The first is that religious life,
whose heart is the mystical feeling, requires *communication*. This
communication seems to be not an equal one but, despite what is
implied by the element of passivity, it is mutual, requiring some activity and springing from a deep feeling of relatedness. The second
claim is that this contact must bear some fruit, must be *effectual* for
us, if we are to treat it as something real and not mere delusion. The
moment of contact allows some kind of "work" to be done. This
might be primarily psychological work, but it is nonetheless deeply
influential. In Jamesian philosophy, the real is what really works.
Though modern people can hardly entertain the view that prayer has
any external, miraculous effect on the natural world, one cannot deny
that prayer profoundly affects one's position in it. James offers a
pragmatic criterion for any kind of religious experience: can we observe any marked, positive changes in the person's way of life?
Indeed, "positive" is inescapably derived from a given system of
values, but so are all other scientific and particularly psychoanalytic
definitions of "health." In his examples, James speaks of greater
optimism, aliveness and a better ability to cope with what one might
encounter in life. This bears some similarity to Eigen's "openness to
experience." Interestingly, both thinkers believe this "openness" to be
both the cause and the effect of mystical experiences.

  For both thinkers, there seems to be an inherent tension between
viewing mystical experience as unique, on the one hand, and speaking
of it as located on a continuum, on the other; as an inherent part of
the human array of experiences. James avows that the healthy psyche
must have some sensitivity for what he terms the "*mystical group*"
(James, 1902/1987, p. 344; my italics). While mystical moments are
peculiar and unique, they are also part of a spectrum. James holds
that there is a wide range of phenomena containing the mystical
element, starting with those that are utterly void of religious

overtones, such as being fascinated by art or falling in love. A person who has no mystical ability whatsoever cannot therefore feel the magic of life at all and, in a manner of speaking, is psychically dead:

> Most of us can remember the strangely moving power of passages in certain poems read when we were young, irrational doorways as they were, through which the mystery of fact, the wildness and the pang of life, stole into our hearts and thrilled them. The words have now perhaps become mere polished surfaces to us; but lyric poetry and music are alive and significant only in proportion as they fetch these vague vistas of a life continuous with our own [...] we are alive or dead to the eternal inner message of the arts according as we have kept or lost this mystical susceptibility. (ibid, p. 345)

For James and for Eigen, the mystical is there for anyone capable of feeling. At its peak, it is experienced as a dramatically different and mysterious state of consciousness, but some mystery is always there, permeating, perhaps, every aspect of the living human soul.

Martin Buber's mysticism of the human encounter

I will now introduce another thinker who will accompany us throughout this book and serve to elucidate nonreligious mysticism and its deep connection to the therapeutic encounter. Martin Buber, an Austrian-born Jewish philosopher, was deeply interested in religious phenomena from his own unique perspective. While he explored many religious subjects – including, for example, the Jewish Hasidic movement – his chief focus was the mysteries of the human encounter. One can argue that his unique thinking, which founded the dialogic movement in philosophy, has made the most explicit connection between human contact and the mystical.

The heart of Buber's philosophic innovation lies in the claim that there are two fundamentally different modes of human existence, which are derived from the way one relates to the Other – to other human beings and to God, but also to animals, plants or even inanimate objects or the world in general. The manner of relating to an Other creates an ontological difference, a difference in being. In his most influential work, named after his central concept, *I and Thou*, Buber claims that whenever the word "I" is pronounced, it entails a certain relation to the Other: either an I-it or an I-thou relation. This relation also defines the essence of the "I" itself: "When a primary word is spoken [the I] the speaker enters the world and takes a stand in it" (Buber, 1923/2010, p. 4).

The difference between the two "stands" is that the I-it relation renders the speaker a lone subject in world of objects. She may observe these objects, want them and use them for her needs, such as food, sex, technological manipulation, self-aggrandizement, and so on. As a Kantian subject, her consciousness is always preoccupied with some object of perception, knowledge or desire. But, according to Buber, she herself is actually only one more object – a dead thing in a world of dead objects. She lives by the laws of blind, physical cause-and-effect and her relations cannot be mutual. She may "know" many things about the qualities of her objects, obtaining the kind of "objective" knowledge that is vital for scientific and technological advancement. But, despite all its practical uses, this is not real knowledge: the "I" knows *about* a thing, but does not know *it*. In contrast, in the I-thou relation, the "I" becomes a living being, which inhabits a living world alongside other subjects. Only this kind of position allows for true relating, which addresses the Other's very essence, and it is only possible when the "I" is invested with all her being. The I- thou position is inevitably mutual, demanding that both parties be fully present. It is a unique, irreplaceable moment of contact with the Other, without any barrier or reservation. As a mutual relation, it is not up to the "I" alone. It is a matter of both "will and grace" (p. 7).

What follows is Buber's description of an I–Thou moment with a surprising partner – a tree:

> I can classify it in a species and study it as a type in its structure and mode of life. I can subdue its actual presence […] recognize it only as an expression of law […] It can however, also come about, if I have both will and grace, that in considering the tree, I become bound up in relation to it. The tree is now no longer *it*. I have been seized by the power of exclusiveness. To effect this it is not necessarily to give up any of the ways in which I consider the

tree [...] Rather, is everything, picture and movement, species and type, law and number indivisibly united in this event [...] the tree is no impression, no play of my imagination [...] but it is bodied over against me and has to do with me, as I with it – only in a different way. Let us not attempt to sap the strength from the meaning of the relation: relation is mutual. The tree has a consciousness then. similar to our own? of that I have no experience [...] I encountered no soul or dryad of the tree, but the tree itself. (ibid, pp. 7–8)

This bold description of "meeting" a tree demonstrates several important points about the I-Thou relation. First, it is unique. It is not about how Buber feels about trees in general; it is a special moment of connection with this particular one. It is also important to note that this link is mutual, though obviously not symmetrical. Buber acknowledges that the tree "has to do" with him in a different way. Buber anticipates potential ridicule and notably resists every reduction of the essence of the tree or the nature of the moment. He does not try to explain away the possibility of this unique moment by reducing it to some psychological (or psychopathological) event or postulating some metaphysical being, such as "tree soul" or "dryad" to supply some kind of fantastic, dualistic explanation which would be equally repugnant to his system of thought. For him, entering the I-Thou realm means living in a new kind of reality, without disconnecting from the former one. He may still retain his scientific knowledge about the tree, but he can no longer objectify it. A new possibility for relating and for truly knowing that particular tree has opened up for him.

Scholars of Buber's thinking have been debating whether his notions about the I-Thou could be termed mystical, especially considering his radical use of the term in describing a meeting with a tree or a cat (ibid, p. 97). Without diving into the depth of this debate, the question of how to define what is mystical is intimately related to understanding the human encounter, including, as I would claim, the therapeutic one.

Various authors commonly differentiate between Buber's early and explicitly "mystical" period, in which he discussed ecstatic, unifying mysticism, and his later "dialogic" thought, to which *I and*

*Thou*belongs. Some say he had neglected the mystical in favor of the dialogic; others argue that some mystical fragments remained in his mature thought; still others claim that there has never been a non-mystical Buber and that the misunderstanding lies in the interpretation of the term "mystical." Scholem (in Koren, 2002) argues that even Buber's dialogic philosophy of meeting is based on a mystical definition of revelation. Moreover, it is clear that God, the "eternal Thou," (p. 75) has a central place in Buber's dialogic philosophy. According to Buber, every living creature is a part of the "eternal Thou" that enable one to "meet" all parts of creation. At the same time, everyone has something unique and individual about them, something that can be truly "met."

In Buber's (1923/2010) words:

> The extended lines of relations meet in the eternal Thou. Every particular *Thou* is a glimpse through to the eternal *Thou* [...] Through this mediation of the *Thou* of all beings fulfillment and non fulfillment, of relations comes to them: the inborn *Thou* is realized in each relation and consummated in none. It is consummated only in the direct relation with the thou that by its nature cannot become it. (p. 75)

True contact with God is always an I-Thou encounter, which is never merely rational. God can never become an "it." An encounter with God is only possible with all of one's being. In contrast, I-Thou encounters between creatures are transient. They are exquisite moments that light up the world for those who share them; transformative moments, in which a new reality is created. But they do not last. People slip back into the technical world of I-it and only sometimes, in blessed moments, are they able to find their way back to real contact.

This belief in the possibility of such contact and the ethic of striving for it mark Buber's mature thought, which is our present focus. This is contrasted to his early endorsement of ecstatic moments of detachment and the wish to distance himself from the faults of this world, which conforms perhaps to the more familiar form of mysticism. His dialogic philosophy, however, repudiates such detachment, indorsing the very opposite – deep, unmitigated connection.

Koren (2002) claims that identifying mysticism with a solipsistic, detached mode that blurs self-other boundaries is a false equation and a methodological error that ignores the typology of mystical states. Moreover, he maintains that Buberian mystical encounters were always understood as sustenance for the self's unfolding and growth. What actually changed in his late period was the determined objection to the "detached" brand of mysticism. In Buber's late writings, mysticism entails direct contact with reality, which is embraced instead of being negated. This is an immanent mysticism of "this world," by which transcendence, transformation and even revelation are achieved through deep contact with the fullness of the Other's reality.

Buber described different facets of life, where such moments of revelation can occur. Those are immanent, but also "magical" aspect of our lives. He outlined the specific characteristics of I-Thou relations with art forms, with nature or with human beings. He even envisioned groups and communities sharing I-Thou intimacy. Unsurprisingly, much like James, Buber viewed such moments of encounter as having varying intensities. On this spectrum, the more "religious" kind of encounter is viewed as a liminal, particularly dramatic phenomenon. But, unlike James, the dialogic Buber (1923/2010) was more interested in milder, less ecstatic, and more involved moments. He wrote:

> what the ecstatic man calls union is the enrapturing dynamic of relation not a unity arisen in this moment of the world's time that dissolves the I and the Thou. [...] here then, on the brink, the relational act goes beyond itself; the relation itself in its vital unity is felt so forcibly that its parts seem to fade before it, and in the force of *its* life, the *I* and the *thou* between which it is established are forgotten. Here is one of the phenomena of the brink, to which reality extends and at which it grows dim. But the central reality of the everyday hour on earth, with the streak of the sun on a maple twig and the glimpse of the eternal thou, is greater for us then all enigmatic webs on the brink of being. (pp. 87–88)

Due to his ethical stance regarding involvement in the world, Buber warns about the allurements of the extreme phenomena on the spectrum of encounters. His warning is equally apt when he is depicting the opposite temptation – that of the apparent "stability" of the I-It world, that can be scientifically measured and manipulated. A true meeting is a singular phenomenon that, by its very nature, lacks the "reliability" and "replicability" required by science. For Buber, however, stability belongs only to objects that can be captured because they are part of a dead world. In the I-Thou realm, an alternative path to knowledge is revealed.

The "Weltanschauung" of in-between mysticism

In rejecting the scientific approach as a way to know the living world, Buber offers a different epistemology. Koren (2002) claims that Buber's mysticism of meeting should be viewed as entailing an essentially different conception of knowledge. It is a nonrationalistic but also nonescapist philosophy that expresses the possibility of direct contact with the world. This alternative epistemology is rooted in the nature of the Buberian encounter, which, as he claims, creates a new sphere of existence – the "in-between." This sphere is neither "individual" nor "collective" – a conceptual dichotomy which Buber views as fundamentally erroneous. For Buber (1947/2014), both the individual and the "aggregate" are mere abstractions; real human life takes place where there is meeting:

> The individual is a fact of existence in so far as he steps into living relation with other individuals. The aggregate is a fact of existence in so far as it is built of living units of relation. The fundamental fact of human existence is man with man. What is peculiarly characteristic of the human world is above all that something takes place between one being and another the like of which can be found nowhere in nature. Language is only a sign and a means for it, all achievements of the spirit have been incited by it; Man is made man by it; but on its way it does not merely unfold, it also decays and withers away. It is rooted in one being turning to another as another, as this particular other, in order to communicate with it in a sphere which is common to them, but which reaches out beyond the special sphere of each. I call this sphere which is established with the existence of man with man

but which is conceptually still uncomprehend, the sphere of "between". Though being realized in very different degrees, it is a primal category of human reality, this is where a genuine third alternative must begin. The view which establishes the concept of "between" is to be enquired by no longer localizing the relation between human beings, as is customary, either within individual souls or in a general world that embraces and determines them, but in actual fact between them. (p. 203)

Here we can see that Buber's theory of meeting distinguishes between what is uniquely human and other forms of I-Thou. Meeting another person is not like meeting a tree. There is a special quality to a human encounter that is not only the result of humanity but also its creator. The ability to truly encounter one another, perhaps by using another uniquely human trait – language – as a platform, is what makes a person human, enabling true knowledge and true creativity. For Buber, it is the "stuff" which love is made of; furthermore, all spiritual achievements are rooted in the human encounter, where soul touches soul and both change, becoming more human, living more acutely, more meaningfully.

According to Buber (1923/2010), the following characteristics are found in every type of true encounter: first, the person receives the "grace" of the encounter, with all the bounty it entails, without knowing (in the intellectual sense) exactly what it is; second, the encounter gives life a profound meaning. The receiver no longer needs to inquire about the meaning of life; life becomes pregnant with meaning. This is not necessarily a happy feeling, for such meaning springs from one's deep connection to other lives and may involve sobering feelings of responsibility. These originate not in guilt, but in the deepest connection. In whatever emotional tone, life is full of meaning and, very often, of beauty – the beauty of the essence of the Other. Still, this meaning cannot be put in words: "you do not know how to exhibit and define the meaning of life [...] and yet it has more certitude to you than the perceptions of your senses" (ibid, p. 110).

The resemblance to James' definition of the mystical moment is striking. Especially if we bear in mind that an encounter is indeed a moment that both unfolds and "decays and withers away" (p. 203), and that it exists on a spectrum of varying intensity. The distinctively

Buberian characteristic is that the meaning we find in such moments belongs to "this world." Buber's mysticism acquires a definite human flavor, especially in his definition of the "between." Buberian mysticism is about the mystery of human connection.

As a phenomenon of life, rather than a subjective feeling, the sphere of "between" has its own ontic characteristics and its unique epistemological potential stemming from the fact, that the "between" is something that both parties create and which lies beyond both of them, without diminishing the uniqueness of either.

> It takes place between them in the most precise sense, as it were in a dimension which is accessible only to them both [...] if I and another come up against one another, "happen" to one another [...] the sum cannot exactly divide, there is a remainder, somewhere, where the soul ends and the world has not yet begun, and this remainder is what is essential. This fact can be found even in the tiniest and most transient events which scarcely enter the consciousness. (Buber, 1947/2014, p. 204)

This unique ontic sphere offers the only possibility for truly, deeply knowing the Other with whom this moment is created. This "knowledge" is obviously not scientific, not necessary verbal and sometimes not even conscious. Like any other mysticism, Buber's mysticism revolves around the Noetic moment except that, in this case, the "knowledge" being imparted is knowledge of another person: "that essence of man, which is special to him, can be directly known only in living relation" (1947/2014, p. 205). By sharing the sphere of "between," each party is granted intimate knowledge of the Other's very core. Buber also challenges the validity of any study of human beings – including, of course, psychoanalysis – which does not stem from real encounters.

It is important to note, that not only passive "knowledge" is acquired in the I-Thou encounter. The issue here is "ontic" because the "between" is a creation of something new – the "between" and the "I" are both created together: "I, moreover, exists only through the relation to the Thou" (1947/2014, p. 205). In other words, the I-Thou relation is the birthplace of the self. In every fresh moment of encounter, the self transforms and undergoes developmental growth – the "I" is reborn.

This touches on one of the interesting paradoxes in Buberian philosophy: his view that the "between" can only happen to two individuals while, at the same time, individuality can only emerge from a true relation. In developing the concept of "between," Buber treats it as a "primal category" both in the history of the individual and that of humanity at large. A human baby is born into an environment of true relating, where it and its mother live in soul to soul contact that starts with the deep shared-living and inter-penetration of pregnancy. Life at the dawn of human existence can also be described as an intimate involvement between people and nature. This developmental view, reminiscent as it is of the psychoanalytic mother-baby model, differs from how Buber views the fully developed state of meeting, which requires two individuals, who cannot be reduced to what is created between them, just as the "between" itself cannot be reduced to the partaking individuals. Buber even hints that the ability to form "full" I-thou relations is a kind of criterion for humanity.

These concerns about the ability to establish full human contact and the possibility of knowing the Other's essence in an encounter are profoundly psychoanalytic concerns. So is the "developmental" view, which sees the human personality as the product of its relations. Buber himself addressed the question of the therapeutic relation and wondered whether it is an I–Thou encounter. He avowed that therapy can only happen if something beyond the formal roles of doctor and patient is attained. And yet, Buber argues, a connection between therapist and patient, or teacher and student, cannot be symmetrical: the teacher or therapist must devote themselves to the development of the Other. Still, if it is to be an I-Thou moment, it must be mutual. The therapist cannot remain anonymous. In the "between," both sides inevitably "touch souls," and attain intimate knowledge of each other.

To conclude, the true human encounter is a mysterious, revelatory moment. At the same time, it is an immanent part of human experience and human development. It can be dramatic or mild, but it is always Noetic, always meaningful. Buber's I-Thou reinforces Eigen's application of the word mysticism to a wide range of human experiences, including the all-too-human therapeutic encounter, suggesting that the mystical is found in the basic defining moments of humanity.

The mystical encounter in therapy – A definition

As we have seen, the definition of the mystical goes beyond the religious context; its boundaries extend to embrace moments of human-to-human revelation. In Jamesian and Buberian thought, therefore, the word "mystical" may be wide enough to contain what Eigen spoke of. As the following chapters will show, this view might shed new light on many well-known yet still mysterious psychoanalytic concepts, including projective identification, empathy, reverie, the analytic third and transitional space.

Unlike Otto's religious philosophy, which views contact with the Numinous as a distinct part of the mind, compartmentalizing the mystical element from the rest of psychic life, James' and Buber's view of a spectrum of phenomena presents a clear alternative. This alternative sees religious mystical encounters as peak, liminal phenomena within a "family" of occurrences that are open to those who have some sensitivity to the mysterious facet of life.

Both James and Buber believe that this kind of occurrence is an encounter with some "Other" that is made possible by the person's openness or striving for openness. This, however, is not a sufficient condition. The encounter cannot simply be willed. For Buber, people "happen" to each other; in James' definition, there is an element of "passivity." Still, James speaks of a sensitivity to what may be called the mystical "spectrum" and Buber describes the ability of the fully formed human personality to make in-depth contact with another person's essence.

This knowledge of the Other is acquired in a nonscientific way; it cannot even be ascribed to particular sensory impressions. Yet, it is a powerful, insightful revelation. This combination can bestow on this kind of knowledge a mysterious aura, sometimes frightening or deeply touching – generating, perhaps, some of the "mysterium tremendum" quality described by Otto.

Nevertheless, it seems that the more impressive, spectacular phenomena on the mystical spectrum differ from the experiences encountered in the consulting room. The latter originate from human-to-human contact and not from an encounter with what may be a divine being. These two situations are likely to be different in terms of contents as well as intensity. Experiences in therapy may be pleasant or disturbing, but they are often subtle and elusive. In Buber's words: "how delicate are the appearances of the Thou!" (1923/2010, p. 98). Though experiences of immersion – either joyful or frightening – as well as feeling overwhelmed by Otherness can occur even in this thoroughly human encounter, they differ from the immense joy or fright inspired by contact with the holy. However, according to Buber, the encounter cannot be reduced to the emotion it generates or to its intensity. The quality of contact is the heart of the matter; the transcendence of everyday I-It detachment and the transition into a new sphere, one that generates a Noetic experience – a deep, internal knowledge of a new, shared reality.

In the spirit of James' parsimony and generalizability, I offer a definition of what I see as mystical concepts in psychoanalysis. I suggest certain potential criteria for characterizing the uniqueness of the mystical in psychoanalysis, as well as bringing it into the fold of the mystical spectrum or "family" of phenomena. Mystical concepts seek to capture meaningful experiential phenomena that (1) often elude verbalization but, nevertheless, (2) possess a Noetic quality; that are (3) part of a communicative process, entail (4) an element of transcendence and (5) are experienced as transformative.

The elements of this definition are interrelated. In "an element of transcendence" I mean that the participants of the communicative process transcend their former selves to truly meet the Other, in a Buberian sense. The self is not the same as it was before this meeting with the Other. It is a transformative moment for both. In a therapeutic context, it is a moment of developmental growth. The knowledge, the Noetic element or "insight" acquired have a life changing meaning and are experienced as a developmental achievement.

Such transformation naturally entails great emotional force. The emotional impact of the meeting is both the cause and the effect of the transformation. Unlike Buber, who viewed emotions as secondary to the meeting, in my view emotions are the "stuff" the meeting – and its mutual impact – are made of. It is a deeply meaningful emotional experience, though this meaning often resists definition.

The nonverbal quality is important, because this is not an intellectual realization – what Bion (1970) would call "transformation in K." Neither is it similar to any other nonverbal experience. There is a wide range of nonverbal experiences both within therapy and outside it. Listening to music, for example, can be a deeply meaningful, even powerful experience, which may even trigger a mystical experience. Indeed, many religions often used music to evoke or resonate sublime emotions. However, this is not enough to qualify listening to music as a mystical moment. For the experience to be mystical, the Noetic element – the feeling of having acquired deep and transformative knowledge – is essential. This is the "mystery" element: life-changing, fateful knowledge has been acquired, but not in a conscious, accessible or verbalizable way. This knowledge is inseparable from a transformation of the self – what Bion would call "transformation in O" or "becoming O."

In James' description, the mystery lies in communication with an Other who is experienced as both infinitely greater than – and intimately connected to – the mystic (Barnard, 1997). In contrast, in the interpersonal mystical moment that concerns us here, the mystery does not lie in the identity of this "other side" of the meeting. It is, nevertheless, a meeting with an Other; a meeting that deeply transforms the self. In spite but also because of its all-too-human context, such meeting offers the opportunity for psychic growth and grants knowledge that resonates throughout one's entire being – yet remains ineffable.

References

Barnard, G.W. (1997). *Exploring Unseen Worlds: William James and the Philosophy of Mysticism*. Albany: State University of New York Press.

Ben-Shlomo, J. (2012). *On Links between Religion and Mysticism*. Jerusalem: Carmel. (Hebrew).

Bion, W.R. (1970). *Attention and Interpretation*. London: Karnac.

Black, D.M. (Ed.) (2006). *Psychoanalysis and Religion in the 21 Century*. London & New York: Routledge.

Buber, M. (2010). *I and Thou*. Tr. R.G. Smith. New York: Martino Publishing. (Original work published in 1923).

Buber, M. (2014). *Between Man and Man*. Tr. R.G. Smith. New York: Martino Publishing. (Original work published in 1947).

Eigen, M. (1993) *The Electrified Tightrope*. Ed. A. Phillips. Northvale, New Jersey, London: Jason Aronson Inc.

Eigen, M. (1998). *The Psychoanalytic Mystic*. London & New York: Free Association Books.

James, W. (1987). The varieties of religious experience. In Bruce Kuklick (Ed.), *William James Writings 1902–1910* (pp. 3–482). New York: The Library of America. (Original work Published 1902)

Koren, I. (2002). Between Buber's Daniel and His I and Thou: A new examination. *Modern Judaism, 22*:169–198.

Otto, R. (1950). *The Idea of the Holy*. Tr. J.W. Harvey. London: Oxford University Press. (Original work published 1917).

Chapter 2

A brief history of the mystical in psychoanalysis

In the beginning, psychoanalysis viewed religion and mysticism as inseparable. Unlike James (1902/1987), who clearly distinguished between formal institutionalized religion and personal religious experience, Freud made no distinctions in what he saw as a form of collective immaturity bordering on social pathology. Inheriting this distaste for what is clearly a central human phenomenon, psychoanalysis has thus spent most of its history engaging in little dialogue with professional literature on religion or mysticism, which may have informed finer distinctions. Freud's derision, together with his famous falling out with the mystically inclined Jung and Ferenczi, effectively barred most systematic thinking about religious experience in psychoanalysis until roughly the 1970s. Despite this conceptual taboo, the mystical element in psychoanalysis has been present from the very birth of the new discipline and, as this chapter will demonstrate, is paradoxically inherent in its core assumptions. Yet, as few ventured to look behind the doors Freud chose to keep closed, the mystical facet of psychoanalysis remained mostly hidden.

In contrast, when reading contemporary psychoanalytic writings, one discovers that the mystical has become a fashionable topic, finally disentangled from traditional religions and, while still somewhat dissociated from mainstream psychoanalytic thought, discussed quite freely. Nevertheless, this virtually diametric reversal involves the same original sin: a lack of real integration by means of a systematic study of the mystical phenomenon in its own right and its connection to psychoanalysis. Rather than being viewed as either refutable or exotic, the mystical experience should be studied and explored more deeply,

DOI: 10.4324/9781003200796-2

especially since, as I would argue, it is intimately related to psycho-analytic practice and core theoretical assumptions.

This chapter retells the history of psychoanalysis (with a focus on British and American developments) from a new perspective: that of the mystical element. What follows is an introductory analysis – that is, naturally, far from exhaustive – of the historical relation between the overt discussion or denial of the mystical experience and its evolution and expression in core psychoanalytic concepts.[1] We will begin, naturally, with Freud.

Freud: The mysterious unconscious

Freud was the progenitor of a new science of the mind which claimed that the human personality was a battlefield where mighty forces wrestled for dominance: the instincts and their mental representatives as well as society's ethical demands, mediated by a sense of the possible and the expedient. Across different layers of meaning, desires, and counter-desires determine who we are and what kind of symptoms we will present with. Many of the main conflicts shaping our existence were seen as situated in the unconscious part of the mind. This was Freud's great discovery. With all the changes psychoanalytic theory has undergone, this notion of the unconscious, involving multiple meanings and ways of being and thinking, is still perhaps the central axis that unites the different psychoanalytic schools.

In his many writings, Freud describes various ways of approaching this mysterious psychic "organ" that is the root of psychic life and psychic suffering. One such way, which Freud saw as central, was the study of dreams. Many hold that the publication of *The Interpretation of Dreams* marks the dawn of psychoanalysis. The book describes the unconscious as a talented storyteller, masterfully hiding meaning in a tapestry woven of the day's residues and symbols of repressed desires. This work of art simultaneously hides and expresses dream-thoughts that seek to escape the prison of repression. However, many of Freud's readers often overlook the fact that we are hereby introduced to a world of an "underground intelligence" and, moreover, one that is working against yet another underground intelligence (that which chooses what to repress and what kinds of compromises to make). Both these intelligences are operating outside of their "owner's" conscious awareness: the resulting picture is quite different from the vortex of desires and animalistic instincts that eventually became commonly associated with the unconscious.

It is in *The Interpretation of Dreams* that nascent psychoanalysis had made one of its most important discoveries: there is a deeply meaningful, hidden knowledge that mysteriously encodes itself into obscure symbols and communicates itself to the conscious person in cryptic ways. This knowledge becomes lost, unclear even to its owner, until the analyst peals away the layers and decodes its hidden meaning. This process of deciphering is also the means of curing and achieving transformation. Although the analyst is portrayed as an almost all-powerful discoverer of meanings, Freud (1900) also says that something unknown and unreachable will remain in every dream, resisting all attempts at understanding.

> There is often a passage in even the most thoroughly interpreted dream which has to be left obscure; [...] at that point there is a tangle of dream-thoughts which cannot be unraveled and which moreover adds nothing to our knowledge of the content of the dream. This is the dream's navel, the spot where it reaches down into the unknown. (p. 525)

Here, at the heart of Freud's supposedly positivistic thought, we encounter the first intimation of the mystical in psychoanalysis: the interpretation of dreams is a Noetic experience of revelation. Like an internal oracle, dreams enigmatically reveal the secrets of the psyche in the context of analytic communication. Though the work of interpretation is done through a verbal medium, Freud knew that the resulting transformation is emotional and experiential: mere intellectual understanding is not enough. Moreover, even when a dream is thoroughly analyzed, there will always remain a mysterious, elusive kernel that refuses to give in to verbal understanding, an umbilical cord to the unknown.

Another tool Freud discovered was free association. Unlike deliberate speech, speaking without self-monitoring may slacken the guarding forces that keep the repressed from surfacing. Freud believed that so-called "free" associations reveal unconscious connections between thoughts (Freud, 1900), like a trail of breadcrumbs leading home to some hidden meaning. The analyst approached dreams and any other analytic objects in the same manner: by listening to associations and trying to reconstruct an internal road map of symbols laden with unconscious meaning.

A third crucially important discovery was transference. Unlike dreams and associations, transference, as an enactment of former relationships, recreated unconscious material in a more direct and palpable way in the consulting room. It did so by casting the analyst in the role of father, mother or any other important figure from the patient's past, involving them in an emotional drama that had shaped the patient's personality. Working through transference, which is an immediate and emotionally powerful experience, allows the analytic pair to recreate the very conditions in which psychopathology was created and seek out a different ending for the patient's story. Such recreation is more powerful and effective than any verbal, conscious exchange.

All these analytic tools, designed to lead to the mysterious unconscious, share a common feature: they are asymmetrical communication processes, in which the analyst is the receiver and interpreter of material and emotional intensity originating in the patient. The analyst is an expert who knows how to put together the puzzle pieces revealed to her through dreams, associations, slips of tongue and the transference relationship. However, unlike other experts, the analyst cannot rely solely – or even mostly – on her knowledge and on accessible forms of expertise. In "Recommendations to Physicians Practicing Psychoanalysis," Freud (1912) writes about the function of the analyst:

> To put it in a formula: he must turn his own unconscious like a receptive organ towards the transmitting unconscious of the patient. He must adjust himself to the patient as a telephone receiver is adjusted to the transmitting microphone. (pp. 115–116)

In "Two Encyclopedia Articles" (1923), he further avows that

> Experience soon showed that the attitude which the analytic physician can most advantageously adopt was to surrender himself to his own unconscious mental activity, in a state of evenly suspended attention, to avoid as far as possible reflection

and the construction of conscious expectations, not to try to fix
something in his memory, and by these means to catch the drift of
the patient's unconscious with his own unconscious. (p. 239)

These quotes clearly indicate that the work of the analytic "physi-
cian" is quite different from that of the medical doctor or the scientist. A deep understanding of the patient does not result from
scientific observation grounded in empirical data. Rather, it is a
wholly different type of insight that depends on the same mysterious
and uncontrollable agency in the analyst that she strives to "understand" in her patient.

As Bollas (1999, 2007) emphasizes, these passages in Freud's
writings represent a completely different theory of the unconscious
than its prevailing equation with the animalistic Id and those parts of
the Ego and Super Ego that try to keep it in check. According to
Bollas, Freud – ironically enough – repressed his own theory of the
unconscious. The unconscious as depicted here is intelligent, receptive, and communicative, even empathic and creative. In *The
Interpretation of Dreams*, Freud describes the inner dreamer and attributes it with the creativity of waking life as well, claiming that
intellectual and artistic accomplishment draw heavily on unconscious
processes. According to Freud, this is why artistic innovations and
inventions often seem to simply spring to mind, practically complete.
In Freud's later writings, the qualities of this "clever" unconscious
fade before the "seething cauldron" of instinct, an image that better
conforms, perhaps, to the dominance of positivistic science, to which
Freud aspired to contribute.

The "repressed" Freudian unconscious is an active, perceptive,
empathic, and creative system. To a significant extent, it is this very
notion that unites many psychoanalytic theories today and that
serves as the most prominent aspect of Freud's legacy. Moreover, this
view of the unconscious as intelligent and communicative – through
dreams, associations, and transference, but also through means that
do not reach consciousness – is the seed of the mystical element, that
would later evolve, though mostly in a "repressed" mode, away from
psychoanalysis' center of attention.

Keeping in mind this notion of the unconscious, let us recall the
definition of the mystical experience: meaningful experiences that

elude verbalization; that possess a Noetic quality; that are part of a communicative process; that have an element of transcendence; and are experienced as transformative. Can Freud's notion of the unconscious thereby be considered mystical? The answer is somewhat ambiguous.

The various expressions of the unconscious – dreams and transference phenomena – are dramatic creations, with a potentially powerful emotional impact that often escapes full verbalization, at least before they are analyzed. The Freudian analyst tries to comprehend their hidden massage through the verbal method of free association, which sends the patient into a semi-dreamlike state, an in-between area of consciousness, where they supposedly slip into the unconscious realm.

It is certainly a communicative process. If the analyst fails to grasp the meaning of transference phenomena, they may remain in the form of mere repetition compulsion; the dream will remain a massage lost in a masquerade, never to become an analytic object. The analyst is thus the true medium of the unconscious. Within the context of therapy, these omnipresent phenomena – seeing as people always dream and are constantly projecting their past relationships onto present ones – pass through the analyst's unconscious, striking her inner cords and eliciting a response. If the analyst practices evenly hovering attention and listens to her own unconscious, this response will presumably help her to arrive at a pertinent and curative interpretation. Freud never elaborated on how unconscious communication eventually results in a verbal, causal, and historical interpretation. This process has remained a kind of "loose end" in his theory, stemming perhaps from his repression of the intelligent unconscious. If one were to read only his "Recommendations to Physicians," one might have been led to believe that Freud did not put much emphasis on *conscious* understanding.

However, taking into consideration his entire corpus and especially his dictum about making the unconscious conscious, it is unlikely that he viewed unconscious communication as transformative in and of itself. Perhaps he only saw it as a preliminary stage of information gathering. If so, Freud's unconscious communication does not fully meet the criteria for a mystical concept because the letter requires transformation. Nevertheless, as we will see, a later evolution of his concepts is less ambiguous in its mystical quality.

Freud's discovery of the unconscious mysterious form of communication is certainly the beginning not only of psychoanalysis but also of a mystical seed that would grow and develop to imbue many of its core concepts. For Freud, psychoanalysis offers a chance for the emergence of meaning, for the kind of development that leads to deep transformation. These revelations are made possible by the analytic relationship, which makes interpretive use of unconscious attunement. Inseparably from the founding principles of psychoanalysis, therefore, Freud discovered (perhaps unconsciously) its mystical way of working: one unconscious relates to another, informing and perhaps transforming it through a singular form of encounter, shaped by Freud's technique.

Freud the man of science and the Jungian threat

As Freud was very reluctant about those elements in his theory that did not fit the scientific zeitgeist, he is mostly known for espousing a view of the unconscious as the immature, thoughtless, and instinctual part of the personality. The role of the psychoanalytic cure was to uncover what was going on "down there" and submit such primitive material to the control of rational, conscious thinking.

Freud's ambition to secure his position in the lucrative circles of positivistic science probably played a key role in his unequivocal rejection of religion and his reductionist treatment of both religion and mystical experience. Freud often addressed the question of religion in his writings, thus revealing its prominence in his thinking. He offered both psychological and semi-anthropological perspectives on it, as in *Totem and Taboo, Civilization and its Discontents, The future of an Illusion* and *Moses and Monotheism*. In all of these writings, Freud locates the religious feeling in the primitive, infantile layer of the mind. Religion is associated with the child's awe of his father and the mystical "oceanic experience" – on which Freud's friend, Romain Roland, asked him to comment in his account of religion – was treated as a regressive, narcissistic wish to merge with the mother.

In his lecture, "The Question of a Weltanschauung," Freud (1933) is not only content with a reductionist description of the roots of religious experience but also portrays it as a dangerous force, undermining humanity's striving toward enlightenment, and rationality. Freud is optimistic, however, in anticipating that science and its newest addition, psychoanalysis, will safely lead mankind out of the darkness of ignorance created by its own infantile instincts and anxieties. In *The Future of an Illusion* (1927), he writes:

> Most of these infantile neuroses are overcome spontaneously in the course of growing up, and this is especially true of the obsessional neuroses of childhood. The remainder can be cleared up later still by psycho-analytic treatment. In just the same way, one might assume, humanity as a whole, in its development through the ages, fell into states analogous to the neuroses, and for the same reasons – namely because in the times of its ignorance and intellectual weakness the instinctual renunciations indispensable for man's communal existence had only been achieved by it by means of purely affective forces. [...] Religion would thus be the universal obsessional neurosis of humanity; like the obsessional neurosis of children, it arose out of the Oedipus complex, out of the relation to the father. If this view is right, it is to be supposed that a turning-away from religion is bound to occur with the fatal inevitability of a process of growth, and that we find ourselves at this very juncture in the middle of that phase of development. (p. 42)

It seems that Freud viewed the task of leading humanity to the light as part of the purpose of psychoanalysis and he devoted much of his intellectual zeal to it. In one dramatic moment in psychoanalysis' history, he even denounced his close friend and chosen successor, Jung, because the latter's theory of collective unconscious had undermined Freud's sexuality-based, biological view of the human psyche. Jung's rich worldview, with its openly mystical assumption of unconsciously shared archetypes of human experience, which connect all of humanity and underpin both the individual personality and collective human life, remained external to what became the canon of classical psychoanalysis. Jung founded his own school, where he and his successors independently developed a deeply spiritual branch of psychoanalysis. There, Freud's intimation of the communicative unconscious was fully acknowledged and could evolve in a markedly different manner than the subversive or repressed route it had taken in Freud's lineage of thought, which is the focus of this book.

Before exploring what happened to the mystical element at the hands of Freud's successors, it is important to point out how deeply this famous rift shaped the history of psychoanalysis. Binyamini (2008), in sketching the differences between Freud and Jung, states that, whereas for Freud the subject must accept that they are separate, partial, and lacking, for Jung the subject's task is to understand that they are complete, one with humanity and with God. The developmental process Jung termed "individuation" is aimed at recognizing this unity, one's participation with the divine and the unity between the particular and subjective level and the transcendent level that contains it. This is a platonic view of human destiny: we are born with the goal of corresponding to a preexisting ideal that is our true nature. For Freud and, for a long time, his successors as well, development and particularly individuation meant almost the opposite: the acceptance of separateness, the ability to invest libido (love) in separate objects and the attainment of disillusioned ego-autonomy. In this vision of human life, the only hope of gaining a reasonably balanced relationship with the "other" within us, the unconscious, is coming to terms with the id and governing it more effectively. One could say that Freud and Jung profoundly and fatefully disagreed about what it meant to achieve psychic maturity.

As I will demonstrate throughout this book, the mystical never wholly disappeared. It kept resurfacing in the Freudian lineage in more or less disguised forms. Although Jung went on a separate path, Freud and his followers could never wholly banish what can be ironically termed, borrowing from Jung's archetypes, "the shadow theory" of the wise unconscious and its capacity for mystical connectedness. However, this divorce (and, later, the similar rift with Ferenczi) held back the developmental understanding of the mystical element and psychic connectedness for many decades. For years, following Freud, the mystical was understood simply as a very primitive, narcissistic union, which posed a threat to libidinal development, which is meant to be outwards-reaching and object-seeking. In Freud's eyes, the Jungian alternative seemed like some mythical siren that calls one back into primordial existence and thus, as Freud explicitly said, a danger to individual sanity (Binyamini, 2008, p. 312) and to the growth of a rational culture.

As will be shown later, it was not until Winnicott that an alternative was born: deep connectedness without merger. This understanding, at least in terms of the mystical element, had to wait for later developments by contemporary authors such as Reiner (2017), who, based on Ferenczi, Bion and to some degree Winnicott, suggests an important distinction between an infantile or traumatic union with divine truth that abandons the self and the growth-promoting experience of an integrative adult ego, which can better understand and learn from the experience. In trauma, mystical experience only serves to escape the self's reality and "bleed out into an infantile mental universe in manic identification with a now canonized mother/God" (p. 137).

Meanwhile, in the Jungian lineage, Erich Neumann wrote as early as the 1940s about the mystical journey of development: from the "uroboric" phase, in which self-other boundaries are fluid and dissolve into each other (a phase which Neumann, much like Buber, viewed as escapist, immature, even pathological mysticism), toward "the mysticism of transformation in the human world," which does not negate this world and lives in the creative tension between conscious and unconscious. For Neumann (1968), human beings are "homo mysticus," since the mystical journey is identical to the developmental journey of becoming a self that is a creative, alive, and capable of agency. With every developmental leap, one must submit to a radical mystical experience through which the self's boundaries are reorganized.

Both Freud and Jung were rather deterministic in their thinking. However, much like the famous painting by Raphael, "The School of Athens," one master (like Aristotle) pointed downward to "earthly" matters, while the other (like Plato) gestured upward, toward the divine. For Freud, it was materialistic determinism; for Jung, a spiritualistic belief in a predetermined divine destiny of the self. In a way, they were each other's theoretical "shadow": Jung accused Freud of confining humanity to its basest parts, favoring the pathological and denying the divine in our nature (Jung, 1933; Binyamini, 2008); Freud proclaimed that the mystical is infantile, narcissistic, even psychotic. Though my knowledge of the Jungian school is too limited to determine the price it paid for their "materialistic" shadow, beyond exile from the classical cannon, it is quite clear that, in the Freudian lineage, the shadow of the mystical has led to fear and even censorship of certain ideas and thus to the under-development or late development of certain key notions. Freud's narrow view of the mystical strictly as primitive oceanic feeling significantly slowed its understanding as intimately related to the core psychoanalytic issue of the development of self-other boundaries.

Even after this rift with Jung, Freud could not eliminate the idea of transpersonal human connectedness, which he expressed through his notion of a hereditary mythology that shaped the human race in *Totem and Taboo (1913)*. Though this vision bears the marks of materialistic ideas and Lamarckian genetics (Binyamini, 2008), it is quite clear that both thinkers agreed, on a deep level, on the communicative, perhaps even unifying and universal nature of the unconscious.

It seems that it is precisely because of the deep implications of his own ideas that Freud considered such a spiritual direction as a great threat to the legitimacy of his theory, perhaps even greater than the other dissenting voices he declared as nonpsychoanalytic, such as those of Adler and Rank. It is no wonder, then, that when his deep commitment to the scientific *weltanschauung* seemed to clash with some of his own findings, like the communicative, intelligent unconscious, a painful conflict ensued. The external symptoms of this conflict were his falling out with Jung (and later with Ferenczi) and his immediate successors' relative obliviousness of this "shadow theory" of the unconscious and its mystical implications. But there were also internal signs of struggle, not so easily resolved, which resulted in textual tensions and inconsistencies in Freud's extensive body of writing. These will be analyzed in greater depth in chapter four. Those conflicts were perhaps inevitable. Freud was the creator of a new, daring and initially doubtful field, who wished to hide, even from himself, the mysterious, almost telepathic, qualities of his fundamental finding – the unconscious. Freud's courage facilitated the study of psychic life in a predominantly materialistic era. It remains for his successors to find further courage to question the validity of the reductionistic worldview that guided him in this quest.

Klein and Bion – The mysticism of thinking together

Klein's appearance on the psychoanalytic stage fundamentally changed psychoanalytic theory, shifting its center of gravity toward the early mother–infant drama and away from the notion of the solitary child struggling with erotogenic development. The Kleinian concept of projective identification describes a process of depositing parts of the self in the Other, either in order to get rid of them or for safe keeping. In phantasy, they remain in the Other until the child is ready to face them. In the meantime, they are neither dangerously present as a part of the self nor too far as to become completely detached. This means that the Other – the mother – is not completely separate either. Though Klein was criticized for undervaluing the importance of the actual relationship with the mother, and the importance of her actions, such importance, if not stressed, is implied. The mother can succeed in her role of containment or fail in it (Klein, 1946), impairing the child's ability to achieve integration and leaving him to reap the bitter fruit of the victory of his own death instinct.

Kleinian theory deepened our understanding of the landscape of the unconscious and of the early formation of the personality through an unconscious connection with the caretaking Other. As the actual reciprocity of this connection was underemphasized, the mystical element had only an embryonic existence in Klein's thought. Klein describes the infantile inner world as dominated by powerful nonverbal experiences of bliss as well as possession and prosecution. In health, these become integrated and thus fundamentally transformative and growth-promoting states. Nevertheless, the element of communication is almost altogether absent and one can hardly argue that Klein's descriptions of the baby's frightful, haunted world, outline any kind of Noetic experience. Much like in Freud's thinking, the element of unconscious communication remained in the shadow, waiting for other times and other thinkers.

As for Klein's concept of projective identification, Bion was the one who fully realized its revolutionary potential, both in terms of the "classical" psychoanalytic goal of understanding mental development and for the evolution of the mystical element. In many ways, Bion is a unique character in the history of psychoanalysis. On the one hand, he is certainly a central figure and, judging from the number of publications relying on and elaborating his ideas, his influence seems to be growing steadily. Many eminent psychoanalytic writers, such as Ogden, Symington, Grotstein as well as Eigen, Brown, Reiner, Vermote, Ferro, and Civitarese see themselves as his conceptual successors. On the other hand, he is also perceived as an eccentric (Reiner, 2012; Grotstein, 2016) whose ideas have made his fellow Kleinians very uncomfortable about what is now termed his "late" period, in which his thinking became more overtly mystical. I believe that this split between the consensual "early" Bion and the controversial "late" Bion can serve as a strong example of the way mystical ideas often grow in the heart of psychoanalytic consensus, but generate so much anxiety in the psychoanalytic community that they are treated as redundant, embarrassing or even outright alien.

Bion developed a theory of thinking which, unlike other psychoanalytic theories, stressed the function of thinking itself rather than its contents (Ogden, 2009). One of Bion's key concepts is that of the alpha-function, a psychic process that metabolizes sensations into meaning and thoughts and which is primarily unconscious and dream-like. By postulating that dream thought is the central and crucial locus of processing and giving meaning, Bion essentially turned the Freudian project of making the unconscious conscious on its head. Rather than seeing the unconscious as the hiding place of primitive instinctual experience, he saw it as the primary channel for listening, understanding, and transformation in analysis. Throughout his writings, Bion developed these notions – reminiscent of Freud's ideas in "Recommendations to Physicians" – more consistently and in a broader scope, positing dream-work as a constant process on which the elaboration and signification of not only the analytic situation but also the entirety of human experience, depended.

Another revolutionary feature of Bion's theory was the claim that these unconscious thought processes are carried out by more than one individual. According to Bion, it takes at least two people to think, most of all in early life. Bion redefined projective identification as a form of direct unconscious communication and as a trigger of this joint thinking process. The baby (or patient) does not merely phantasize about transferring their feelings and parts of their self to the Other; they actually *make* the Other (the analyst or parent) share their unconscious predicament, by producing the relevant feelings in them. If the receiver can tolerate these seemingly unbearable states and think them – not through some conscious and logical process, but through the dream-like and unconscious process of *reverie* – the sender (baby or patient) would then be able to reclaim these parts as something thinkable and, therefore, bearable. Moreover, this shared cycle of projective identification and reverie allows the baby to acquire the function of thinking (or alpha-function) itself. Later in life, there may be thoughts that are beyond the capacities of one's alpha function, requiring its further development or elaboration. Then, once again, we need an Other to think with us and for us, not through conscious problem solving or brainstorming, but by having them dream our undreamt dreams.

Despite postulating an exchange and transformation of mental content by unknown, intangible means, this theory was not met with objection in the professional community. Bion's containment theory became consensual alongside his view of projective identification, which became the predominant understanding of this term. The striking assumption of mutual unconscious influence – a stronger claim then Freud's unconscious receptivity – seemed to somehow pass under the rider of the professional community's notice.

Later on, however, Bion began discussing his notion of O – "The ultimate reality, ultimate truth, the godhead, the infinite, the thing-in-itself" (1970, p. 26) – as the heart of analytic work (for a more comprehensive discussion of Bion's O, see chapter 5). To make matters worse, he stated that O cannot be reached by any sensual means and that the work of the analyst most resembles that of the mystic, by striving for "at-one-ment with O." Bion's colleagues could no longer ignore such scandalous "mystical" connotations. In response, they preserved much of what was valuable in Bion's thinking by splitting him into his "good," solid period of analytic theorizing and his dubious mystical musings. By doing so, just like in the mental processes of splitting and projective identification described-ironically enough – by Kleinians and Bionians, they had bought time for other thinkers (like Ogden, Grotstein, Reiner, Eigen, Brown, and others) to elaborate the psychoanalytic community's alpha-function so that it could contain, process, and grant meaning to Bion's previously intolerable thoughts.

Though this process of mentally digesting and understanding Bion is still ongoing, there is less and less doubt that Bion, even the "late" Bion, is crucially important for psychoanalytic thought. In the history of the mystical element hereby traced, Bion's contribution is critical. He is not only one of the first analytic thinkers to use the word "mystical" un-apologetically in the context of psychoanalytic work but also the first to explore its meaning as a powerful communicative process taking place through intangible, nonsensual means and affecting deep transforma-tion through Noetic, experiential knowledge.

Bion began the transformation of psychoanalysis from an already daring and novel field of inquiry, that explored the mysteries of the unconscious mind, into an adventurous journey into an even less charted territory: the area of mental overlap between human beings. His theory is based on the unconscious sharing of experience by at least two people (as discussed in his writings on groups). Moreover, he put forth the idea that the most unique and revered of all human qualities, thinking, is actuality acquired through a mysterious form of communication, and requires a constant striving for contact with the ineffable.

Winnicott – The mysticism of playing together

Like Bion, Winnicott is one of the most influential figures in the history of psychoanalysis and the founder of a great and profoundly revolutionary lineage of thinking. Unlike Bion, Winnicott was never explicitly "mystical." On the contrary, he is often portrayed as a pacifying figure, modestly presenting his contributions in the context of Freud's and Klein's theories. However, he sparked what is perhaps the greatest revolution concerning our view of human beings after Freud. As shown in the chapter dedicated to Winnicott, this re-volution entails both clinical insight and an epistemological under-standing of what psychoanalytic knowledge – or human knowledge in general – is. Both aspects of this revolution are closely related to the Winnicottian transformation of the mystical element.

Winnicott essentially postulates two distinct ways of co-existing in a shared mental field: first, through his notion that "there is no such thing as an infant" (1960, p. 587); and second, through his focus on play in potential space, where "such a thing as an infant" as well as "such a thing as a mother," begin to emerge. These two ways, and especially the latter represent a profound and, despite the prominence of Winnicottian thinking, underappreciated revolution in the history of psychoanalysis.

The first mode of mental sharing Winnicott presents is a symbiotic one. The mother, entering the phase of primary maternal preoccupation, is so attuned to her baby that it does not even need to signal its needs by crying. She just "feel herself into her infant's place" (Winnicott, 1956, p. 304). Winnicott stresses that signaling belongs to a different phase, when the baby releases its mother from this "semi-psychotic" state. I think that it is fair to say (this point will be more meticulously addressed in chapter 6) that Winnicott is referring to something reminiscent of a telepathic connection, or more accurately, a psychosomatic bond that allows an almost first-hand knowledge of the Other. Winnicott explains that this phase is a natural extension of the pregnancy, in which mother and baby were, in fact, one. Nevertheless, how can such communication be accounted for? Winnicott himself states that any reference to hormonal changes or "maternal instincts" is insufficient. Thus, the biological aspect of maternity is only part of the story or, perhaps, a cover story for an inexplicably powerful experience of emotional sharing. This symbiotic phase, however, lasts a very short while and both mother and baby emerge from it as two beings who live together but are not one and the same. Transitional phenomena begin to emerge because baby and mother can exist at first (and throughout life in a way) only in a liminal zone between inside and outside, between shared objective reality and what is subjective, sacred, and personal. There, in the creative field between mother and baby, a new way of being and knowing begins to form. Baby and mother can now know each other: not because they are merged, but because they participate in a mutual act of creation – play.

Though it differs from the dramatic totality of the "oceanic experience," in which baby and mother or God and man are one, the Noetic experience arrived at through play enables a more mature and intimate dialogue with the world. This new way of knowing something through creative contact is perhaps the only true way of knowing. By postulating a third zone of reality, which is neither subjective (and thus magically omnipotent) nor objective (and thus separate and containing isolated beings that are encapsulated in their own skin), Winnicott paves the way for a new philosophy of knowing and a new era in psychoanalysis. Either implicitly or explicitly, Winnicott's successors embraced this basic assumption of a common psychic field that people can share without eliminating separateness and uniqueness.

A kind of "overlapping psychic field" theory has existed, albeit in the shadows, from the very beginning of psychoanalysis, starting with Freud's conversing unconscious. But it was mostly a unifying field, where baby and mother were collapsed into one (with the mother containing the baby, as in Bion's theory), limiting the field of psychic contact to a primitive, merged existence. Because the intimation of Freudian "primary narcissism" phantasies embedded in this form of mysticism was found abhorrent, the "field" assumption was thoroughly negated and abandoned. This negation was historically necessary both because of the "unscientific" quality it might have lent to psychoanalysis and, perhaps, because it posed a major threat to the experience of individuality (Kohut, 1984; Ogden, 1994/1999). After Winnicott, however, one is no longer forced to refute either the experience of psychic contact or the reality of separateness. In my view, both these poles of human existence are empirically present in the consulting room and in human experience in general. Winnicott's potential space has freed us from falsely having to choose which of the two is more "real."

Thus far, Winnicott's contribution was mainly applied to the clinical context. My claim is that it is the concept of potential space - which introduces a unique ontological position, neither "inside" the inner world nor "out there," in the realm of scientifically measurable objects – which makes his theory such a groundbreaking achievement in understanding the phenomena of subjectivity, intersubjectivity, and religious experience. The human psyche is never solipsistic. Winnicottian subjectivity is the fruit of a uniquely human function that preserves the tension between aloneness and profound sharing. In metaphorical terms, the existence of the "Winnicottian God" does not have to be "objective" in a scientific sense, as identically perceived by everyone. But it must be real, a living God of shared experience.

American ego-psychology and Kohut – The painful choice between poles

Across the Ocean, away from direct Kleinian influence, the current of psychoanalytic thought took another turn. For a long time, the

American ego-psychology school dominated the psychoanalytic scene in the United States. For the mystical element, its decades-long reign was a time of almost complete suppression. Ego-psychology seems to have inherited only one side of Freud's conflict, the side that had won the battle – waged in his mind – between the mysteries of the unconscious and the scientism of his age. Accordingly, the Ego-psychology analyst was viewed as a scientist, objectively observing the patient's materials. Analyst and patient were perceived as observer and observed. The former was detached and objective in accordance with the medical model. The analyst's aim was to enable the patient to control their childish, instinctual unconscious derivatives by fortifying their Ego and becoming a kind of observing and critical scientist in their own life and a master of their own psyche. Among other factors, this notion of analysis may have stemmed from the fact that the American Psychoanalytic Society barred its doors to non-physicians, in defiance of Freud's opinion. The communicative unconscious was, as Bollas claims, pushed into the shadows and quite forgotten.

It was in this climate that Kohut began to offer his widely different view of psychoanalysis. His theory was a direct rebellion against key Ego-psychology values, especially those of separateness and independence. He maintained that human beings begin and end their life in an empathic matrix that sustains them. One never achieves full autonomy from the empathic nourishment provided by others, nor should one aspire to such autonomy. This, Kohut claimed, would be as ridiculous as wishing to live without air (1984, p. 77). He coined the term "selfobject" to denote an object that is not wholly separate from the self and that answers the self's narcissistic needs. For him, development is not about shifting from narcissism to object-relations, but about transforming one's relations with one's selfobjects (1984, p. 52). In early life, dependence is absolute: the child needs a selfobject that would enjoy her existence and admire her; she also needs a selfobject that *she* herself could admire, one with whose power (even greatness) and trustworthy calm she could merge. Later, the form of this primitive relationship changes, but the empathic bond persists. Thus, the adult person can relate to people who appreciate her, without the need for constant admiration. She may use cultural objects such as art or moral values instead of the omnipotent idealized figures of childhood. Moreover, the healthy adult self is capable of expanding and including other people in its empathic circle, so as to serve as a selfobject for others. It is able to channel its narcissism in order to preform creative feats, commit to selfless ends and, in its most advanced form, merge with the universe by transcending isolation and the fear of death and attaining a sense of all-encompassing unity that Kohut (1966) termed "cosmic narcissism."

Kohut was well aware of the revolutionary character of his work. Unlike Winnicott, he felt his contribution to psychoanalysis was so fundamental that he founded a distinct school of thought. But his path was not smooth. He had to combat his colleagues' ridicule for offering a "love therapy" (1984, p. 102), a struggle that might have had an impact on his definitions of what works in psychoanalysis, Inclining him toward what he called "tool and method snobbishness" (ibid, p. 104).[2] Like in Freud's case, Kohut feared that his new theory might sound "unscientific," thus hampering its claims for recognition. According to Kulka (2005), Kohut was particularly sensitive to being criticized as "mystical" – a claim that could easily be made against his concept of cosmic narcissism. But even without this particular term, Kulka views Kohut's theory as aiming for the dissolution of the self in an empathic matrix, with the self's expansions serving to unite it with others: not just as an ethical position or a therapeutic tool, but as a growing awareness of an ontological state of unity.

Indeed, Kohut's landmark 1966 paper presents a developmental theory stemming from the concept of empathy as a main axis. A baby starts its life in a kind of a porous state, in which it can feel its mother's states of mind and vice-versa: the two are empathically united. After the healthy adult has achieved a cohesive self, the empathic mode of relating is no longer overwhelming. Now, the self can expend at will and give itself to others, up to a complete dissolution of boundaries, approaching an "oceanic" unity with the object of merger.[3]

In discussing the fundamental contributions of self-psychology to psychoanalysis, and the future of the former, Kulka (1991) maintains that Kohut had brought about a revolution in the psychoanalytic paradigm of knowledge, shifting from the positivistic model to one where the method of investigation – namely empathy – corresponds to the material being investigated: human experience. He further claims that one of the greatest objections self-psychology still encounters has to do with this unique method of knowing and affecting the patient, granted only to those who would submit to the strenuous requisite of relinquishing separateness without transgressing any boundaries:

> The experiential significance of the situation for the analyst is one of great loneliness, at times a complete abrogation of [...] narcissistic satisfaction, a virtual giving up of one's own psychic space – a kind of acceptance of "being erased" which is not identical with being nothing [...] on the contrary, this is a situation that demands a most intensive psychic presence, having a complex characteristics of passive activity and the dissolution of boundary between self and other without breaking a single boundary. I know that this dialectical presence, which moves between totally contradictory poles, sounds at times verging on mystical romanticization; but this is not the case, and it requires a very persistent theoretical and clinical effort to decipher the complex elements of the special therapeutic presence required. (ibid, p. 180)

Kulka does not explain why this view, which advocates complete selfless dissolution, is not a "mystical romanticization." Does he mean to imply that the presence of a theoretical method and the requirement for study refute this accusation? Certainly, some mystical disciplines involve much study and practice and may have related theological theories. Indeed, Kulka (2005) himself writes that some of Kohut's remarkable courage wavered in the face of the accusation of being "mystical and unscientific," and he retracted his acknowledgment of the radical implications of his concepts.

Kohut's story is yet another example of the conflict psychoanalysis had to face, from its very beginning, concerning its position in the field of human knowledge. For Kohut and his contemporaries, as well as for Freud before him, science or, more accurately, the positivistic model of science was a beacon of truth, which one must strive to reach. Any apparent break with its principles was shameful. While Freud seems to have decided to follow this beacon and repress the more "obscure" aspects of his theory, Kohut is caught in a more conscious struggle. Unlike Bion, who boldly embraces these "obscurities," or Winnicott who shows few signs of awareness or concern about the mystical implications of his thought, Kohut seems to be well aware of the troublesome connotations of his concepts. In particular, his concept of "empathy" as a way of truly knowing the not-fully-separate Other, and the "expandable," transcending self. If the mystical is defined as a Noetic moment that generates transcendence in the self, then, as the foundation for narcissistic transformation, Kohut's notion of empathy certainly qualifies. The Kohutian analyst is capable of knowing the Other "from the inside" by transcending herself to an awareness of their psychic unity.

Kohut explains the fierce opposition he has encountered as a result of this very point, which shattered people's belief in their separateness. He believes that, like Freud, he was facing the consequences of a narcissistic wound that his ideas have inflicted on his generation. He questions Freud's claim that the key injury psychoanalysis caused was demonstrating that no one was master of their own psyche. He claims that Freud's conclusion stems from his preoccupation with knowledge and that this would not necessarily constitute such a great affront for later generations. Meanwhile, Kohut's (1984) revolution is indeed a shattering one:

> Man of our time is the man of the precariously cohesive self, the man who craves the presence, the interest, the availability of the self-cohesion-maintaining selfobject. It is the very intensity of this need that via a wall of secondary prideful disavowal accounts for the fact that he may experience our theory that the self's autonomy is only relative, that, in principle, a self can never exist outside a matrix of selfobjects, as a serious narcissistic blow. Could it be that some of the intense antagonism that self psychology has aroused, that some of the distorting ridicule to which it is exposed, can in part be explained by this factor? (p. 61)

Of course, it can be argued that the shift between Freud's and Kohut's positions was achieved, among other things, through Freud's discoveries and the fact that he dared to inflict what had been a severe wound at the time. One way or another, the difference between the two described offences is not that great: both thinkers complain about their culture's reluctance to accept their ideas because these are undermining core values such as autonomy, separateness, and control.

Kohut, Bion, and Winnicott – Differences and agreements about unity, truth and faith

Kohut's place in the evolution of the mystical element should be understood in the terms he himself suggested. He had brought the challenge on human autonomy to an extreme level. Unlike his contemporaries in the British object-relations school, he was not satisfied with demonstrating how crucial one's first relationships are and how influential these remain throughout one's life due to internalization processes. Kohut believed that human beings remain deeply connected to others – although the term "others" is not fully applicable to the unifying selfobject function – throughout our entire existence.

Kohut's (1984) descriptions potentially indicate that he views some degree of mental unity as omnipresent, although most of us are so engaged in the nonempathic perception modalities required by adult life that we are seldom attuned to it or even aware of it (Kohut, 1966, 1984). Nevertheless, when we do apply it, empathy becomes a Noetic tool that utilizes our fundamental unity in order to know the not-wholly-separate Other. In some ways, this is similar to Bion, who advocates giving in to reverie, to dreaming the Other's dream. For both thinkers, the analyst should engage in an act of discipline that allows her to transcend herself and come in contact with the emotional truth of the patient. Both believe that *the* truth is out there and that one can grasp it (either fully or, according to Bion, only partially) through the empathic matrix or the emotional containment we provide the patient.

There is a notable difference, though: for Bion, the truth is not only in a continues flux but also unreachable. We can only become aware of and use some transformation of it. All we can aspire to is an asymptotic approximation to absolute truth (O) and, although this quest will forever be frustrated, we must commit ourselves to it, despite being imperfect containers for *the truth* (Bion, 1970). For Kohut, however, matters seem to be simpler. Knowledge of the Other is achieved through "vicarious introspection" (Kohut, 1984, p. 82), which is one of his definitions of empathy. By sharing the empathic matrix with the Other, we can know them almost as we know ourselves. Therefore, empathy is both an ontological fact of existence and an epistemology of "observing from zero distance" (Kulka, 1991, p. 177). If something is blocking our knowledge, it is usually our lack of commitment to the selfobject function and to empathic unity.

The possibility (or, for Bion, the inevitability) of being an imperfect container, of striving for but never reaching at-one-ment with the truth may stem from the fact that the patient's truth always retains a solid core of Otherness. However, the notion that this Otherness paradoxically co-exists with psychic connectedness was one of Winnicott's accomplishments. In describing the first days of life and the baby's complete dependence and merger, Winnicott resonates with Bion and even with Kohut's radicality. Nevertheless, with the onset of transitional phenomenon, as we have seen, the person can no longer be considered either fully separate or totally dependent. Rather, the baby's caretaker acquires a new, exciting quality as both "me" and "not-me."

Kohut, Bion, and Winnicott all describe a kind of psychic overlap between baby and mother, and later on, between patient and therapist. But Winnicott's version of what I would name the *psychic overlap paradigm* differs in stressing separateness as an ontological fact that is no less important than that of union. In fact, I chose the term "overlap" precisely in order to capture the Winnicottian reality of mystical contact that is free of the omnipotence and omniscience characteristic of merger.

Interestingly, some authors acknowledge that the revolution brought about by Bion, Winnicott and Kohut is a fundamental one, a paradigm shift in psychoanalysis (Brown, 2011; Eshel, 2019, Grotstein, 2016; Kulka, 1991; Reiner, 2012) but Grotstein and Reiner speak of Bion alone, while Kulka and Eshel who mention Winnicott as well, emphasize the radical unity between the patient's and the analyst's psyche in the analytic situation – both as an epistemological shift but mainly as a powerful clinical tool, while minimizing the role and even the reality of separateness. For example, Eshel (2019) compellingly describes how Bion and Winnicott revolutionized psychoanalytic technique. To capture the scope and significance of this revolution, she offers the term "quantum psychoanalysis" which, through an analogy to the quantum revolution in physics, describes "the fundamental organization of unbroken wholeness that underlies our perceived world of separateness" (p. 268). Like in the physical world, according to some interpretations of quantum mechanics, the deeper reality of psychic relatedness is unity. Eshel does not mention the concept of transitional space as part of this paradigm shift. For her, the essence of the Winnicottian shift involves going back to the primordial unity by allowing a state of radical regression in therapy. While I agree with this view, I think it is a partial one, and one that fails to do justice to the full scope of Winnicott's revolution, by downplaying the importance of his portrayal of later phases of development. While this emphasis on deep connectedness is indeed important and innovative, it only tells half the story. It leaves out Bion's *Caesura*[4] and Winnicott's potential space: the dialectics of separateness and union and the qualities of *psychic overlap* as opposed to *psychic merger*.

It is curious that these three thinkers, Bion, Winnicott, and Kohut, who are so crucial to the evolution of the mystical element in psychoanalysis, entered the stage of psychoanalytic history at more or less the same time. Moreover, each one of them has profoundly revolutionized psychoanalytic theory and technique and, pertinently to their treatment of the mystical element, its epistemology. Bion straightforwardly rejected the positivistic paradigm in favor of "faith." Winnicott uses the word "trust" but, as Eigen (1981/1999) has noted, his theory also requires faith in the Other and in the nature of reality as a prerequisite for play, object-use, and creative engagement with one's surroundings. I would add that the mother and the analyst must also have faith in their abilities to properly feel their baby/patient. *The analyst should not act solely according to her "objective" observations or her theories, but through her faith in the analytic connection and the "knowledge" it yields.* Though Eigen (1981/1999) did not mention Kohut in his seminal article about faith and psychoanalysis, Kohut certainly asks us to believe in our (disciplined) feelings about the patient as a way of knowing the patient's mind. He celebrates empathy as a renewed scientific tool: the only tool suitable for understanding the human psyche.

For all three thinkers, the assumption of psychic overlap is essential for psychoanalytic technique, for understanding human development and, crucially, for knowing and transforming the human psyche. For all three, it is that mysterious contact between souls that provides the only true knowledge (be it limited or complete) that is possible, and that can facilitate change. The work of these thinkers has forever changed the way in which psychoanalysis understands how it works and how it "knows" anything at all.

The mystical element in contemporary psychoanalysis

The obvious successor to this approach is the American relational movement. Bion and Kohut criticized the psychoanalytic aspiration to know the psyche through the methodology of positivistic science. The relational movement, following Winnicott's incipient lead, questioned the analyst's ability to "know" anything that is not co-created with the patient. The analyst was no longer a scientific observer, nor a pure container reaching for absolute truth, free from memory and desire, nor an empathic selfobject, free from countertransference distortions. Regarding the relational notion of the transference-countertransference matrix, I think it is fair to say – paraphrasing Winnicott – that we shouldn't ask neither the analyst nor the patient whether they found or created the Other, or even themselves in relation to that Other. Both answers are true. For the relational approach, analytic "knowledge" had lost its classical meaning and had become irrevocably attached to mutual experiential involvement.

This relational matrix (Mitchell and Aron, 1999) is described as continuously changing, as co-created through the constant negotiation of self-other parts and their different external and internal relationships, with both parties influenced by and influencing each other. This notion has brought the analyst, as a full human being, out of the "closet" that had compelled her to hide all that was uniquely human about her. Following this dramatic change, other elements in psychoanalysis likewise emerged from the darkness of repression. Among them was a new-found interest in mystical and religious elements and their relation to psychoanalysis.

In fact, we are now witnessing the opposite of repression: an unprecedented outpour of professional writing about religion and mysticism, either within the relational movement or in its wider field of influence. The contemporary zeitgeist of pluralism and tolerance deeply influenced even nonrelational writers, such as Symington and Grotstein, two prominent Bionian analysts who wrote extensively on these subjects. Lev (2017, p. 212) even speculates that this shift might mark the emergence of a new psychoanalytic tradition. Moreover, he argues that psychoanalysis has always been a spiritual practice, even before "the spiritual turn in society" that allowed these aspects to be openly discussed. In any case, the extent of the present outpour of writing seems to indicate that we are witnessing a response to some deep, long-unsatisfied need in the psychoanalytic community. One might wonder what this need is exactly, and how is it currently being answered. While the first question is addressed in the following chapters, I will now address the second question by briefly outlining the current "spiritual" trend in psychoanalysis.

Many contemporary writings take the form of comparisons between certain aspects of psychoanalysis and various spiritual traditions, such as Buddhism (Brickman, 1998; Cernovsky, 1988; Ghent, 1999; Peled, 2005; Rubin, 1985) or Jewish Kabbalah (Berke, 1996; Eigen, 2012). Another recurrent theme is the exploration of mystical, religious, or spiritual ideas or aspects in the writings of prominent analysts, mostly Bion, but also Winnicott, Lacan, Loewald, and Bollas (Brickman, 1998; Eigen, 1998/1999, 1998; Gordon, 2004; Grotstein, 2000). Alongside such writings, which take a clear stand by focusing on "spiritual"[5] issues, there are also texts that do not necessarily address religion or mysticism as their main subject matter but rather use rich religious, mythical, or theological imagery and terminology to convey psychoanalytic ideas. Such use is evident in Bollas' writings, most notably in *The Shadow of the Object*, and in Grotstein's "mythological" language. Yet another "genre" is the psychoanalytic analysis of religious experience. After Freud's rather derisive contributions, this type of exploration was left relatively untouched until the late 1970s and early 1980s, which saw the publication of two innovative books: Rizzuto's *The Birth of the Living God* (in Black, 2006), that discussed the uses of God imagery from an object-relations perspective; and Meissner's *Psychoanalysis and Religious Experience* (1984).

Meissner, both a psychoanalyst and a Jesuit priest, has reached two important achievements in this virtually untouched field of interdisciplinary discourse. The first is the very formation of such a shared field and the establishment of a genuine interdisciplinary dialogue between psychoanalysis and theology. He did so in a way that demonstrated how we could draw on these two disciplines to enriching each other, instead of striving to use one in order to "explain away" the Other. His second achievement is introducing a nonreductionist developmental perspective on religious experience. He claims that it is a mistake to treat religion exclusively through its most primitive facets, as Freud did. According to Meissner, Freud has neglected his own great innovation: the developmental understanding of the human mind. Religion, like many other human phenomena, changes in accordance with the different phases of human development. As Meissner explains, drawing on object-relations and Kohut, these different developmental aspects of religious experience go far beyond the stage of childish, wish-fulfilling fantasy.

Meissner's bold move involved the attempt to understand religious experience using psychoanalytic tools – a complementary strategy to that employed by the current surge of writings, which try to explain or merely compare certain analytic elements to specific spiritual traditions. Finding parallels with Buddhism or Judaism seem to have become a playful new trend. These evocative ideas, however, seldom amount to more than a miscellaneous collection of anecdotal references. They have failed to develop into a specialized field of study within psychoanalysis, such as sexuality, narcissism, object-relations, countertransference, etc.

A handful of authors have taken matters further than this by exploring whether the two fields of "spirituality" and psychoanalysis share something more fundamental in common. Such authors (including Brickman, 1998; Brown, 2011; Eigen, 1998/1999, 1998; Gordon, 2004; Grotstein, 2000) have begun to speculate on a larger scale, claiming that "spiritual" ideas can be seen as a significant common thread that runs through main analytic ideas, or as connected to psychoanalysis' very essence. This book is inspired by these pioneering works and aims at deepening, organizing, and expanding them in a systematic way. This task of addressing a central, though often disavowed, psychoanalytic theme has long been left unattended. The following is brief overview of some of these theoretical beginnings.

Eigen and Ghent – The mystical as inherent in the psyche and the psychoanalytic cure

Ghent and Eigen, two influential figures in contemporary psycho-analysis, have both contributed to the first volume of *Relational Psychoanalysis: The Emergence of a Tradition*, and thus share a prominent place in informing the psychoanalytic spirit of our time. Moreover, both of their papers explicitly introduce the mystical element and, in a novel and inspiring way, illuminate its importance in psychoanalytic thought.

Eigen's paper, "The Area of Faith in Winnicott, Lacan and Bion" (1981/1999), explores the centrality of what Eigen calls "faith" in key psychoanalytic theories – and his personal sources of inspiration – Lacan, Bion, and Winnicott. A more detailed analysis of this paper is found in Chapter 9. However, it is important to mention Eigen's revolutionary notion that these central theoreticians – some of the most important figures in post-Freudian psychoanalysis – have placed faith at the center of their developmental theory and their definition of the curative factor in psychoanalysis. While this is per-haps more readily apparent in the writings of the overtly mystical "late" Bion, who openly discusses faith, Eigen's penetrating reading of Lacan and Winnicott exposes the crucial role of faith in their conceptualization of the human voyage toward developing awareness of self and Other; being authentic and creative; and attaining intimate knowledge of and closeness to the Other, alongside tolerance for the gap that separates the self from its objects. Moreover, Eigen reads Bion, Lacan, and Winnicott as protesting against the exclusive con-finement of images of the ideal and the sacred to parental introjects. For Eigen, the sources of human creativity depend on an ideal image, which goes beyond the internalized relationship with one's actual parents. In fact, Eigen argues that the numinous is present within us and must be dealt with as an ontological as well as a psychological fact of human existence.

Ghent also plays a major part in retrieving Faith from its confined "religious" niche in the psychoanalytic basement of repressed ideas. He does it by suggesting a new term, "surrender," that brings to-gether spiritual needs and more commonly discussed developmental vectors. Ghent believes we all have a need to be profoundly known

and benignly penetrated by the Other. This longing to be fully recognized, down to the very core of our being – sometimes by a human
Other and sometimes by a greater Otherness – is, according to Ghent,
a basic developmental need. As such, it also evokes our greatest fears.
For Ghent, this need drives the quest for spiritual life, as well as for
object-relations and intimacy. He touches on the subject of western
culture's autonomy bias, which makes it difficult to even find a
proper term for this state of intimate, total contact with a trustworthy
greater Other. He thus provisionally chooses the term "surrender."

However, Ghent's main focus in "Masochism, Submission, and
Surrender" is *not* this revolutionary statement but an innovative
perspective on the phenomenon of masochism, which he explains
as the perversion of the need to surrender. Ghent binds the development of this spiritual need and the more familiar and well-
studied notion of object-seeking. Throughout most of the paper, he
leaves the former aside to trace the fate of the need to surrender to
an object. As a result, his startling idea loses some of its impact by
being woven so well into the familiar object-relations framework.
In spite of Ghent' concise treatment of the subject, this paper is still
of profound importance because it offers a view of the spiritual
need as an independent and, at the same time, fundamental psychic
element. While it is intricately intertwined with the development of
object-relations, it cannot be reduced to it. Ghent's thesis develops
Winnicott's ideas about the relation between the environment and
the core self and about object-use. He beautifully illuminates some
of the mystical facets of Winnicott's theory, which hitherto remained unnoticed. Ghent's own creative "use" of Winnicott's ideas
is another example of the implicit evolution of the mystical element
within the explicit revolution propagated by the British middle
school.

The importance of these pioneering ideas by Eigen and Ghent is that
they go against the grain of the reductionist treatment of the "spiritual." It seems that the main rift between the more "mystically inclined"
analysts and "mainstream" psychoanalysis involves this very reductionism: can religious, mystical, or other "spiritual" experiences be
reduced to known psychoanalytic descriptions of psychosexual development, object-relations, narcissistic needs, etc.? Or, alternatively,
might such experiences be understood as an independent psychic

phenomenon which, though naturally intertwined with these other elements (like any other psychic aspect), merits investigation in its own right?

The mystical element after the relational revolution

Despite the current popularity of "spiritual" themes, the main corpus of psychoanalytic writing maintains its silence on the matter and sometimes even actively negating it. This includes authors who develop the concept of the communicative unconscious to its full capacity, such as Ogden (1994/1999). Ogden maintains that therapist and patient exist as such only through their dialectical tension with a third "being" – "The Analytic Third": a shared psychophysical field that allows the therapist, by sharing in this "third," to gain intimate knowledge of the patient's psyche (or, more accurately, their shared psyche). However, Ogden hastens to reassure his readers that such contact with the emotional truth of the session has "nothing magical or mystical" about it (p. 548). Apparently, he felt that such reassurance was particularly needed given the boldness of his ideas. Ogden is not alone. McWilliams (2011) feels that similar caution is in order when discussing how patients induce feelings in the therapist through such processes as projective identification (p. 35) and tries to ward off the suspicious "mystical" flavor sticking to this rather conventional concept.

This caution and recoiling are a response to the omnipresence of mystical concepts in psychoanalytic writings. It is hard to imagine a contemporary psychoanalytic paper that does not profoundly rely on the assumption of multilayered, conscious and unconscious, verbal and nonverbal communication between patient and therapist. Moreover, the relational movement holds, as one of its core assumptions, that there is a mutual, conscious, and unconscious "dance," where both parties co-create a new relational reality, which is dynamic and changing and unique to each therapeutic couple. It seems that the relational climate is particularly friendly to the mystical element, not only because it encourages a more open approach to a broader range of ideas but also in its core assumptions. The idea of a meaningful, nonverbal, yet Noetic and transformative experience seems to fit the relational notion of how psychoanalysis works.

One reservation seems in order. The presence of the Noetic element – the element of knowledge – is put in question by post-modern skepticism about *any* knowledge, particularly within any authoritative approach that favors what the therapist "knows." Still, it is quite clear that the experiences generated in this mutual relational dance *do* have a Noetic status. The truth may be dynamic, co-created, even multiple, but the relational analyst learns about the patient's psychic reality by looking into her own and assuming that there is significant overlap. Moreover, working through this area of overlap is the key to transformation. In fact, this understanding of therapeutic "knowledge" may sharpen the difference between the more conventional use of the word – as something clear-cut that can be indicated, defined and subjected to the "either-or" structure of formal logic – and the Noetic experience as characteristic of moments on the mystical continuum: a complex, nonverbal experience of therapeutic contact and deep familiarity.

Given that the relational outlook is such a dominant perspective in contemporary psychoanalytic writing, the lack of interest in the various ways in which this mysterious, unconscious communication occurs and the disregard for its meta-theoretical implications are curious. Psychoanalytic silence on this matter stands out against the backdrop of the comprehensive study other psychoanalytic issues have merited: sexuality, object-relations, the necessary environmental conditions for the healthy and creative development of inborn potential, trauma, etc.

Once again, this position that treats unconscious communication as central while ignoring its implications or even the need to explain its workings, goes all the way back to Freud. In his "Recommendations to Physicians" (1912), his advice is that the analyst should surrender to the workings of her unconscious as the only way of reaching the patient. He does not, however, explain how this is accomplished, except by noting that one should not pursue conscious memory or knowledge. He also offers the metaphor of the telephone receiver, which, though it sounds mechanical, denotes perfect perception by unknown and certainly nonmechanical (at least to the best of our knowledge) means.

Subsequent authors have rarely dared to explore the assumptions underlying this telephone metaphor. Even now, when we are witnessing an unprecedented outpour of writing about spiritual life as psychic contents and the possibility of mutual enrichment between psychoanalysis and various spiritual traditions, the neglect of the mystical element as an "inherent" psychoanalytic issue remains virtually undisturbed. This is all the more surprising given the wide acceptance of Bionian, Winnicottian, and Kohutian ideas that have promoted an understanding of psychoanalytic treatment as grounded in "intuition" or even "faith." Phillips (1994) scoffs at the psychoanalytic tendency, following Freud, to escape the mysterious by trying to provide "scientific" legitimacy to the concept of the unconscious which, according to Philips, *is the mysterious*. But, even Philips' poignant criticism of the splitting and denial at the very heart of psychoanalysis failed to stir the psychoanalytic community into taking a serious, investigative look at its mysterious core.

In fact, this core is now hiding in the best hiding place of all: in plain sight. Contemporary analytic authors who write about mysticism need not fear the fate of Jung, who was thrown out of the analytic society, or of Ferenczi, who died a shunned and ridiculed figure. Some, such as Eigen and Ghent, may even gain a prominent place. But still, references to the mystical, though plentiful, are mostly anecdotal and sporadic and fail to raise serious interest. It did not become a field of systematic analytic study. Moreover, many authors continue to develop Bionian and Winnicottian ideas about nonverbal communication and even psychic merger, without even a mention of their potentially "mystical" implications – some of which are developed in groundbreaking papers like Eigen's. It is difficult to imagine any other psychoanalytic field receiving similar treatment: not being mentioned in relevant contexts, even merely as a point of disagreement.

The "official" position of the analytic community, which combines tolerance and acceptance with conspicuous avoidance, shows that the mystical element was never really "metabolized" and integrated into the psychoanalytic organism. Tolerance, even generous, respectful acceptance, is not the same as genuine openness to dialogue with a historically abject issue. The treatment of the "spiritual" brings to mind the status of a step-son or, harsher still, of an interesting and amusing pet: who are barely considered full members of the family.

It might be that the colorful, provocative language used by some of the "spiritual" authors, who do not always confine themselves to formal, systematic discussions of their concepts and prefer a more associative style, facilitates such treatment. Alternatively, it could be argued that the current atmosphere of tolerance – existing alongside the relative absence of serious discussion, be it approving or critical – is actually barring the way to fruitful dialogue. The new "spiritual" movement is not challenged enough to feel the need to clarify its concepts. Thus, acceptance serves as a kind of dismissal – a most affective one, for it remains politely disguised, provoking no antagonism.

Notes

1 Many important theoretical developments, such as the contributions of Balint, Coltart and Milner, had to be left out due to limitations of scope.

2 In all probability, he is referring to the textually adjacent and somewhat entangled discussion he offers of why empathy, his key concept, was not enough. The role of psychoanalysis is to facilitate the growth of a self-esteem regulating "structure" in the self. The basic therapeutic unit therefore is "understanding and explaining" (Kohut, 1984, p. 94–95), i.e. providing an empathy-based interpretation that would promote this "structuring" of the self – a language reminiscent of Ego-psychology's preoccupation with the ego's "structure."

3 Kohut (1984) clearly refers to Freud's "oceanic experience" when writing that some echoes of the primordial oceanic experience with the mother, when she and the baby were united, may later be utilized in a mature self's empathic modality, this time not in a passive or transient way, as in the oceanic experience, but as a lasting choice.

4 While most of Bion's texts emphasize a unitary view ("at-one-ment" with the patient's O), *Caesura* is a notable exception, a unique paper that seems to be the germ of a new way of thought that stresses the tension between union and separateness (see chapter 5). Still, Bion did not elaborate this theoretical notion of union versus separateness as fully as Winnicott did.

5 I use this term loosely as referring to many religious, mystical, and metaphysical ideas that appear in various psychoanalytic writings as part of the above-mentioned trend. The diverse nature of these writings makes a more accurate term difficult to find and, by using this one, I wish to give the sense of this variety being a part of the same phenomenon in psychoanalytic publications, as well as stressing its wide, unspecified nature.

References

Berke, J.H. (1996). Psychoanalysis and Kabbalah. *Psychoanalytic Review*, *83*:849–863.

Binyamini, I. (2008). Freud and Jung – From merger to separation between two ethical systems. In *Sigmund Freud Carl Gustav Jung Letter Exchange 1906–1914*. Tel Aviv: Resling. (Hebrew).

Bion, W.R. (1970). *Attention and Interpretation*. London: Tavistock.

Black, D.M. (2006). *Psychoanalysis and Religion in the 21ˢᵗ Century*. London & New York: Routledge.

Bollas, C. (1999). *The Mystery of Things*. London & New York: Routledge.

Bollas, C. (2007). *The Freudian Moment*. London: Karnac.

Brickman, H.R. (1998). The psychoanalytic cure and its discontents: A Zen perspective on "common unhappiness" and the polarized self. *Psychoanalysis and Contemporary Thought*, *21*:3–32.

Brown, L.J. (2011). *Intersubjective Processes and the Unconscious*. London and New York: Routledge.

Cernovsky, Z. (1988). Psychoanalysis and Tibetan buddhism as psychological techniques of liberation. *American Journal of Psychoanalysis*, *48*:56–71.

Eigen, M. (1998). *The Psychoanalytic Mystic*. London & New York: Free Association Books.

Eigen, M. (1999). The area of faith in Winnicott, Lacan and Bion. In S.A. Mitchell & L. Aron (Eds.), *Relational Psychoanalysis: Emergence of a Tradition* (pp. 1–38). New York & London: The Analytic Press. (Original work published in 1981).

Eigen, M. (2012). *Kabbalah and Psychoanalysis*. London: Karnac.

Eshel, O. (2019). From extension to revolutionary change in clinical psychoanalysis: The radical influence of Bion and Winnicott. In *The Emergence of Analytic Oneness* (pp. 237–272). London and New York: Routledge.

Freud, S. (1900). The interpretation of dreams. *SE, IV*, ix–627.

Freud, S. (1912). Recommendations to physicians practicing psychoanalysis. *SE, XII*, 109–120.

Freud, S. (1913). Totem and Taboo: Some points of agreement between the mental lives of Savages and Neurotics. *SE, XII* vii–162.

Freud, S. (1923). Two encyclopedia articles. *SE, XVIII*, 233–260.

Freud, S. (1927). The future of an illusion. *SE, XXI*, 1–56.

Freud, S. (1933). New introductory lectures on psycho-analysis. *SE, XXII*, 1–182.

Ghent, E. (1999). Masochism, submission and surrender: Masochism as perversion of surrender. In S.A. Mitchell and L. Aron (Eds.), *Relational Psychoanalysis: The Emergence of a Tradition* (pp. 211–242). New York and London: The Analytic Press. (Original work published 1990).

Gordon, K. (2004). The Tiger's stripes: Some thoughts on psychoanalysis, gnosis, and the experience of wonderment. *Contemporary Psychoanalysis*, 40:5–45.

Grotstein, J.S. (2000). *Who is the dreamer who dreams the dream? A study of psychic presences*. New York and London: Routledge.

Grotstein, J.S. (2016). Bion crosses the Rubicon: The fateful course – and curse – of "O" in psychoanalysis and the furies left in its wake. In A. Reiner (Ed.), *Of Things Invisible to Mortal Sight: Celebrating the Work of James S. Grotstein* (pp. 251–268). London: Karnak.

James, W. (1987). The varieties of religious experience. In Bruce Kuklick (Ed.), *William James Writings 1902–1910* (pp. 3–482). New York: The Library of America. (Original work Published 1902).

Jung, C.G. (1933). Freud and Jung: Contrasts. In *Modern Man in Search of a Soul* (pp. 115–124). New York: Harcourt Brace.

Klein, M. (1946). Notes on some Schizoid mechanisms. In Roger Money Kyrle, in collaboration with: Betty Joseph, Edna O'shaughnessy and Hannah Segal (Eds.), *Envy and Gratitude and other Works* (pp. 1–24). New York: The Free Press, 1975.

Kohut, H. (1966). Forms and transformations of narcissism. *Journal of the American Psychoanalytic Association*, 14:243–272.

Kohut, H. (1984). *How Does Analysis Cure?* Chicago and London: The University of Chicago Press.

Kulka, R. (1991). Chapter 12: Reflections on the future of self psychology and its role in the evolution of psychoanalysis. *Progress in Self Psychology*, 7:175–183.

Kulka, R. (2005). Between tragedy and compassion. In H. Kohut, *How Does Analysis Cure?* (pp. 13–52). Tel Aviv: Am Oved. (Hebrew).

Lev, G. (2017). Getting to the heart of life: Psychoanalysis as a spiritual practice. *Contemporary Psychoanalysis*, 53(2):222–246.

McWilliams, N. (2011). *Psychoanalytic Diagnosis*. Second Edition. New York and London: The Guilford Press.

Meissner, W.W. (1984). *Psychoanalysis and Religious Experience*. New Haven: Yale University.

Mitchell, S.A. and Aron, L. (1999). Preface. *Relational Psychoanalysis: The Emergence of a Tradition*. New York and London: The Analytic Press.

Neumann, Erich (1968). Mystical man. In J. Campbell (Ed.), *The Mystic Vision* (pp. 375–415). Princeton: Princeton University Press.

Ogden, T.H. (1999). The analytic third: Working with intersubjective clinical facts. In S.A. Mitchell and L. Aron. (Eds.), *Relational Psychoanalysis: The Emergence of a Tradition* (pp. 459–492). New York and London: The Analytic Press. (Original work published 1994).

Ogden, T.H. (2009). *Rediscovering Psychoanalysis.* New York: Routledge.

Peled, E. (2005). *Psychoanalysis and Buddhism.* Tel Aviv: Resling. (Hebrew).

Reiner, A. (2012). *Bion and Being.* Great Britain: Karnac.

Reiner, A. (2017). Ferenczi's "astra" and Bion's "O": A clinical perspective. In A. Reiner (Ed.), *Of Things Invisible to Mortal Sight: Celebrating the Work of James S. Grotstein* (pp. 251–268. London: Karnak.

Phillips, A. (1994). Secrets. *London Review of Books, 16*(19):3–5.

Rubin, J.B. (1985). Meditation and psychoanalytic listening. *Psychoanalytic Review, 72*:599–613.

Winnicott, D.W. (1956). Primary maternal preoccupation. In *Collected papers: through Pediatrics to Psychoanalysis* (pp. 300–305). London: Tavistock Publications, 1975.

Winnicott, D.W. (1960). The theory of the infant-parent relationship. *The International Journal of Psychoanalysis, 41*:585–595.

Chapter 3

Psychoanalysis, pragmatism, and the epistemology of faith

If Psychoanalysis is indeed "mystical," if something unfathomable is part of its very nature, can it still be considered an academic discipline? How does this view affect psychoanalysis' long and bruising struggle to prove its validity? Before attempting to address this question, let us take a quick look at the history of this struggle.

Freud believed that the field he had created was a science. In his paper, "The Question of Weltanschauung," he proudly announced his creation as the newest addition to the edifice of science and the latest scientific nail in the coffin of such nonrationalistic world views as religion. But his welcome to this edifice was never warm or complete. In 1962, philosopher Karl Popper (1962) delivered an almost mortal blow to the psychoanalytic aspiration of belonging to the scientific community. He claimed that psychoanalysis failed to measure up to the crucial criterion that defines all science: refutability. It did not provide clear statements that could be either supported or refuted by empirical evidence. It is, rather, a theory that may employ its imprecise terms to explain any outcome – notoriously avoiding any refutation – and, therefore, a pseudo-science.

Though Popper's critique is taught in many textbooks as a devastating blow to psychoanalytic validity, it is not the only possible definition of what science is. Nor, for that matter, is "being a science" the only way to achieve validity. The focus of this chapter lies in exploring such an alternative path, without wholly abandoning the spirit of the scientific tradition. Its main goal is to argue in favor of a *pragmatic epistemology of faith* – an epistemological stance of faith in the ineffable aspect of psychoanalytic practice, while still adhering to

DOI: 10.4324/9781003200796-3

the rational criteria of expected and discussable, if not measurable, results. This paradoxical worldview will be offered as the most suitable for the current *weltanschauung* of psychoanalysis.

With this goal in mind, the chapter briefly reviews the different epistemological solutions offered for psychoanalysis thus far – mainly the scientific and the hermeneutic solutions. It will be argued that given the hybrid nature of psychoanalysis, its liminal position between the natural sciences and the poetic, the metaphoric and the mysterious – alongside its obligation to cure, neither of these solutions is satisfactory. William James' pragmatic philosophy, his ideas about rationality and validity will be presented as a possible starting point for an alternative epistemological anchor. Such an anchor can allow psychoanalysis a more comfortable place within interdisciplinary discourse without compromising its unique, multifaceted nature. Following the previous chapters, the parallels between James and Buber's thought will be analyzed in order to crystallize their view of knowledge as stemming from intimate connection – Their "intimate universe" worldview. It will be argued that faith is a precondition for achieving the mystical state as well as true therapeutic empathy. Buber and James' definitions of "faith" will be discussed in order to illuminate its place in the therapeutic encounter. Finally, a new synthesis of Jamesian, Buberian, and Winnicottian ideas will be presented, suggesting a novel way of understanding the question of knowledge in psychoanalysis. This synthesis is the *"epistemology of faith"* and its more moderate version – *"pragmatic faith"* which, as I would argue, is particularly suitable to the nature and inherent paradoxes of psychoanalysis.

Empirical results versus good stories

A rivalling position to that of Popper was presented by another philosopher of science, Thomas Kuhn (1962), who holds a more holistic view. He sees scientific theories in terms of paradigms, which are a kind of lens through which we view reality. Though successful predictions are certainly a crucial feature of a good paradigm, Kuhn claims that no paradigm is rejected because of a single failed statement. If this were so, says Kuhn, no paradigm would ever endure. Instead, paradigms are replaced only when there is a viable alternative, that usually answers many, not just one, of the questions left open or the problems left unresolved by its predecessor. Moreover, a new paradigm necessarily offers an alternative point of view, raising questions that had never been asked before. Psychoanalysis is certainly a prevailing paradigm, a lens that is often used to examine many questions in the social sciences and the humanities. To date, no rivaling "lens" has provided a better alternative – a richer, more comprehensive view of human nature. But does this make it a science? Kuhn briefly touches on the question of the "humane sciences," that are constantly preoccupied with their status and caught in the controversy about their right to claim their place under the lucrative title of "science." He expresses his doubts about whether this question can be resolved by a simple, exclusive definition of what science is. He believes it is rather a matter of consensus among a group of experts, about what should be considered achievement and progress. In the case of "young" sciences, this community of experts, which considers itself and is considered by outsiders as an authority, may not have been formed yet. Is that the case with psychoanalysis and its external (but also internal) strife among different "schools?"

Lately, it appears that psychoanalysis has given up on this point in favor of embracing an alternative view of itself. This new identity is often based on the hermeneutic field, that deals with the construction of meaning rather than the discovery of a certain, preexisting truth. The relational revolution played a major role in this epistemological shift (Mitchell, 1993), that situated psychoanalysis closer to the humanities than to empirical sciences and pushed it further away from its birthplace as a branch of medicine. The hermeneutic tradition was developed to meet the need to understand texts, sometimes old texts (originally, scripture) and was tasked with reconciling the inevitable subjectivity of the reader and their entanglement in the conventions of their time and culture, with the demands of the text, which had been written to be understood, not just projected onto. This dance between text and reader, the potential for a multiplicity of interpretations created through their encounter, has appealed to a group of analysts, who began to see their professional role as co-creators of meaning.

But, as human beings are more than written texts and the understanding of their "text" in the psychoanalytic setting might have direct implications on their wellbeing and mental health, the hermeneutic paradigm has serious limitations as an alternative anchor to psychoanalysis. The hermeneutic approach to texts might be a good working metaphor, but embracing it as full epistemological solution is problematic. While it is not relativistic in spirit, as its supporters constantly argue (for example, Sass and Woolfolk, 1988; Clarke, 1997; Bouchard, 1995) because it strives to meet the text and not simply suggest whatever interpretation suits the reader's fancy, it fails to produce any criteria that are good enough for a field that has a practical goal – to promote mental health and alleviate suffering. Strenger (1991) argues that hermeneutic criteria, such as internal consistency and meaningful construction, are insufficient for psychotherapy. Some of the best, most consistent, collectively constructed and emotionally meaningful stories have proved to be very dangerous throughout human history. This is clear enough if we think of political and religious ideologies, but Strenger gives a powerful example that is closer to home, from the history of treating the mentally ill: the understanding of psychosis as demonic possession and "treating" it through rites of exorcism. The demonic explanation is meaningful, emotionally powerful, coherent and had been consensual for centuries. Though its emotional meaningfulness might be of some therapeutic use, perhaps in terms of what medicine calls "the placebo effect," this would not be our treatment of choice today. It is not enough to tell a good story.

In addressing these vulnerabilities of the hermeneutic approach, Clarke (1997) offers Gadamerian hermeneutics as an epistemological anchor for psychoanalysis. He speaks of the Gadamerian/relational view of the meeting of horizons, of mutual co-creation and contextualized understanding as safeguards against relativism. Still, he finds it necessary to join the hermeneutic view to pragmatism, specifically to the contemporary pragmatic philosopher Hilary Putnam. Putnam speaks of "lower case" realism, the kind that must depend on human judgment and human intuition. According to Putnam, it is an error to assume that all judgments of reality could, or even should, be decided through scientific tools. Following James, he demonstrates that in some of the most important issues of our lives this cannot be the case. In disciplines such as psychology, anthropology, sociology and so on, intuition and empathy are central tools, but they must be kept in check and overseen. Such oversight, however, is also performed through human tools rather than the microscope and telescope of the natural sciences. For Putnam, this does not mean relativism; to think that a discipline ascribes to either positivism or "anything goes" philosophy is, as he aptly puts it, an adolescent kind of error. But Gadamer, though not a relativist, was not a pragmatist either. Clarke argues that a pragmatic view can be deduced from his writings, but any clear method for examining our intuitions is not inherent in the hermeneutic approach – though its emphasis on meeting, mutuality, and rechecking our ideas is a step in this direction. It is clear, then, that the hermeneutic view cannot serve as a sole epistemological anchor for psychoanalysis, not without some adjustments.

The call for necessary adjustments is also loud and clear from the other, "scientific" side of the efforts made to find a proper "home" for psychoanalysis. Fonagy (2000), for example, proposes an approximation of "scientific culture," if not of the classical methods of science. He maintains that arguing about whether psychoanalysis is a science or not is a futile debate. It is more important to ask whether it is relevant. Much like Kuhn, he suggests that what is considered scientific is an abstraction based on many different fields that are accepted as sciences, not all of which fully conform to the ideal Popperian standard. Fonagy states that trying to approximate to this ideal will distort the nature of psychoanalysis beyond recognition. As an analyst and a researcher, Fonagy is aware of the inherent difficulty in trying to operationalize psychoanalytic concepts. Still, he does not despair, but offers some conditions, which, if fulfilled, will achieve a better approximation to scientific culture and therefore to interdisciplinary relevance. He advocates clear logical connections between theory and technique, a deductive and not merely inductive connection between clinical material and theory, a clearer use of concepts, avoidance of the redundancy created by many schools grappling with the same clinical phenomena, interest and involvement in multidisciplinary research, reliance on multiple sources of information and, finally, greater availability of clinical material to public scrutiny. This last point is obviously laden with difficulties, but it is clear that the spirit of Fonagy's approach is understanding psychoanalysis as a hybrid discipline and trying to find a philosophy of knowledge (epistemology) that is akin to the well-tried scientific culture, but that will satisfy psychoanalysis' complex needs.

Psychoanalysis is not a positivistic science, nor, if it wants to be taken seriously as a therapeutic method, can it be a mere "narrative" – an interesting story about the human psyche. This story, or group of stories, which comprises psychoanalytic discourse must prove itself useful and relevant – yet without aspiring to the kind of proof dictated by the natural sciences. How is it possible to partake in "scientific culture" without negating subjectivity, without sacrificing the poetry of psychoanalytic practice and the mystery of the unconscious? Can we be relevant to interdisciplinary discourse without losing our unique identity?

The pragmatic answer

Questions about relevance and usefulness are classic pragmatic concerns, which are systematically and methodically addressed, regarding very specific issues, by the empirical sciences. But the question of usefulness is important for any conceptualization, not solely for ideas that can be tested within the scientific framework. The pragmatic philosopher William James aspired to widen the scope of pragmatic thinking beyond the possibility of testing and manipulating the natural world. He tried to find a place for the psychological, the highly subjective, even the mystical, in what Fonagy would call "scientific culture."

James was one of few modern philosophers who tried to deal with what is most meaningful to human beings – their personal experience, including religious experience, faith, and intuition – without sacrificing the role of rationality and valid methodology. Unlike many of his contemporaries, he refused to choose between "rationality" and "meaning" and dealt with the challenge of holding the philosophical rope at both ends. Though he saw himself as a successor to the tradition of British empiricism, he rejected the sterilized approach of analytic philosophy (the other obvious successor of the empiricists), which sought to eliminate metaphysical concepts which they deemed meaningless. James resisted this rejection of concepts which may hold the most meaning for human life. Yet he also confronted idealistic philosophical approaches that tended to make assertions without drawing on lived experience. James thus presented an important attempt to heal the old philosophical rift between idealism and empiricism. Moreover, as I would claim, his view can serve as a philosophical home for psychoanalysis, whose very essence resonates this rift.

I will briefly review some of the central tenets of his philosophy and then connect these to Buberian thinking, in order to suggest an outline of what I call a "pragmatic epistemology of faith" – an epistemology that accepts and deals with the liminal concepts dwelling in this rift.

Experience as "materia prima" – An epistemological question and answer

The concept of experience is the alpha and omega of James' philosophy. The anchor for every valid question and attempted answer. Nothing should be placed "beyond" or "above" human experience, nor should any parts of this experience be left behind because of their apparent complexity or "subjectivity." James' pragmatic philosophy is a method of thought suggested for navigating what he termed "the stream of consciousness" (James, 1890/1950) – a stream of sensations and perceptions, thoughts, memories, emotions, conceptualizations, motor activities, and the feedback about their results, that comprise our moment to moment experience.

James spoke of "radical empiricism" which, unlike classical British empiricism, accepts every part of experience, including the connections between different sensations, that where denied by Hume. This evades the "atomistic" dead-end as well as the absolutist fantastic solution suggesting extra-experiential monistic beings that connect everything, like in Hegel's philosophy. The connections between feelings, between natural events, between living beings and humans are there, within the scope of our experience, requiring no imagined external glue. On the other hand, disconnections are also a part of our experience. James' "radical empiricism" is a nondualistic, pluralistic theory, an achievement reached after years of grappling with the difficulties of both monistic and dualistic philosophies. James argued against a clear-cut distinction between "external" and "internal" reality as well as the idealistic tendency to abolish any difference altogether, thus negating our experience of "living in our own skin," our individuality, and sometimes even loneliness. He claims that the solution he has worked out solves the longstanding philosophical problem of perception. In the world of radical empiricism, the dualistic distinctions between objective and subjective or inner and outer reality lose their essentialist status and become a matter of context. In what context is it useful to distinguish between "outer" and "inner" reality? According to James, *a posteriori* introspection allows us to make this distinction, but before it, there was just a "pure" bit of experiencing: "the instant field of the present is at all times what I call the 'pure' experience. It is only virtually or potentially either object or subject as yet. For the time being, it is plain, unqualified actuality, a simple *that*" (James, 1912/1996, p. 23).

The simple *thatness* of experience is there before there are subject and object, before there is any context that would assign it to either classification. Instead of an "I" facing an "external world," there is, in James' view, only an immense variety of experiences: tastes and smells, moral judgments, mathematical measurements, and day-dreams. This miscellaneous variety of experiences maintains a complex and changing network of connections among themselves, a tapestry of "pure" experiences and second-level experiences of conceptions. Conceptions include the assigned meaning and placement of these experiences, such as "outside" and "inside," with their accompanying feelings – all in a continuous flux. The universe we live in, in its entirety, is "made" of this experiential tapestry.

Placing experience at the center of his thought had freed James from the traditional dichotomies that stress one pole of human experience and devalue the other. The following will demonstrate how this methodical placement of experience at the heart of both ontology and epistemology helps to solve not only the philosophical problems James wrestled with, but also the conundrum of psychoanalysis' place in the field of knowledge. As a field primarily dealing with the study of experiential truth which is, by nature, unique and transient, resisting "scientific reliability" – in terms of replicability in an artificial trial setting – psychoanalysis needs a philosophy that allows for the kind of validation that is inherent in experience and that resists both the presumption of objective detachment as well as the laxity that fails to ask any pragmatic questions about relevance, usefulness and progress.

James on the question of validity

If experience is indeed the "materia prima" of all reality, then knowledge, according to James, is a connection between one part of experience – "the concept" – and other parts of experience that "validate" it (James, 1909/1987c, 1912/1996, 1907/1987b). As Slater (2008) put it, this is the Jamesian version of "truth as compatibility." James describes a chain of connections as "physical or mental intermediaries connecting thought and thing [...] To know an object is here to lead to it through a context that the world supplies" (James, 1909/1987c, p. 854). In other cases, when the "object" is present, "to know immediately then, or intuitively, is for mental content and object to be identical" (p. 856). A successful "leading to a phenomenon" is achieved when there are compatible implications between the concept and experienced phenomenon. The concept must lead, if not to the target itself, then to its "neighborhood" and allow one to witness the expected results of its existence. For example, our concept of dark matter should lead us to observable gravitational affects, even though we cannot experience dark matter directly. Similarly, our concept of projective identification should lead to a better understanding of the therapeutic situation when the described phenomenon is present and, consequently, to a better chance of properly addressing and treating this intensity of emotion and possible therapeutic deadlock.

According to James, the validity or the truth of an idea is not some inherent characteristic of it. It is a function of how well it appears to serve us in dealing with our experience. His provocative saying, "truth happens to an idea" (1907/1987b, p. 574), means that an idea that proves useful in our dealings with bits of our experience is therefore found to be true. Truth is the *result* of a validation process. The populistic representation of pragmatism is, to some extent, correct: pragmatic truth is *what works*.

This chain of validation might also be entirely conceptual: we can perform a mental experiment or a logical deduction without ever using our sense organs or motor reactions in the process. But, according to James, concepts are only relevant if they can be reintroduced into experience and meet it in an efficient way, even potentially. One of James' examples is that we can know about tigers in India without ever having visited India and actually having seen them. But there is a real possibility of doing so, without which the whole chain would collapse. Most of our "truths" are never directly checked in this manner. Instead, as James writes, truth lives on a "credit system" (ibid, p. 576): we cannot possibly verify everything and, in our daily lives, we trust astronomers about dark matter and zoologists about tigers in India.

Unlike many other philosophers, James rejects the possibility or the desirability of constant doubt. When our ideas help us run smoothly through daily experience, they are not challenged. It is only when something interferes with this harmony that further investigation is warranted. Moreover, one of the central criteria that affects the acceptance of a new idea is its compatibility with the rest of our knowledge. Much like Kuhn, James conceived of knowledge as a system rather than a series of isolated propositions. Only when there is a cumulative pressure of opposing evidence as well as a viable alternative will the system/paradigm be questioned.

I believe this holistic view of a theory's destiny is particularly suitable to psychoanalytic culture. Psychoanalysis is a comprehensive system of understanding of the human psyche, which lives on the "credit system" provided by clinical experience (and the compelling force of other cultural derivatives of psychoanalytic thinking, for example, in literary studies or education). The concepts that form part of this system are embraced or gradually abandoned and taken out of common circulation, so to speak, according to their felt usefulness for the psychoanalytic community, either in the clinic or in current theoretical trends. James' pragmatic approach allows for such "organic" growth of knowledge and may help bring a little more precision and regulation to the natural development of this community of experts.

The will to believe and the sentiment of rationality

So far, James's ideas are akin to the kind of thinking we are used to applying in science and in dealing with common-sense problems. But what makes him capable of tackling such "subjective" issues as mysticism and what grants his view relevance as an epistemological anchor for psychoanalysis, is his uniquely wide notion of "implications." James agrees with the positivistic view that a proposition or an idea must have practical implications, if it is to be accepted as meaningful. But the difference concerning what might be considered as such "implications" is profound. Perhaps it may be summarized by stating that, in the positivistic view, they must be measurable and repeatable, while in James' broader pragmatism they must be meaningfully experienced. Giuffrida and Madden (1975), in describing the difference between positivism and Jamesian pragmatism, explain that according to the "classic" positivistic view, a proposition is either shown to be true analytically (such as saying that all bachelors are unmarried) or found to be true if it has results that can be publicly demonstrated in a reliable, replicable and preferably measurable way. Otherwise, it is meaningless. As metaphysical propositions do not have such consequences, they are therefore meaningless (Giuffrida and Madden, 1975, p. 19).

In comparison, James (1909/1987c) writes in *The Meaning of Truth* that:

> The pragmatic view, on the contrary of the truth relation, is that it has a definite content, and that everything in it is experience-able... The workableness which ideas must have, in order to be true, means particular workings, physical or intellectual, actual or possible, which they may set up from next to next inside of concrete experience. (p. 827)

This is a very wide definition of "workings" – that can even be "potential." For example, James asks the following question: what difference does it make in the world, if people believed in salvation or not? His answer is that the more optimistically driven and possibly more responsible actions of such believers may indeed "save" the world. This approach allows him to philosophically handle meaningful problems that elude scientific formulation like religion, ethics and the mystical experience without giving up on rational discourse.

Yet, even rationality is defined anew. In two exceptionally eloquent written papers, *The Will to Believe* and *The Sentiment of Rationality*, James demonstrates the "rationality" of faith and, if you will, the element of faith in rationality by showing it to be a "sentiment" – as dependent on personal feelings and preferences as it is on logic. He defines his oxymoronic term, "The Sentiment of Rationality," in the following way:

> This feeling of the sufficiency of the present moment, of its absoluteness, this absence of any need to explain it, to account for it, or justify it – is what I call sentiment of rationality. As soon in short, as we are enabled from any cause whatever to think with perfect fluency, the thing we think of seem to us *pro tanto* rational. (1896/1992b, p. 505)

This seems like a deeply personal matter. Who can tell what makes a particular person think with perfect fluency? Indeed, James provocatively states that it can happen for "whatever cause." What then, is left of rationality in all of this? Can the "sentiment of rationality" result from outright delusion? Theoretically, yes, of course. We may imagine that a paranoid schizophrenic might feel that "everything falls into place" once he had "understood" the plot against him and might feel that this cognitive path is running with "perfect fluency." Yet James was a pragmatist and, although he insisted that there can be no absolute and final judgment that is authorized to decide what the truth might be, there certainly are some guidelines that would appeal to the common-sense of most and that have a greater chance of resulting in public appeal or even consensus. For James, public opinion is no guarantee for the truth, but if something appeals to the "sentiment of rationality" of the many, it serves as an important rule of thumb distancing us from the errors inherent in the subjectivity of all judgments.

James offers a set of criteria that usually evoke the sentiment of ratinality most of which are concordant with what is considered sound theorizing in science and philosophy. These are all logical or common-sense rules, but James also shows how their interpretation is inevitably subjective. His starting point is a situation in which two theories equally satisfy the demands of logic. They will now be tested, says James, according to how well they satisfy people's practical and esthetic demands. Among those consensual tests he lists predictability, which he discusses as a basic human and even biological need to anticipate and gain control over one's environment. This, of course, is a basic demand for scientific theories, but when logic cannot decide between rivaling theories, such as the materialistic and the religious outlooks, some people may feel more in control in a mechanistic universe where nothing can surprise them or upset their assumptions about the laws of nature, while others need a divine being to guarantee a happy ending. It all depends on one's philosophical and psychological inclinations. Another common criterion is parsimony – by which "causes converge to a minimum number, whilst still producing the maximum number of effects" (1896/1992b, p. 506). But alongside it, there is the "sister passion" of detailed acquaintance with the parts and not just the whole. This "loyalty to clearness and integrity of perception" (ibid, ibid) may, for some minds who share this esthetic preference, prevail over abstraction. A good theory should provide both needs, but sometimes there is a marked inclination toward one of these poles. Thus, according to James, the philosophical world is divided between those who prefer empirical multiplicity and those who find excitement in far-reaching abstractions, such as Hume, at one extreme, and Spinoza at the other.

Finally, James discusses a criterion that is both esthetic and practical – "awakening of the active impulses" (ibid, p. 513). In James' view, humans crave the feeling that the universe somehow responds to our active powers and echoes those parts of ourselves that we hold most dear, such as our values. Most importantly, we need to feel that we have "something to press against" (ibid, p. 518), to feel that the universe does not remain indifferent to our efforts – be they technological, intellectual or ethical. For example, James believes that materialism, as a philosophical outlook that denies that people's actions have any meaning and explains away their motivations through objects that have no emotional significance, will never be universally adopted. The universe it presents is too eerie a place, condemning humanity to a permanent sense of *unheimlickeit* (ibid, p. 519). Inferring perhaps from his own psychological makeup, James argues that an appeal to human agency is a decisive factor in the acceptance of any theory.

Ultimately, in all his writings, James convincingly demonstrates the intimate connection between feelings and knowledge. Knowledge is a practical need, which is naturally followed by action. But even before any action is taken, knowledge effects a sense of agency – a feeling of having impact on the universe, a sense of connection to it. Like his notion of "implications," James' idea of how deep this connection is, how significant is the resonance between human beings and their world, is far-reaching. This idea is discussed through James's notion of "humanism" and his treatment of the centrality of faith in people's relation to the universe.

The role of faith and the humanistic universe

These two papers, *The Will to Believe* and *The Sentiment of Rationality*, provide tools for approaching "metaphysical" questions and describe the conditions under which one has no choice, logically or morally, but to yield to faith. The essence of the argument presented in *The Will to Believe* is that when there is no logical way to resolve an important and unavoidable question, then choosing what "feels like" the truth – an act of faith – is the inevitable, but also desirable course of action. James stresses that this applies to problems that lay outside the reach of science. Another criterion is that the said question or problem must also be deeply meaningful and unavoidable. Finally, the options one is choosing from must be "living options" – not some remote and obscure possibilities, but such that carry emotional impact. Religion, in James' opinion, fulfils all these conditions. According to James, one cannot choose to suspend judgment upon the religious question and wait for scientific results, even if those where obtainable. Living a secular lifestyle in suspended belief is a choice in itself. To be or not to be religious is not a choice one can avoid. Choosing either way or neglecting to choose will have immense consequences on one's lifestyle, worldview and possibly emotional health – not to mention the "eternal" implications, if those indeed await us. The choices must nevertheless be "living." In his lecture, *The Will to Believe*, James said he supposed that most of his listeners could not maintain Islam as a living option, but might be preoccupied with deciding between different Christian movements. Culture obviously plays a major role in supplying choices. But these must be poignantly felt, regardless of their source.

Sometimes, one has to make life-changing decisions that are unrelated to religion but have everything to do with faith. James gives the example of a man who is standing at the top of cliff and must decide whether to jump to the other side. If he stays, he will certainly freeze to death eventually. If he jumps, he might fall and die. The choice depends on whether the man believes he can successfully complete the jump. He cannot wait for "evidence" about his ability to jump, nor has he had any experience with similar jumps. It is a matter of faith. If the other choice is freezing to death, the logical decision would be to try and jump. But, if the man jumps in desperation, says James, his chances of safely reaching the other side are lower. If, on the other hand, this man has faith in himself, this may empower his jump and increase his chances of surviving the ordeal.

While it sounds less immediately dramatic than the above example, the decision about whether to view psychoanalysis as valid has deep and widespread implications. For western culture, where psychoanalytic thinking permeates not only the world of psychotherapy but also educational thinking, the arts, literature, and philosophy, this decision, if it could indeed be made, has considerable impact. Providing the best care for suffering is not the only thing at stake. The validity of psychoanalysis concerns our very perception of humanity: should we view human beings as complex, multilayered creatures, with conflicting wishes and different levels of consciousness, whose personality is shaped by an intricate interplay of forces – internalized images of past relations, significant memories, esthetic choices, varying levels of maturity and so on? Can we ignore all this richness, because it cannot be demonstrated in a lab? Would it be more productive to treat humans as rational creatures, or perhaps as something to be directed and designed by behavioral methods, even by "taming?" The endless debate around psychoanalysis demonstrates that this is very much a "living" choice and that its resolution may deeply affect our culture. On the other hand, can it be decided by "faith" alone? Can people be expected to pay psychoanalytic therapists on the basis of "faith?" Is this a matter in which logic and evidence play no part? Otherwise, what kind of evidence can be expected? I will try to address this question further, but it does seem that, though some aspects of psychoanalysis can be submitted to scientific scrutiny, the question of psychoanalysis' validity – with all its widespread consequences – remains *de facto*, for most people, a matter of faith.

James' point is that in matters of life decisions, which are crucial and imperative, faith is the proper, unavoidable, and desirable way to make a choice. Scientific methods of investigation are irrelevant here.

One must trust one's deepest feelings. Importantly, James believed that faith affects reality, like in the case of the man forced to jump to save his life. He demonstrates the matter further through common-sense examples of a mainly social nature: A confident man, who has faith in his own charm, is much more likely to be successful in wooing women; a friendly person, who believes in the good of others would, most probably evoke friendly behavior in them, thus confirming her belief; a suspicious person would cause others to keep their distance too, likewise confirming their expectations about others. But James goes much further. He uses "the social metaphor" for understanding man's place in the universe. Might it be, askes James, that like in the social sphere – where one's stretched hand may find another reaching out toward one – the same reciprocity holds true for one's relation to God? Might it be that instead of the passive model of salvation, human beings have their place in the grand scheme of things? That by having deep faith – the kind that motivates action – humanity can change the course of the universe and tilt the scales toward good? Can man meet God halfway? James confessed to believing that he can and that there is a kind of mutual, though not an equal re-lationship, with God. In essence, even apart from religion, James sees reality as existing in dialogue with us, shaping and being shaped by human beings. This is applied to our physical (for example, techno-logical) engagement with the world, as well as our intellectual com-prehension of it and, finally, our spiritual contact with it. He writes:

> Laws and languages at any rate are [...] man made things. Mr. Schiller applies the analogy to belief, and proposes the name of 'humanism' for the doctrine that to an unascertainable extent our truths are man made products too. Human motives sharpen all our questions, human satisfactions lurk in all our answers, all our formulas have a human twist [...] It is fruitless to define it [the world] by what it originally was or by what it is apart from us. It *is* what is made of it. Hence, the world is plastic. He adds that we can only learn the limits of plasticity by trying. (James, 1907/ 1987b, p. 592)

The world and what we make of it are inseparable. It is hard to see where one ends and the other begins. Truth is not transcendent to people. Human beings design not only the concepts that attempt to capture these truths but, to a large degree, also shape the reality to which these concepts refer. Still, James distances himself from the implied relativism: the world is not infinitely plastic; it offers "resistance." Some concepts will fit it more than others and will be of better use in our endless mission of navigating the stream of consciousness. This stream is largely comprised of sensory data – the element which is least susceptible to being shaped by us. Offering concepts that do not fit these sensory elements or act in a way that defies them would be metaphorically, and sometimes literally, hitting a wall. Of course, some walls are harder, less "metaphorical" then others.

James was very insistent on the Peircean principle of fallibilism – knowing that we can err, that some other, more suitable concept for useful dialogue with reality may come along. Still, some concepts are so well rooted in our history of thought that it is highly unlikely that they would ever change. Kant's *a priori* categories of time and space, for example, become, in James' thought, not structures of mind or of reality, but ways of relating to reality which are so useful and so fundamental to the comprehension of other concepts, that they are the least changeable part of the human legacy of contact with the world.

Our beliefs shape our experience and are shaped by them. Those beliefs sometimes must spring from faith, but even faith should not be blind. We must be guided by our "sentiment of rationality" – an intuition informed by logic and esthetics, which can be considered as generally recognizable rules of thumb. Most "sane" and certainly "sensible" people, while they may not necessarily agree with each other – indeed, given the inevitably subjective facet of "rationality," general agreement is impossible – would at least find mutual anchors to guide their debate.

Because of the irreducibly human nature of all truth, having been formed through faith and what "feels right," we cannot aspire to get rid of this inherently subjective aspect. Objectivity, in its classical sense, is meaningless. If something is completely detached from us, then we can have no connection to it, no way of ever perceiving and knowing it. The best we can aspire to, according to James, is disciplined thinking that will take into account, as much as possible, our motives and aspirations when we are trying to reason on the grounds of logic and evidence – at least, when such reasoning is possible, when it is not a "will to believe" matter.

I believe psychoanalysis resides exactly in the in-between zone, between the scientific (the empirical science of psychology) and the philosophical, poetic and mystical – in an area of faith. It is a field that, by its very nature, lives on a caesura. This liminal position is suitably addressed by the unique epistemological features of James' thought. For example, in his view, the phenomenon of different psychoanalytic "schools" may never disappear, nor should we wish it to. However, some guidelines to our internal discourse, some ability to account for the contextual usefulness of different psychoanalytic terms, could and should be found, perhaps by employing some of James' guidelines for informing our professional "sentiment of rationality." Such anchors can serve the discussion of psychoanalytic beliefs in interdisciplinary discourse, as well as in the intradisciplinary one, and perhaps foster the establishment of the consensual "community of experts" described by Kuhn.

The pluralistic universe as an intimate place

Lamberth (1997) suggests that James introduced a new philosophical principle: intimacy. In his view, James portrayed "an intimate universe," where human beings are deeply connected to their perceived surroundings. According to Lamberth, the principle of intimacy became the measure of the value of things and of their truthfulness – supplementing the traditional philosophic concept of rationality. In my view, however, it would be more accurate to say that intimacy is the only true way to rationality in James' universe.

In his analysis, Lamberth mainly refers to James' book, *A Pluralistic Universe*, where James openly discusses his personal religious views, in contrast to his more "neutral" voice in *The Varieties of Religious Experience*. In *A Pluralistic Universe*, James shares his sympathy with Fachner's pan-theistic pan-psychic belief in a "world soul" or "earth consciousness" (1909/1987a, p. 700) – a belief that suggests that we all share in some kind of global, even universal consciousness, without compromising our individuality, uniqueness and, even in some cases, separateness. He supposed that some parts of the universe are truly disconnected and may never become part of the whole. This seemingly inelegant idea served James as a way of avoiding any kind of negation – either of the notions of good, unity and intimacy or those of evil, disharmony and loneliness, or even the plain and simple thought that reality, in fact, does not have to subscribe to any final conception or esthetic structure.

James criticizes "the commonest vice of the human mind," which is "its disposition to see everything in yes or no, as black or white, its incapacity for discrimination of intermediate shades" (ibid, p. 665). According to the "black or white" view, if we acknowledge our empirical evidence of difference and diversity, we must forsake equally compelling evidence of connections, deep similarities and even mystical intimacy with the world. But this supposed "choice" is an error of thought, because, as he states: "abstract oneness as such *doesn't* change, neither has it parts – anymore than abstract independence as such interacts. But then, neither abstract oneness nor abstract independence *exist*" (ibid, p. 656; italics in origin).

James' notion of radical empiricism is applicable to religious ideas as well as to the concepts we should form about nature. No aspect of religious experience – not that of intimate closeness to God, nor that of transcendence and awe, is to be neglected. It seems that, for James, the mystical experience is a way of directly and intimately experiencing – and therefore a way of deeply "getting to know" – these different facets of reality. Because we are connected, we can really come to know each other and the universe. Because we are likewise irreducibly different, having our own perspective, our own way and, even, our own degree of connectedness to this postulated shared consciousness, we can all err. We are fallible. Even more interestingly, we can all be right in different, irreconcilable ways, because reality is multifaceted and pluralistic.

The pluralistic and intimate universe in James and Buber

James' "American" and democratic view of the deep structure of reality is surprisingly similar to that of German-born Jewish philosopher Martin Buber.[1] Even though the romantic Buberian view seems to belong to a wholly different philosophical world than that of the father of pragmatic thought with his direct, plainly spoken messages. Nevertheless, both thinkers speak of a deep connection between irreducibly unique individuals and both view the nature of our connection to the universe as dialogical. Both call for deep involvement in the world from an ethical, but also from an epistemological point of view. For Buber and James alike, our intimacy with the universe and with other human beings is the only path to true knowledge. This intimate connection that allows free thinking and meaningful, affective action is, in fact, the essence of "the sentiment of rationality."

The sentiment of rationality requires a felt correspondence between some concept or theory and experienced reality. It stands, therefore, on two legs: the emotional and the rational. In this context, one should note that James (1890/1950) discusses two kinds of knowledge: the first is "knowledge by acquaintance," a direct, intimate way of experiencing things, a category in which Barnard (1997) classifies mystical experience. It is a theoretical moment that takes place before concepts and other preexisting knowledge come into play. The latter belong to another category of knowledge, termed "knowledge about." The mystical moment, according to Barnard's analysis of James, is a wholly new experience, one that cannot be encompassed by our preexisting "knowledge about." Later on, it engages in an interplay with this kind of knowledge, seeking appropriate preexisting concepts or sometimes compelling the mystic to come up with new ones, thus prompting religious innovations. This view explains the power of the mystical experience. According to Barnard, this experience carries with it a compelling quality of "otherness." At the same time, the concepts used to contain it may derive from an erroneous system of thought, just like the errors made by our ancestors in interpreting their compelling sensory data to conclude that the earth was flat.

It appears that here we arrive at an unreconcilable difference between James and Buber since, for Buber, what happens in the "between" area of meeting is a matter of fact, of ontological presence, and not of feeling or experience. According to James, the latter could just as well be illusory and should be examined in relation to context, consequences, and impact. The difference, however, is not as great as it appears. Even in the essentialist system described by Buber, I-Thou moments spark and wither away. In their wake, they imbue everyday life with a sense of magic and a meaningfulness that evokes deep involvement. The meaning of I-Thou moments is therefore "interpreted" by daily life, depending on practical contact with reality in a way that resonates with James' insights. Thus, for both thinkers, these two modalities of existence are understood as being intimately intertwined, dynamically interchanging and even mutually dependent: "every real relation in the world is consummated in the interchange of actual and potential being. Every isolated *Thou* is bound to enter the chrysalis state of the it to take wings anew" (Buber, 1923/2010, p. 100; italics in origin).

Buber's "second period" was all about involvement in "this world": loving the real world with all of its beauty and all of its horror (1923/2010, p. 94). The center of this involvement was the I-Thou relationship between human beings. Similarly, according to Barnard, James' notion of the mystical does not only relate to one's relation with what may lie "beyond" man, but to what happens between human beings as well. The mystical – as direct, unmediated contact with reality – is essentially an empathic mode of understanding. According to Barnard, James viewed the empathic ability as inherent in mystical experiencing. It is possible that empathic people are more prone to having mystical experiences or that one of the gifts of such experiences is empathic sensitivity. Be that as it may, the two are deeply connected as the mystical experience is an empathic way of understanding Otherness and appreciating its essence.

James (1899/1992a) discussed the worldview of poets and of lovers, who forsake the distanced, mundane view of things, in order to reveal the beauty and magic in life. Being in love means seeing the Other in a special, sacred light, adoring their uniqueness, while recognizing their flaws. It is about real knowledge, not blindness as common wisdom argues. When one truly loves, one truly knows who the loved one is. For James, poets and lovers carry a message of the foremost pragmatic importance to human society – a message of tolerance and deep respect for difference. The mystical experience takes us beyond ourselves to a different kind of appreciation of the Other that could not have been achieved otherwise. According to Barnard's reading, mystical states reveal our mysterious connection to other people. They grant us a sort of direct contact with the Other's inner world that nourishes both our ability for empathy and our ethical commitment. It is in our everyday perception that we are blind – guided by preconceptions, prejudice, and self-interest. In surprisingly Buberian language, Barnard (1997) writes that "this mystical insight into another person's inner world keeps us from making an 'it' out of the person and forces us to recognize that, instead, he or she is a 'Thou' – someone like ourselves, someone to be treated with respect and understanding" (p. 68–69).

Thus, as James argues, "true realism always and everywhere is that of poets" (1899/1992a, p. 846), because empathy, for both him and Buber, is the only way of truly knowing a living thing. However, even though James includes telepathy in his range of mystical experiences, this poetic and empathic vision does not equal omniscience. On the contrary, the mystical view is a kind of openness that can tolerate the encounter with Otherness, including what is unknown about it. The principle of fallibilism holds even for one's interpretation of a mystical moment, be it an encounter with divinity or an interpersonal empathic connection. One of the reasons for this constant risk of error is that, for both thinkers, separateness survives this touching – or even partial union – of souls. James (1899/1992a) writes:

> We have unquestionably a great cloud bank of ancestral blind-ness weighing down upon us, only transiently riven here and there by fitful revelation of the truth. [...] our inner secrets must remain for the most part impenetrable by others, for beings as essentially practical as we are necessarily short of sight. (p. 862)

In similar terms, Buber declares that:

> Every real relation in the world rests on individuation, this is its joy, for only in this way is mutual knowledge of different things won – and its limitations – for in this perfect knowledge and being known are foregone. But in this perfect relation my Thou comprehends, but is not myself, my limited knowledge opens into a state in which I am boundlessly known. (1923/2010, pp. 99–100)

For James and Buber alike, the meaning of life lies in our ability to find joy and relish the magic in the Other. This is made possible through "fitful" moments that tear the veil of "practical" reality and

reveal the truth of deep connectedness alongside irreconcilable difference. This "interpersonal" mysticism suggested by James parallels
Buber's second period, which does not concern a mysticism of union
or solipsistic experience, but a mysticism of encounter: a meeting that
is an equally new epistemological opportunity, leading to the
revelation of ontological truth.

What kind of truth is that? To sum up, for both Buber and James,
reality exists in the tension between union and separateness. This
tension peaks in moments of meeting, where, for a brief moment, a
new reality is created. This reality is the consummation of human
creative and ethical activity in the world, which is made possible by
our capacity for empathic, unmediated contact. The two thinkers can
be seen to speak in one voice regarding some of their key principles.
For both, the universe is neither enmeshed nor consisting of isolated
parts. It is neither dualistically split between "spirit" and "matter"
nor is it materialistic. The classical philosophical traditions tried to
solve the riddle of the existence of the human spirit in a materialistic
world by stripping one or the other of their actuality. Such efforts are
no longer needed: James and Buber's thought presents an "intimate"
universe, where lives converse with each other, interpenetrate and
thus create and reaffirm their human uniqueness.

James, Buber and Winnicott: The ontology and epistemology of transitional space

It can now be readily demonstrated how James' theory of truth and
validity is the philosophical "twin" of the current, post-Winnicottian
understanding of the psychoanalytic encounter. Through his description of transitional space, Winnicott introduced into psychoanalysis a much-needed nondichotomous notion by proposing a
realm of reality which is neither internal nor external. In this realm,
the question of whether something was revealed or created is irrelevant – it is both. The assumption that the cardinal area of life lies
between the objective and subjective opened up a new way of practicing psychoanalysis. The notion of practice shifted from an archeological excavation site to a playground of meanings that does not
forsake the materials of its play – namely "external" reality.
Moreover, a fresh perspective on human understanding was

established, one that does not chase its own tail with questions of "objectivity." This revolutionary epistemology will be discussed further in the chapter about Winnicott. Our main focus now is the convergence of pragmatic, Buberian and Winnicottian views of knowledge, a convergence that can remedy psychoanalysis' "homeless" state and offer an epistemology that is more suitable for psychoanalysis than previous attempts, that had focused on either the "objective" or "subjective" pole.

In *The Meaning of Truth*, James Writes:

> We have here a quasi paradox. Undeniably something comes by the counting that was not there before. And yet, that something was *always true*. In one sense you create it, and in another sense you *find* it. You have to treat your count as true beforehand, the moment you come to treat the matter at all. (1909/1987c, p. 876)

Similarly, Winnicott's famous text reads:

> Of the transitional object, it can be said that it is a matter of agreement between us and the baby, that we will never ask the question: "did you conceive of this, or was it presented to you from without?" The important point is that no decision on this point is expected. The question is not to be formulated. (1971, p. 17)

Finally, Buber's intermediate area is similar to Winnicott's even in name. But the similarity does not end there. As we have seen, it is an area where the human personality is both created and expressed, where its capacity for encountering the Other generates a new ontological reality, where everything can be intimately known through mutual transformation. In this sense, from Winnicott's and Buber's texts, it is quite clear that the terms "knowing" and "creating" are mutually interchangeable. For Buber (and for James, as well), any other kind of knowledge is but pseudo-knowledge of a dead world. The reality of meeting is what permits true knowledge.

All three thinkers agree, therefore, on the convergence of ontological and epistemological questions. They all speak of the paradoxical nature of truth and all see closeness and intimacy as a precondition for knowledge – what Lamberth called the *criterion of intimacy* in James' thinking. To truly know something in an intimate universe, one must have a trusting relationship with it – that is, in the broadest sense, to have faith. The next section discusses this precondition, leading to the proposed term of *epistemology of faith* and, finally, to what it means to have a *pragmatic epistemology of faith*.

Faith and trust: Toward a new epistemological anchor

In my native Hebrew, the words faith and trust are similar, stemming from the same root: *emunah* and *emun*. This affinity goes beyond the peculiarity of one language. To have Faith is to trust in the object of one's faith, to trust their abilities, intentions, and motivations. To have religious faith, for example, is to have some kind of trusting relationship with God and with his universe. Trust in someone or something often goes beyond the realm of rational knowledge; for example, I trust someone with a secret because she seems trustworthy to me, not necessarily because I have proof of her past conduct with secrets. Even if I do, some element of faith is necessary on every new occasion where I must put my trust in someone.

Buber and James alike speak of a kind of trusting relationship with the world that is required in order to really get to know it and which is manifest in being open to experience (James) or to I-Thou relationships (Buber). Perhaps their notion of faith/trust is somewhat similar to Ghent's concept of *surrender*, but with a less passive connotation. For Winnicott, the trust created in the first two years of life is the *sine qua non* of the ability to live in potential space and to develop a capacity for object-use. Trust has certainly been a cornerstone of the psychoanalytic understanding of early development and the development of the therapeutic relationship. I wish to argue that trust is likewise closely connected to therapeutic *knowledge*. In the following sections, the connection between faith, trust, the mystical experience, and therapeutic epistemology will be further illuminated.

Faith and trust in James' writings

In *The Varieties of Religious Experience*, James (1902/1987d) favorably quotes Leuba, who identifies the state of faith with the mystical state:

> When this sense of estrangement [...] breaks down, the individual finds himself one with all creation. He lives in the universal life; He and man, he and nature, he and God are one. That state of confidence, trust, union with all things [...] is the *faith state*. [...] as the grounds of assurance here is not rational, argumentation is irrelevant [...] The ground of the specific assurance in religious dogmas is then an affective experience. (p. 227)

According to Barnard (1997), most scholars of Jamesian thinking missed the fact that, for him, the state of faith and the mystical state are closely connected, even interchangeable. James defines faith in the following way: first, as a loss of anxiety and fear through the individual's felt sense of unity with the universe; second, as an apprehension of an ineffable truth about the nature of reality; and third, as effecting a transformation of one's perception of the external world (1997, p. 183). Contrary to Barnard's opinion, only the second criterion is identical to James' definition of the mystical, while the other two refer to what James often described as the consequences of mystical enlightenment. Personal religion springs, for James, from personal experience – the mystical experience – and is its "fruit." It is the state of mind or, rather, the stance and disposition toward life that are left in the wake of the transient mystical moment. The faith created by a mystical experience is the ability to deeply understand and love the beauty of the world, to have empathy toward it and, therefore, to live a more optimistic and moral life.

On the other hand, James also viewed faith as a precondition of the mystical state. In his *Varieties*, James says that we can prepare ourselves for the mystical moment – though we cannot will it – through certain practices that promote openness to it. But even those who work hard to achieve enlightenment must reach a stage where they simply surrender in order to receive the external blessing. For James, surrendering to a higher power or, in other words, having faith in one's relationship with it, trusting it with one's very soul, is a necessary (though not sufficient) condition for this special state of mind and for the more stable state of faith that will ensue. Similarly, James speaks of the need to reach out to the universe, to outstretch our hand and be emotionally committed, if we wish to attain both psychological support and true Noetic (empathic) knowledge. Much like

Buber, James believes that a meeting depends on both will and grace. Having faith and knowing the Other are intimately connected.

Faith and trust in Buber

In his book, *Two Paths to Faith*, Buber (1950/1961) writes:

> There are two, and in the end only two, types of faith. To be sure there are very many contents of faith, but we only know faith itself in two basic forms. Both can be understood from the simple data of our life: the one from the fact that I trust someone, without being able to offer sufficient reasons for my trust in him; the other from the fact that, likewise without being able to give a sufficient reason, I acknowledge a thing to be true. In both cases my not being able to give a sufficient reason is not a matter of a defectiveness in my ability to think, but of a real peculiarity in my relationship to the one whom I trust or to that which I acknowledge to be true. It is a relationship which by its nature does not rest upon 'reasons', just as it does not grow from such; reasons of course can be urged for it, but they are never sufficient to account for my faith. (p. 1)

Buber distinguishes between believing something without proof and trusting in someone, God or man, as a form of interpersonal connection. He is thus casting trust as a form of faith. For Buber, the two forms are classically represented by the Jewish model (faith as trust, as a relationship with God) and the Christian model (faith as belief in something without rational proof). But it is important to understand that, for him, faith in its two forms is part of daily life, not only of religious experience. Moreover, religion is not a separate sphere of existence: faith is the way every I-Thou relationship is formed; it is a precondition for a true meeting.

Buber (1950/1961) claims that faith and trust are made possible when someone gives their "entire being" (p. 2) to their object of trust or believes in the truthfulness of something with "the totality of [one's] nature" (ibid, ibid). Obviously, one form of faith may evoke the other. Both these processes also take place in a psychoanalytic encounter. The first kind would be the deep trust a patient develops for her therapist: a link to which no rational explanation can do justice and which is created before the patient feels any improvement and is an essential condition for a good therapeutic outcome. A patient may be able to point to occasions where she felt understood by the therapist, to the pleasure of being contained, to the therapist's felt devotion and so on. But all these cannot fully account for the real experience of a trustful link and the quality of the encounter. There is something ineffable about it. The other kind happens constantly and is the grounds for interpretation and insight. Patients and therapists alike often believe something to be true, without knowing exactly why. This has been called therapeutic "intuition." There may be some evidence in the clinical material for a particular belief. Such evidence may even be compelling, but to know something deeply and meaningfully enough for it to be transformative, it must go beyond verbalized data. Thus, *Noetic experience – knowing with all one's being that something is true – is the stuff therapeutic insight is made of.*

This coincides with the Jamesian "sentiment of rationality." The triggers for this sentiment can be shown to have certain characteristics or match certain criteria, which cannot be dispensed with, perhaps, if one is to achieve this "sentiment" of pleasurable, uninterrupted flow of ideas. As James had shown, it is usually triggered by parsimonious explanations that have esthetic and practical value and that free one for action. These criteria for good theories are equally applicable to good interpretations. But the feeling of rationality cannot be reduced to a process of logical reasoning. Again, there must be something "beyond" these to make an idea feel right.

Buber demonstrates that the two paths to faith can be interconnected – one is naturally more prone to accept as true something that comes from a source one trusts. It is equally reasonable for one to be more likely to form a trusting relationship with someone who utters things one believes in. In the first case, says Buber, the relationship is the center and the belief is derivative; in the second, the center is the recognition of truth and a relationship with the source is the derivative. In either case, there is a living, unmediated relationship with the *object of faith* (a certain belief, person or God), a sharing of one's being with it.

The epistemology of faith in psychoanalysis

In an ongoing therapeutic process, therapist, and patient both experience moments of unmediated contact with each other. If we accept Winnicott's Ogden's and Brown's (2011) line of thought, they
share a field of connected psychic living or, as I would call it, *a field of
psychic overlap*. The experiences created in this field, where both
parties are "living an experience together" (Winnicott, 1945, p. 141)
or where the "analytic third" resides, are compellingly powerful and
meaningful and are felt to hold a psychic "truth," though it might not
always be readily put into words. These experiences often create and
are created through deep mutual trust. This kind of trust and emotional intimacy is, in turn, likely to generate more shared experiences,
to increase the openness and receptivity of both parties and broaden
their field of psychic overlap. These profound experiences of trust and
intimate connection – in short, of faith – are both the precondition
and the result of mystical experiences in psychoanalysis: faith is what
makes Noetic moments possible.

In the therapeutic context, faith can be defined as both an emotional and an epistemic stance. It is what Buber and James viewed as
a way of relating to the world, of approaching reality. It is a stance of
deep trust toward the Other or toward the therapeutic process, which
paves the way to an I-Thou encounter, to the interpersonal mystical
moment in therapy. It means trusting in the value of the experiences
created in this encounter – believing in their informative and transformative potential, even when faced with insufficient "proof." In the
epistemology of faith, validation is almost a circular process because
the experience created in the encounter, which is believed to generate
a field of psychic overlap, is its own "proof." We know psychic reality
because we share it. This circular validation process is suited for the
reality of an I-Thou encounter which is, to a large degree, nonverbal,
and non-"rational" (in Otto's sense), to the same extent that the
empirical and dualistic subject-object model suits the field of positivistic science.

It is *almost* circular, however, because there is an imminent danger –
that of treating our interpretations, our secondarily derived understandings of the mystical experience in therapy as omniscient, thus
transforming faith into delusion. When we rely on our experiences

because they are believed to somehow be part of a shared psychic truth and, therefore, come to believe that we know the patient's truth as well as we do our own, we expose ourselves to all the problems of treating subjective experience as indication of an "external" reality, the kind of confusion that has led people to believe in a flat earth or in witches. Such delusions are precisely the thing that positivistic science labored to deliver us from and the reason that Freud viewed science's mission as so noble. The epistemology of faith, therefore, is essential, but not in itself sufficient for psychoanalysis.

For this reason, I suggest adopting a stance of *pragmatic faith*, the kind of faith that is not afraid to constantly check-in with reality – the kind of love that is not squeamish about meeting the beloved in their full form, with all the imperfections of body and soul. This means having deep faith in the relevance, even the sanctity, if you will, of the shared experience in the consulting room, without forgetting that our interpretations of it are always fallible. We must constantly check with our playmate – the patient – how our interpretations are received. Do they promote her creativity? Make her think? Support her well-being inside and outside the session? Many potential criteria have been put forth by different psychoanalytic traditions for therapeutic success, some of which will be reviewed in the following chapters. Nevertheless, whatever the criteria or the underlying theory, all psychoanalytic interpretations must capture our, the patient's and/or the analytic community's sentiment of rationality. Is a given theoretical construct elegant? To what degree does it capture past and present or explain multiple phenomena without being too abstract and out of touch with emotional reality? Most importantly, as James would claim, does it free us for action, promoting agency and further faith in the meaningfulness of our actions?

Of course, most clinicians do just that. They follow their intuition, but check it both with the patient – whether through verbal or behavioral response – and with the existing body of psychoanalytic knowledge that informs our intuitions and allows the interpretation of the immediate or the mystical moment by engaging "knowledge about." Psychoanalytic practice has always been pragmatic, just as it has always been mystical – albeit unknowingly so. Nevertheless, no organized pragmatic meta-psychology had been systematically discussed by theoreticians, certainly not as a possible answer to psychoanalysis' supposed epistemological "homelessness."

Psychoanalysis cannot remain in the mystical moment alone. Though there will always be some part of the analytic experience that no interpretation or theory can fully account for, part of the paradoxical task of psychoanalysis is to communicate the ineffable, to give words to what is yet to be verbalized. This is true concerning our patients – for whom psychoanalysis remains a "speech therapy" and has the obligation of verbalizing the deepest, most elusive emotions, while acknowledging the limitations of words. This is equally true for our internal and external discourse. Psychoanalysis needs to be able to talk and be talked about in the interdisciplinary academic community, without forfeiting or further negating its mystical core. Either withdrawing from interdisciplinary discourse or negating the mystical elements that make such discourse a challenge, exposes psychoanalysis to the critique of being pseudo-science, a "philosophy" or a set of "metaphors" with a limited claim to validity. We must, therefore, hold on to our paradoxical task – of being both mystical and rational, of maintaining a stance of pragmatic faith, of being open to a pragmatic discussion about our faith, of using rational tools while remembering that rationality (especially in psychoanalysis) is a *sentiment* – a sentiment that, if we are rational, we can have faith in. This paradox is inherent both in the sentiment of rationality and in psychoanalysis. The paradox of pragmatic faith is a way to be true to our unique place in the field of knowledge; a way to fight for the true place of our "impossible task" in the interdisciplinary arena.

In the spirit of this endeavor, the following chapters offer examples and demonstrations of how different psychoanalytic theories can be shown to have a mystical core assumption, around which their concepts "revolve" – and that these concepts can nevertheless be pragmatically analyzed in terms of their contextual applicability and clinical meaning.

Note

1 To my knowledge, the affinities between these two philosophical figures have never been explored before.

References

Barnard, G.W. (1997). *Exploring Unseen Worlds: William James and the Philosophy of Mysticism*. Albany: State University of New York Press.

Bouchard M.A. (1995). The specificity of hermeneutics in psychoanalysis: Leaps of the path from construction to recollection. *International Journal of Psychoanalysis*, 76:533–546.

Buber, M. (1961). *Two Types of Faith*. Tr. N.P. Goldhawk. New York: Macmillan.(Original work published in 1950).

Buber, M. (2010). *I and Thou*. Tr. R.G. Smith. New York: Martino Publishing. (Original work published in 1923).

Brown, L. (2011). *Intersubjective Processes and the Unconscious*. London and New York: Routledge.

Clarke, B.H. (1997). Hermeneutics and the "relational" turn: Schafer, Ricoeur, Gadamer and the nature of psychoanalytic subjectivity. *Psychoanalysis and Contemporary thought*, 20:3–68.

Fonagy, P. (2000). On a relationship of experimental psychology and psychoanalysis commentary by Peter Fonagy. *Neuropsychonalysis*, 2:222–232.

Giuffrida, R. and Madden, E.H. (1975). James on meaning and significance. *Transactions of the Charles S. Peirce Society*, 11(1):18–36.

James, W. (1950). *The Principles of Psychology*. New York: Dover. (Original work Published 1890).

James, W. (1987a). A pluralistic universe. In Bruce Kuklick (Ed.), *William James Writings 1902–1910* (pp. 627–819). New York: The Library of America. (Original work Published 1909).

James, W. (1987b). Pragmatism. In Bruce Kucklick (Ed.), *William James Writings 1902–1910* (pp. 481–624). New York: The Library of America. (Original work Published 1907).

James, W. (1987c). The meaning of truth. In Bruce Kucklick (Ed.), *William James Writings 1902–1910* (pp. 823–974). New York: The Library of America. (Original work Published 1909).

James, W. (1987d). The varieties of religious experience. In Bruce Kucklick (Ed.), *William James Writings 1902–1910* (pp. 3–482). New York: The Library of America. (Original work Published 1902).

James, W. (1992a). Talks to teachers on psychology and to students on some of life's ideals. In Gerald Myers (Ed.), *William James Writings 1878–1899* (pp. 705–888). New York: The Library of America. (Original work published 1899).

James, W. (1992b). The will to believe. In Gerald Myers (Ed.), *William James Writings 1878–1899* (pp. 445–704). New York: The Library of America. (Original work published 1896).

James, W. (1996). *Essays on Radical Empiricism*. Lincoln and London: University of Nebraska Press. (Original work published 1912).

Kuhn, T. (1962). *The Structure of Scientific Revolutions*. Chicago: The University of Chicago Press.

Lamberth, D.C. (1997). Interpreting the universe after a social analogy: Intimacy, panpsychism, and a finite God in a pluralistic universe. In R.A. Putman (Ed.), *The Cambridge Companion to James* (pp. 237–259). Cambridge: Cambridge University Press.

Mitchell, S.A. (1993). *Hope and Dread in Psychoanalysis*. New York: Basic Books.

Popper, K.R. (1962). *Conjectures and Refutations*. New York: Basic Books.

Sass, L.H. and Woolfolk, R.L. (1988). Psychoanalysis and the hermeneutic turn: A critique of narrative truth and historical truth. *Journal of American Psychoanalytic Association, 36*:429–454.

Slater, M. (2008). Pragmatism, realism and religion. *Journal of Religious Ethics, 36*(4):653–681.

Strenger, C. (1991). *Between hermeneutics and science*. Maddison, Connecticut: International Universities Press.

Winnicott, D.W. (1945). Primitive emotional development. In *Collected Papers: Through Pediatrics to Psychoanalysis* (pp. 145–156). London: Tavistock Publications, 1975.

Chapter 4

Freud and Ferenczi – In the beginning there was a split

How did the state of affairs described in Chapter 2 come to be? How was it possible that one of the basic assumptions of psychoanalysis – the existence of psychic overlap and its mystical implications – could have been overlooked for so long by the brilliant minds who founded the field of psychoanalysis, a field whose cornerstone is self-awareness? Was it, in fact, overlooked? Was it unconsciously repressed and split off or simply consciously denied? This chapter focuses on a key episode in the formative years of psychoanalysis: it discusses the internal conflict concerning religion and mysticism in the minds of Freud and his chosen intellectual heir, Sandor Ferenczi, as well as the external conflict between them, which resulted in alienation and a split that shaped psychoanalytic history.

Whereas the Freud-Jung conflict led to Jung's establishment of an alternative, relatively independent school, Ferenczi was ridiculed and eventually partially suppressed. At the same time, however, Ferenczi's ideas had an undeniable influence on prominent analysts. Some of these did not acknowledged his influence, while others treasured his heritage and carried it on. The most notable of the latter is Michael Balint, who taught Ferenczi's ideas, publicly defended him against Jones' accusations that he was not of sound mind in his final years and kept his diary until he felt the time to publish it was right. In the united states, his ideas were carried on by his analysand, Clara Thompson, one of the founders of the American interpersonal school. Such analysts carried the torch until Ferenczi was fully "resurrected" and celebrated as an honorable founding-father of the contemporary relational movement. In many ways, this story resembles that of the

DOI: 10.4324/9781003200796-4

mystical element itself, making Ferenczi an important and intriguing figure in the quest to uncover the mystical element's history.

This chapter is composed of several parts. The first part is devoted to Freud's internal conflict, as it can be reconstructed from his texts. His disparaging view of religion and mysticism, manifest in formal contexts, is presented in sharp contrast with another, less familiar side of Freud. An analysis of certain Freudian texts reveals a fascinating process he had undergone regarding the phenomenon of telepathy. Following that analysis, the connection between the definition of the mystical and Freud's telepathic unconscious is explored further. We then turn to the figure of Ferenczi, by drawing on his clinical diary to unfold his tormenting conflict around mysticism. His direct engagement with the mystical facets of the analytic bond is presented and his view of the question of mysticism and psychopathology is explored. This is followed by a discussion of Ferenczi's developmental theory and its close connection to mysticism. Next, his developmental theory is tied to his preoccupation with the "feminine principle" in nature and the human personality, a principle he came to represent himself, through his therapeutic approach and mystical inclinations. This is discussed in light of the split between the "feminine" and "masculine" in psychoanalytic history, in the wake of the Freud-Ferenczi rift. The effects of this split on the analytic encounter and the form the mystical element took in those early, formative years of psychoanalysis, is discussed through a Buberian point of view at the end of the chapter.

Freud – Religion as mass pathology

In *The Future of an Illusion*, Freud (1927) discusses the power of religion and its puzzling capacity to exist independently of reason. As we have seen, Freud asserts that the religious feeling stems from the small child's fear, his helplessness, and his Oedipus complex. The child loves and fears his father and his notion of the father as both a protector and as a menace results in a life-defining conflict. This turbulent ambivalence never subsides completely, especially when man discovers the awful power nature holds over him, a power that recreates his childhood helplessness. Religion offers a consoling, consensual solution: where there was once an earthly father, imagined as all-powerful, there is now a divine one, who inspires even more awe, but promises to wield his power justly. The individual mind is greatly relieved as both his complexes and his fear of natural and human cruelty are soothed. Ritual and piety replace childhood neurosis.

In *Totem and Taboo*, Freud (1913) offers a psychological-anthropological theory that uncovers the "missing link" between the child's internal turmoil and the overarching universal structures of religion. The origin of human society, Freud argues, can be traced to a primitive tribe controlled by an all-powerful father who terrorized his sons and took possession of all the females. One day, his sons revolted and killed him to gain access to the females. But they could not enjoy the fruit of their crime: they were overcome with remorse and longing for the dead father. Moreover, they needed laws, however, arbitrary their enforcement had been. The band of brothers then created its own set of laws and forbade themselves to engage in sexual relations with the tribeswomen – the wives and daughters of the great father. This is how exogamy and the incest prohibition came to be.

The murdered father, in the meantime, began to be revered as a symbol of the whole tribe and became embodied in a totemic animal. The eating of its flesh was only permitted on special ritualistic occasions. Later on, the totemic animal evolved into more anthropomorphic gods and eventually took the form of a monotheistic abstraction. But the love/hate ambivalence toward the great father never changed; it constituted the foundation of human civilization and fueled its religions. The origins of the human family and human religion are the same – an archaic crime that haunts the fantasy of every human child; a legacy he must confront in order to become civilized.

I will not dwell here on the familiar critiques of the fantastic story Freud offers as a solid, almost unavoidable anthropological theory. Nor will I discuss the critique of Freud's reductionistic view of religion. Rather, what I wish to stress is his exclusive focus on the origin of institutionalized religion and the fact that he gives little thought to the personal religious experience. In *The Future of an Illusion*, Freud (1927) dedicates but a few lines to this alternative:

If the truth of religious doctrines is dependent on an inner experience, which bears witness to that truth, what is one to do about the many people who do not have this rare experience? One may require every man to use the gift of reason which he possesses, but one cannot erect, on the basis of a motive that exists only for very few, an obligation that shall apply to everyone. If one man has gained an unshakable conviction of the true reality of religious doctrines from a state of ecstasy which has deeply moved him, of what significance is that to others? (p. 27)

Feeling that this is merely a rhetorical question, Freud swiftly returns to his attack on institutionalized religion. He disputes the validity and relevance of personal feelings or "intuition" (p. 31) in dealing with life's great questions, which he lays at the doorstep of science. If science cannot answer them yet, there would no doubt come a time when it could; but the only hope for nonillusory answers to such questions lies in science.

Nevertheless, Freud finds himself obliged to return to the question of personal religion in answering a letter from his friend, the novelist Romain Roland. Roland commented on *The Future of an Illusion*, saying that he could easily agree with Freud's evaluation of religion, if it were not for the fact that he ignored the true origins of religiosity. Seeing religion as a mass neurosis applies to religious doctrines, but not to personal religion. In Roland's opinion, it is this personal feeling of sacredness that institutionalized religion exploits. While this feeling of something limitless and boundless, which Roland calls "oceanic," contains no promises of eternal life or any other set of beliefs in and of itself, it can be harnessed by religion and subjugated to the set of beliefs critiqued by Freud.

Freud's "Civilization and its Discontents" (1930) opens with this correspondence with Roland and the reader is led to believe that the paper has been written to address the question of personal religious feeling. However, this long and rich essay only touches on the question brought up by Roland in its first few pages and then seems to dismiss it and forget about it altogether. Freud talks of the oceanic feeling as a feeling of indissoluble unity with the world. He declares that he himself had never experienced it, but this is no reason not to consider it as the source of religion. He suggests, with some un-certainty, that the origin of this feeling lies in the baby's "narcissistic unity" with its mother. He then expresses even greater uncertainty about whether such an archaic feeling can still be present enough in the adult psyche to adequately explain religious feeling. Freud considers various archeological and physiological analogies of long-surviving structures (the embryonic past, the relics of Rome) and concludes that only in the mind can such remnants of a long-lost past endure. He is, however, rather reserved about this possibility: "Perhaps we are going too far in this. Perhaps we ought to content ourselves with asserting that what is past in mental life *may* be preserved and is not *necessarily* destroyed" (1930, p. 71; italics in origin). The hesitant quality of this conclusion seems very strange for a thinker whose theory is, to a great extent, based on the assumption that residual childhood conflicts have considerable influence on the adult mind.

Freud's next step is to claim that even if such an archaic relic does indeed exist, it is unlikely to play so central a role as the emotional origin of religion:

> To me the claim does not seem compelling. After all, a feeling can only be a source of energy if it is itself the expression of a strong need. The derivation of religious needs from the infant's helplessness and the longing for the father aroused by it seems to me incontrovertible, especially since the feeling is not simply prolonged from childhood days, but is permanently sustained by fear of the superior power of Fate. I cannot think of any need in childhood as strong as the need for a father's protection. Thus the part played by the oceanic feeling, which might seek something like the restoration of limitless narcissism, is ousted from a place in the foreground. The origin of the religious attitude can be traced back in clear outlines as far as the feeling of infantile helplessness. There may be something further behind that, but for the present it is wrapped in obscurity. (p. 72)

It is interesting that, despite all his poignant ridicule of formal religion, when Freud contrasts the longing for the father (as the ostensible foundation of religion) and the narcissism that underlies the oceanic feeling, the latter is presented as much more contemptible. At least the need for the father is an understandable, universal feeling that is present throughout our lifetime – Freud merely asks us to fight against the temptation to fulfill it in an illusory manner, like the one offered by religion. Narcissism, on the other hand, is seen as contemptible in and of itself. It is a state of mind originating in early unity with the mother – a figure that is conspicuously missing from Freud's discussion. This suspicion is strengthened by Freud's claim that the child abandons the oceanic feeling in favor of the father's stronger and more significant protection. Moreover, it is useful to remember in this context that Freud sees even mature women as only capable of narcissistic love, until their love is "drawn out of themselves" when they become mothers. Freud thus views female love and love *for* the female/the mother – not as a sexual object but as the "early" oceanic mother – as infinitely primitive.

In contrast to the nonsexual need for the mother, who is not even directly named, the longing for the father is the strongest need Freud recognizes. This view is one of the greater points of dissent between classical Freudian theory and the object-relations theory. In both object-relations and self-psychology, the relationships of early infancy are seen as the infrastructure of the mind. As we have seen in chapter two, both the acceptance and the rejection of the centrality of early relationships are closely related to the perceived centrality or marginality of the mystical element in psychoanalysis.

The connections between Freud's notion of femininity, its psychic role, and the mystical element were aptly discussed by various authors (Meissner, 1984; Phillips, 1994; Neuman, 1948/1968). For our present purposes, it is interesting to note how this important part of psychic development, which bore a "feminine" mark, was also perceived as nonscientific and had been left out and pronounced irrelevant for being "too infantile" to merit further psychoanalytic inquiry. The "mystical" part, lost in the haze of early childhood, was left in the hands of those who were to become likewise excluded from mainstream psychoanalysis.

Though it is easy to agree with Freud that the feelings of the few cannot serve as an epistemological justification for the beliefs of the many, does this render such feelings unworthy of psychoanalytic investigation? Given the many reports of mystical feelings throughout history, there is serious reason to doubt Freud's justification in treating them as a mere idiosyncrasy, especially if, by his own account, they are rooted in the universal experiences shared by all babies. But even supposing Freud was right in considering the mystical as a marginal phenomenon – Still, Freudian psychoanalysis offers a broad theory of the human psyche, ranging from rare and abnormal conditions (such sexual perversions and even the idiosyncratic expressions of particular symptoms) to the universal psychic and cultural structures, including a frequent discussion of the role of religion in these diverse contexts. Can't the mystical experience find its place, even if it is indeed small, in such a comprehensive project? Is it not strange for the founder of this ambitious theoretical system to treat such a pervasive human phenomenon, with an undeniable historical impact, as irrelevant – especially when it is potentially tied to the question of religion, which clearly occupied much of his thought?

Freud later accepts some of Roland's critique by saying that *The Future of an Illusion*, indeed, only dealt with the layman understanding of religion – which emphasizes its promises of comfort and eternal life – rather than the deep origins of religious feelings. Here, again, the reader is seduced to believe that this gap would now be filled. Instead, Freud abandons the topic once more and turns to his favorite habit of attacking the intellectually ridiculous and neurotically based religious doctrines. From there, he dives into a discussion about the formation of civilization, the role of drives in it and the riddle of the super-ego. The oceanic feeling is never mentioned again.

The peculiar structure of this text gives the reader reason to believe that Freud has great distaste for this topic, which he was only led to consider by the urgings of his prominent friend. He flees from it as soon as possible with little excuse and moves on to subjects nearer to his heart where, for him, the facts are "irrefutable." He even shares with his readers some of his feelings of relief about not being "mystically-attuned" himself, quoting Schiller's ballad: "let him rejoice, whoever draws breath in the roseate light!" (1930, p. 12). It seems that, for Freud, these mystical/narcissistic experiences feel somewhat like a suffocating cave (the maternal womb?), from which one must escape in order to breathe and enjoy the light of day.

The "Other Freud" – The saga of the telepathic unconscious

A direct support for Bollas's (2007) claim, that Freud had suppressed his own theory of the receptive unconscious (as discussed in chapters 2 and 8) can be found in Freud's texts about telepathy. These texts were rarely mentioned by Freud's immediate successors, as they go against the grain of psychoanalysis' scientific pretenses. In fact, Freud himself had the same concerns (see Eshel, 2019, for a captivating review of the history of these texts and the opposition Freud met with from Jones in publishing them). A chronological analysis of these texts reveals the fascinating process their author underwent with regard to the role of the "occult" in his newly found discipline. The first of these texts is also the least known and one which had been actively hidden by Freud: "Psychoanalysis and telepathy" (1921). This paper was never meant to be published: Freud wrote it as a presentation to his intimate circle of colleagues, all of five people including himself. It is written as a friendly discussion, including Freud's confession that he had forgotten his notes about one of the cases supporting telepathy at his house in Vienna. He interprets this forgetfulness as a result of his great aversion to this area of study. In fact, it seems that he takes pride in his resistance, offering it as proof that his evidence should have more weight, because he introduces it reluctantly. He entreats his friends to find arguments to dismiss what he himself could not – the existence of telepathy in his case histories. He lists the dangers and the latest attacks made against psychoanalysis, referring among other things to the defection of Adler and Jung. Freud emphatically points out the "occult" as a great and potentially devastating threat to psychoanalysis and to science as a whole, even to scientists from more traditional fields who object to psychoanalysis: "this time it is something tremendous, something elemental, which threatens not us alone but our enemies perhaps, still more. It is no longer possible to keep away from the study of what are known as 'occult' phenomena..." (1921, p. 177).

It might be supposed, says Freud, that the "occult" and psychoanalysis would have much in common, because both have suffered ridicule and rejection at the hands of traditional science. Moreover, psychoanalysis is "to this day [...] regarded as savoring of mysticism" because it has discovered the unconscious, which is "looked upon as one of the things between heaven and earth which philosophy refuses to dream of" (ibid, p. 178). According to Freud, however, he shuns any association with the occult because the differences between it and psychoanalysis are deeper than such similarities. The champions of the occult, some of whom have approached Freud for support, come with unshakable convictions and seek science's confirmation only in order to destroy it. While scientists seek to maintain their connection to the materialistic worldview, the occultists would rejoice in proving it wrong, in rising above the laws of physics and chemistry.

Here, Freud demonstrates the confusion James warned about, between science as a method of investigation and science as a particular content, or as a set of beliefs held by the scientific community – namely materialism. In a subsequent paragraph, however, Freud voices the wider understanding of science as an ethics of commitment to evidence, of whatever sort. He asserts that the psychoanalyst must resign himself to the evidence that supports telepathy if it is *forced* upon him. This wording speaks strongly of Freud's struggle. His apocalyptic prophecy about what might happen should such evidence be accepted speaks even stronger:

> There may follow a fearful collapse of critical thought, of determinists standards and of mechanistic science. Will it be possible for scientific method [...] to prevent this collapse? It is a vain hope to suppose that analytic work, precisely because it relates to the mysterious unconscious, will be able to escape such a collapse in values as this. (ibid, p. 180)

This dramatic statement is followed by his explicit decision to keep this matter away from public attention. He then proceeds to tell his colleagues of two fortune-telling incidents, wherein the prophecy did *not* come true, but nevertheless suggested the presence of telepathy. In both cases, though the prophecy itself had failed, it remained emotionally significant to Freud's patients. While trying to decipher this psychoanalytic mystery, Freud and his patient reached the understanding that the prophecy was connected to the patient's wishes, which entailed intimate biographical details of great emotional importance. Freud rules out the possibility that the fortune-tellers could have known anything about his patient's future (and indeed, they did not) or "read" anything in their palm or date of birth (the means they employed).

Freud is thus left with two final possibilities: either the patients misrepresented their encounter with the fortune-teller – a possibility he dismissed, at least in one case, because of the character of the patient – or a telepathic exchange had indeed taken place between the patients and the fortune-tellers. Freud tells his colleagues that, in one of these cases, he was so shocked that he could not proceed with the psychoanalytic inquiry. However shocked at the time, Freud does not forget to stress psychoanalysis' unique capacity to illuminate even such dubious maters:

> The application of analysis to this case [...] further increases its significance. It teaches us that what had been communicated by this means of induction from one person to another is not merely a chance piece of indifferent knowledge. It shows that an extraordinarily powerful wish harbored by one person and standing in a special relation to his unconscious has succeeded, with the help of a second person, in finding conscious expression in a slightly disguised form – just as the invisible end of the spectrum reveals itself to the senses on a light sensitive plate as a colored extension. (ibid, pp. 184–185)

This sounds like a new encounter with the unconscious as it is presented in *The Interpretation of Dreams*, where meaningfully saturated content is somehow understood by the Other, who serves as a medium. Much like in the case of dreams, the content must be potent indeed if it is to cross the gap between minds, as well as the conscious/unconscious boundary in the originator's mind. Here, because the receiving end is an analyst, it was possible to understand the hidden meaning of the message. But the reception itself, the telepathic exchange, is not restricted to the analytic situation: the "fortune-tellers" had received the telepathic message just the same; the unique power of analysis lies only in deciphering the received information.

Freud's second paper, "Dreams and Telepathy" (1922), was written very shortly after the above address to his colleagues. Unlike its predecessor, however, it was written in order to be published and this intention explains its widely different character. Here, Freud warns his readers that, if they expect to learn anything new about telepathy, they are going to be disappointed. He declares he has neither anything to say about this phenomenon nor any opinion to give regarding its veracity. His goal is to discuss the relation between telepathy, if it does actually exist, to the psychoanalytic theory of dreams, in an attempt to answer the question of whether the supposed existence of telepathic dreams contradicts the analytic view of the dream as wish-fulfilment. His answer is negative.

As an example, he analyzes a dream that might be considered telepathic and demonstrates how it is nevertheless wish-fulfilling: Freud's friend dreamed that his wife gave birth to twins. The dream occurred on the same night that the friend's pregnant daughter gave birth to twins and news of this reached him the following morning. Freud interprets the switch in the mother's identity in terms of his friend's wish that his daughter, to whom he is close, would give him a child, rather than his emotionally estranged wife. Freud argues that a dream may or may not utilize a telepathic massage that had reached the dreamer in his sleep. When asleep, Freud explains, we are more susceptible to stimuli which, in a waking state, are usually screened by daily demands. He does not rule out the possibility that such stimuli may include telepathic communication as well. But, what of it? the dream might just as well use any other stimulus – like entanglement in one's bedsheets or a need to go to the bathroom; anything might serve as material for the story-weaving aimed at fulfilling the unconscious wish.

Freud's dry and neutral tone in this paper is in sharp contrast to the emotional turmoil he shared with his friends behind closed doors. From a grave threat to all the achievements of modernity, telepathy becomes a seemingly marginal matter, brought up solely because of a technical question regarding its compatibility with the psychoanalytic theory of dreams. If one reads this paper without knowing of Freud's previous one, which had been kept secret at the time, it might seem somewhat puzzling: how can such an evocative topic as telepathy be treated as a peripheral matter, as mere background for Freud's claims about the wish-fulfilling function of dreams? How can it be equated with being entangled in one's sheets? And is it truly possible that the author (and a very opinionated one, at that) has no opinion about it whatsoever?

Some readers may perhaps believe that Freud was simply so pre-occupied with protecting his theory that he was blinded to the importance of other matters, despite their clear significance to the study of the psyche. Those who have read the first article, however, cannot be convinced by Freud's assumed position of cool, disinterested observation. Rather, the chronological proximity of the two papers reinforces another hypothesis: after discussing the threat of telepathy with his friends, Freud decided to tackle it with the weapon of indifference, to make it unimportant, a nonissue, at least as far as psychoanalysis is concerned. Moreover, Freud tried to avoid being tainted by association. Perhaps with this intention in mind, a 1925 appendix to *The Interpretation of Dreams* concerning telepathic dreams did not appear in any of the subsequent editions.

Unlike both its predecessors, Freud's (1933) final paper on telepathy, written over a decade later, was published in a prominent place as a part of the section about dreams in *The New Introductory Lectures*, and was titled "Dreams and Occultism." The straightforwardness of its publication as well as its content indicate that the writer has come a long way from his initial position, though the struggle is by no means over. Here, Freud once again voices his conflict, but this time it is out in the open and in a much more level-headed tone. He now publicly acknowledges that the psychoanalytic unconscious is deeply connected to some of the arguments made by occultists. He presents all the objections that might be raised about this association and discusses the advantages and disadvantages of prejudice against the occult: a critical viewpoint may save us from wasting time on improbabilities, but might also obstruct exploration and, with it, the chance for new findings. Once again, Freud warns that advocates of the occult might harbor reactionary tendencies against science and rationality. Humanity had only recently escaped the danger of religious dogma imposing itself on reason – a singular accomplishment that the "occult" may render fragile. Even if one is willing to conduct a nonprejudiced investigation of such phenomena, one encounters the intentional vagueness in which the 'medium's' performance is carried out and the antiscientific caveat that the observer's very skepticism might preclude the emergence of the phenomenon in question. Freud surprisingly concludes, that while human phantasy is profoundly invested in the occult realm and thereby exploited by many a charlatan, in ways which mask any potential grain of truth – the most probable hypothesis is that such a grain does indeed exist! Furthermore, Freud claims that the study of dreams shows that, of all the various "occult" phenomena, telepathy is the one that merits serious attention.

Despite this conclusion, Freud's internal conflict is not reconciled even in this 1933 paper. His language remains markedly inconsistent: on the one hand, he still insists that he did not commit to the truthfulness of the phenomenon; on the other, he presents its validity as an almost certain conclusion. In yet another place, he says it is an undecided matter but urges his readers to accept the "telepathy hypothesis."

The 1933 paper finally presents the case omitted in the 1921 address and makes it easy to understand the original omission. The case involves telepathic communication with a patient, and it is the patient who "reads" Freud's mind.[1] Freud discusses this case in great earnestness and detail and presents the arguments for and against considering it as evidence of telepathy. While he offers alternative explanations for every "mysterious" aspect of this story, Freud still chooses to believe that telepathy is the correct one. This is very different from his state of mind in 1921, when he declared himself eager for a refutation. As in previous papers, Freud celebrates the aptitude of the psychoanalytic method in exposing the telepathic nature of what might have been construed as insignificant events by uncovering the unconscious truth of their messages. In this paper, however, the figure-background relation is not as strikingly odd as in "Dreams and Telepathy" and Freud seems fully aware of the importance of telepathy and honest about his own struggle. He admits both his repulsion and his earlier disavowed fascination: "if one regards himself as a sceptic, it is a good plan to have occasional doubts about one's skepticism too. It may be that I too have a secret inclination toward the miraculous which thus goes halfway to meet the creation of occult facts" (1933, p. 52).

Importantly, in "Dreams and Occultism" Freud makes his first connection between telepathy and the heart of analytic treatment: transference. He quotes another paper to demonstrate that he was not the first to experience "thought transmission" during an analytic session and that this phenomenon is connected to transference. He then quotes yet another paper describing telepathy between mother and son that was also observed in an analytic setting. According to Freud, if these observations are confirmed "we would be bound to put an end to the remaining doubts on the reality of thought transference" (ibid, p. 55). But even in this bold move, connecting telepathy to the core of the analytic process, Freud makes his point in two short paragraphs, without fully explaining so important a topic. How does the connection between transference and telepathy "work?" – the question is left unanswered. In addition, He attributes the discovery to Deutsch. Freud, a pioneer in so many things, does not wish to be remembered as a pioneer in the research of telepathy. Though Deutsch's paper concerning transference and telepathy is published in 1926, five years after Freud's shocking discovery is reported to his friends, Freud would rather be seen as having been forced, in the footsteps of others, to acknowledge the existence of telepathy, let alone its connection to psychoanalysis.

Nevertheless, there is a clear change. Freud frankly discusses his former concerns about the destructive power of these findings and admits that it was a mistake to doubt the strength of the scientific worldview and to conceal data. He further claims that:

> [...] so far as thought transference is concerned, it seems actually to favor the extension of the scientific – or as our opponents say, the mechanistic – mode of thought to the mental phenomena which are so hard to lay hold of [...] What lies between these two mental acts may easily be a physical process into which the mental one is transformed at one end and which is transformed back once more into the same mental one at the other end. The analogy with other transformations, such as occur in speaking and hearing by telephone, would then be unmistakable [...] It would seem to me that psychoanalysis, by inserting the unconscious between what is physical and what was previously called 'psychical' has paved the way for the assumption of such processes as telepathy. (ibid, p. 54)

Freud's ardent desire to adhere to the materialistic worldview and to technical examples in spite of or, actually, because of his compromising discovery, is evident. The phone analogy, however, is familiar to his readers from his "Recommendations to Physicians" paper, where he defines the attitude the analyst must adopt: "to put it in a formula: he must turn his own unconscious like a receptive organ toward the transmitting unconscious of the patient. He must adjust himself to the patient as a telephone receiver is adjusted to the transmitting microphone" (1912, pp. 115–116). Thus, the 1933 paper finally closes the circle; the meaning of Freud's telephone metaphor from twenty years earlier, which was overlooked (at least consciously) by most of his immediate successors, is brought to light: the transference of meaningfully charged thoughts from patient to analyst (and vise-versa) is immanent to the analytic process. Being in a receptive position to such "thought transmission" *is* the analyst's stance and a basic requirement of her profession. The similarity between these two texts, separated by more than two decades, brings into question the novelty of Freud's position regarding telepathy. I believe that this analysis of Freud's writings about telepathy shows that the position expressed in the *New Introductory Lectures* was not wholly new, but merely the softening of a conflict – the same conflict described by Bollas as resulting in the suppression of the received unconscious. The 1933 text shows that, perhaps as he was nearing the end of his days, Freud was more aware of both sides of this conflict or may have felt that openly admitting his opinion is no longer so great a threat to psychoanalysis. Indeed, Freud himself raises the possibility that this change has to do with his old-age and his having grown soft and credulous at the end of a "strictly scientific" career. He states, however, that this is not the case; he simply had to bow his head before the facts (p. 56).

If we listen to the different levels at which Freud is discussing telepathy, as his analytic method urges us to, we will realize, in accordance with Freud's 1933 admission, that the birth of psychoanalysis necessarily revisits the phenomenon of telepathy. Even if psychoanalysis has yet to address Freud's hope of elucidating this phenomenon, there can be little doubt that a mysterious, unconscious nonverbal connection between two minds was at the heart of the psychoanalytic project from the very beginning.

Mystical experience and telepathy

This conclusion raises a new question: does telepathy necessarily constitute a mystical experience, in line with the definition presented in previous chapters? It is justifiable to group these two terms to-gether, especially in light of Freud's unequivocal rejection of the mystical? Let us revisit the suggested definition: a mystical experience is a meaningful experience that occurs as part of the process of analytic communication; it is nonverbal or difficult to verbalize, has a Noetic quality, requires transcendence and is transformative.

As a nonverbal part of the communication process, the mystical experience coincides with Freud's (1933) notion of telepathy as transmission of thoughts through unknown nonverbal means. The definition of the mystical is, however, broader than mere "thought transmission": it requires the communication to possess a Noetic quality; it must feel deeply meaningful. Even if we accept it as gen-uine, simple "mind-reading" like that demonstrated by magicians does not qualify. Mystical experiences are not about "reading" which number or card someone had in mind; they involve the transmission of transformative, possibly life-changing knowledge. One theme that stands out in all of Freud's papers on telepathy is the emphasis on its meaningfulness, on the great subjective weight of the message that was telepathically exchanged. In his 1921 and 1933 papers, Freud even suggests that this kind of communication is more likely to occur between people who are emotionally close to each other. While this is not a defining attribute of telepathy, he shows it to be important for the occurrence of telepathy in psychoanalysis. Perhaps this is how telepathy is related to transference, though Freud makes no explicit mention of this. Important thoughts "go through" and people who are important to each other are more likely to be receptive to these thoughts. For Freud, the category of meaningful thoughts mainly involves libidinal wishes, which are presumably powerful enough to cross the gap between separate minds.

The requirement that this knowledge should be transformative is closely related to its personal importance. The communication must be deeply meaningful, so that it may generate actual transformation. It is easy to imagine that the experience of unconscious-to-unconscious contact is potentially transformative, either in itself or, as Freud would probably argue, because it enables the therapist to offer an accurate interpretation. The distinction is of course a fine one: if Freud is right in assuming that all telepathically transmitted messages are meaningful, could such information *not* involve transformation? Some contemporary analysts, such as Ogden, believe that unconscious communication is never trivial. Moreover, in crossing the boundary between souls, this communication has already affected some change in both. In her innovative paper discussing the telepathic dreams patients have about their therapists, Eshel (2019) claims that such dreams are like a "search engine." They are utilized by particularly traumatized patients (p. 143) in an attempt to mystically transcend analyst-patient separateness by realizing the "possibility of primary, unmediated patient-analyst interconnectedness, or analytic oneness, revealing its power and radical quality" (ibid). For her, this moment of union and transcendence of separation creates the *potential* for growth, for preventing the unimaginable agony of further loss – this time, the loss of the therapist. Thus, in itself, it is not necessarily transformative but more like a wake-up call for the therapist, albeit one that is difficult to ignore. We can conclude, therefore, that even if telepathy, in the narrow sense of "thought exchange," is not necessarily a mystical experience, it is fair to say that, phenomenologically, at least in the consulting room, the two are closely related.

It is important to note, though, that there remains a certain irreconcilable difference between Freud's notion of telepathy and the suggested definition, namely concerning the nonverbal and often ineffable quality of the mystical experience. Freud speaks of a rather clearly defined information – an instinctual wish – that *can* be put into words. Such content might be embarrassing and therefore eagerly suppressed, but it is not formless or beyond verbalization. Moreover, Freud markedly discusses "thought transmission" rather than the communication of experiences. Still, it is Freud (1933) himself who bridges the gap to the realms of nonverbal experience, by suggesting that telepathy is an archaic method of communication that served our ancestors before the development of speech and that still serves some animals. Within a large crowd or in the minds of young children, this primitive means of communication is more dominant and observable.

This hypothesis can be clearly linked to Freud's anthropological speculations in *Totem and Taboo*, which raise the inevitable question of how the guilt-complex over the original crime against the father is perpetuated throughout the generations? It is clearly not enough to assume the existence of a verbal tradition. Well aware that he is verging on Jung's notion of a collective unconscious, Freud writes (without mentioning the latter) that: "no one can have failed to observe [...] that I have taken as the basis of my whole position the existence of a collective mind, in which mental processes occur just as they do in the mind of the individual" (1913, p. 157).

If we try to piece together the puzzle of Freud's view of the unconscious, it becomes clear that he thought of it as a communicative "organ," both at the "micro" level of the consulting room, where two people engage in nonverbal communication, and at the "macro" level, where the whole of humanity is apparently connected in some way. The latter is an implicit assumption which rarely surfaces as it does in the above quoted passage. Nevertheless, it is a deeply influential assumption, permeating the central tenets of Freud's psychoanalytic theory – the unconscious, the formation of dreams and structure of civilization – and one that clearly caused Freud much distress.

Perhaps this is why we are still grappling with the tension between the "wise" unconscious – which creates the dream, communicates and receives highly complex experiences – and the animalistic unconscious – which is full of instinctual wishes and impervious to logical thought. This Janus-faced faculty creates the elaborate artwork of the dream but, according to Freud, does so with the sole purpose of hiding a libidinal wish. It may be that the materialistic spirit of the animalistic unconscious helped Freud disguise his mystical notion (or wish) within the more acceptable, yet still very daring artwork of psychoanalytic theory. In any case, the mystical Freud or, in more conservative language, the Freud who believes in telepathy, would likely surprise many of his successors, who have retained an image of him as a fierce fighter for materialistic, positivistic thought, who does not hesitate to denounce his closest friends for their "mystical" tendencies. It is small wonder that some of the more mystically inclined analytic authors still use this image of Freud as the grounds for their rebellion. Indeed, it was only many years after his death that the "law of the materialistic father" that he (or, at least, his better-known public figure) had imposed, began to fade.

The Freud–Ferenczi rift – Law of the mother versus law of the father

Sandor Ferenczi is a tragic figure in the history of psychoanalysis. He was one of Freud's two "princes," chosen as his next heir after Freud's falling-out with Jung. In 1932, Ferenczi presented his thesis about "the confusion of tongues" between adults and children; Freud found the notion shocking and unsettling and demanded that it should not be published (Dupont, 1988). Following a bitter dispute, Ferenczi declined to head the International Psychoanalytic Association. His attempts to gain the support of his analyst and intellectual father – Freud – for his "deviant" ideas had failed. Deeply hurt, Ferenczi wrote in his dairy: "must I (If I can) create a new basis for my personality, if I have to abandon as false and untrustworthy the one I have had up to now? Is the choice here between dying and rearranging myself and at the age of fifty-nine?" On the last page of his diary, he answers these questions as follows: "a certain strength in psychological makeup seems to persist, so instead of falling ill psychically, I can only destroy, or be destroyed, in my organic depth" (Dupont, 1988, p. xi).

Ferenczi was, indeed, "organically destroyed" seven months later, when he died of pernicious anemia. In the rather romantic opinion of many in the psychoanalytic community, he had died of a broken heart, torn between his true self and his ambivalently beloved mentor. He was proclaimed crazy by his own analysand, Ernest Jones, and became infamous for his forbidden experiment in mutual analysis. Jones seemed bent on suppressing Ferenczi's legacy even after his death, preventing the publication of his ideas in English and insisting that he had been mentally ill. Balint fought publicly against this allegation, attempting to paint a more balanced picture of Ferenczi, one that acknowledged his genius and his deeply humane approach alongside his mistakes (Mészáros, 2003). This approach also lived on in the American interpersonal school which Clara Thompson, after experiencing Ferenczi's respectful, self-inquisitive and nonauthoritarian approach in person (Wolstein, 1989), helped establish. Though his heritage lived on through these influences, Ferenczi's clinical diary, in which he documented his experiments about mutuality in psychoanalysis, his ideas and tormenting conflicts, went unpublished for many years and was entrusted into the hands of Michael Balint, who only saw fit to publish it long years after Freud's death.

The 1980s and the 1990s witnessed a renaissance of Ferenczi's ideas (Berman, 1996). Once repressed and directly or indirectly influencing prominent analysts some of whom, like Klein, did not acknowledge this influence, Ferenczi's ideas are now celebrated as precursors to modern psychoanalysis. He is considered an honorary father of relational psychoanalysis, having been the first to identify the importance of mutuality and countertransference in the analytic relationship.

As the best testimony for the conflict that tormented Ferenczi and eventually became a historical split in psychoanalysis, I chose to focus on Ferenczi's clinical diary. Much like the other disputes between Freud and his followers, his rift with Ferenczi concerned the rejection of what Freud considered the cornerstones of psychoanalysis: the instinctual origins of motivation and the phantasmatic background of neurosis. Ferenczi questioned both: he treated severely disturbed patients who reported sexual abuse and believed them. While Freud's own theoretical journey took him away from exploring actual memories and toward the discovery of phantasy, leading to the invaluable contribution of charting the internal world, Ferenczi's choice to highlight the reality of incest memories seemed not only shocking but also a veritable theoretical regression. Moreover, his interactions with these patients illuminated the great importance of actual early relationships (not just phantasmatic ones), of being treated with affection and genuineness both in one's early years and in the analytic relationships – a discovery which challenged the supremacy of sexuality as an exclusive motivation. His discovery of the centrality of early relationships in structuring the psyche, which later served as the foundation for the object-relations school, was the very rock against which the Freud-Ferenczi relationship crashed.

As the first "object-relations" analyst, it should come as no surprise that Ferenczi was also the first to discover the mystical element in the early mother-infant relationship and the analyst-patient one. As his clinical diary clearly shows, this discovery was an agonizing one. Therefore, we will now trace Ferenczi's fascinating journey, which for him had been a *via dolorosa*, to the mystical heart of human connection.

The clinical diary

The diary contains a record of several cases of mutual analysis as well as Ferenczi's theoretical and emotional dilemmas, many of which directly concerned Freud. It is written in a highly personal manner, frequently and irregularly shifting between the theoretical and the personal and jumping from one patient to the next. Reading it is an emotionally absorbing experience: Ferenczi writes beautifully and the esthetic needs of the reader are answered even when one is horrified by the emotional suffering of sexual abuse victims and, above all, when one delves into Ferenczi's own emotional torment. One cannot help but be touched by the exposed nerves of such unprecedented self-disclosure.

The diary is rife with words like "mystical," "metaphysical," "sixth sense," "telepathic" and the like, which are constantly accompanied by Ferenczi's repeated expression of shame about their use. As the diary unfolds, however, the reader witnesses Ferenczi's growing conviction concerning the inevitability of such use. He avows that his realization about the mystical element in clinical reality took him by surprise while he was working with severely disturbed patients. He discovered it in extreme interpersonal situations – those of abuse and betrayal in the outside world and those of complete devotion to the Other in the consulting room, the kind of devotion he himself en-gaged in during mutual analyses. Struck by what he encountered, Ferenczi describes mystical experiences reported by patients as well as the mystical qualities of the therapeutic relationship itself. Finally, he attempts to offer broad generalizations about the meaning of these phenomena, which nearly amount to a complete metaphysical theory of the "feminine principle" in the universe.

In what follows, we will analyze the context in which these "mystical terms" appear and classify the phenomena Ferenczi de-scribes in order to understand the nature of the mystical element in his thinking.

Emotional coldness and the porous existence of the self

Ferenczi (Ferenczi and Dupont, 1988) begins his diary with a severe critique of the formal and distant stance the analyst assumes when meeting his patients:

Mannered form of greeting, formal request to 'tell everything', so called free floating attention, which ultimately amounts to no attention at all, and which is certainly inadequate to the highly emotional character of the analysand's communications, often brought out with the greatest difficulty. (p. 1)

After this opening statement, Ferenczi goes on to list the ill effects of this professional hypocrisy: the patient is offended and perceives the analyst's cold response as a personal rejection; she internalizes this aloof object, further deepening her self-destructiveness and questioning the veracity of her own history. Essentially, this analytic stance is a re-traumatization that exacerbates existing pathology and, as an avoidance of one's humanity, is closely related to its etiology.

Ferenczi provocatively stresses his claim regarding such lack of humanity being a pathogen, by redefining hysteria. He disputes the Freudian definition of hysteria as the bodily representation of psychic conflicts, arguing instead that it is manifest when the body takes over the psyche. It means thinking with one's body: after the psyche had collapsed due to an unbearable attack, due to the cruel inhumanity of another, it gives way to a primordial, bodily form of thinking and being. To illustrate this, Ferenczi uses metaphors from the physical world, such as "solidity," "flexibility" and "diffusion." Positive emotional connection is viewed as a "consolidating" agent for the human personality. On the other hand, abusive relations "breach" and "shatter" the personality structure. In the case of hysteria, the personality becomes half "fluid," even "gas-like." It then becomes more susceptible to outside influence; for example, to the thoughts and feelings of others and even to distant events. Interestingly, Ferenczi associates this pathologically increased susceptibility with the origination of clairvoyant perception (ibid, p. 8).

Alongside this "physicalization" of the psyche, Ferenczi also animates the body and even inorganic matter. To him, all matter has the potential for a sort of primitive psychic life:

So it appears that in human beings, given certain conditions, it can happen that the (organic, perhaps also the inorganic) substance recovers its psychical quality, not utilized since primordial times. In other words, the capacity to be impelled by motives, that is, the psyche, continues to exist potentially in in substances as well [...] under certain abnormal conditions it can be resurrected. (p. 5)

Once this primordial force is awakened, it is very hard to suppress it again. Ferenczi postulates a universal intelligence, which he termed "Orpha," which takes over the helpless, attacked personality. Orpha serves as one of the "fragments" of this torn personality, the other two being a purely suffering, wholly dissociated personality, and a "soulless" body. Ferenczi defines Orpha as:

A singular being, for whom the preservation of life is of "coûte que coûte" significance. (Orpha). This fragment plays the role of a guardian angel: it produces wish fulfilling hallucinations [...] it anesthetizes [...] In the case of a second shock, this maternal part could not help in any other way than by squeezing the entire psychic life out of the inhumanly suffering body. (p. 9)

Later (p. 54), he defines Orpha as an intelligence that transcends time and space, and therefore individuality: a trans-individual force. The brake with Freud is clear. Whereas Freud views hysteria as an illness originating in phantasy, here it is seen as the result of an actual traumatic relationship. The body takes over, guided by a mysterious, transpersonal intelligence that controls living organisms and perhaps even nonliving matter. As Ferenczi describes it, once the human realm had failed the victim, they turn to the nonhuman or, perhaps, the super-human. The essence of this transformation is that the child gives up on herself and her needs and wants, in favor of complete adjustment to external conditions. This unimaginable sacrifice gives her access to the abilities of this nonhuman universal intelligence, with which she is now merged:

This moment probably signifies the relinquishment of self preservation for man and his self inclusion in a greater perhaps universal stare of equilibrium. In any event these reflections open the way to an understanding of the surprisingly intelligent reactions of the unconscious in moments of great distress, of danger [...], or of mortal agony. See here also the often quoted incidents of clairvoyance. (pp. 7–8)

In accordance with Ferenczi's physical metaphors, it seems that the dissolution of the self increases its surface area, opening it to a universal reservoir of knowledge, which is inaccessible under normal circumstances. In this context, the figure of Orpha is continually developed in the diary as a transpersonal, all-knowing, distinctively feminine intelligence that supports all life. Ferenczi depicts it as able to grant the child the ability to anticipate the mind of her attacker. The body becomes de-humanized and dissociated and the psyche, likewise dissociated from personal existence, crosses over to the super-human. The only part of the psyche that is personal is in unthinkable agony and remains inaccessible. Ferenczi presents a girl who went through this process as his first mutual analysis patient. What he learned from this case and implemented in others might be described as the way to reverse this devastating process. The effect of a kind, trustworthy relationship that Ferenczi describes as metaphysical:

> Now something "metaphysical": some patients have the feeling that when this kind of mutual peace is attained the libido, released from conflict, will, without any further intellectual or explanatory effort, have a "healing" effect. They demand that I should not reflect quite so much, I should just be there; [...] The two unconsciousness thereby receive mutual help: the "healer" himself would gain some tranquility from the healed, and vice versa. Both emphasize that this mutual flux be taken in the substantial sense and not merely explained in terms of psychology. [...] The psyche that has been fragmented [...] feels love [...] flowing toward it and enveloping it, as if with a kind of glue: fragments come together into lager unites: the entire personality may succeed in again becoming united. (p. 12)

Anticipating many later thinkers such as Winnicott, Kohut, Balint and others, Ferenczi finds that, even without any sophisticated interpretive activity, a "holding" (Winnicott) or "empathic" (Kohut) human presence may "rebuild" or revitalize a deeply damaged self. This is a passive power, a basic, motherly human presence, that

Balint (1968) later equated with the earth and the water. It requires the analyst to assume a stance of total devotion. This is fundamentally different from Freud, who, despite being the first to describe and stress the importance of unconscious contact, had difficulty in acknowledging the basic transformative quality of this mutual flow, which is unmediated by interpretation. Freud saw the early maternal bond as a primitive stage, destined to disappear almost without trace and to give way before the power of the father. The "metaphysical" here is the non-Freudian notion that the healing factor is not "insight." Instead, it lies in the union between souls – the unconscious flux of exchange between patient and therapist. The latter can remain completely passive and still the transformative moment may come. It is "metaphysical" also because, according to Ferenczi, both patient and analyst demand that this bond of minds should be taken in essential, literal terms, and this, indeed, requires a metaphysical theory. This contact is not hallucinatory or merely phantasmatic; it is a reality that both patient and therapist share and experience as meaningful. This is perhaps similar to Buber's notion of the "ontological reality" of an encounter, to the unmistakable feeling of precious reality inspired by sharing the in-between area.

In the above quoted passage, Ferenczi's "metaphysics" – namely, his pioneering recognition of the mysterious facet of human relations – corresponds to what I define as mystical in psychoanalysis: a meaningful experience that is nonverbal or hard to verbalize, but is Noetic, transcendental, and transformative. Ferenczi describes a powerful, though often soothing experience of nonverbal, even nonconscious connection. It requires transcendence – in the form of complete devotion to the therapeutic relationship. It is certainly transformative – as it gives birth to the self, that can now exist as a whole unit through the Other's loving presence. The mutual flow is experienced as real and as having Noetic significance. Both patient and analyst know that something of great importance has transpired between them, though this experience often cannot or even should not be intellectually defined.

Ferenczi is not always as naïve as he may sound. Right after this dramatic description, he admits that most of what is attained through this mystical connection withers away when the session ends. He wonders whether the reason for this "Penelopean" repetition (p. 12) lies in the fact that therapy, despite all the blurring of boundaries that

Ferenczi is willing to practice, still ends with the session and that what therapists can offer is but a faint echo of the love that was needed in childhood. Seeing as honesty is Ferenczi's central therapeutic value, he suggests that a frank discussion of these limitations with one's patients is both unavoidable and curative. In the same vein, throughout his quest, Ferenczi is always experimenting, trying to make contact, trying to be true to his experience in exploring what he describes as the perilous connection between two unconscious minds.

The qualities of the mystical connection: Healing or madness?

Why is such a connection perilous? Essentially, because similar contact between minds was initially created through unimaginable suffering, through the violent tearing of the child's "psychic skin," which left her traumatically over-sensitive to the rest of the universe. Do similar horrors lurk in the consulting room? Is unconscious contact inevitably and always associated with pathology, even madness?

Ferenczi's diary suggests that the danger is there, even for the analyst. His second diary entry makes another mention of Orpha. This time, it is unclear if he is talking about the patient's personality being replaced by her, or her taking over the analyst-patient mental bond. He speaks of the analytic couple's mutual position of need, of the therapist's powers being depleted by the analysis:

> Our psyche, too, is more or less fragmentated and in pieces [...] it needs such repayment now and again from well disposed patients who are cured or in the point of being cured.

Intellectual activity at the time of each physical change

This activity is at rest if nothing disturbs it from outside. Resistance (defiance, non comprehension) to every assault, time and space determined by this resistance. Intellect itself is without time and space, therefore supra-individual. "Orpha." (p. 13; enlarged line and italics in original)

This passage, like many others in the diary, attests to a blurring of boundaries between patient and analyst, perhaps leading to (or resulting from) a more general blurring of the outline of the personality and its relation to time and space. Whose personality has given in to Orpha – the patient's? The analyst's? Both, as they become connected? Who is resisting? The fabric of space-time slips away; it does not exist where Orpha reigns. She does not live in the "actual" world, that involves an "outside" and an "inside" that can offer resistance to each other.

The union facilitated by Orpha threatens one's contact with reality. It destroys the boundaries necessary for maintaining one's connection to the paradoxical fullness of a limited world. Perhaps this is why the notion of Orpha and mutual analysis has disappeared from the psychoanalytic landscape. Ferenczi himself recognizes some of these dangers and oscillates, throughout his diary, between total devotion and "unambivalent love" toward his patients and feelings of absolute hate for them, for being so demanding. In still other passages, he seems mindful of the threat embedded in boundless devotion and occasionally tells us about setting limits for his patient's demands.

Inseparably from this dilemma, Ferenczi pondered the question of the mystical element. Is total psychic union curative? Is it a prerequisite for a healthy psyche? Can it even be necessary for maintaining a healthy society? Or is it a maddening and dangerous state? Ferenczi's experiment brought him close to the maddening suffering of his patients. Their union with others or with "Orpha" has its sinful birth in their horrible torture. Ferenczi's own danger in getting so close to them is evident not only in the content of his writings, which manifestly express that danger, but also in their form, which shifts between clear and sound arguments and vague, sometimes almost meaningless paragraphs, confusing different topics and interchanging patient and analyst.[2]

According to Ferenczi, two of the four patients on whom his diary entries are based had a deep interest in the occult that had clear pathological aspects. Ferenczi writes about one of them: "At this point I succeeded in diverting the patient away from one sided interest in ghosts and metaphysics, yet bound up with a great deal of anxiety, to two sided interests (remaining friends with the spirts, but also being able and willing to provide helpful assistance in the real

world)" (pp. 15–16). The other patient thought of herself as possessing mysterious powers and imagined she could guess other people's
thoughts, especially Ferenczi's. She told him that, as a child, she had
scanned the universe in search of a soul that could understand and
cure her in the future – and that this soul was him. Ferenczi, well-
aware of the narcissistic and delusional aspects of such beliefs,
nonetheless sees them as having a grain of truth. He thereby expresses
an original and bold view of "madness":

> Naturally, everyone will say that this is megalomania, but to this
> the patient retorts that whoever has not been there himself does
> not know how right madmen are and how obtuse intelligent
> people can be. It is advisable […] if one wishes to understand
> anything about mental illness or traumatic shock, not to be to
> quick in the draw with one's rationalistic weapon […] but to keep
> in mind the grain of truth they [the assertions] do contain in a
> quasi-medium-like fashion, precisely in the mentally disturbed
> persons whose hypersensitivity is outwardly oriented. In any case
> an opportunity is offered for gaining insight not only into the
> psychic content of the fragmented unconscious but also into the
> ways and means of fragmentation itself. Whether one should go
> further and search for supramaterial, metaphysical intuitions in
> the form and content of mental disorders […] is something each
> must decide for himself. (p. 29)

Ferenczi clearly believes that at least some part of his patients'
"mystical" hypersensitivity is indeed a form of perception and not
mere phantasy. The word "mystical" here refers to a state of transcendence (beyond one's suffering self) that entails a consciousness of
being connected to the universe, which is a meaningful, Noetic experience. The "grain of truth," according to Ferenczi, lies in the essence of mental illness – which involves the fragmentation of the
personality and the subsequent dispersal of its fragments on a
"cosmic" level of existence. But there can also be some truth in the
content of psychotic thoughts. Elsewhere in the diary, he proposes
that psychotic phantasies about telephones and telegraphs represent
the truth of mystical communication, in a psychotically twisted form.
The possibility of "going further," that Ferenczi leaves open to the

judgment of his readers, seems to be more about exploring whether these intuitions are evidence of something immaterial or "supranatural" than whether they are real or not.

Ferenczi is greatly concerned by the question of materialism but does not find as straightforward an answer as Freud's. Ferenczi refers to himself as a complete materialist, who is disturbed by his findings. He attempts to make certain amendments to the materialistic world view by linking the hypersensitivity of mediums with an archaic, animalistic function, that is similar to an overly sensitive olfactory ability that had been lost throughout human evolution (pp. 86–88). This rather strange theory, connecting clairvoyance with the sense of smell, is not developed further and remains no more than a feeble suggestion, made perhaps by Ferenczi's vanquished internal materialist.

This desperate need to ground these discoveries in biology is better understood if we think of the grave danger that lies in accepting mystical reality. It threatens Ferenczi's ties with Freud and the analytic community and perhaps even his own sanity. Can anyone who risks his soul through intimate contact with hideous suffering remain psychically intact? Moreover, does such contact threaten one's sanity in itself, regardless of its contents? Can the very experience of mystical reality be dangerous? Has Jones' slander concerning Ferenczi's sanity touched upon a grain of truth of its own – an abyss Ferenczi had stared into?

Madness, wholeness, transcendence

Ferenczi writes:

> In all this the question remains unresolved and unanswered: To what extent do those who have "gone mad" from pain, that is, those who have departed from the usual egocentric point of view, become able through their special situation to experience a part of that remains inaccessible to us materialists? And here the direction of research must become involved with the so-called occult. Cases of thought transference during the analysis of suffering people are extraordinarily frequent. One sometimes has the impression that the reality of such processes encounters strong emotional resistance in us materialists; any insights we

gain into them have the tendency to come undone, like Penelope's weaving or the tissue of our dreams.

It is possible that we are facing here a fourth "narcissistic wound" namely that even the intelligence of which we are so proud, though analysts, is not our property but must be replaced or regenerated through the rhythmic outpouring of the ego into the universe, which alone is all knowing and therefore intelligent. (p. 33)

On the one hand, this passage describes the connection between the mystical experience and moments of extreme suffering and madness. On the other hand, this experience is also seen as the agent of change. It is the source from which even the proud, materialistically inclined analyst derives his insight. Again, this raises the question of the analyst's personal risk. If one can gain access to cosmic intelligence through great suffering and madness, is the opposite direction also possible? Might the analyst, in trying to connect to the soul of his patient and gain access to universal "Orphic" knowledge, go mad? Can this be the real reason why Ferenczi's experiment was forbidden and he himself cast out of the psychoanalytic community, while his ideas continued to exert a covert influence because "in a manner which to us appears mystical, the ego fragments remain linked to one another, however, distorted and hidden the link may be" (p. 176). After all, Ferenczi explicitly says that the devotion needed for mutual analysis and the connection of minds involves a great sacrifice, which he is willing to make, but one that leaves him in need of support from the patient – in a circle of interwoven suffering and mutual rehabilitation (p. 13).

Be that as it may, Ferenczi argues that the true connection to another person's mind is made possible through recourse to a transpersonal intelligence, a cosmic mind. Even if we reject this metaphysical notion, the innovation is clear: *the unconscious connection* (to the patient, to the universe, to the cosmic intelligence through the therapeutic connection) *is the curative factor*. The mystical experience is placed at the very heart of psychoanalysis.

This notion is reminiscent of Buber's description of the I-Thou relation as enabled by the "eternal Thou," the Buberian parallel, perhaps, of Ferenczi's cosmic intelligence. For both thinkers, it is this connection that enables the creation of new meaning, the wholeness of the human self and any kind of human creativity. It is no wonder that Ferenczi saw it potentially capable of dealing a narcissistic blow to humanity in general and to analytic pride, in particular.

The above passage represents the beginning of the distinction Ferenczi is slowly discovering between the "mad" aspect of mysticism and its curative potential. While the distinction is still nascent, one can nevertheless sense the difference between the language used to describe the victim's mystical experience – fragmentation of the soul and self-abandonment – and the intelligence gained by the "rhythmic outpouring of the ego into the universe." This choice of words suggests something less violent, more harmonious and regenerative – perhaps a healthier circle that involves both transcending the self and returning to it.

There seem to be two more points of difference between the "mad" and the "curative" mystical experience. The first is that the "mad" experience is usually described in more dramatic and colorful terms. For example:

> The soul passes through a hole in the head, into the universe and shines far off in the distance like a star (this would be clairvoyance, which goes beyond understanding the aggressor and understands the entire universe so to speak, in order to be able to grasp the genesis of even such a monstrous thing). Thus under the pressure of the shock a part of the personality leaves the selfish spheres of earthly existence, and becomes all knowing. (pp. 206–207)

Ferenczi's experiences with his patients have a calmer tone and usually do not entail such visually impressive imagery. Still, when a patient reports a mystical experience in a session, it might include some similar elements, as when a patient reported seeing Ferenczi's aura coming out to meet her. In general, experiences within the sessions seem to be less dramatic and colorful as well as less violent. It is more about the soul "going out" to reach another than being ripped out of the body.

A more important difference is that the curative experience take place as part of a communication process, within the context of therapy, while the "mad" experience happens to the patient alone, outside the consulting room, as a more solipsistic experience. A second glance, however, revels a more complicated reality. The mystical experience which is external to the session has happened in the context of the sexual assault or of the victim's recollection of it. I believe this means that these experiences also happen in the context of a connection between two minds – in this case, an evil and destructive one. Ferenczi speaks of transcending the self because of the need to understand the attacker and "the genesis of such a monstrous thing," to fathom the roots of evil.

It seems that some kind of a connection between two people is requisite for a mystical experience, though each of them may experience it differently. Even within the consulting room, the visual experiences of seeing auras, for example, are confined to the patient alone and Ferenczi does not share the same perceptions. In fact, he claims that as far as the patient is concerned, he may even fall asleep. What is shared between patient and therapist is not a certain content or perception; it does not even require a full waking state. Therefore, we are not talking about "mind reading" per se, but rather an experience of deep psychic connection, even merger, between two people – patient and therapist or attacker and victim. This connection transforms both parties, and even if each of them perceives and experiences it in their own way (for example, with or without visual sensations), both share an overlapping psychic reality, a nonverbal emotional experience that encompasses both.

Ferenczi repeatedly explains how the process of identification with the aggressor occurs: the attacked child cannot feel anymore; instead of complete psychic annihilation, she merges with the only one who is allowed to feel, or even exist in the situation: her attacker. His parasitic presence lingers on within the child even after the attack, like a *dybbuk*, a demonic procession. On his part, he needs to fill her with unbearable emotions such as terror and appropriate her childish innocence.

> The result of this process is, on the one hand, the implanting of psychic contents in the psyche of the victim [...] causing pain and tension; at the same time, however, the aggressor sucks up, as it were, a piece of the victim into himself, the piece that has been

expelled. Hence the soothing affect on an enraged person of the explosion of his rage when he succeeds in causing pain to the other. (p. 77)

The transformation of both parties takes the form of a vampiric attack instead of a benevolent sharing. This is Ferenczi's description of a process that Klein eventually termed "projective identification," without crediting Ferenczi. His description constitutes a fuller and a mystical account of this process, a facet that had been lost until Bion's elaboration of the term.

For Ferenczi, therefore, a connection that carries "psychic parts" from one person to another is neither an anomalous nor an exceptional event; it is part and parcel of interpersonal reality. It can tend toward benevolence or malevolence (Ferenczi does not deny the possibility of some destructiveness even in therapy), toward a curative sharing that nurtures the personality or a force that violently shatters it.

A developmental theory

After making its initial appearance in the middle of the diary, Ferenczi's developmental theory, though scattered in fragments, continues to develop. Put together, the fragmented passages constitute a budding theory which is rooted in a more systematic metaphysical approach. Ferenczi writes:

> The idea of the still half dissolved state [...] tempts the imagination to suppose that the childish personality is in much closer contact with the universe, and therefore, its sensitivity is much greater than that of the adult, crystalized into rigidity. It would not surprise [us ...] if some day it were to be demonstrated that in this early state, the whole personality is still resonating with the environment. [...] So called supernormal faculties [...] may well be ordinary processes [...]. (p. 81)

Ferenczi thus begins to view the "dissolved" state as a normative developmental stage. He speculates, much like Freud, that these capabilities have remained active in animals and also mentions thought transmission between mother and fetus. He claims that mediums, if they have legitimate achievements, owe these to a regression to this infantile phase. Later on, the diary presents a further theoretical step, explaining the transition from infantile "dissolution" to the adult "crystalized" state:

> But the physical embrace also allows her, or forces her, to convert her personality, which has been dissolved in the universe, into a real thing existing of this world, and more or less withdraw her libido from the universe [...] one can claim [...] that the narcissism that is indispensable as the basis of personality – [...] the recognition and assertion of one's self as a genuinely existing, valuable entity of a given size, shape and significance – is attainable only when the positive interest of the environment, let us say its libido, guarantees the stability of that form of personality by means of external pressure so to speak. Without such counter-pressure, let us say counterlove, the individual tends to explode, to dissolve itself in the universe, perhaps to die. (pp. 128–129)

This is the essence of Ferenczi's developmental theory. The loving embrace of the human environment coalesces this unformed, "liquid" infantile existence, solidifying it by giving it form and significance. Without this external pressure, the child and the eventual adult may be omniscient, but they will have no personal existence. Such unimpeded dissolution is tantamount to the death of subjectivity. Years later, Winnicott will write about holding and, more specifically, both he and Kohut will extensively discuss the role of the mother's gaze in giving shape to the child's personality. Here, Ferenczi stresses the plain and simple, unmediated act of hugging. Perhaps it was part of his own total "hands on" investment in his patients and his belief in the power of love, without the need to hide it in "professional" terms. This love acts as a shield, keeping the fortunate adult unaware of the mystical reality. Only babies and, in adulthood, the most miserable souls are exposed to this reality.

A page later, Ferenczi suggests a different view:

> (it is impossible to foresee what the consequences would be for knowledge if people were freed from this anxiety and dared to examine and recognize the world in its own quite self evident form; how much further it could lead than even the most audacious of

what nowadays we call fantasies. Really mastering anxiety [...] might perhaps make us quite clairvoyant, and might help humanity solve apparently insoluble problems. This may be a deferred verification of the self-assurance which impresses as megalomania, in R.N.'s declarations.) Furthermore, no analysis can succeed if we do not succeed in truly loving our patients. (p. 130)

Ferenczi does not explain his shift from seeing clairvoyance as a result of trauma to viewing it as an achievement attained by *overcoming* fear. Rather, he offers a new vision of the immense benefits that humanity could attain by daring to see reality for what it is, its "simple truth" – the truth of deep contact with others and perhaps with the whole universe.

Finally, Ferenczi reaches a more consolidated view:

The effect achieved by such [...] incompletely developed life, thus brings to mind the achievements attained in later life only by exceptional people of outstanding moral and philosophical nature. Religious people are selfless, in that they renounce their own selves; primordial life is selfless, because it does not possess a developed self as yet. To a considerable extent the selfish person seals himself off from the external world with the help of his stimulus-barrier [...] In infants these protective devices are not yet developed so that infants communicate with the environment over a much broader surface. (p. 148)

Ferenczi now makes a clearer connection between normal and pathological clairvoyance and bridges the tension between the two poles of the mystical experience mentioned in the diary. The baby is in touch with the universe because her self is in a liquid state, still free of rigid defenses. The victim of abuse is likewise susceptible to a wide range of contact, because her self was broken in pieces. But here a new figure appears, the religious person, who is capable of mystical contact not because of regression but, on the contrary, due to her capacity to transcend the boundaries of the self as a result of an ethical choice and a philosophical achievement.

Though Ferenczi does not explain in detail how one can reach such a "philosophical" stage of development, he associates it with the selflessness practiced by the devoted analyst. Moreover, he suggests that, since he views thought transference in analysis as more common than chance would allow, it is likely that "transference relationship could quite significantly promote the development of subtler manifestations of receptivity" (p. 85). Freud (1933) reached a similar conclusion about the connection between transference and "thought transference," but, as we have seen, he chose to attribute this idea to another author and never developed it further, even though transference was already well-established as the heart of the analytic process and everything relating to it surly merited investigation. Ferenczi, on the other hand, is much clearer in suggesting that emotional closeness and, therefore, real analytic devotion, open up one's psychic "pores" to the person one is attuned to.

It is now easier to understand the connection Ferenczi makes between the knowledge acquired in the mystical state and his vision of solving humanity's hitherto unsolvable problems. He writes:

> The somewhat daring hypothesis regarding the contact of the individual with the whole universe must be viewed from the standpoint not only that this omniscience enables the individual to perform extraordinary feats, but also (and this is perhaps the most paradoxical assertion that has ever been made) that such a contact can have a humanizing effect on the whole universe. (Ferenzci and Dupont, 1988, p. 147)

We have before us a statement of faith that mystical contact is not just some archaic leftover from humanity's past; it can also shape its future. Openness to the "intimacy principle," that Lamberth (1997) found in James' writings, can promote new levels of empathic understanding. If one mind can truly touch another, mankind can perhaps be in touch with its surrounding nonhuman environment as well, promoting, the evolution of James's humanistic universe. Ferenczi's developmental theory transcends "analytic faith" in the individual and expands it to embrace the entire human race and beyond.

The feminine principle and its split

It seems that what helped Ferenczi establish his unfinished bridge between the regressed and the more evolved mystical experience was the development of his own metaphysical world view. We first en-counter it in his daring hypothesis about the archaic psychic life of matter. Later, alongside his developmental theory, Ferenczi presents the idea that development, being dependent on love, is made possible by a fundamental feminine principle – a passive, giving, even sub-missive altruistic principle that governs maternity, feminine sexuality, and even existence itself – the life of the universe.

He rejects the split between the physical and the spiritual and offers an adjustment to the dualistic Freudian metaphysics of the life and death instincts. He introduces a masculine principle of self-assertion and a feminine principle of conciliation. For him, the interplay of these two forces defines the workings of the universe, but it is nevertheless the feminine principle that sustains life. According to Ferenczi, being a woman, giving life, experiencing the joys of mo-therhood – all require submission and a certain degree of suffering. In its extreme from, this drive may turn into masochism, as the extreme form of the masculine drive turns into sadism. In addition, Ferenczi challenges Freud's notion of sublimation, arguing that love is not a transformation of animalistic drives but a basic reality, without which the universe could not have sustained life.

As mentioned above, this universal feminine principle or "Orpha" is what allows the child to evacuate herself completely in the face of her attacker. In this extreme masochistic scenario, however, she is deprived of her selfhood, which could only have developed as an interplay be-tween the two forces. The dialectic structure that Ferenczi ascribes to both the human personality and the universe stresses his view that a deep, intimate connection between souls is a basic principle for all forms of existence, including the human psyche. This interaction can take the form of a complete breach of boundaries, when the male principle sa-distically violates another's subjectivity, leaving it no choice but to re-sort to the feminine extreme, in the form of masochistic self-annihilation. It can also take the form of an intimate mutual contact that "consolidates" the personality and nurtures it. Both cases involve an interpenetration (either loving or violent) of psychic boundaries; if you will, these are "evil" and "benign" forms of mystical union. It seems that Ferenczi, in his mutual analysis experiment, experienced these heavens and these hells and came back to tell us of the grave dangers, as well as the great potential, of such boundless union.

It would be beyond the scope of this discussion to comment on Ferenczi's metaphysics or his pro-feminine bias. For our present purposes, it suffices to point out that it is a *counter bias* to Freud's bias, manifest in the conspicuous absence of the feminine principle from his writings. While Ferenczi expresses an almost religious reverence toward what in ancient times might have been considered the great mother-goddess (Eliade, 1957), Freud stresses the power of the father and the love and awe he inspires, in relation to which the longing for the mother (except as an object of libidinal wishes) is depicted as archaic and primitive. Many of Ferenczi's diary entries make it quite clear that he sees Freud as having a greater affinity to the masculine principle, while associating himself with the feminine one. He sees himself as an analyst who completely "gives in" to his patients. Freud, on the other hand, is quoted in the diary describing himself as egoistic and narcissistic, lacking the patience to stay with his patients where they are and rushing them to become, through an educational process, more like himself. In this great battle between the two principles, it was the feminine side of psychoanalysis that was the first to "lose" (at least until the British middle school gained influence), fading from conscious knowledge and practice but remaining extremely influential in the background – much like Ferenczi's own neglected figure.

Concluding remarks: The fate of the mystical element in early psychoanalysis

Looking at the dawn of psychoanalysis from the perspective of the mystical element, it is clear that this element was one of the fundamental forces shaping the new discipline. As a modern attempt to grasp human complexity, psychoanalysis necessarily confronted its predecessors, including religious and mystical traditions and their notions of the psyche. Freud shares with us his concern that these traditions are reactionary and dangerous. His choice, therefore, was to try and cast his new field in the mold of science. He dismissed not only religion but also philosophical attempts that were not grounded in empirical verification (Freud, 1933). Nevertheless, the absence of a philosophical toolbox was sorely felt when psychoanalysis faced the need to build a bridge between Freud's (materialistic) idea of science and the recognition, forced upon Freud and Ferenczi both, that the therapeutic connection – perhaps like all close human relationships – entails a "telepathic" exchange of experience and psychic states.

Both Freud and Ferenczi report having "stumbled" onto this re-cognition and feeling the shock that came with realizing the funda-mental change that would ensue if this idea were to have been assimilated. For Freud, this fundamental finding was ironically marginalized in his writings: he never made any systematic attempt to integrate it into his own theory, viewing it as a threat to his con-ceptualizations. He did have some hope of integration, however, manifest in the vague statement that the unconscious, a term that combines the bodily and the psychic, may point the way to an in-tegration of telepathy into a materialistic point of view (Freud, 1933). Ferenczi, on the other hand, was willing to face the consequences of this discovery and even pay the price that any disciple must pay for defying his teacher. But the price was not confined to the reaction of the analytic community. Freud (1933) wrote that whoever wished to delve into the study of the occult will inevitably become wholly en-grossed in it, and that the analyst's task is difficult enough as it is. Perhaps part of this task means facing a skeptical world, even without invoking mystical claims. The mere focus on the psyche, instead of on the organic brain, might have been enough of a chal-lenge for early 20th century industrial society. Freud, as we know, has had more than his fair share of this kind of struggle.

The nature of the mystical element in early psychoanalysis

Freud felt that "telepathy" was a foreign body for his theory, alter-natively appealing and interesting or deeply menacing. Accordingly, while the "materialistic" drive-based structure of the unconscious came to the fore, the mystical facet of the unconscious became a disavowed reality – perhaps the *unheimlich* of psychoanalysis.

The person who came to embody this *unheimlich* was Ferenczi: he was the mystic, the feminine, the disavowed. For generations, he was also the "shadow" who had dared to perform the forbidden experi-ment of mutual psychoanalysis; his name was tied to what should never be. This was, in part, justified. But the mystical element he championed, though tormenting, was not foreign; rather, it was all too close. He practiced the mysticism of union, of boundlessness. In his admiration for the feminine ideal of total devotion, he risked loss of self and certainly the loss of his analytic stance – by needing that his patients "refuel" him. This is perhaps the archaic, "oceanic" form of union with the mother, which Freud found so revolting.

From a Buberian perspective, neither form of psychoanalysis – Freud's "objective" observation or Ferenczi's dissolution of self-boundaries – constitutes a true I-Thou meeting. The former because of its distanced observer-observed stance and the latter because of its threat to the separateness of the self. In the dialogic I-Thou connection, two selves deeply touch each other, at their core. They create a shared reality, but remain separate. Buber (1923/2010) was clear about this point, especially in addressing caretaking relationships. He spoke specifically about mental health, hinting at psychoanalysis. For him, if the doctor only tries to analyze the patient, to "bring to light unknown factors from his [the patient's] microcosm" (p. 122), he may hope to effect some change, but no real transformation will occur, for he will never truly understand the patient. Understanding can only be attained in a "face to face position" (ibid, ibid). On the other hand, the doctor must never forget his position as a healer and convert this essentially mutual relationship into a fully equal exchange: "one only can heal or educate if he stands face to face and infinitely far away at the same time" (ibid; author's translation). Inferring Freud and Ferenczi's technique from their writings,[3] the psychoanalytic meeting, at the time of its invention, was not structured to facilitate I-Thou moments. The immanent presence of intimate "soul to soul contact" that arose in the consulting room was either pushed away with horror or basked in, at the risk of losing the analytic boundaries.

Still, Ferenczi never lost himself completely to the experience of mutuality, just as his teacher could never wholly escape it. He survived with the full mental capacity required to report it and to draw invaluable conclusions. But part of his legacy, even after its great value has been acknowledged, is that his experiment of mutual analysis must never be repeated. Coming close to a state of psychic merger means exposing oneself to all the dangers lurking in two people's unconscious – as well as the magic therein. Ferenczi reports both mutual calm and beatific experiences of unity as well as a terrifying feeling that his patient might engulf him. Eventually, his "feminine" alternative was no less problematic than Freud's original "masculinity."

Between delving into archaic and oceanic mysticism and denying any trace of mysticism by playing the part of the "dispassionate surgeon," psychoanalysis still grapples with these two extremes, represented by its founders. Perhaps the relational formula of "mutual but not symmetrical" owes part of its popularity to the resolution of this historical split. Accordingly, perhaps it is now time to invite the "shadow" back, to be united in a thoughtful and more integrated way into the body of psychoanalysis.

Notes

1 It took decades after Freud himself had passed away before any other analyst dared to present a similar case, which includes the repudiated phenomenon of countertransference, as well as the arguably telepathic exchange of unconscious material between therapist and patient.

2 Naturally, this is a personal diary that was not originally meant for the public eye. Still, some parts of it seem more carefully constructed than others, more beautifully written and inviting, while others are hard to decipher. Some passages even contain neologisms, shifting between "I," "we" or "one" and between masculine and feminine when referring to patients (Editor's Note, 1988). I believe it is fair to suppose that this reflects not only the idiosyncrasies of a man writing to himself but may also mirror the fluctuations in the sense of self resulting from Ferenczi's experiments in mutual analysis.

3 Given that Freud and Ferenczi were both very complex and gifted, it is hard to assume that either of them always kept the same inflexible stance. We know for a fact that Freud's personality had a warm side and that he cared deeply about some of his patients; just as we know that Ferenczi was not always the giving and devoted "mother earth." Moreover, Ferenczi was never completely "merged" with his patients and never stopped asking questions and evaluating the dangers, as well as the benefits, of his method. Still, for clarity's sake, they are treated as wholly representative of their chosen ideals.

References

Balint, M. (1968). *The Basic Fault: Therapeutic Aspects of Regression.* Evanston: Northwestern University Press.

Berman, E. (1996). The Ferenczi renaissance. *Psychoanalytic Dialogues*, 6(*3*):391–411.

Bollas, C. (2007). *The Freudian Moment.* London: Karnac.

Buber, M. (2010). *I and Thou.* Tr. R.G. Smith. New York: Martino Publishing. (Original work published in 1923).

Dupont, J. (1988). Introduction. In S. Ferenczi and J. Dupont, *The Clinical Diary of Sandor Ferenczi* (pp. xi–xxvii). London: Harvard University Press.

Eliade, M. (1957). *The Sacred and the Profane*. New York: Harcourt inc.

Eshel, O. (2019). From extension to revolutionary change in clinical psychoanalysis: The radical influence of Bion and Winnicott. In *The Emergence of Analytic Oneness*. London and New York: Routledge.

Ferenczi, S. and Dupont, J. (Ed.). (1988). *The Clinical Diary of Sandor Ferenczi*. Tr. M. Balint and N. Zarday-Jackson. London: Harvard University Press. (Original work published in 1932).

Freud, S. (1912). Recommendations to physicians practicing psychoanalysis. *SE, XII*, 109–120.

Freud, S. (1913). Totem and Taboo. *SE, XIII*, vii–162.

Freud, S. (1921). Psychoanalysis and telepathy. *SE, XVIII*, 173–194.

Freud, S. (1922). Dreams and telepathy. *SE, XVIII*, 195–220.

Freud, S. (1927). The future of an illusion. *SE, XXI*, 1–56.

Freud, S. (1930). Civilization and its discontents. *SE, XXI*, 57–146.

Freud, S. (1933). Dreams and occultism. *SE, XXII*, 31–56.

Lamberth, D.C. (1997). Interpreting the universe after a social analogy: Intimacy, panpsychism, and a finite god in a pluralistic universe. In R.A. Putman (Ed.), *The Cambridge Companion to James* (pp. 237–259). Cambridge: Cambridge University Press.

Meissner, W.W. (1984). *Psychoanalysis and Religious Experience*. New Haven: Yale University.

Mészáros, J. (2003). Could Balint have done more for Ferenczi? *American Journal of Psychoanalysis, 63*(3):239–255.

Neumann, E. (1968). Mystical man. In J. Campbell (Ed.), *The Mystic Vision: Papers from the Eranos Yearbooks*. Princteon, NJ: Princeton University Press. (Original work published in 1948).

Phillips, A. (1994). Secrets. *London Review of Books, 16*(19):3–5.

Wolstein, B. (1989). Ferenczi, Freud, and the origins of American interpersonal relations. *Contemporary Psychoanalysis*, 25: 672–685.

Chapter 5

Bion: Doubt and faith – Dreaming the ineffable truth

For Bion, one of the greatest architects of contemporary psycho-analysis, as well as one of the most esoteric authors psychoanalysis has ever known, psychoanalysis was about grappling with the un-known; even more so, with the *essentially* unknowable. At the same time, Bion spoke of ultimate truth, a truth that can never be reached, but must be perpetually strived for. In this seemingly impossible emotional and epistemic position, he believed the proper stance from which the analyst should practice is that of *faith*. Faith in the ex-istence of an ineffable truth. Bion chose to denote the ultimate *truth* with the neutral, ostensibly geometric denotation – O: the point of origin for any coordinate system (Bion, 1965). Truth as a starting point. Unburdened with any other values. At the same time, it is also seen as the most meaningful thing – a denotation that points to the ultimate meaning, as well as to none – the alpha and the Omega of experience.

Bion defines O as follows:

> I shall use the sign O to denote that which is the ultimate reality, represented by terms such as the ultimate reality, absolute truth, the godhead, the infinite, the thing in itself. O does not fall in the domain of knowledge or learning save incidentally; it can 'become', but it cannot be 'known'. It is darkness and formless-ness, but it enters the domain K when it has evolved to a point where it can be known through knowledge gained by experience, and formulated in terms derived from sensuous experience; its existence is conjectured phenomenologically. (1970, p. 26)

DOI: 10.4324/9781003200796-5

In his advice to analysts, similar in content to and perhaps surpassing in influence even Freud's recommendation to physicians, Bion states that to achieve contact with O, the analyst must relinquish memory and desire. This injunction was enthusiastically embraced by many, perhaps because it coincided with the analyst's traditional austerity. This statement became representative of Bion, almost like a slogan. However, what he recommended instead of memory and desire, remained both enigmatic and much less celebrated:

> It may be wondered what state of mind is welcome, if desires and memories are not. A term that would express approximately what I need to express is 'faith' – faith that there is an ultimate reality, and truth – the unknown, unknowable, 'formless infinite'. This must be believed of every object of which the personality can be aware: the evolution of ultimate reality (signified by O) has issued an object of which the individual can be aware. (ibid, p. 31)

I think it is safe to say that no other psychoanalytic concept, including Freud's death drive, has ever caused so much controversy, drawn to itself so much lively interest (in the form of either fascination or aversion), and sparked such an extensive body of literature debating its meaning, as Bion's O. Adding insult to injury, the "faith" which is required for engaging O is a provocative term, with a distinct religious air. The concept of O served as the divide between the consensual early Bion an the late "mystical" Period. A great many of Bion's contemporary followers are themselves outstanding analytic authors, including Ogden, Grotstein, Eigen, Vermote, Symington, Ferro, Brown and Reiner. The fact that some of them are fascinated precisely with the late Bion, makes the early-late split more difficult to maintain today, in comparison with Bion's own time. It has therefore become a point of great emotional momentum to determine whether Bion was indeed mystically-inclined and what it means if he was.

Can one keep faith with Bion while "throwing out" the mystical as merely a metaphor or some nonessential feature? If the split does not hold, and one cannot negate Bion's importance, what is to become of psychoanalysis? Is the transformation that would await it (borrowing Bion's own terms) if it were to fully face the meaning of O, too catastrophic to be made a reality? Perhaps it is too great a change: O, heralded by Bion as the only thing psychoanalysis should concern itself with, is completely unempirical, by definition, since it is non-sensual. Bion points to this shocking conclusion himself: "the central phenomena of psycho-analysis have no background in sense data" (ibid, p. 57).

Just as Freud's 1933 paper, "The Question of a Weltanschauung" is surprisingly determined to affiliate psychoanalysis, in spite of its distinguishing features, with the same worldview as that of chemistry and physics, so does Bion stand out in his equally extreme and dia-metrically opposed position. Through a Bionian lens, psychoanalysis may not only appear to be a nonempirical field of study (in that, it may at least be listed among the humanities), but seem a completely spiritual endeavor. For, as Bion (1970) writes, "non-sensuous phe-nomena form the totality of what is commonly regarded as mental or spiritual experience" (p. 91). At first glance, at least, it seems that there is little in common between Bionian *psychoanalysis* and the original, Freudian sense of the term. This position was fully devel-oped in *Attention and Interpretation*, the second major book of Bion's "mystical period" and his final theoretical one. It unfolds an epis-temic outlook that touches upon metaphysical systems of thought, such as Kantian and Platonic philosophy, mysticism and the re-ligious, artistic, and scientific worldviews, as means for determining the elusive subject matter and methodology of psychoanalysis.

This chapter analyzes this late Bionian position, as reflected in this book and in his paper *Caesura*, in an attempt to elucidate Bionian mysticism and its place in psychoanalysis' theoretical and me-tatheoretical development. Moreover, in order to answer the question of "what is the Bionian 'O,'" I will also discuss a possible disparity between Bion's original mysticism and various contemporary at-tempts to conceptualize it, examining whether such attempts – which position Bion as one of the most influential analysts in contemporary psychoanalysis – indeed do justice to the original spirit of O.

The field of the ineffable: Science, religion and mysticism

Bion, much more than Freud, views psychoanalysis as a completely unique and peerless field. Unlike Ferenczi and Kohut, this distance from the sciences does not seem to cause him any pain. On the contrary, *Attention and Interpretation* is, in a way, a proud manifesto celebrating this uniqueness.

At the beginning of the book, Bion (1970) tackles psychoanalysis' close neighbor or, we might say, its "motherland" and place of birth – medicine. He rejects the medical model as unsuitable for psychoanalysis for several reasons, the main one being its dependence on the senses:

> The physician is dependent on realization of sensuous experience in contrast with the psychoanalyst whose dependence is on experience that is not sensuous. The physician can see and touch and smell. The realizations with which a psycho-analyst deals cannot be seen or touched; anxiety has no shape or colour [...] for convenience, I propose to use the term 'intuit' as a parallel in the psychoanalyst's domain to the physician's use of 'see', 'touch', 'smell' and 'hear'. (p. 7)

Bion stipulates intuition – which Freud treated with so much suspicion – as the analyst's main tool and a counterpart to the senses. For him, "intuition" is an *ad hoc* term for a means of fathoming the ineffable. For Freud, intuition, as a derivative of one's hopes and fears, serves the pleasure principle and leads one away from the reality principle. For Bion, it is the other way around: focusing on one's senses is what obscures the analyst's path to the truth. He admits that anxiety, passion or any other emotional experience may have physical indicators, like accelerated pulse, perspiration, etc., but such sensuous derivatives are *not* anxiety or passion. These cannot be reduced to their physical manifestations. Bion thus completes the severing of psychoanalysis from the body of medicine, a process that was begun by Freud.

Bion discusses important parallels between psychoanalysis and science, but also with art and religion. Nevertheless, his conclusion is fascinating and unequivocal: "it is absurd to criticize a piece of psychoanalytic work on the ground that it is 'not scientific' or 'not artistic'. It is not any of these things [...] The critical formulation for which there is no substitute is that it is 'not psycho-analysis'" (ibid, p. 62). For Bion, psychoanalysis is a unique human endeavor to reach psychic truth, which is essentially different from the kind of truth sought by the empirical sciences. Psychic truth does not produce (except as a remote derivative) any sensuous affects that can be measured scientifically or represented artistically. It does resemble religion, however, in its subject matter – the attempt to reach the ineffable, ultimate truth.

Is religion, then, the proper peer for psychoanalysis? Bion's text does present an affluence of religious metaphors, and sometimes perhaps more than metaphors: concepts like "the Godhead" which, he claims, the two fields share. Nevertheless, he warns his readers against an "early saturation" of O with religious or mythical content, since this would lead to pseudo-knowledge – the antithesis to the possibility of achieving contact with O and, therefore, to growth:

> A further source of distortion is the tendency to link F with the supernatural because of lack of experience with the 'natural' to which it relates. The tendency to introduce a god or devil that F [Faith] is to reveal (or that is to 'evolve' from O). The element F, which is to remain unsaturated, becomes saturated and unfitted for its purpose. (ibid, p. 48)

Moreover, in terms of its method or, perhaps more accurately, in terms of its ethics, Bion sees much more affinity between psychoanalysis and science than between psychoanalysis and religion. This is shown in the following Bionian fable concerning religion and science:

> The liars showed courage and resolution in their opposition to the scientists, who with their pernicious doctrines bid fair to strip every shred of self-deception from their dupes leaving them without any of the natural protection necessary for the preservation of their mental health against the impact of truth. [...] It is not too much to say that the human race owes its salvation to that small band of gifted liars who were prepared even in the face of indubitable facts to maintain the truth of their falsehood. Even death was denied and the most ingenious arguments were educed to support obviously ridiculous statements that the dead lived on in bliss. (ibid, p. 100)

However, Bion does not offer a systematic discussion of the similarities and differences between these fields and his position must be
extracted from among scattered, sometimes seemingly contradictory
statements. Still, it appears that he considers psychoanalysis and religion similar in their object of pursuit: an intangible truth. Indeed,
the manner of this pursuit is widely different, and it is not difficult to
identify the religious establishments and doctrines as the "liars" in the
above fable. Science, on the other hand, is defined by Bion as an
approach that holds that "the truth is of overriding importance and
that reason should be harnessed for its elucidation" (p. 100). Unlike
Freud, then, Bion did not consider materialism as the heart of the
scientific endeavor, but rather the search and commitment to truth.
Thus, the repudiation of comforting lies, be they materialistic or
spiritual, is at the core of Bion's recommended ethical/psychoanalytic
practice. The difference between psychoanalysis and science lies in the
use of the senses, as Bion openly declared, or, as the above quote
suggests, also in one's reliance on reason. To "intuit," after all, is very
different than to reason.

For Bion, the single parallel that resembles psychoanalysis both in
aim and in method/ethics is the striving of the mystic. He writes:

> This does not mean that psycho-analytic method is unscientific,
> but that the term 'science,' as it has been commonly used hitherto
> to describe an attitude to objects of sense, is not adequate to
> represent an approach to those realties with which 'psycho-
> analytical science' has to deal. [...] The criticism applies to every
> vertex, be it musical, religious, esthetic, political; all are inade-
> quate when related to O, because, with the possible exception of
> the religion of the mystic, these and similar vertices are not
> adapted to the sensuously baseless. (pp. 88–89)

The parallel to mysticism is even more pronounced in other passages, but here it is evident that Bion, having surveyed various
methods of representation or "vertices" used by humanity, finds
that the vertex of the mystic is psychoanalysis' only possible peer. In
this context, he makes a clear distinction between mysticism and
formal religion: the mystic, according to Bion, is the very antithesis
of established doctrine.

The Messianic idea and the (psychoanalytic) establishment

Bion proposes the mystic as a source of inspiration that could help elucidate the role of the analyst. The mystic defies the shackles of prejudice and pseudo-knowledge and strives to become one with the ultimate, nonsensuous, ineffable truth. This must also be the aim of the analyst. Bion explores terms which he sees as somewhat adjacent to the term "mystic," such as "genius" and "messiah." He declares a preference for the connotation of the term "mystic" over those of "genius" (ibid, p. 147), because the former claims to have reached unity with O. It seems that Bion deliberately evokes and rejects the more easily acceptable secular term "genius," just as he invoked the term "science," whose relevance to psychoanalysis he both accepted and rejected. This suggests that, even if the term "mystic" was not meant to be taken literally when applied to the analyst's work, it was nevertheless carefully selected with the clear intention of evoking associations to this particular semantic field.

As for the term "messiah," which is taken from the same field of associations, Bion takes it up in order to elucidate the mystic's social role. The mystic/messiah, after becoming one with O – the ultimate truth, also becomes the bearer of a new idea – one that undermines and threatens the establishment. Much like Prometheus, he carries the light of truth to human beings and might pay a heavy price for doing so. According to Bion, the analyst, like the mystic, must strive to become one with O. The analytic relationship, in trying to couple a human personality with its truth, resembles the relationship between the messiah and the group. The new idea the messiah introduces is always an earthquake for the group. It may lead to destruction (if the group rejects and destroys the messiah to protect its own stability or if the group institutions crumble under the weight of the new idea) or to growth-promoting change.

For Bion, who keeps oscillating between the individual and the group levels, that which distinguishes the healthy from the psychotic (on both levels) is the relation to truth: the nonpsychotic stance is tolerant of truth. The psychoanalytic or mystical mission transcends this, in that it is the analyst's/mystic's duty to encounter the truth which, in their case, is ineffable. What distinguishes the psycho-analytic/mystical practice is that it is based on *faith* in the existence of such ultimate truth – even if it cannot be reached, only aspired to – and the willingness to bear the consequences, whatever they may be, of striving for that truth. This faith drives the Bionian mystic to surrender herself to the truth, even before it takes any (approximate) form. This form can be scientific, religious, or psychoanalytic. Bion asserts that:

> No psycho-analytic discovery is possible without recognition of its [O's] existence at-one-ment and evolution. The religious mystics have probably approximated most closely to expression or experience of it. Its existence is essential to science as to religion. Conversely, the scientific approach is as essential to religion as to science and is as ineffectual until a transformation from $K \rightarrow O$ takes place. (p. 30)

It seems from this quote that, for Bion, faith, and an inquisitive position (doubt) may need each other and compliment each other, but that both are only meaningful when combined with the courage to leave behind K (knowledge) and enter the ineffable, formless and infinite O. More certain, however, is that he views the assumption regarding the existence of truth, its sanctity and the need to pursue it as the basis of perhaps any worthwhile human undertaking. Accordingly, Bion's examples of such messianic figures spans many fields and cultures – he mentions Jesus, Luria (the Jewish Kabbalah mystic), and Newton.

His discussion of Newton is particularly interesting. Newton is remembered and celebrated for his fundamental discoveries in physics. However, he also had a lively interest in the mystical sphere and had left writings containing his ideas about religion, alchemy and the occult. In fact, he had written more about religion than about science. According to Bion, the establishment eagerly embraced Newton the scientist, while ignoring his research into the occult. Moreover, his name became synonymous with a materialistic, mechanical world-view. Bion suggests that Newton's scientific genius sprung from his "mystical matrix" and the latter cannot therefore be viewed as some negligible, unrelated part of his corpus.

One cannot avoid the analogy to Bion's own fate in some parts of the psychoanalytic establishment, which failed to see the deep connection between his "mysticism" and his more consensual ideas and rejected the former with great zeal. When Bion discusses the destructive/growth-promoting relationship between the messiah and the group, it is at times quite clear that he sees his own ideas as a "messianic" seed that threatens the psychoanalytic establishment.

On its part, the psychoanalytic community is still dealing with the shockwaves Bion had caused. A 2019 volume of *Psychoanalytic Dialogues* offers a fascinating discussion – in terms of content and from a sociological/historical perspective (the history of ideas) – about whether Bion was indeed mystically oriented. Civitarese, who in another paper (2019a) stated emphatically that viewing Bion as mystically oriented was "a gross misunderstanding," wrote a long, rich, yet self-contradictory paper with the sole purpose of proving that O is not a mystical notion. As in most psychoanalytic writings, he does not bother to define the term mystical, but rather treats it as something he must save Bion's name from being affiliated with, at all costs. He engages in an elaborate exploration of western philosophy, musing about what O might be. This "tour" is indeed enriching and interesting, but while Bion ends his musings about science, religion and art by rejecting these as adequate metaphors for psychoanalysis and proclaiming that the work of the mystic is closest to that of the analyst, Civitarese, without any reference to Bion's own conclusion, tries to show why Bion's "real" meaning is anything but mystical. Through extremely intricate argumentation, invoking many different thinkers from Kant to Wittgenstein but, surprisingly, making almost no references to Bion's own discussion of O, Civitarese tries to show that O is either "language" or "the esthetic," though both of these options were explicitly rejected by Bion as proper vertices for psychoanalysis (1970, pp. 88–89).

Civitarese (2019b) does not try to reconcile or even admit the possible contradiction or tension between the two, or between either of them and a third option he mentions – a wordless sharing in which patient and analyst engage in unison. Instead, he vacillates between the two (or three) possibilities with the sole purpose of avoiding a mystical interpretation of O, whatever that might mean for him. A typical line of argumentation runs as follows:

Bion quotes from the 13th century Flemish mystic [..."] God in the godhead is spiritual substance, so elemental that we may say nothing about it" [...] could this sentence not be taken as a reference to the spiritual substance of language, and its being fundamental and in the sense of foundational, for humanity as opposed to animality? And isn't language something that by definition transcends the individual? Couldn't the doctrine of incarnation [...] express the emergence of a single human mind from a collective preconception, ultimately manifesting its cultural or linguistic nature? Could the event of this phenomenon – the subject having the opportunity to grasp or represent in itself the happy reunion of this pre-individual background of meaning be called: Deity, God, Language, Unconscious, thing in itself, or person in itself, infinite being etc.? In my view all these questions are rhetorical. This can be deduced from Bion's writings and from the implicit interpretations that are discovered in the play of the cross-references of his various definitions of O. If we want to support *outside* Bion, we could think of a number of places. (p. 394; italics in origin)

Surprisingly, what could be called Civitarese's free associations to O – for they are not grounded in any solid reference to Bion's text, except for the very contradictory quote of the mystic referring, ironically, to what we can say nothing about – is so evidently connected to "language" that any question about it is considered rhetorical. As the paper progresses, Civitarese once again asserts that seeing O as "language" is the obvious conclusion and that the word Godhead is a metaphor for what transcends the individual, because it is shared by all humanity, precedes every human being and is the basis of every individuality. While I agree with Civitarese's view regarding the fundamental role of language – indeed, I believe few will disagree with it – how does this have anything to do with Bion's "play" with the "many meanings of O," of which Civitarese conveniently offers no examples? Maybe because most of these instances of "play" stress the darkness, the "formless infinite" and insist on O being unknown and unknowable, undefined. Indeed, Civitarese hurries to leave Bion's own text with this flimsy allusion and sails off to "support *outside* Bion," again displaying his impressive knowledge of western philosophy, but with little substantial connection to Bion's actual words.

Civitarese's commentators exhibit trends that are just as interesting. While it is not possible to encompass here all the richness of their discussions, it is worthwhile to note that both commentators commend Civitarese for finding a nonmystical and "pragmatic" definition of O. They do so without wondering what this mystical option might be and whether Civitarese has indeed successfully proven that Bion could not possibly have aimed for a mystical understanding, in spite of his insistent and recurrent use of the word. While Goldberg (2019) notices some of Civitarese's contradictions, he treats the task of disproving the mystical understanding as successfully accomplished and very important. It seems that, for all three, pushing psychoanalysis in general and the revered figure of Bion in particular away from any mystical connotations is a noble crusade. Goldberg notices how Civitarese is vacillating between language and the non-verbal facet of psychoanalysis and fixes on the latter as the meaning of O – particularly the bodily-sensual, or what he calls co-sensuality – an equally mysterious notion of mutual induction and sharing at the most basic bodily-sensory layer. Steinberg (2019), on her part, clarifies and crystalizes Civitarese's ideas while expanding his notion of language to include the semiotic layer (an interpretation he fully agreed with in his reply paper), thus softening the contradictions. For Goldberg, O is the (co)sensual. For Civitarese and Steinberg, it is symbolic (and semyotic) meaning, derived from language in its broadest sense, which transcends the individual and can be accessed by any member of the *socium*.

Nevertheless, Bion expressly said that O cannot be known and is nonsensual. In fact, he maintained that psychoanalysis' subject matter cannot be accessed through the senses and that this is what sets it apart and renders it similar to the mystical experience. Bernat (2018) offers an interpretation of late Bion that, in my opinion, is much more respectful of Bion's textual choices and methodology. He states that Bion went beyond language, understanding that we cannot express emotions without transforming them. To expand upon this claim, it is clear that, since we think through language (as Civitarese would doubtlessly agree), we can never "know" emotional truth but only "be" it. Bernat points out that one of Bion's sources of inspiration is negative theology – a tradition of negating any concepts associating God, as a way of emphasizing the ineffableness of religious and mystical experience. According to Bernat, Bion sought a deeper stance of doubt than the one offered by the positivistic scientific tradition. The methodology of negative theology requires a negation of *conscious awareness itself*, as a method of reaching the truth. That truth is ineffable and forever bears "the mark of the mysterious" (p. 20), requiring that the analyst maintain both this deep state of doubt in his conscious thought and perceptions, as well as his faith in the absolute truth and the ability of the unconscious to reach at-one-ment with it.

Bion himself clearly went to great lengths to avoid the saturation of O with any premature meaning, be it physical or metaphysical. Nevertheless, the discussion of his concept of O by Civitarese and his commentators almost seems to be desperately grasping at *any* conceptual saturation (extending the term "language" to include even music [Civitarese, 2019c] and anything else that could carry subjective meaning), from either the cultural or physical spheres, in an attempt to supplement the word "mystical," a word Bion probably evoked, among other things, in order to avoid the danger of early saturation and to stress the mysteriousness of the psychoanalytic project. However, all three authors and especially Civitarese are very conclusive in "knowing" what O is, thus ostensibly acting-out the very anxiety Bion implored us to tolerate.

Bion's O and the epistemology of faith

What then, is the Bionian O? Can it be explained in any other terms and still remain faithful to Bion's definition as "truth in itself," "Godhead," "darkness," and "formless infinite?" Although O was *meant* to stay obscure and elude any limiting definition and despite the fact that Bion's references to it are even somewhat contradictory, I believe it is still possible to pinpoint the main ideas Bion wanted to convey through this mysterious term. The key lies in his statement that the problem of psychoanalysis is the problem of growth: "the psychoanalytic problem is the problem of growth and its harmonious resolution in the relationship between the container and the contained, repeated in individual, pair, and finally group (intra and extra psychically)" (1970, p. 16). Bion speaks here of growth and the problem of "harmoniously" allowing it in the relationship between container and contained on all levels – from the individual to the group – both as internalizations and in concrete pairs and groups. This implies that the task of psychoanalysis – promoting growth – may threaten the basic relationship of containing, which entails the process of thought, the internalized mother–baby dyad, the group as a container, and the psychoanalytic relationship itself. Thus, it is the responsibility of psychoanalysis to facilitate growth at a tolerable pace, so that the container grows instead of, presumably, breaking down and attacking itself and others.

Bion also states that psychoanalysis' subject matter is O, which is the ultimate truth. That which should be contained is the truth and, if this is done successfully, such containment promotes growth. The importance of *the truth* in the Bionian corpus is well established. He was preoccupied with truth and lies, considering the former to be the mind's nourishment and the latter its poison. The nature of this truth is intangible and ineffable; it cannot be known, but one must strive to be one with it.

Further, we have Bion's notion of transformation and invariance: the idea that psychoanalysis should promote transformations – changes – in O, rather than in K (knowledge), while other things stay the same. Bion stresses the dynamic nature of O, noting that it changes with every transformation; for example, when some part of it is transformed into K by a good interpretation. That interpretation immediately becomes irrelevant, for O had already undergone transformation. Finally, we know that it is through faith alone – as opposed to memory and desire – that we can aspire to make contact with O.

After summarizing these main ideas, I think it becomes evident that O is not any particular object, but a process of growth. Its "end point" is merely theoretical, as the search for growth-promoting mental truth never ends. I think this entails striving for one's true "form" and, even though it can never be reached, the search for it must never be abandoned. "Faith in O" is the faith "that there is an ultimate truth." Seeing as Bion was preoccupied with psychoanalytic truth, the truth of the session or of the patient, I think this should be seen as *one's* ultimate truth, one's form, the goal toward which their path of growth leads – the achievement of their final, completed personality, as an obviously impossible aim. Still, it is an aim that everyone is ethically bound to seek – as a quest for their inner truth, purpose, or form of being, for their invariant, that allows for their many transformations in the world – and is also arrived at through those transformations. It seems that, for Bion, transformations both express O and partake in its evolution; every transformation (a representation, a picture, an interpretation) both expresses and immediately changes O, having done some "work" on it.

This claim, which views O as a growth process aiming toward the "ultimate truth" of the personality – may be supported by Bion's reference to Plato, linking O to Platonic forms (ibid, p. 89). According to Plato, while the forms themselves are perfect, complete and eternal, there are many replicas in the phenomenological world that are accessible to humans. In Platonic philosophy, one must strive to resemble the human "form" and this endeavor is the most sublime purpose of human existence. Of course, for Plato, there is but one, preexisting truth for all humans. All other variations of it, any instance of individuality, are a kind of unwanted deviance, an error imposed by this imperfect world. For Bion, in contrast, truth is dynamic and seems to undergo a continuous form of evolution – "transformations in O." Still, there seems to be a super-human quality to it, which makes it difficult to say to what degree Bion agreed with Plato's disdain for individuality.

This uncertainty springs from Bion's peculiar discussion of the messianic idea, truth, and lies. Bion had introduced a most provocative notion of thoughts that precede their thinker and are searching for one to serve as their container. The roots of this idea lie in a more acceptable notion of Bion's containment theory – namely, that sensual and emotional experiences developmentally precede the "alpha-function" that can properly "think" them. Still, it seems that, in *Attention and Interpretation*, such "thoughts without a thinker" have indeed broken loose of any recognizable psychoanalytic form and are running wild. Bion speaks of the messianic idea as a deeply meaningful truth that is independent of the person expressing it. It is merely "reincarnated" in a certain person, much as Jesus was the incarnation of divinity. Bion uses this powerful religious example to assert his notion about the relationship between the messiah and the establishment. Whether this relationship is constructive or destructive, as mentioned above, the task of the person expressing the truth or of the establishment challenged by it is one of *containing*, not of partaking in its creation.

Bion maintains that truth does not require a thinker; only lies do. Thus, a strong hallmark of individuality is also a strong hallmark of a lie. Between lies and truth, Bion poses the notion of falsity as a kind of compromise-formation between the truth and its imperfect human container, which inevitably introduces some distortion of the complete truth. Falsity, however, is essential for the person/establishment to achieve some contact with the truth and make use of it. A good interpretation is a falsity – hopefully not too far from O to be useful. Lies, in contrast, are completely personal and are devastating to psychic or social health. They poison every connection (for example, the therapeutic one). Obviously, distinguishing lies from falsities becomes an imperative, though very complex task. Since truth is dynamic and changing, the distinction depends on the context. While Bion discusses this distinction extensively, I wish to address two criteria that he posits for distinguishing truth from lies:

> The Ps↔D reaction reveals a whole situation which seems to belong to a reality that pre-exists the individual who has discovered it. The lying discovery lacks the spontaneous bleakness of the genuine Ps↔D. The lie requires a thinker to think. The truth, or true thought, does not require a thinker – he is not logically necessary. (ibid, p. 102)

One criterion, therefore, that helps spot a lie is an idea which is too happy. For Bion, there is always something bleak about the truth. This may be understandable if we think of the kind of truth that *must* search for a thinker, a truth whose containment is a challenge. This calls to mind the Hebrew prophets, who were forced to deliver God's horrible massages of destruction. Indeed, Bion thought that the truth, at least the kind that matters analytically, may bring about a "catastrophic change." It is therefore avoided and such avoidance of the truth is a psychotic act. In contrast, if it is accepted, the result – in the wake of catastrophe – might be the gloomy realization of the depressive position.

The other, more challenging criterion is the need for a thinker. For Bion, a lie can be recognized according to how much of one's personal tendencies – even one's creative ability – was required. This goes against every modern sentiment of appreciation of human creativity and is close to the striving of the classical world for the divine origin of every creative act. It even brings to mind Plato's disparaging treatment of artists as liars. Bion mentions Plato's thoughts on this matter, but his own opinion remains somewhat obscure. He does state that myths and art are a kind of necessary falsehood, rather than a lie. Still, this makes it clear that Civitarese was quite wrong in determining that O was "the esthetic"; Bion certainly meant what he said about the artistic or esthetic vertex being unsuitable for psychoanalysis. Moreover, in discussing the role of the analyst, he is much less ambiguous then when speaking of the poet, arguing explicitly that the analyst's individuality only gets in the way:

> Since the analyst's concern is with the evolved elements of O and their formulation, formulations can be judged by considering how necessary his existence is to the thoughts he expresses. The more his interpretations can be judged as showing how necessary *his* knowledge, *his* experience, *his* character are to the thoughts as formulated, the more reason there is to suppose that the interpretation is psycho-analytically worthless, that is, alien to the domain O. (ibid, p. 105; italics in origin)

Here Bion is in complete agreement with Platonic metaphysics: the truth exists in some pure, ideal form, independently of humanity. At most, humans may have a share in the truth by expressing it, as faithfully as they can. In passing through the human medium, an unavoidable distortion occurs, but not to the truth itself, only to its formulation. Bion Writes:

> The absence of memory and desire should free the analyst of those peculiarities that make him a creature of his circumstances and leave him with those functions which are invariant, the functions that make up the irreducible ultimate man. In fact this cannot be. Yet upon his ability to approximate to this will depend

> his ability to achieve the 'blindness' that is prerequisite for 'seeing' the evolved element of O. (ibid, p. 58)

Bion is thus coupling the classical psychoanalytic ideal of neutrality with even more "classical" philosophical and religious thought: the notion that people strive to imitate the eternal Platonic "form" or ideal man or God (Jesus, Buddha), but always fall short of it. Through this connection, Bion returns to the image of man as a receiver rather than a creator of truths. In contrast with James' "pragmatic humanism," in which man and reality mutually affect and even create each other, the Bionian therapist in *Attention and Interpretation* must train herself to be a passive container. The model for such passivity is the mystic becoming one with the truth, merging with God.

But is the mystic's and the analyst's truth the same kind of truth? After all, Bion was an analyst and I believe he searched for a pure, mystical transcendental model of knowledge in psychoanalysis, not a psychoanalytic pathway to religious life. He deliberately invokes blunt religious associations, but nevertheless tries to fathom psychoanalytic content. He constantly cites emotional experience as examples:

> The platonic theory of forms and the Christian dogma of the Incarnation imply absolute essence which I wish to postulate as a universal quality of phenomena such as 'panic', 'anxiety', 'fear', 'love'. In brief, I use O to represent this central feature of every situation that the psycho- analyst has to meet. With this he must be at one; with the *evolution* of this he must identify so that he can formulate it in an interpretation. Certain states of mind obstruct this. (p. 89; italics in origin)

It seems that, contrary to religious institutions, which tried to mobilize the world of human emotion in support of religion, Bion is trying to evoke reverence for the numinous, the infinite, the unknown, in order to appreciate the full moment of *human emotions* – in their ineffability as the *mysterium tremendum* of the human sphere. Perhaps it is the Platonic form of the *human being* that remains unreachable for every concrete person, who nonetheless must abide by its terrible power and its demand of him – the demand to contain it, to be one and transform with O, no matter the cost.

This seems like a paradox. Panic, love, etc., are human emotions, at once poignant and, while they are not physically tangible, they are certainly felt to belong to a concrete empirical "I" (in this context, the patient). But Bion seems to refer to Truth with a capital letter, to a truth that transcends the individual and that will forever remain unfathomable. Bion demands that we empty ourselves of what makes us concrete human beings in order to be in touch with it. But what is "it?" – the *Truth* of emotions like panic and love. We seem to be running in circles. I think there is an inherent contradiction between the Platonic view of truth as an eternal form and Bion's allusions to O as dynamic, dependent on context and, above all, evolving. I believe Bion himself never reconciled these aspects of his thought.

I wish to return here to my suggestion that O should be understood as a process of growth, aimed at an ultimate, unattainable *personal* form. While the word "personal" contradicts Bion's assertion that the individual's impact can only distort contact with O, this understanding is supported by his references to growth. Furthermore, it is grounded in the emotional, even Passionate experience that Bion demands of the analytic couple in oscillating between Ps. (the paranoid-schizoid position) and D. (the depressive, more integrated position) when some temporal "form" (or formulation) has been reached. Moreover, it is consistent with the fact that Bion is still writing for analysts and describing – indeed, in quite radical terms – the analyst's task as being in touch with the *patient's* truth and facilitating transformations in it ("transformations in O") and, thus, personal growth. There is certainly an inherent tension in Bion's text between the awe-inspiring, transcendental Truth and the all-too-human emotional truth encountered through the struggle for personal growth. Perhaps, among other things, these two kinds of truth are united by the mysteriousness of the analytic process, that transcends what can be sensually known. More importantly, there seems to be a more intimate connection between the seemingly different kinds of truth that requires further elucidation.

Between the religious and the psychoanalytic – The epistemology of faith

I believe that the religious language Bion insists on using indicates his belief that very human and personal truths, such as anxiety, belong at the same time to a transcendental super-human order. He saw this personal evolution, the quest to achieve one's "form," as a kind of moral, even religious duty, perhaps as part of more general human evolution. I think that what he was repudiating was not individuality *per se*, but its enslavement to the ego's wants and needs. The possibility of separating ego from individuality is another matter and here I think Bion has made a great philosophical and practical mistake; after all, there can be no thoughts without a thinker, no invariant of the patient without a patient. Otherwise, it is not a psychoanalytic truth that we are after, but a religious or Platonic one, and Bion would be adding nothing new beyond Plato's old doctrine. However, as mentioned, I suggest viewing O as a process of human evolution, in which every individual *as an individual*, with their own peculiar truth – a truth that is not given or known in advance – is required to partake, even in spite of themselves. This view is supported by Bion's constant reference to the individual psyche and the group as metaphors for each other – and to both as facing the challenge of serving as a suitable container for the truth or the messianic idea. Eigen often writes about Bion's challenge to the individual and to humanity: how much truth can we bear? I completely agree with this interpretation of Bion and would add, in line with Eigen (1981/1999), the importance of faith in this respect. As O, *the truth* is not only unknown, but unknowable; because the path to it is duty-bound and tormenting – even destructive – it takes *faith* to traverse this *via dolorosa*. Bion says that faith should be put in O – in the fact that *there is* an unknown and unknowable truth. In accordance with my interpretation, this faith is faith or trust in the process of growth; in other words, since the problem of psychoanalysis is the problem of growth, it is *faith in the analytic process*, which according to this understanding has both an individual and a collective meaning.

For the therapist, faith means that she must trust her intuition, if it is free from memory and desire, meaning, if it is indeed attuned to the needs of the patient's growth process. *Faith* in the Bionian context is a form of the *epistemology of faith* – the term I suggested for the analyst's trust in the knowledge created in the analytic experience. For Bion, Faith is both an ethical and an epistemological position – a total commitment to the truth of the Other's emotional experience and growth. If my view is correct, this faith is also placed in the analytic *relationship* – as perhaps the only thing that can help one cross the "valley of the shadow of death," to undergo the catastrophic change that stems from scorching contact with the truth. To use another biblical metaphor, faith in the analytic relationship is required in order to face the ultimate truth – of the individual, and of his part in the evolution of humanity – which, like the face of God – no one may look upon and live. Perhaps the analytic relationship, when based on faith and trust, can facilitate transformations that are more tolerable to the human mind and, at the same time, conductive to its evolution. If you will, this is the therapeutic version of the biblical burning bush that appeared before Moses and ultimately delivered the Hebrews from bondage.

A Jamesian reading of Bion

If we apply James' criteria of "the sentiment of rationality" to Bion's O, we might discover that it does not conform to any of them. This may explain its reluctant reception by the psychoanalytic community. At face value, the Bionian theory of truth sees human beings as passive receivers – as vessels for a divine massage, who take no part in shaping truth, save for the risk of distorting it. Such a view denies what is, for James, the most basic human need – the need to be an active agent, whose activities matter and resonate in a friendly universe.

Moreover, Bion seems to reject any practical, measurable, sensual, or conceptual implication of truth as the "thing in itself," thus seemingly depriving it of any pragmatic value. Another Jamesian criterion is the theory's ability to efficiently connect us to the everyday details of that aspect of experience we are discussing – to the empirical richness of experience. Throughout the Bionian description of O, the reader finds that their expectation for a connection between the proposed definitions of O and the actual richness of the clinical experience is constantly thwarted. This is perhaps the greatest weakness of this definition, although, as we shall see later, in this weakness also lies its strength. Bion resists any reduction of O to other terms and uses lofty phrases – like "Godhead" and "formless infinite" – to define it. He also resists offering clinical examples for the same reason – the concern that O will be restricted, reduced or, in Bion's words, saturated too early. This lack of detail and operational implications naturally renders Bion's O of little use when predicting anything in the analytic situation, thus failing in yet another important criterion of rationality. In fact, predictability is foreign to the nature of O, as something which can never be known, certainly not in advance; and to the well-known Bionian recommendation of practicing "without memory and desire."

But despite its failure in measuring up to pragmatic criteria and despite its partial, though passionate, rejection by some of Bion's contemporaries, O is an extremely productive idea, which has yielded a most impressive body of psychoanalytic thought. Was James mistaken, then, in his suggested criteria for a theory's acceptance? James was well aware that the acceptance of a theory is a complex matter, depending as much on the personal proclivities of the receivers as it is on any definable criteria. In applying James' psychological analysis of "philosophical tempers," it seems that Bion's theory speaks to those who prefer the thrill provided by abstractions over what James termed the "sister passion" of distinguishing and learning the details of actual experience. James (1896) believed that the passion for abstractions was more prevalent and this is how he explains the attraction to such an overwhelming abstraction as Hegel's "world spirit." James himself was not immune to its charm. In his *Pluralistic Universe*, he attempts to offer a more pragmatic version of the idea of the absolute, his own "world soul" and reconcile this idea of unity with the equally fundamental plurality of its parts. Apparently, the notion of some great, all embracing essence, an absolute truth of all things that forever escapes the feeble powers of our language, has held a lasting allure for the human mind throughout history.

Similarly, Bion (1974) believes that religiosity, in its broader sense, is a basic human impulse. He wonders why psychoanalysis has been ignoring so basic a force in human history and activity, one that, to his mind, is no less prevalent than sexuality. Moreover, he wonders whether any personality can be considered fully human if it is lacking such a basic facet of human mentality. Speaking of a "religious impulse" might perhaps explain the allure of the absolute or "ulti-mate truth" in different terms than those of Freud's discussion, which frames religion as having the surprising power to still survive in de-fiance of all logic. If all people can be described as "homo religiosus" (Eliade, 1957), then perhaps those for whom the dogmas of existing religions do not resonate with their "sentiment of rationality" will seek to fulfill this basic need in other ways, potentially turning to philosophical terms, such as the world spirit, or psychoanalytic ones such as Bion's O. The many therapists and analytic thinkers who were enchanted by Bion's ideas, perhaps even especially taken by his late mystical turn, may have recognized something in his words, obscure as they were, that struck their innermost chords; something apparently "felt right."

Importantly, the works of the late Bion, such as *Attention and Interpretation* and "Notes on Memory and Desire" appeal to the reader's own *experience*. At the beginning of *Attention and Interpretation*, Bion states that his claims can only make sense to a practicing analyst. He refers his readers to their analytic experience in order to understand his meaning and make use of it, though he hardly ever offers his own. It seems as though he is wishing for each reader to have their own unsaturated O, that will serve as a function of their own growth process as analysts. Thus, O is perhaps some-what like a Rorschach stain: it has no preexisting meaning, yet it does not yield to any interpretation either. Its not an "anything goes" matter. The analyst is required to believe in the patient's ul-timate "form" and not force or project anything onto it that defies the contours (blurry as they may be) of the evolving design. Indeed, O's obscurity has yielded the need for further interpretation by many different writers, who believed in O's "form" in spite of its vagueness. Its very obscurity gave birth to so many enriching texts that it is impossible to deny O's messianic role in the evolution of psychoanalysis.

But why would anyone be so fascinated with such an apparently impractical term to begin with? Bion's reference to every analyst's experience brings to mind Otto's appeal, in the beginning of his book, that it should not be read by those who have had no experience of the sacred. It seems that analysts, at least some of them, *do* have an experience of something powerful and perhaps sacred in their work, something that does not conform to other, more conventional analytic concepts. Returning to James, I think some analysts make a "will to believe" choice in accepting such a claim about the ineffable facet of their work, which does not offer even the possibility of proof. As both James and Bion suggest, the proof lies, paradoxically, in the experience of the limitless and the ineffable, of what cannot be proven. It seems that Bion finally gave voice to a sentiment shared by many therapists: that there is something, something essential, in their work that could not be defined in words or reduced to anything other than itself without a crucial loss of meaning.

Psychoanalysis was already equipped with rationalistic concepts that were based on a mechanistic worldview. Later on, it also acquired concepts depicting the deep, meaningful relationships that shaped the human personality from early life. But something was still missing. The religious aspect of the human personality, assuming that Bion was indeed right in postulating it, and the "religious" aspect of the psychoanalytic relationship, had been silenced. Bion's thinking brought to light Freud's "shadow theory" of the wise unconscious. In fact, it may be seen as a negative of Freud's theoretical choices, in bringing the dream-thought to the foreground and marginalizing the importance of what can be understood, verbalized and brought under the ego's control.

Before Bion, no one expressed the sense of psychoanalytic mystery so poignantly. Ferenczi's mystical notions had been mostly forgotten; Jung's had become some of the distinguishing features of a separate school. Moreover, their language was more saturated to begin with. They developed metaphysical theories and hypotheses regarding matters about which Bion chose to remain silent. In contrast, Bion insisted on bringing to light the essential darkness, the opaque. He brought a sense of the *mysterium tremendum* – the numinous – into psychoanalysis. Some parts of his writings, like those discussed next, have yielded more easily to subsequent attempts to offer more practical interpretations or to elicit elements that are "user friendly" and suitable to contemporary interpersonal and relational trends. Nevertheless, if we look at the main body of his late writings, and especially *Attention and Interpretation*, we must acknowledge that it is the most extreme expression of the mystical element in psychoanalysis: it presents an unyielding sense of mystery, presents mystery as a moral decree, posits the ethical value of accepting the mysterious, and claims that the essence of the human personality, the essence of the psychoanalytic encounter, perhaps even of all reality, is the unknown and unknowable.

The absolute O and the possibility of meeting

Bion was familiar with Buber's works and probably appreciated and was influenced by it. In one of the best-known papers from his late period, *Caesura*, he draws on the following quote from Freud: "there is much more continuity between intra-uterine life and earliest infancy than the impressive caesura of the act of birth allows us to believe" (Bion, 1977, p. 37). In this same paper, he also repeatedly quotes Buber. Immediately following the above quote from Freud, which opens the paper, Bion offers the following quote from Buber:

> The prenatal life of the child is a pure association, a flowing towards each other, a bodily reciprocity; And the life horizon of the developing being appears inscribed and yet also not inscribed, in that of the being that carries it; for the womb in which it dwells is not solely that of the human mother. (ibid, ibid)

The mother and child are interdependent, but they are not the same. Their inseparableness survives the impressive Caesura of birth, yet they were never wholly merged to begin with. The womb surrounding the child is more than his mother's physical womb; he also belongs to and develops in another, super-human order. Bion offer several other quotes from Buber, in which the latter speaks of the developing human being as resting in "the womb of the great mother, undifferentiated" (ibid, p. 38) and presents the Jewish myth about the universal knowledge the baby acquires in his mother's womb (p. 39). It seems that in the spirit of O, a concept which is not mentioned in this paper, Bion wishes to emphasize the caesura between human beings and absolute truth – we are capable of being one with it and at the same time are irreparably distant from it. Bion also makes the same point about closeness to and separateness from other human beings; Caesura is presented as an omnipresent fact of life.

This frequent reliance on Buber is not surprising, since this paper discusses "Buberian" concerns. It addresses the connectedness/separateness relation between different life periods (intra-uterine existence, infancy and adulthood), between different mental realms (such as conscious and unconscious, a mental state and its different transformations), and between human beings (the containing relationship of mother and baby). Most of all, it is this connection between human beings that is intimately related to Buber's philosophy of encounter. Bion himself may be described as a theoretician who has been preoccupied – throughout his entire career – with the possibility of encounters and what might hinder them: the encounter between the baby's mouth and the mother's breast, the penis and the vagina, or, in psychological terms, between container and contained, thinker and thought, analyst, and analysand and, finally, the mystic and the group. What all these encounters have in common is the idea of containment, which was one of Bion's most valuable contributions to psychoanalysis.

In a caesural encounter, however, the notion of containment no longer prevails. In a containing relationship, separateness is minimal and sometimes experienced as nonexistent: from the baby's point of view, it and the mother are one; from the Catholic church's point of view (that had endured for centuries), it was the one true "container" or interpreter of the word of God. This is not the case with the caesura: a caesura is not oneness or merger, nor is it separateness; it derives meaning from the very tension, from being the middle realm.

"Caesura" is a unique text, which signifies a novel, not fully developed turn in Bion's thinking, even though Aharoni and Bergstein (2012) argue that it highlights a long-existing depth structure in Bion's thought, maintaining, if you will, that the caesura between this paper and the rest of Bion's texts is not so pronounced. In any case, Bion turns his inquiry away from the containing relationship and argues that everything of interest to the analyst may be found in the caesura model. For example, he stresses the connection between the rational and the more experiential-emotional facets of the mind. He strongly criticizes the "overly sane" position of some people who negate the caesura and flee to the realm of rational thought because they are terrified of madness. In this critique, the idea of O (though not the concept itself) reemerges:

Rational interpretations might be adequate if they were the only important ones, but what may appeal to the human mind because it seems to be logical, or fit in with such powers of logic as we have, may be by no means the correct interpretation of the factual situation which is beyond our comprehension or experience. To distort the experience in order to make it fit into such capacities as we have is a dangerous thing. (Bion, 1977, p. 52; italics in origin)

This quote is somewhat reminiscent of religious thinking, which views the human mind as inadequate for grasping divine reality and our feeble mental tools (such as logic) as ill-equipped for fathoming the numinous. Religious or not, it is still a valuable and typically Bionian warning against the dangers of pseudo-knowledge. Any limitation of an experience because it does not wholly "fit" in with our conceptual or rational tools is a distortion of reality. For Bion, in order to refrain from distorting reality, we must live with this partial connection. The relation between the rational and experiential, between primary and secondary thinking, and between O and what we can fathom, should be caesural, not split off. Concepts cannot contain experience in its entirety, but they might have a valuable relation with it. Concepts and experiences have their own separate, yet interdependent realms in mental life.

The same applies to the connection between human beings. Between mother and baby, therapist, and patient, there is a caesural realm in which they may have a real, in-depth, meaningful, yet painfully partial connection. Bion's paper ends with an uncharacteristically dramatic appeal:

Rephrasing Freud's statement for my own convenience: There is much more continuity between autonomically appropriate quanta and the waves of conscious thought and feeling than the impressive caesura of transference and counter-transference would have us believe. So...? Investigate the caesura; not the analyst; not the analysand; not the unconscious; not the conscious; not sanity; not insanity. But the caesura, the link, the synapse, the (counter-trans)-ference, the transitive-intransitive mood. (ibid, p. 56)

In this passage, Bion mentions three caesuras:

a. The caesura between the physical and the mental world. The physical world is merged with what was supposed to be the word "unconscious," since the quote associates the "autonomically appropriate quanta" with the "waves of conscious thought."
b. The conscious-unconscious caesura.
c. The patient-analyst caesura.

Without any explanation or even acknowledgment of this shift, the first two caesuras merge in the beginning of one sentence, while the third joins in last. Bion is playing here with the relation between the physical, subatomic (quantic) scale that becomes the intra-psychic (conscious-unconscious), and the inter-psychic (transference and counter-transference), as different perspectives, the differences between which are blurred, until they become one.

This enigmatic phrasing is perhaps designed to convey the idea of a threefold comparison between the physical world, in its most basic yet mysterious sub-atomic/quantic level, and the workings of the unconscious and, consequently, of the unconscious contact between people. The quantic world is indeed a somewhat "crazy" reality, at least from the perspective of classical physics: uncertainty is a prin-ciple, a basic (ontological) fact; the existence of a spectator alters the outcome; and two particles departing from the same place continue to affect each other even when they are light years apart. This is not a bad metaphor for both unconscious primary thinking and for un-conscious connection. But perhaps this is more than a metaphor. Through the peculiar structure of his sentence, Bion wishes to de-monstrate how these different scales of reality depend on each other and are intimately connected, without any of them being wholly defined by or reduced to the other. He describes a caesural relation between faculties of the mind, between minds, and between the unconscious mind and the physical world.

Perhaps this explains Bion's choice in quoting those passages by Buber, which posit a connection between the womb of the human mother and that of a "great mother," who brings the unborn baby in touch with universal knowledge. Perhaps Bion is alluding to quantum physics in order to further elucidate how Buber's "eternal Thou" or, in this case, "great mother" connects all beings, a connection which makes possible every individual I-Thou moment. Perhaps this is Bion's way of arguing (much like Ferenczi, in a way) that a universal connection underlies every Noetic moment between two people. Naturally, this is mere speculation, for Bion does not discuss the quotes with which he chose to open his paper. There is no doubt, however, about his intention to argue that there is an ontological connection between different realms of reality, in particular those of patient and analyst (which, in the above quoted passage, are reduced – or perhaps transcended – to the mental experiences of transference and countertransference).

In this "quantic" transference-countertransference connection, the analyst is no longer a passive container, whose activity is restricted to an ascetic act of discipline that robs him of his uniqueness in favor of merger with the great reality of O. In the caesural model, countertransference is essential as one of the two connected particles that define the system. This anticipates the relational view of the analytic dyad. It also supports many contemporary interpreters of Bion (such as Ogden and Eigen), who equated Bionian reverie, the openness to O, with an attentiveness to the analyst's own experience, to her countertransference in its widest sense. Bion writes:

> As things are at present, giving an interpretation means that the analyst has to be capable of verbalizing statements of his senses, his intuitions and his primitive reactions to what the patient says. This statement has to be affective as a physical act is affective. (ibid, p. 44)

Here, Bion speaks of something in the patient that affects the therapist deeply, evoking physical or primitive reactions. From this deep level of sharing, the interpretation the therapist can give is so precise, so powerful, that it is as affective as a physical act. Still, there is not enough evidence in the text to suggest that Bion was referring to the mutual influence of a full Buberian encounter. It seems more likely that he was preoccupied with the roots of the I-Thou possibility. He explored this, among other things, through Buber's ideas about the broad, cosmic meaning of pregnancy – where the embryo develops alongside a placenta, within a caesura between him and mother and between him and the rest of creation. The placenta is lost after birth, but the possibility of physical and psychic sharing, according to Buber's and Bion's view, is somehow still there.

In the paper's conclusion, Bion declares that he cannot go further than an emotional appeal to investigate the caesura, because he lacks "the very evidence which have not yet been discovered or elaborated" (ibid, p. 56). I understand this statement to mean that he is on the verge of something new, the view of which is still mostly obscured. From this position, standing on a metaphorical mount Nebo, catching a glimpse of what lies ahead but not being able to enter the promised land himself, Bion is pointing out the embryonic state of his understanding of the caesura.

Bion's descriptions have not amounted yet to a Buberian encounter where two full, separate personalities meet and jointly create a new truth. But, according to Buber, the potential for I-Thou moments grows from the primitive connectedness between mother and child or between pretechnological humanity and its natural environment. Furthermore, the Buberian idea of "in between" shares significant characteristics with the Bionian caesura. The "in between" is where an encounter with the true essence of another takes place. It is a most intimate touch, by which the individuality of each party is both re-tained and enriched. This is the "synapse" where patient and analyst meet. Still, in Bion's paper, the fate of the analyst's individuality in the analytic session remains unclear. Does she remain truly separate? Does she grow alongside the patient? Do the primitive reactions she must notice originate in the patient alone?

In contrast, in *Attention and Interpretation*, the answer to these questions seems clearer and contact with the (analytic) truth is por-trayed differently. The analyst and analysand are in a container-contained relation, where the analyst must rise to become united with some absolute-Platonic idea of truth. There, Bionian truth is *The Truth* – something grand and awe-inspiring, which in certain passages seems to precede its human carrier. If one is willing to adhere to a "no memory and no desire" discipline, one may hope to experience oneness with it – though always partially and without ever *knowing* it rationally. While this is not explicitly stated in *Attention and Interpretation*, it is clear that the analyst also grows – for she becomes one with O and expands her alpha-function through her fearless striving for the truth. But it seems that this truth – transient, valid only in the moment – was, at the same time, there to be found, thus not necessarily created in the encounter and certainly not mutually created. Being in contact with O may be tantamount to having a classical mystical-Noetic experience (which suits James' criterion of passivity), but it does not amount to having a Buberian encounter with the Patient.

"Caesura" was written after *Attention and Interpretation*. The latter is the most cohesive statement of the late Bion, as well as his last theoretical book. The former, meanwhile, is the beginning of an idea – demonstrating a clear "caesura" with his other writings. But although, as mentioned above, meeting and linking were always Bion's primary interest, "Caesura" does not offers a "fully baked" notion about how this separateness works alongside connectedness and how exactly do caesural relations differ from his well-developed containment thesis. Still, though it is an unwarranted conclusion to say that a Bionian notion of psychotherapy is akin to the Buberian encounter, Bion's followers *did* interpret him that way, stressing mutual creativity and mutual, though asymmetrical, contribution and growth. With all the abovementioned caveats, it seems that "Caesura" is one of their greatest sources of support. In it, Bion claims that the potential for growth lies in a connection which is also a gap. His language, his reference to countertransference and especially his dramatic closing appeal, point toward mutuality more than his texts about containment. More than anything, it seems like an intimation of an approaching future in psychoanalysis, an unfolding roadmap for future generations; a somewhat nebulous prophetic statement, that was later creatively developed as Bion's legacy.

Conclusion

Bion brought to light a central psychoanalytic facet, a great truth which many of his colleagues felt, but could not articulate. This truth was absent from mainstream psychoanalytic texts after the Freud-Ferenczi rift. Only certain traces were left of Freud's "wise" unconscious, not enough to leave a sufficiently strong conscious impression.

Still, Bion did not provide his followers with enough landmarks to guide them through the path he saw. He only left us with an idea. He was a prophet or, in his own words, a mystic, a messiah. He pointed in the direction of truths that deeply shocked the analytic community. It was never the same again. But the messianic idea must be utilized and fashioned anew so it does not destroy the container, the psychoanalytic community. Moreover, for Bion's ideas to be understood as a legitimate theory of psychoanalytic practice – as ideas that are capable of transformation into usable "formulations" – his followers had to translate, even "domesticate" his notion of O and soften the unrelenting austerity of his "no memory and no desire" understanding of the analytic position.

Bion was a mystic, certainly not a pragmatist. He left the task of tackling the many practical clinical and theoretical questions raised by his theory to others. It seems that he himself was aware of the difficulty inherent in such a theory as his – one that refuses to deal with the friction of its encounter with real, down-to-earth analytic work:

> I may be able to make [something] clearer while at the same time being misleading. Alternatively, I can resort to something which is so sophisticated that has very little, or no feeling... I can either be comprehensible and misleading or truthful and incomprehensible. (quoted in Reiner, 2012, p. 75)

Bion chose to be truthful and obscure. His theory, though creating a great deal of powerful "feeling" did not help his readers understand this sentiment (transformations in K). Perhaps, like the theory's subject matter – O – Bion did not feel that what he spoke about could be known or reduced to manageable concepts. One (actually, many in the psychoanalytic community) just felt that it was the *Truth*. It became the task of the next generations to be clearer, though perhaps at the cost of some unavoidable distortions of the (Bionian) truth.

References

Aharoni, H. and Bergstein, A. (2012). On 'the' Caesura and more Caesuras. In H. Aharoni and A. Bergstein (Eds.), *Caesura* (pp. 7–24). Tel Aviv: Tolaat Sfraim. (Hebrew).

Bernat, I. (2018). Negation as a method for psychoanalytic discoveries: Bion's turning point in "Notes on Memory and Desire" and beyond. *Sichot*, *33*:11–22. (Hebrew).

Bion, W.R. (1970). *Attention and Interpretation*. London: Karnac.

Bion, W.R. (1974). *Bion's Brazilian Lectures I*. Rio de Janeiro: Imago Editora.

Bion, W.R. (1977). Caesura. In *The Grid and Caesura*. London: Karnac.

Bion, W. R. (1984). *Transformations*. London: Karnac. (Original work published 1965).

Civitarese, G. (2019a). A preface and some "frog" thoughts. In L.J. Brown, *Transformational Processes in Clinical Psychoanalysis* (pp. xiii–xxiii). New York: Routledge.

Civitarese, G. (2019b). Bion's O and his pseudo-mystical path. *Psychoanalytic Dialogues*, *29*(4):388–403.

Civitarese, G. (2019c). Reply to Goldberg and Steinberg. *Psychoanalytic Dialogues*, *29* (4):427–434.

Eigen, M. (1999). The area of faith in Winnicott, Lacan and Bion. In S.A. Mitchell & L. Aron (Eds.), *Relational Psychoanalysis: Emergence of a Tradition* (pp. 1–38). New York & London: The Analytic Press (first published in 1981).

Eliade, M. (1957). *The Sacred and the Profane*. New York: Harcourt.

Freud, S. (1933). New introductory lectures on psycho-analysis. *SE, XXII*, 1–182.

Goldberg, P. (2019). Where are we when we are at one? Discussion of Bion's O and his pseudo mystical path. *Psychoanalytic Dialogues*, *29*(4):404–417.

James, W. (1992b). The Will to Believe. In G.E. Myers (Ed.), *William James Writings 1878–1899* (pp. 445–704). New York: The Library of America (Original work published 1896).

Reiner, A. (2012). *Bion and Being*. London: Karnac.

Steinberg, B. (2019). Civitarese on O: Bion's pragmatic and aesthetic-intersubjective theory of truth, the growth of the mind, and therapeutic action: Discussion of Bion's O and his pseudo mystical path. *Psychoanalytic Dialogues*, *29*(4):418–426.

Chapter 6

Playing and unity: The Winnicottian revolution

Many therapists feel the work of D.W. Winnicott, one of the most influential and likeable thinkers after Freud, to be their theoretical "home." It might be surprising, therefore, to claim that within his well-recognized contributions to our clinical understanding, so deeply assimilated in today's theory and practice, lies a fundamental and unsettling revolution, one that is far from being fully understood. Winnicott's silent revolution introduces a new, magical element into psychoanalytic thinking. At the same time, he treats the reality of magic as an immanent part of psychoanalysis and even of everyday life.

My claim is that Winnicott's (1971) concept of potential space – a phenomenon he referred to as "sacred," (p. 139) because it is at the core of "the magic of imaginative and creative living" (p. xvi) – contains within it a twofold revolution: one in the meaning of psychoanalytic knowledge and, closely related to this, one in the mystical element, whose fate and vicissitudes in psychoanalytic history we have been following. *Transitional epistemology*, as I would call it, is a qualitatively different way of approaching old questions about the nature of knowledge: what does it mean to know something about one's patient, to have a theory about child development? What does it mean to know anything human? These questions are at the heart of psychoanalysis' long struggle to find its place. Winnicott, perhaps unknowingly, offers psychoanalysis an entirely new plane to stand upon; one that is different from both the classical, scientific view and from the various solutions that limit the possibilities of sharing an interdisciplinary field of discourse. He does this by postulating an

DOI: 10.4324/9781003200796-6

alternative, third reality: essentially, he illuminates an unrecognized, yet well-trodden path to an intimate and involved knowledge of the Other.

Unlike the mystical element that can be traced in the work of the other thinkers reviewed so far, Winnicott's (1971) *transitional mysticism*, as I call it, is non-oceanic; it is not restricted to the infantile experience of being held by a great mother. Instead, it is about the magic of a true meeting, one that does not blur subjectivity but rather nurtures it and requires its uniqueness as a necessary ingredient. While Winnicott himself did not stress these broad, interdisciplinary aspects of his thought, leaving them for others to develop, he was evidently aware of at least some of their implications. Winnicott's (1971) own intuition of the deep connection between the concept of transitional space and the realm of metaphysical thought is expressed in his introduction to *Playing and Reality*:

> It is of course possible to see that this [...] intermediate area has found recognition in the work of philosophers. In theology it takes special space in the eternal controversy over transubstantiation. It appears in full force in the work of the so called metaphysical poets [...] (ibid, p. xv–xvi)

Here, Winnicott hints at the crucial relevance of what had been long recognized (or at least acted upon) in religion and in metaphysical poetry to his study of psychological development and to what is, in his view, a vital ability of the healthy personality: The ability to live in the "transitional" place between the inner world and outer, shared reality. This ability holds the key to both revolutions.

In order to understand this, we will move along Winnicott's proposed timeline of infant development. This will help us see the ways in which Winnicott's "mystical element" resembles that of his predecessors as well as where a real paradigm shift occurs. In the first three parts of this chapter, the Winnicottian developmental milestones will be explored in light of their relevance to the evolvement of the mystical element and the epistemological stance. This refers both to the growing infant and, by extrapolation, to the development of the psychoanalytic way of meeting and knowing. The third section of this part, "Magic and the third reality," presents and contrasts two forms of mystical experience that arise from ways of sharing experience and experiencing the Other throughout the course of development. These issues of the mystical and epistemological aspects of the encounter are then discussed through several of Winnicott's foci of interest: Transitionality ("true magic") versus madness, the incommunicado core and its paradoxical pairing with essential togetherness, religious experience as a transitional phenomenon, and the centrality of paradox to the human psyche. Following this last topic, which was particularly close to Winnicott's heart, the Winnicottian revolution will be fully presented and contrasted with pre-Winnicottian, nonparadoxical Psychoanalysis.

Next, the section titled "The mystical experience and the mystic of experiencing" will touch on the difference between mystical experience, which is often associated with religious life and what could be understood, in light of Winnicott's revolution, as an essential part of the psyche. Lastly, the chapter's two final sections offer an interdisciplinary analysis of Winnicott's thought, weaving together the subject of mystical experience and the questions of epistemology and ontology. The essence of Winnicott's unrecognized and, therefore, novel view of the human self and human knowledge, is integrated with its striking parallels in the philosophies of James and Buber. As the readers wind their way on this thematic journey, they will come in contact – hopefully both experientially and intellectually – with what Winnicott calls "magic." This word keeps appearing in Winnicott's writings, bearing different meanings in different contexts, the study of which is most revealing. It unveils some of Winnicott's understanding of the magical part of life and sheds some light on Winnicott's own "magic" – the one that has ever worked on his readers.

The magic of unity

In the beginning, as Winnicott (1960) tells us, there is no such thing as an infant, only a unified field of experience. Winnicott's famous statement goes beyond the idea of the baby's complete physiological and psychological dependence, which he often stressed as a basic fact of life. For Winnicott, baby and mother, baby and surrounding environment are one. Winnicott thereby exposes his readers to an alternative experience of reality. In the beginning, unity is the living reality for the mother as well as the baby. The mother enters a unique state of consciousness that Winnicott (1956) calls "primary maternal preoccupation." This state allows her to feel – almost to "know" – her baby's needs: a kind of telepathy. This is possible because post-partum psychological reality is continuous with the biological unity of pregnancy (Winnicott, 1956). What does this really mean? Well, no one remembers. Winnicott claims this state of consciousness is akin to madness and that women forget it as soon as the baby's maturation allows them to recover.

Here, in an affinity with this "mad" form of empathy, the word *magic* appears. Mothers, according to Winnicott (1960), possess an "almost magical" (p. 593) capacity to understand their babies. He also mentions the "almost magical" abilities of people with early deprivation, who did not enjoy the privileges of merger and cannot relinquish it. These persons have remarkable empathic capabilities. They may be, for a time, a great "mother" to others and possess "magical healing powers" (Winnicott, 1949, p. 245). Yet their fragility, their actual need to receive that very nourishment from others, become apparent when they break down or approach breakdown, when others really rely on them. Winnicott thus shares Ferenczi's (Ferenczi and Dupont, 1988) and Kohut's (1966) intuition that pathology in the early, merged state of the mother–baby relationship may give rise to a remarkable empathic, almost telepathic ability. This ability reigns in early infancy but lies dormant in most adults, until one is called upon to be a mother. Compared to the "normal" extent of adult interpersonal understanding, these abilities are "magical." When unsupported by a mature personality, this ability is soon overwhelming. According to Winnicott, only a mother with a healthy personality can enter this special state and relinquish it when the baby needs her to do so. This merger is limited in terms of time and purpose, a temporarily granted magical ability that later sinks into oblivion. Merger with others is magic, but it is also dangerous, insane.

Winnicott (1960) writes:

> In the management of infants there is a very subtle distinction between the mother's understanding of her infant's needs based on empathy and her change over to understanding based on

something in the infant [...] that indicates need. This is particularly difficult to mothers because [...] children vacillate between
one state and the other. One minute they are merged [...] while
the next they are separate and then if she knows their needs in
advance she is dangerous, a witch. It is a very strange thing that
mothers who are quite uninstructed adapt to these changes [...]
this detail is reproduced in psycho-analytic work [...] in all cases
at certain moments of great importance where dependence in
transference is maximal. (p. 594)

Clearly, for Winnicott, there is no external signal that might help us
understand how the mother performs her magic. This is why mo-
therhood cannot be taught. This is why words with "supernatural"
connotations appear in Winnicott's texts. The mother has a witchlike
ability, but she is felt to be a witch only if she works her magic after
the baby is ready to separate. Then, her magic is no longer beneficial,
it is felt to be obtrusive, witchcraft. Thus, the mother must know
when she is not allowed to know her baby. Paradoxically, realizing
when this is so requires a fine, preverbal empathic sensitivity.
"*Preverbal*," however, is not enough to capture Winnicott's meaning:
crying is preverbal; so are laughter, gestures, and smells. Those, at
least as signals, belong to a later period, when the mother must let her
baby communicate his needs. Before that, Winnicott leaves us with
an utterly mysterious, perhaps telepathic way of "knowing." Similar
to the mother, an analyst must also possess strong empathic abilities:
she might be required to enter a state of merger, or the trickier,
fluctuating state between merger and separateness, without the biological preparation mothers are endowed with by nature. Both cases
– parenting and therapy – involve a mature adult who is devoted and
stable enough to let herself become ill. Psychic merger is a field of
experience that allows the caretaker to wield a powerful, dangerous,
and exhausting magic. The mother/analyst submit to it as an
expression of love for the child or the patient.

Two ways of living together

Although devoted, loving investment is a necessary condition, the
experience of blissful unity is not a matter of choice for either mother

or baby. Much like the passivity criterion James (1987b) offers for the mystical experience, it is something that happens to them, experienced by both as a sudden, profound transformation. For Winnicott (1945), the critical moment for this life-supporting unity is a shared experience:

> In terms of baby and mother's breast [...] the baby has instinctual urges and predatory ideas. The mother has a breast and the power to produce milk and the idea she would like to be attacked by a hungry baby. These two phenomena do not come into relation with each other, till the mother and child live an experience together. The mother, being mature [...] has to be the one with tolerance and understanding so it is she that produces the situation that may, with luck, result in the first tie an infant makes with an internal object [...] from the infant's point of view. I think of the process as if two lines came from opposite directions liable to come near each other. If they overlap there is a moment of illusion – a bit of experience which the baby can take as *either* his hallucination *or* a thing belonging to external reality. (p. 141)

Mother and baby possess a predisposed phantasy world, designed by biology (and, in the mother's case, culture as well), that prepares them for a meeting. But this complementary similarity between their phantasies is not enough. For the two lines to meet, luck is needed – a lucky occurrence for the baby, which requires emotional maturity and boundless, sensitive devotion on the part of the mother. Still, for both, it is not a moment they can choose or plan.

As depicted by Buber (1923/2010), a meeting is a matter of both grace and will, or of both luck and striving. One hand is held out to another, which is extended to meet it from the other side. For the very immature baby, much striving is impossible, except by the instinctual movements of a mouth seeking a breast. The work is done by the mother. Later, a partial overlap may exist between the experience of mother and baby, enabled by this history of merger. The baby can now reach her hand out too. This is how two worlds, two options of living and connecting, present themselves: the baby may entertain the illusion she is the creator of the breast; in a later period, she may acknowledge that the breast has been offered to her and that she and mother share the experience of nursing. In both cases, though in different ways, baby and mother "live an experience together." This latter form of togetherness is made possible by the "magic" of transitional space. It is the place that allows the breast to be both me and not me, both created and found. Mother and baby can then be united and separate at the same time, within a shared experience. Winnicott's metaphor of the two lines that come together does not express mere similarity between two separate psychological events. Rather, much like the moment of unity, it is "luck" that provides a meeting place for experience.

Magic and the third reality

In his description of the first few days and weeks of life, Winnicott differs very little from other theoreticians who speak of merger and view the birth of psychological life in similar terms to (though later than) biological life: psychological life emerges from that state of unity which is experienced, perhaps, as the "oceanic" type of mysticism. This state of oneness can feel like the magic of a tender, maternal embrace, holding the baby in a safe, soothing, blissful place. Later, it might become the "black magic" of the witch, who keeps impinging on the baby, the mother who is unable to separate, peering into the child's soul while the latter seeks autonomy and individuality. One way or another, this kind of magic can operate when true, full subjectivity has yet to be born.

However, Winnicott has a unique, revolutionary view of the transition between this "oceanic" state and adult personality. This transition involves a new, "non-oceanic" type of mysticism. Winnicott (1971) calls this the "intermediate area" or "transitional space." This use of spatial terms indicates that this "transitionally" is not just a phase; rather than being temporary, it holds a special "place" in the human experience of reality:

> My claim is, that if there is a need for this double statement [about inner and outer reality] there is also need for a triple one: the third part of the life of a human being, a part that we cannot ignore, is an intermediate area of experiencing to which inner reality and external life both contribute. (p. 3)

Winnicott considered the intermediate area to be the real scene where everything distinctively human happens, where human culture, as well as individual selves, live. It is where creativity happens and, for Winnicott, human life is necessarily creative. To illustrate how strongly he felt about this point, consider the following quote: "Everything that happens is creative, except in so far as the individual is ill" (1971, p. 91). This claim goes beyond Kohut's (1966) view of creativity as a sign of health. For Winnicott, this is not optional; creativity is just what a healthy person does or even is. It can range from a simple act of breathing to an elaborate work of art or scientific invention. The crucial point is that creativity is a personal investment, a lively connection between a person's inner world and their external environment.

The ability to make this connection starts with child's play. Playing is the first spark of the lifelong potential for meaningful contact. For example, some dirty rocks a child has picked up on the street can become the eggs of a powerful dragon. At the same time, they preserve their shared quality as rocks. Unlike the phase in which baby and mother are one, objective reality is now just as valid as the subjective one. Their meeting place is precisely what allows the dragon eggs to be so special, so magical. In one of Winnicott's favorite examples, the communion ceremony provides some adults with the very same alchemy. For adults, artistic, or religious experience – or, in a broad sense, cultural experience – is a place where things have both a shared and "objective" quality and, at the same time, a very personal, "subjective" meaning.

These moments of illusion, these "magical" creations, are the fruit of the ability to play. Playing, in turn, necessarily relies on trust. As Winnicott (1971) writes:

> Play is immensely exciting. It is exciting *not primarily because the instincts are involved,* be it understood! The thing about playing is always the precariousness of the interplay of personal psychic reality and the experience of control of actual objects. This is the precariousness of *magic* itself, *magic* that arises in intimacy, in a relationship that is being found to be reliable. To be reliable, the relationship is necessarily motivated by the mother's love, or her love-hate, or her object relating, not by reaction-formations. (p. 64; italics added)

Without trust, the tension of keeping the inner and the outer worlds playfully connected would crumble under the weight of the fear each of these worlds might inspire. The mother (or other primary caretaker) is the object of this trust, but her role, the way she discharges the trust put in her hands, keeps changing. In "The Use of the Object," Winnicott (1971) adds yet another requirement for the object to be considered trustworthy. He states that the person serving as a protective environment must survive the child's phantasy world, which is sometimes necessarily destructive:

> The subject says to the object: "I destroyed you" and the object is there to receive the communication. From now on the subject says: "hullo object! I love you. You have value for me because of your survival of my destruction." (p. 120)

"The object is there to receive the communication" means that this person must be in some way or other truly affected by the child's inner world, in touch with it, yet not merged and not wholly dependent on its primitive forces. By means of this complex process of "surviving," reality is created for the child. Now, it can be engaged with, played with, without fear of it being destroyed or becoming destructive. By being meaningfully connected but not merged, by maintaining the tension, "the object" is there for every creative act, for every moment of aliveness and, most importantly, for "living an experience together" without being one. Thus, trust, intimacy, and human love are what allow magic to happen.

I would claim that in this, our second encounter with the term *magic*, Winnicott's use of the term is not merely metaphorical. "Magical" here refers to the "ordinary magic" that sometimes blesses day-to-day life, the magic of a true meeting with another person. This meeting is "magical" because it creates something new and allows true contact (not only in phantasy) between the inner and outer worlds and, in some cases, between two people's innermost selves. It is as if Winnicott is revisiting the Cartesian question: he agrees that a connection between the inner and the outer presents an insurmountable philosophic difficulty when one assumes that "me" and "not me" is all there is. Winnicott's innovation lies in the claim that reality is not binary, that there is a third realm of reality, the essence of which is connection. Like Buber, Winnicott's thinking leads to a new ontology. The meeting is reality in itself, living on its own terms, irreducible to its parts. It is momentary and transient, it is fragile. It is created and fades away according to the availability of intimacy and trust.

A familiar example is the art of literature. There is no point in asking whether *Alice in Wonderland* is real. "Reality," in this sense, is not a relevant perspective to apply to any work of art. Alice derives her success from some kind of emotional truth that Charles L. Dodgson (writing under the pseudonym Lewis Carroll) has been able to share with his readers. An intimate, creative relationship is formed between the text and those who enjoy it. A less familiar application of Winnicott's thought is, ironically, the meaning it bears on psychoanalytic knowledge, specifically regarding how we "know" the patient's feelings or how we come to sense the various layers of meaning in her communications. We are able to do so because we share the same area of experience with her: Not by way of psychic merger, as in the first days of life, but because we share – and, as Ogden (1994/1999) would say, cocreate – a special field of reality. We do not empty ourselves to feel, with perfect infallible empathy, another person's mind. Rather, we meet it. We can never grasp the Otherness before us in its entirety. Nor can we "know" the patient's thoughts. But, as cocreators of the same play environment, we "get a feel" for the psychic reality of our play-mate – especially if, as therapeutic practice requires, the patient takes the lead in designing the playground.

Magical thinking versus "true magic"

We see madness, Winnicott explains, when someone demands that we acknowledge their private illusion. Yet, the very foundation of human connection and the formation of communities lies in the area of overlap between illusions. Winnicott (1971) writes:

> *Playing has a place and a time.* It is not *inside* by any use of the word [...] nor is it outside, that is to say, it is not part of the repudiated world, the not-me, that which the individual decided to recognize (with whatever difficulty and even pain) as truly external, which is outside *magical* control. To control what is outside, one has to do things. Not simply to think or wish, *and doing takes time.* Playing is doing. (p. 55)

It is interesting to note that, here, the word "magical" bears a different, almost opposite meaning to that in the previous quote, in which Winnicott refers to "the precariousness of magic" as the essence of play. In the above quote, the word "magic" means what it usually does in psychoanalytic, Kleinian thought: phantasmatic destruction and restoration of objects that has nothing to do with external reality. In Winnicott's terms, it is what happens when object use is not possible or is yet to be achieved. Here, the word bears the negative connotation of primitive defenses that are detached from reality, whereas in the previous quote, "magical" refers to the exact opposite: the achievement of real, authentic connection with the "objective" world, creating that precious bridge between otherwise estranged realities. In a world dominated by phantasy, that of the very young child or the psychotic, thought and reality are equivalent, and Thoughts possess "magical" power. In play, on the other hand, the individual must relate to outside reality and change it through her creative efforts. The psychotic kind of "magic" is a prison build of phantasy, which detaches the sick person from their human environment. But when two or more persons share an illusion, it is "true" magic, in the sense that it connects two phenomena that are otherwise considered almost hopelessly separated.

We each live in our own skin. In a deep sense, we are alone. But for Winnicott, this aloneness, though just as essential, can at moments be transcended. A shared illusion – or more accurately, an area of overlap between private illusions – is the foundation of all that we as individuals, as well as groups and communities, hold most dear. When there is an overlap between areas of play, a joint reality is created. This reality is both subjective and objective. It creates and changes culture, which is shared and is therefore, in this sense, "objective." Religious symbols, for example, may evoke powerful emotions which stem from a person's private relationship with their God. Yet they are cultural symbols, parts of "objective," institutionalized religious language. The "third" reality is that of experiential connection. In Winnicott's potential space, it is not about sameness or merger. Neither is it a coincidental similarity. A proper geometric metaphor would be circles that share an overlapping field while each retains a separate area. This is a most intimate meeting of souls that depends on the tension of separateness no less than the joy of contact.

Irreducible loneliness and underlying relatedness: the paradox of transitional mysticism

Winnicott is one of several thinkers renowned for insisting on the crucial importance of human relatedness. At the same time, he believed we are all essentially alone. This Winnicottian paradox is what makes his "mystical element" novel, bringing psychoanalysis closer to the Buberian "I-thou" encounter than ever before. On the one end of the paradox, there is the importance of maintaining continuous authentic contact with others throughout life. The baby is completely dependent, but the adult is also in continuous need of a human environment to meet her in her endeavors, to share at least some of her illusions. Intimacy, as the matrix of creativity, pervades every human activity. Winnicott (1971) writes: "No statement that concerns the individual as an isolate unit can touch this central problem of the source of creativity" (p. 96). Much like electric potential, which comes alive when tension is created between two poles, Winnicott believed that the ability to create something new emerges when intimacy and confidence are established between individuals, on various levels – toward a mother, a close friend, a receptive audience, perhaps even a state that permits and encourages free speech.

Since Winnicott views creativity and, therefore, intimate contact as the heart of human life, it is perplexing to find that he states, strongly and dramatically, that the core of the personality is isolated and lies beyond communication. Moreover, Winnicott holds this loneliness sacred. In his famous paper, "Communicating and not Communicating" (1963), he addresses his readers with a strong emotional tone, demanding that it be respected:

> I suggest that in health there is core to the personality that corresponds to the true self of the split personality; I suggest that this core never communicates with the world of perceived objects, and that the individual person knows it must never be communicated with or influenced by external reality. This is my main point, the point of thought which is the center of an intellectual world [...] Although healthy persons communicate, and enjoy communicating, the other fact is equally true, that *each individual is an isolate, permanently non-communicating, permanently unknown, in fact unfound* [...] in life and living this hard fact is softened by the sharing

that belongs to [...] cultural experience. At the center of each person there is an incommunicado element, and this is sacred and most worthy of preservation [...] Rape and being eaten by cannibals, these are mere bagatelles as compared with the violation of the self's core [...] for me this would be a sin against the self. (p. 187)

In a sense, this dramatic statement is a mirror image of his other provocative saying: "there is no such thing as an infant ," which speaks of total union. Here, Winnicott claims that isolation lies at the core of human experience and, in fact, constitutes the sense of having a core. His language is pointedly religious: the isolate self should not be "desecrated," this would be a "sin." He further claims that, in health, a person needs something more than overt communication with others – something more elusive, more private; something like the silent communication with internal objects that a sick person may use almost exclusively: "There is room for the idea that significant relating and communicating is silent" (ibid, p. 184).

Is Winnicott contradicting himself? Is this earlier paper a reflection of a different thesis than the one we explored in *Playing and Reality*? Is he returning to the primacy of the internal world of objects and phantasy that caused his split from Klein? Not at all. For Winnicott, the isolate self is – through a typical Winnicottian paradox – the product of deep connection, of merger, even, with the environment mother, and as we saw, the isolate self carries with it the potential of a future merger (for example, as a mother or a therapist), possible only for a healthy, mature individual with an isolate core. The paradoxical nature of Winnicott's claim is even more apparent in one of his other texts. In "The Capacity to Be Alone" (Winnicott 1958), he explains that the capacity for aloneness, which is an important developmental achievement, is only acquired because the baby is never really alone. He is alone in the proximity of the mother, who protects his experience of playing; she is either physically present or there are soothing signs of her nearness.

Later, says Winnicott, people can be alone with each other. He calls this ego-relatedness, as opposed to an id-relationship, and views it as the basis of friendship. In friendship, loneliness plays a special role as an important, special other guards one's loneliness and offers a presence which paradoxically gives meaning to being alone.

Aloneness is thus rooted in a deep, intimate relationship with a specific real object. It is a form of communication, though no overt communication is taking place. This is very different from phantasmatic communication with internal objects, evident in schizoid states. In "Communicating and not Communicating," after saying that meaningful communication is silent, Winnicott (1963) goes on to state that:

> Real health need not be described only in terms of residues [...] of what might have been illness patterns. One should be able to make a positive statement of the healthy use of non-communication in the establishment of the feeling of the real. It may be necessary [...] to speak of man's cultural life which is the adult equivalent of the transitional phenomena [...] and in which area communication is made without reference to the object's state of being either subjective or objectively perceived. It is my opinion that psychoanalysis has no other language to refer to cultural phenomena. He can talk about the mental mechanisms of the artist but not about the experience of communication in art and religion unless he is willing to peddle in the intermediate area whose ancestor is the infant's transitional object. (p. 184)

The past and the future of the incommunicado core are, therefore, deeply intertwined with communication or, more accurately, with connection. Its sacred privacy is paradoxically defined with respect to those phases of contact, in which the silent core must express itself for a meeting to take place. Only authentic selfhood is capable of a transitional experience, of creativity. The core self is never alone in its aloneness.

For Buber as well, the "I-thou" area of meeting occurs through the same necessary paradox. In the Buberian meeting, one fully opens his deepest being to another. Actual nonverbal and profoundly intimate knowledge of the Other is therefore possible, because both sides cocreate a new moment in which they are fully present. The Buberian moment is a mystical one, a "mysticism of this world" in which both participants transcend themselves and are transformed, without disconnecting in any way from daily life. Rather, they are staying present and transforming the mundane into something magical. This is only possible, however, for two individuals who have fully established their subjectivity. A person does not lose himself in this newly created joint reality. On the contrary, his personality is further enriched and strengthened. In fact, Buber's (1947/2014) brief account of human development defines these encounters, much like Winnicott's potential space, as the building blocks of human personality. At the same time, paradoxically, only a full "person" – one who already has a self that can contribute to the meeting – is able to share this mysterious realm with another.

Just as Buber left behind his "early period," in which he embraced an ecstatic, "oceanic" kind of mysticism that flees daily life (Kaufman, 2001; Koren, 2002), so the Winnicottian baby – and with it, psychoanalytic theory – moves a step forward: a step that no longer permits it to leave reality and Otherness behind, nor settle for the estranged I-it world. Now, a new way of knowing, of connecting, unfolds: the "I-Thou" realm, or transitional space.

Religious experience and the third reality

The paradoxical structure of human existence and human relatedness is also deeply connected to the relationship a person may have with God, offering a wholly new view of religious experience. The Winnicottian view represents a silent revolution that reshapes Freud's legacy concerning religion. For Winnicott, religion is (or, at least, may be) part of cultural life. It might be an illusion, but it is located in the area of adult "allowed illusion," where illusions are not merely inner phenomena derived from the pleasure principle and the difficulty in accepting the harsh facts of reality. In fact, the opposite is true. In Winnicottian language, this kind of illusion is the place where phantasy meets reality and enriches it. A phenomenon cannot be transitional if it is too instinct-laden or if it denies external reality. Whenever the tension between these two poles is not maintained, whenever the paradox is not respected, the experience of play is destroyed.

Meissner (1984) has pointed out the interdisciplinary implications that Winnicott's work has for the understanding of religion. The idea of transitional space frees the religious person or, by extrapolation, the mystic from having to choose between the complete, unshaken belief that someone is "out there" (and must thus be recognized by others in the same way) and the "realization" that his own mind is fooling him, that perhaps he is mad. There is no need to "prove" the existence of God to justify one's religious experience. In fact, for Winnicott, much like it is for James (1996), experience has its own intrinsic value. The question is, rather, how well does it connect to the other experiences this person is having? Does it bring him closer to or farther away from satisfactory contact with other people? How does it affect, in short, the whole experiential tapestry of his life? On the other hand, personal experiences cannot possess a "factual" quality that must compel others to accept the same "not me" environment. Others can only be invited to share the same playground of thought and feeling if it so happens that their experiences find a meeting place.

Similarly, "transitional epistemology" – as I suggest it can be called, as opposed to the "true" or "false" dichotomy – may, in some cases, free the analyst from the strain of determining "reality" while trying to comprehend an experience that is alien to his own. Rubin (2006) makes a similar point when discussing psychoanalysis' view of spirituality. According to Rubin, Winnicott allows us to refrain from choosing between inner and outer realities and deciding whether an experience is a divine revelation or an illusion. He also sees the relevance of this viewpoint to the psychoanalytic encounter, the meeting place of the patient's and the therapist's "inner" and "outer" worlds and, like Eigen (1998), views it as something that can be "sacred."

The religious experience of connection with God is the offspring of the teddy-bear of infancy. The teddy, in its turn, inherits one's actual relationship with one's mother:

> Of the transitional object, it can be said that it is a matter of agreement between us and the baby, that we will never ask the question: "did you conceive of this, or was it presented to you from without?" The important point is that no decision on this point is expected. The question is not to be formulated. (Winnicott, 1971, p. 17)

The teddy might not have a mind or a soul "in reality," but it is a meaningful expression of the baby's idea of connection between minds. It is the same with transubstantiation. Just as we would never ask the baby whether she had conceived of the object or found it, it is pointless to challenge the idea of transubstantiation. The fact that a worshiper "actually" swallows a wafer does not contradict the communion it allows through the body of Christ. The teddy, we should bear in mind, was there to be found. Winnicott, it is true, does not pretend to solve the question of whether God was "really" there, like mother was, even before the baby was mature enough to perceive her. He contents himself with claiming that if we wish to maintain our cultural life, the question should not be formulated as such (Meissner, 1984). If you wish to enjoy a puppet show, you should not preoccupy yourself with the strings holding the puppets; nor should you forget them entirely. The question of the strings or the wafer may certainly be important for some practical purposes, but not for the sake of artistic or the religious experience. Perhaps it is made even more exciting because of the life now pervading lifeless things that are hanging on strings. The strings are real; but the work of art that uses them is no less so. For Winnicott, it is the most real thing we have.

Winnicott illuminates not only the nature of religious experience but also the nature of the religious subject – in fact, of the human subject in general. To be able to participate in religious or other cultural experiences, a person needs to be alone yet deeply connected. She should stay herself while connected. She can be a part of a religious congregation that shares an illusion yet, at the same time, have her "own" God with whom she maintains silent communication. Winnicott, like James, speaks of what James would call "personal religion," as opposed to mere submission to an institutional religion, which would amount to an aspect of false self. In a personal religion, the believer is personally invested, even if their belief relies on institutional elements. They must have a personal relationship with their religion, share an intimate connection with God.

Paradox: The mystical dwelling place of the human psyche

Both the characteristics of the mystical experience as described by James (1987b) and Otto (1917/1950) and those of the human mind as portrayed by Winnicott are paradoxical. They are both actually "made" of paradox, structured by an unsettled space that exists only as tension between two poles. Both depend for their very existence on a paradox that is essential and cannot be resolved.

The mystical experience is riddled with paradoxes. It is, by definition, a sense of "knowledge" that cannot be expressed in words, yet often pressing the mystic to find adequate expression. At the same time, he feels that words cannot do it justice. The mystical experience might be sought after, but not chosen. It may fill one with dread and awe as well as joy. It is a new revelation that connects the mystic with knowledge that was always there to be found. It is an intimate encounter with something (or someone) infinitely beyond our grasp. This experience is one of many hosted by the human mind which, as Winnicott believed, is itself paradoxical. Moreover, Winnicott (1971) claimed his main contribution lies in pointing out the centrality of paradox in human experience:

> I am drawing attention to the *paradox* involved in the use by the infant of [...] the transitional object. My contribution is to ask for a paradox to be accepted [...] respected, and for it not to be resolved. By flight or split off intellectual functioning it is possible to resolve the paradox, but the price [...] is the loss of the value of the paradox itself. This paradox once accepted, and tolerated has value for every human individual, who is not only alive and living [...] but who is capable of being infinitely enriched by the exploitation of the cultural link with the past and with the future. It is the extension of this basic theme that concerns me in this book. (p. xvi)

Before Winnicott, psychoanalysis had been "flying," as he terms it, toward one of the poles that define our existence. Traditionally, it had chosen the inner world. The great analytic writers who preceded Winnicott had focused on analyzing phantasy, conflicts, and the structure of personality. Even the British school, which argued for the primacy of object seeking, and specifically the middle group, that stressed the importance of the actual relationship, had focused on the internalized object and the various ways in which it was affected by that relationship. In the United States, the interpersonal school preferred to study the external relationship; some critics say it chose the other pole. Winnicott was unique in not choosing to settle on either riverbank. He claimed that all that is interesting happens in the river itself or, rather, in the potential to support a bridge. Connection is what should be of interest; potential space is where creative life happens. Here, we may hear an echo of Bion (1977): "Study the *caesura*," not the patient or the analyst, not the conscious or unconscious, but the fragile, flickering bridge between them.

Even more clearly than Bion, this idea echoes Buber's (1923/2010) discussion of religious life:

> Man's religious situation, his being there in the presence is characterized by essential and indissoluble antinomy [...] he who tries to think out a synthesis destroys the significance of the situation. He who strives to make the antinomy into a relative matter, abolishes the significance of the situation [...] the significance of the situation is that it is lived, and nothing but lived, continually, ever anew, without foresight [...] forethought, without prescription, in the totality of its antinomy [...] if I consider necessity and freedom not in the worlds of thought but in the reality of my standing before god [...] then I cannot try to escape the paradox that has to be lived by assigning the irreconcilable propositions to two separate realms of validity [...] but I am compelled to take both to myself, to be lived together, and in being lived, they are one. (pp. 95–96)

The similarity between Buber and Winnicott is striking, though they apparently did not know of each other's writing. Both spoke of the intermediate area of the authentic meeting as the place where human life happens – where human essence is expressed (Praglin, 2006). Both realized that referring to this area requires moving past the familiar epistemology of logic and the rule of contradiction. This kind of thinking about categories, of "true" and "false," belongs to the "I-it" world and precludes real meeting.

Winnicott's revelation is that paradox is not necessarily a problem. It might indicate an unsolved problem in the natural sciences, but not in the study of the human mind and especially not in treating it. Here, paradox has value; it is a hard-won ability. To live a full life, one must understand external reality (physical and social) with all its limitations, even its determinism. At the same time, we must re-cognize that we are beings who act, initiate and make choices. Consequently, we must view the world as potentially coming to meet us – in other words, we should understand our stay in this world as a creative potential. We have no choice but to tolerate this tension. In Buber's words: the paradox must be lived, not reconciled.

Paradox as a revolution

Freud, the first psychoanalytic revolutionary, undermined man's view of himself as a rational creature. He showed that the deeper layers of our mind are anything but rational. The unconscious does not abide by the rule of contradiction; within it, plus and minus, affirmation and negation, are one and the same. In this sense, the second revolution in the understanding of the human mind is Winnicott's. He uncovered the paradoxical life of the healthy, fully mature human psyche. The existence of potential space defies the rules of logic. It is not internal or external. It requires both impregnable solitude and the deepest, most intimate connection. Nevertheless, it is not some primitive, suppressed part of our personality. Unlike the Freudian unconscious,[1] potential space is not "illogical" in the sense that it rejects logic or lacks the necessary maturity to accept it. It is not a question of primitive thinking, quite the opposite: it is the way a healthy, creative person allows herself to be. It is what makes the greatest human achievements possible, including science and logic. However, the conditions that allow potential space to exist have nothing to do with classical logic. Questions of "true" and "false" are irrelevant; in a playful environment, they are meaningless: if we choose to "answer" them, play ceases to exist.

In addition, the Winnicottian revolution undermines the classical view of the individual as the relevant subject of study in psycho-analysis. Bion and Kohut both showed that there is no point in thinking of the individual without someone(s) who contains him, who thinks for him (Bion), or who supports him as a selfobject throughout his life (Kohut). Winnicott showed that there is no point in talking about a living subjectivity without addressing its connection to the world and to other subjects – not just as supporters, but as co-creators of culture. Herein, of course, lie the seeds of the relational approach. The essential difference is that one cannot speak of an autonomous individual or (in health) about total containment and merger. The healthy person lives in the tension, on the bridge, where the mystery of her life takes place: the mystery of transubstantiation between inside and outside, between determinism and choice. Winnicott (1945) writes:

> The subject of illusion is a very wide one that needs study; it will be found to provide the clue to a child's interest in bubbles and clouds and rainbows and all mysterious phenomena [...] Somewhere here, too, is the interest in breath, which never decides whether it comes primarily from within or without, and which provides a basis for the conception of spirit, soul, anima. (p. 154)

The mystical experience and the mysticism of experiencing

Is this similarity between the structure of the human mind and that of mystical phenomenon coincidental? It certainly does not suffice to say that they are both described in paradoxical terms. Is there a more essential ground for this pairing? Before we can get any closer to answering this question, let us once more examine the definition offered here for the mystical in psychoanalysis: it is a deeply meaningful experience, which eludes satisfactory verbalization yet carries with it a Noetic quality (of knowledge received). These experiences take place within a communication process and have a transcendental, as well as transformative, quality. I suggest that, by this definition, both the primary stage of the baby's life (when it and mother are one) and the later stage (in which transitional phenomena appears – which, with luck, can remain as a lifelong asset) are "mystical." To briefly recap the argument, when baby and mother are merged, they both live the same experience. Full "telepathy" allows the mother to transform powerful, overwhelming emotions into growth possibilities. For this purpose, the mother requires "magical" abilities – the self-transcendence that her temporary "illness" produces. Her experience of the baby (and, if things go wrong, his experience of her) is Noetic. Meaningful, life-changing knowledge is passed wordlessly by mysterious means; it is lived together and transformed inside the baby-mother dyad.

So far, there is no essential difference between Winnicott's mystical element and that of Kohut's, Bion's, Ferenczi's, and other theoreticians' more or less acknowledged mystical thought. Winnicott's critical contribution emerges in the next stage: when the ability to play appears, the self already has boundaries. It has an "inside" an "outside" and an untouchable, deeply personal core, which nevertheless communicates. "Play," as a particular content of potential space (some specific play), relies on the "interplay" between the inner and outer worlds, unity and separateness, on the constant, though ever-changing tension, that constitutes the healthy personality. It is this tension which creates meaning and permits true knowledge of the Other. Meaning depends on a certain distance between the giver of meaning and the object of meaning. At the same time, it depends on their link, on the investment of the self – its issues, its loves, its actions – in an object. Only in this state can real knowledge exist. In merger, there is no point in speaking of knowledge since there is no Other, no object of knowledge. In contrast, in a state of total detachment or purely academic knowledge, real knowledge is equally impossible. I can know how tall a person is, what he wears and what he does for a living, but I would *know* nothing about who he is and would have no chance of touching his soul without risking my own, without engaging in this "immensely exciting" yet "precarious" dance on Winnicott's bridge, woven of "magic itself" (Winnicott, 1971, p. 64).

It is what De Saint-Exupéry (1946) tells us about the risks of growing up: an adult, he complains, would ask all the wrong questions about a friend you try to describe. He would feel he knows your friend after asking how much he weighs, how many siblings he has, and how much his father makes. He would never ask what his voice sounds like, whether he collects butterflies or what his favorite play is. The things one finds out in this manner are less stable than the numbers used to quantify income or height and, as De Saint-Exupery poignantly shows, they demand that we risk enduring a painful loss. Buber (1923/2010) also criticizes the scientific idea of knowing as "freezing" living things and pushing them away. This allows us to know their attributes, but the real Other transcends such measurable characteristics. Real knowledge requires living contact, not "objective" detachment. To achieve this, the self in its entirety must be involved – a real risk must be taken. Winnicott (1949) views intellectual detachment as a dissociative, pathological state in which the mind is lured away from the psycho-soma. Buber (1923/2010) makes a similar distinction between the "worlds of thought" and living.

Knowledge acquired through contact, through intimacy, is not necessarily verbal: "There is room for the idea that significant relating and communicating is silent" (Winnicott, 1963, p. 184). This kind of knowledge calls to mind James's mystical, "Noetic experience," an experience of an extremely important, profound discovery that cannot be verbalized. In the intermediate area, the Noetic experience originates in the fact that a creative act is taking place. A person knows her creation. On the other hand, it is really "knowing," not only "making," because the thing created was there, waiting to be found. This unique state – creating something that in a sense was already there – brings us to the criteria of transcendence and transformation. This is because such deep participation is necessarily transformative. In such an encounter, the self is changed, sometimes dramatically, sometimes only a little. That is why potential space is so valuable a place for the individual: it allows a self-initiated transformation, the only kind of change to the self which is permitted (Winnicott, 1971). A person moves to creatively meet what is outside. Any other way would violate the incommunicado core. For this reason, the intermediate area is where the psychoanalytic meeting takes place: "*Psychotherapy takes place in the overlap of two areas of playing. That of the patient and that of therapist*" (p. 51; italics in original).

The idea of communication, another criterion for mystical experience, is of course critical here. It bears the "transitional" quality between what Winnicott (1971) calls indirect communication and the place where it is unclear whether the word *communication* has any meaning at all, because a state of merger is in effect: "only in playing is communication possible. Except direct communication, which belongs to psychopathology or extreme immaturity" (p. 73). Meaningful communication, which does not have to be verbal but assumes a certain degree of separateness, is at the heart of transitional space. Here lies Winnicott's contribution: he has redefined the most valued human activities – authentic communication and creativity – as something that transcends the objective-subjective polarity.

Everything that is meaningful has the illusory, magical nature of "bubbles, clouds, and rainbows." In them, the soul lives.

If there is any merit in the claim that potential space shares similar qualities with the mystical encounter, this might mean that the mystical modality is essential to the functioning of the healthy personality: the human soul lives where there is a real, creative, transformative encounter between it and the world, between it and another soul. However, it is important to bear in mind the difference between a mystical experience as possible "content" of transitional space – classically, an experience of communication with an Other that might have religious meaning (theistic or pantheistic, with all their possible variations) – and the mystical qualities of transitional space itself. These qualities persist even when the content of play is not "mystical" at all. For example, consider a humorous exchange between two adults. In this case, the objects of humor are not important in themselves and the exchange obviously lacks the dramatic aura commonly attributed to mystical experiences. Still, the deep connection between two people, which allows the exchange of subtle meanings, the dance between understanding and misunderstanding and, perhaps above all, the tension Winnicott describes between intimate contact and aloneness – the elusiveness of the experience, the realization that it may fade at a moment – is a deeply meaningful experience, one that defies definition.

Let us return to Winnicott's multidimensional use of the word "magical." He was familiar, of course, with the usual psychoanalytic meaning of the word – omnipotent phantasy – and sometimes, as we have seen, he himself used the word in the latter sense. Yet, Winnicott also believed in "real magic": real knowledge, inside knowledge of another person's essence and a deep, unmediated connection to the world. This is magical because of the mysterious connection that may be found in intimacy, even after the merger phase. It has a 'telepathic' quality that exists in constant tension with what we will never know about the Other's Otherness, since everyone remains, in essence, alone. It is "real magic" also because this knowledge, the Noetic experience, does not arise merely from what was there before. The very act of knowledge, as a necessary part of creation, changes both the object and the subject of knowledge. Winnicott's uniqueness lies in the realization that magic is an organic part of a healthy psyche and a healthy culture. The mystery of the transformative encounter, which occurs beyond words and sometimes even without them, is at the same time life's "bread and butter" and its most sacred part. Winnicott stresses that he merely points out the regular, day-to-day things that were overlooked by psychoanalytic theory because they had been taken for granted. On the other hand, his language is overflowing with religious allusions and a dreamlike atmosphere. There is fairy-dust sprinkled on daily life. This magic of living, Winnicott claims, cannot be explained away by analytic reasoning. It cannot be reduced to anything else.

Winnicott, pragmatism and James' pluralistic universe

The meaningful experience that occurs mysteriously and subtly between patient and analyst or, in Winnicott's words, in the potential space between them – cannot be captured and measured by regular "objective" means. Now, more than ever, we can see how misguided such an aspiration is. In light of Winnicott's revolution, it is easier to understand why Bion (1970) claimed that psychoanalysis is not a science and that trying to judge it by using scientific tools would be like judging a work of art by scientific criteria. The true psycho-analytic encounter, the creation of an intermediate area that permits transformation, takes place in the "colorful bubble and rainbow" area. You can write down a psychoanalytic meeting verbatim, you may even film it, but you cannot capture its transitional quality. You cannot catch a rainbow. The imaginary spectator of a filmed session may feel that something special, meaningful, and transformative has happened there. But this would be another intermediate area, the one created between the spectator and what they saw: a new moment, not a replay of the first. Scientific reliability is impossible here, only an overlap between areas of play, like the one taking place between an artist and those touched by her art and (as we would like to think) between a therapist and his supervisor, with whom he shares the story of a meeting.

This does not mean, however, that objective criteria should not be set for the psychoanalytic endeavor. Winnicott was a therapist, not a philosopher, and his goal was to create an environment for personal growth. Similarly, James, as a pragmatist and a psychologist, claimed that although mystical experience itself is deeply personal and cannot be viewed from outside, its implications for the lives of those who had it can and should be investigated. Has this person improved their quality of life, their psychological well-being, their moral character? This is the only way in which the value of such an experience can be assessed. Winnicott, too, offers criteria for successful treatment and even for a successful session. First and foremost, a person should feel alive, experience himself as a center of initiative, involved, present. The question of whether a certain interpretation was "correct" is less relevant. What matters is whether something new happened between patient and analyst, something that had "aliveness" in it, something that helped the patient to leave the room more able to play. Nevertheless, if we try to assess the ability to play by using some objective tool (for example, a "quality of life" questionnaire), we would doubtlessly encounter many difficulties. James' similar criteria for the effect of religious experience – aliveness and optimism, like any other psychological variable – challenge the researcher in the same way. This is not the place to discuss operational solutions.

What we have before us is a "pragmatic" analytic thinker (whether or not Winnicott was actually familiar with the pragmatic school of thought) who unveils a fascinating connection between the necessary conditions for analytic theory and practice and those that facilitate psychic life itself. The connection between inner and outer worlds, the freedom from the demand to make an artificial "choice" between the two; the status of human beings as co-creators of reality and, at the same time, the inevitability of accepting limitations and the "resistance" of the "outside" world to their efforts at molding it – all these are hallmarks of Jamesian pragmatism. For James, the distinction between inner and outer worlds is contextual, not absolute. Human beings spend their lives giving form to the stream of consciousness: on the one hand, creators; on the other, creatures of this world, forming something new from their very immersion in their surroundings. An analyst may offer a theory about human development. The concepts she proposes are not her "subjective" view, nor do they represent "objective truth." The question, rather, is the extent to which it fits the flow of psychoanalytic experience, helps to deal with therapeutic challenges, succeeds in forming a creative overlap, a "playground" for other therapists, and to promote new "aliveness" and further dynamics of growth in theory and practice.

According to James, human beings are creators who depend on a tradition of previous formulations deeply rooted in their own history and the history of thought of the human race. Similarly, Winnicott (1971) writes:

> In any cultural field it is not possible to be original except on the basis of tradition. Conversely no one in the line of cultural contributors repeats [...] The interplay between originality and the acceptance of tradition as the basis of inventiveness seems to me [...] one more example, and a very exciting one, of the interplay between separateness and union. (p. 134)

For Winnicott and James alike, human beings depend not only on the legacy of human thought or on parental care as vital, but now passive memories. Rather, James' (1987a) idea of a pluralistic universe supposes constant tension between connection and separateness. In other words, creation and creativity draw both on the vertical axis of tradition and the past and on the horizontal axis of the singular encounter. James speaks of a common "sea of souls" in which every soul is also an irreducible individual. The paradoxical unity of James' (1987a) pluralistic universe is similar both to the conditions that allow for the creation of Buber's meeting in the intermediate area and Winnicott's potential space. For both Winnicott and Buber, only a mature self can truly meet another. Only a real individual can transcend his separateness. All these thinkers point to a "third reality" – a reality of living contact.

The epistemic revolution: New mysticism and pragmatism in psychoanalysis

With Winnicott, psychoanalytic history turns a page. Though it was the relational school that stressed and more thoroughly investigated the idea of a meeting between two subjectivities in the consulting room, Winnicott is the one who is truly behind what Kuhn (1962) would call a "paradigm shift" in psychoanalysis. Psychoanalysis is no longer an investigation of one person's mind through the skill of another. Nor is it only the containment of one person by another, as the self-transcendence of the analyst, putting aside his own needs and desires, allows the patient to grow. At certain points, it is a meeting, where two subjectivities meet in an area of play, which allows the patient to experience life as play. Outside the room, the inner and outer worlds continue their playful dialogue, permitting the creative tension that nurtures life. This Winnicottian or Buberian meeting – which is always new and ever-changing, in which moments of contact constantly emerge and dissolve – is a new stage in understanding knowledge and in the containment of the mystical experience. Actually, it is a new lens through which human experiences of any kind and, therefore, human nature can be viewed.

I believe Winnicott's popularity stemmed, among other things, from the deep need of the psychoanalytic discipline to act prag-matically in the uncomfortable area in which it unavoidably finds itself: the need to not "solve" the paradox on which its very ex-istence depends; not to have to "choose" between internal and ex-ternal, subjective and objective. Being forced to "choose," it might become something it is not, restricting itself to either a poetic de-scription, without any clinical responsibility for outcome, or a pseudo-science. These two poles are psychoanalysis' "false selves," offered by the different thought cultures it encounters. Such "choice" is indeed a pathological outcome of "paradox solving" (Winnicott, 1971, p. 19).

According to Winnicott (1954), there is something intuitive in how an analytic session works, which approaches the idea of psycho-analysis as an art form. Indeed, Winnicott deals with extremely de-licate and elusive facets of experience – not just internal phantasy, but also the moment this phantasy meets reality, leading to the trans-formation of both. This full and rich treatment of subjective life adheres to the Jamesian ideal of respecting experience and relying on it as the foundation of both theory and action (for example, taking therapeutic action). At the same time, in line with the demands of pragmatism, Winnicott (1971) has set clear criteria for transitional experience and for its expected implications, both in a specific session and for the therapeutic process as a whole. In a session, it is "the moment the child surprises himself" (p. 68). From the broadest perspective, the "fruit" of psychoanalysis, as James would put it, is the person's ability to feel real, alive and have a self "to which one can retreat for relaxation" (p. 158).

Notwithstanding the importance of outlining implications and criteria, the essence of Winnicott's thought and its great revolutionary importance lies in the unique, irreducible quality of the transitional moment. Whoever reads Winnicott cannot say that the mystical experience is "actually" something else, be it the fruit of a delirious imagination or divine manifestation. The mystical moment is what it is: both internal and external, a deeply subjective moment, yet one that many people around the globe and throughout millennia have partaken in. It is a part of human experience and we must live with its inherent tension. Now we can also speak of psychoanalysis without reducing it to something else, such as a branch of experiential science, a form of philosophy or art. If we translate Winnicott to James' interdisciplinary standpoint, we should try to find a way to speak about the subjective "objectively," in the shared intellectual world. This we must do, however, without deluding ourselves that our words can capture or explain experience in its entirety. But, paraphrasing Winnicott (1963, 1971), the fact that only poets can capture experience with more fidelity is no excuse for accepting our ignorance and leaving the human psyche in the hands of poetry alone. Only if we undertake this task of living and creating theory in the paradox of "transitional knowledge," can we talk not just *about* psychoanalysis, but *with* it as well. In Buber's terms, psychoanalysis could then be truly met (within the interdisciplinary arena). Inside an area of meeting, with its unique essence – or in Winnicott's words, its true self – psychoanalysis can be more deeply understood and touched, can become more meaningfully transformative for other fields and, inevitably, be transformed itself.

Note

1   In accordance with the distinction made earlier, the reference is to the "animalistic" unconscious and not to the "shadow theory" of the creative unconscious that Bollas rediscovers in Freud's writings.

References

Bion, W.R. (1970). *Attention and Interpretation.* London: Karnac.

Bion, W.R. (1977). Caesura. In *The Grid and Caesura.* London: Karnac.

Buber, M. (2010). *I and Thou.* Tr. R.G. Smith. New York: Martino Publishing. (Original work published in 1923).

Buber, M. (2014). *Between Man and Man.* Tr. R.G. Smith. New York: Martino Publishing. (Original work published in 1947).

De Saint-Exupéry, A. (1946). *The Little Prince.* Tr. I. Testot-Ferry. Herts, UK: Wordsworth Editions.

Eigen, M. (1998). *The Psychoanalytic Mystic.* London: Free Association Books.

Ferenczi, S. and Dupont, J. (Ed.). (1988). *The Clinical Diary of Sandor Ferenczi.* Tr. M. Balint and N. Zarday-Jackson. London: Harvard University Press. (Original work published in 1932).

James, W. (1987a). A pluralistic universe. In Bruce Kuklick (Ed.), *William James: Writings 1902–1910* (pp. 627–819). New York: The Library of America. (Original work published in 1909).

James, W. (1987b). The varieties of religious Experience. In Gerald. E. Myers (Ed.), *William James: Writings 1902–1910* (pp. 3–482). New York: The Library of America. (Original work published in 1902).

James, W. (1996). *Essays on Radical Empiricism.* Lincoln, NE: University of Nebraska Press.

Kaufman, W.E. (2001). The mysticism of Martin Buber: An essay of methodology. *Judaism, 27*(2), 175–183.

Kohut, H. (1966). Forms and transformations of narcissism. *Journal of the American Psychoanalytic Association, 14*(2):243–272.

Koren, I. (2002). Between Buber's Daniel and his I and Thou: A new examination. *Modern Judaism, 22*:169–198.

Kuhn, T. (1962). *The Structure of Scientific Revolutions.* Chicago: University of Chicago Press.

Meissner, W.W. (1984). *Psychoanalysis and Religious Experience.* New Haven: Yale University.

Ogden, T. H. (1999). The analytic third: Working with intersubjective clinical facts. In S. A. Mitchell & L. Aron (Eds.), *Relational Psychoanalysis: The Emergence of a Tradition* (pp. 459–492). New York: The Analytic Press. (Original work published in 1994).

Otto, R. (1950). *The Idea of the Holy.* Tr. J.W. Harvey. London: Oxford University Press. (Original work published in 1917).

Praglin, L. (2006). The nature of the "in-between" in D.W. Winnicott's concept of transitional space and in Martin Buber's das Zwischenmenschliche. *Universitas, 2*(2):1–9.

Rubin, J.B. (2006). Psychoanalysis and spirituality. In D.M. Black (Ed.), *Psychoanalysis and Religion in the 21st Century* (pp. 132–153). London: Routledge.

Winnicott, D.W. (1945). Primitive emotional development. In *Collected Papers: Through Pediatrics to Psychoanalysis* (pp. 145–156). London: Tavistock Publications, 1975.

Winnicott, D.W. (1949). Mind and its relation to psyche-soma. In *Collected Papers: Through Pediatrics to Psychoanalysis* (pp. 243–254). London: Tavistock Publications, 1975.

Winnicott, D.W. (1954). Metapsychological and clinical aspects of regression within the psychoanalytic set up. In *Collected Papers: Through Pediatrics to Psychoanalysis* (pp. 278–294). London: Tavistock Publications, 1975.

Winnicott, D.W. (1956). Primary maternal preoccupation. In *Collected Papers: Through Pediatrics to Psychoanalysis* (pp. 300–305). London: Tavistock Publications, 1975.

Winnicott, D.W. (1958). The capacity to be alone. In D.W. Winnicott and Masud Khan (Eds.), *The Maturational Process and the Facilitating Environment* (pp. 29–36). London: Hogarth Press, 1965.

Winnicott, D.W. (1960). The theory of the infant-parent relationship. In D.W. Winnicott and Masud Khan (Eds.),*The Maturational Process and the Facilitating Environment*(pp. 37–55). London: Hogarth Press, 1965.

Winnicott, D.W. (1963). Communicating and not communicating: Leading to a study of some opposites. In *The Maturational Process and the Facilitating Environment* (pp. 179–192). London: Hogarth Press, 1965.

Winnicott, D.W. (1971). *Playing and Reality*. London: Routledge.

Chapter 7

Ogden: Stepping out of the shadow – The shared psychoanalytic psyche speaks

Thomas Ogden is one of the best-known analytic authors of our times and a leading voice in shaping contemporary psychoanalysis. He is known both for his own innovations and for his mission of "translating," into more comprehensible and accessible terms, the contributions of Bion, Winnicott, and other leading thinkers (such as Klein and Loewald). Through this systematic endeavor, Ogden extended their circles of influence even further and, to a large degree, determined the contemporary understanding of their ideas. In this chapter, Ogden's work will be construed as the voice of a generation of thinkers, who were largely engaged in interpreting and assimilating the thinking of the previous generation – the "architects" of the analytic world view, especially Winnicott and Bion. In his writings, Ogden further develops trends of thought started by Bion and Winnicott, achieving their theoretical maturity or, alternatively, their most extreme form. By Ogden's hand, Winnicottian transitional space becomes alive, almost too concretely; Bionian reverie assumes a defined form and becomes a usable methodology.

By following Ogden's theory of the analytic third – which is the focus of this chapter – it will become clear that the Buberian I-Thou dimension of human relations is at the heart of the analytic process, at least within the new tradition started, to a large degree, by Ogden. Moreover, Ogden paints a specific psychoanalytic portrait of how this kind of mind-to-mind or even psycho-soma to psycho-soma contact works in the therapeutic setting, elucidating its characteristics and implications. This clinical incarnation of Winnicottian, Bionian and, by extension, Buberian ideas dons a clear and fluent form thanks

DOI: 10.4324/9781003200796-7

to Ogden's talent – a form that is, though this is avowedly denied, much more mystical.

As a popular interpreter and developer of the British object-relations school, Ogden's work was also – perhaps inevitably and certainly unwillingly – fertile soil for the development of the mystical element. In his theory of the analytic third, the mystical element reached a rather absurd peak: on the hand, it had never stood out so clearly and, on the other, actively denied by the very author who brought it to light. Ogden is an important figure for our discussion from another angle as well: he is one of the most pragmatic and even didactic theoreticians in psychoanalytic history, while also being a captivating and highly influential author. The great importance of his clarity and pragmatic proclivity, especially for dealing with the mystical element, will be analyzed throughout this chapter.

The analytic third

Among Ogden's original contributions, the theory of the analytic third can be singled out as one of the most widespread and pro-vocative concepts. As these lines are being written, his 1994 paper, "The Analytic Third: Working with Intersubjective Clinical Facts," is ranked 10th on PEP-Web's list of "most popular journal articles" and 7th on the website's list of "most cited journal articles." In addition, it is the highest ranking paper by this very prolific author.

The analytic third may be depicted as a center of gravity in Ogden's work: after it was formed through the accretion of previous ideas, many other theoretical elements came to revolve around it. This is because, for Ogden, the existence of the third both allows for and defines the process of psychoanalysis. This paper was also included in Mitchell and Aron's first volume of *Relational Psychoanalysis: Emergence of a Tradition*, situating Ogden as one of the major springs of this new stream of thought.

Thus, it is more than a key to Ogden's own ideas; it heralded in a new era. Alongside Ogden, other contemporary authors also embraced the idea of thirdness, contributing to this revolutionary zeitgeist. Notable among these is Jessica Benjamin, whose notion of thirdness (2004, 2016), though different than Ogden's, also draws on Hegelian and, to some degree, Buberian notions of mutuality, subject-to-subject recognition and reciprocal constitution. Ogden himself is well aware of the historical significance of the third and opens his paper by taking the metaphorical "pulse" of contemporary psychoanalysis:

> I shall endeavor to address an aspect of what I understand to be 'the present moment of the past' of psychoanalysis. It is my belief that an important facet of this 'present moment' [...] is the development of an analytic conceptualization of the nature of the interplay of subjectivity and intersubjectivity in the analytic setting. (1994b, p. 3)

He then defines his own contribution to this historical moment:

> My own conception of analytic intersubjectivity places central emphasis on its dialectical nature [...] This understanding represents an elaboration and extension of Winnicott's notion that "There is no such thing as an infant" [...] I believe that, in an analytic context, there is no such thing as an analysand apart from the relationship with the analyst and there is no such thing as an analyst apart from the relationship with the analysand. Winnicott's statement is, I believe, intentionally incomplete. He assumes that it will be understood that the idea [...] is playfully hyperbolic and represents one element in a larger paradoxical statement. From another perspective (from the point of view of the other 'pole' of the paradox) there is obviously an infant and a mother who constitute separate physical and psychological entities. The mother-infant unity coexists in dynamic tension with the mother and infant in their separateness [...] Neither the intersubjectivity of the mother-infant nor that of the analyst-analysand [...] exist in pure form. The intersubjective and the individually subjective each create, negate and preserve each other [...] the task is not to tease apart the elements constituting the relationship in an effort to determine which qualities belong to each individual [... but to] attempt to describe as fully as possible the specific nature of the experience of the interplay of individual subjectivity and intersubjectivity.

In the present paper, I shall attempt to trace [...] the vicissitudes of the experience of being simultaneously within and outside the intersubjectivity of the analyst-analysand which I will refer to as 'the analytic third'. This third subjectivity, the intersubjective analytic third [...] is a product of a unique dialectic generated by (between) the separate subjectivities of analyst and analysand, within the analytic setting. (ibid, p. 4)

Ogden is here offering a creative combination of Hegel's idea of the formation of the self through interdependent recognition and negation and Winnicott's more extended notion of how the human environment sustains the emerging self and allows it to become an individual. Winnicottian transitional space is Ogden's stated starting point. He elaborates on the Winnicottian notion of tension between unity and separateness, self and Other, as the place where the psyche lives and on Winnicott's insistence on the acceptance of paradox as a central psychic need. Building on this, Ogden allows himself a most radical declaration: the psychoanalytic process creates a *third subject* that exists in dialectic (Hegelian) tension with the two subjects we recognize. Without that third subjectivity, there can be no analysis and, therefore, no analyst or analysand. It is worth noting that the word "subject" is not in quotes in Ogden's text, nor is there any other indication that it should be taken as a "playfully hyperbolic" statement. Rather, by placing this third subjectivity in dialectic relation to the other two, Ogden strengthens its claim to ontological validation: in a dialectic rela- tion, no pole can be considered more "real" than the other. A dialectic presupposes interdependence, by which one pole derives its definition, even its reality, from its relation to the other. Elsewhere, Ogden (2013) stresses that the third is, of course, a metaphor and should not be understood concretely. Still, it seems that he is referring to the literal understanding that no third "person" has entered the room, while the assumption of a unified psychic field should nevertheless be taken at face value, even if words like "field" and "subjectivity" are inevitably metaphoric. Moreover, it is historically important that the original article did not include such a caveat. I believe that Ogden wished for his choice of words to have its full impact.

The implications of Winnicott's quote are equally definitive: there is no such thing as an analyst or analysand, just as there is no such thing as an infant. The analytic couple depends on that "thirdness" just as the infant depends on the mother. More accurately, if we read Winnicott in an "Ogdenian" way, patient and analyst both depend on the third as much as infant and mother depend on the holding and playing environment created between them (though mainly supported by the mother's efforts). Ogden does not forget the inherent asymmetry in what might seem as an overwhelmingly intimate mutuality.:

> As the analytic third is experienced by analyst and analysand in the context of his or her own personality system, personal history, psychosomatic make-up, etc. the experience of the third (although jointly created) is not identical for each participant. Moreover, the analytic third is an asymmetrical construction, because it is generated in the context of the analytic setting, which is powerfully defined by the relationship of roles of analyst and analysand. As a result, the unconscious experience of the analysand is privileged in a specific way, i.e. it is the past and the present experience of the analysand that is taken by the analytic pair as the principle (though not exclusive) subject of the analytic discourse [...] (the analyst and analysand are not engaged in a democratic process of mutual analysis). (ibid, p. 16)

Clearly ruling out any relation to Ferenczi's experiment (without, however, mentioning him explicitly), Ogden is outlining one of the important features that make his theory a groundbreaking innovation. He speaks of radical unity – an ontological unity – more radical perhaps than any notion put forth by previous authors, without neglecting separateness. Such separateness is manifest both in terms of each party's individuality and in terms of the different roles that deeply influence the analytic "rules of engagement," both consciously and unconsciously. They determine, as Ogden implies, what share each unconscious can have in the analytic third. Moreover, as the above quotes suggests, Ogden even "enlists" Winnicott's agreement that separateness was there from the start; that there was never really a "no such thing as an infant" form of existence. Rather, a thirdness was always there, sustained in the tension between differentiation and merger, though perhaps, in the first weeks of life, privileging mainly the latter. According to Ogden (1992), during the period of primary maternal preoccupation, Winnicott describes a mother that gives up on herself for a while but, at the same time, retains a sufficient sense of subjectivity to be able to "serve as interpreter to the infant's experience, thereby making her otherness felt but not noticed" (p. 620). Indeed, Winnicott (1956) himself states that the mother must have a healthy personality; a fully developed self that she could surrender in her devotion to her baby, and to which she could subsequently return.

Whether "thirdness" was there from the start or not, Ogden is clearly not content with treating it as a mere state of mind, relationship, or process. Rather, he refers to the tension between separateness and merger as a third *being*. He anthropomorphizes the psychic space cocreated by analyst and analysand, granting it a life of its own, the course of which will determine the outcome of analysis. In pragmatic terms, one must ask: what does Ogden stand to gain from such bold, anthropomorphic language? What does the notion of the third accomplish beyond Winnicott's potential space? There seem to be several implications – accomplishments, in my view – to Ogden's potent metaphor; the subsequent sections discuss some of these.

The first accomplishment – Integration

Ogden's third allows an efficient and, to my mind, elegant integration of his two main sources of influence: Bion and Winnicott. For Ogden, the analytic third is an inter-psychic "living" space between patient and analyst, that can be filled in different manners. It can exist in the form of potential space, allowing a playful exchange and directed toward growth. It can also be a "being" that forces itself on both patient and analyst, the offspring of their pathological merger. The latter version, which Ogden dubs the "subjugating third," is in fact an extrapolation of Bion's notion of projective identification. The subjugating third is a form of the third wherein the essential tension between unity and separateness collapses, in varying degrees of severity, toward unity. The third thus takes over the two other subjectivities in a coercive, malignant way. This description is a sharpening of Bion's notion that projective identification is more than a phantasy about controlling the object; it is an actual inter-subjective event that has profound implications for the recipient of the projection:

> It does not suffice to say that projective identification simply represents a powerful form of projection or identification or a summation of the two since the concept of projection and identification address only the intrapsychic dimension of experi-ence. Rather, projective identification can be understood only in terms of a mutually creating, negating, and preserving dialectic of subjects, each of whom allows himself to be "subjugated" by the other, that is, negated in such a way, as to become, through the other, a third subject (the subject of projective identification). What is distinctive about projective identification as a form of analytic thirdness is that the analytic intersubjectivity character-izing it is one in which the (asymmetrical) mutual subjection [...] has the effect of powerfully subverting the experience of analyst and analysand as separate subjects. In the analytic setting, projective identification involves a type of partial collapse in the dialectic movement between subjectivity and intersubjectivity resulting in the subjugation [...] by the analytic third. The analytic process, if successful, involves the reappropriation of the individual subjectivities of the analyst and analysand, which have been transformed through their experience of (in) the newly created analytic third. (Ogden, 1994a, pp. 100–101)

The subjugating third allows Ogden to assimilate his interpretation of the Bionian concept of projective identification within the larger framework of his analytic third theory. Thus, Ogden brings together the thinking of Winnicott, Klein, and Bion by elaborating Winnicott's claim that Klein's descriptions of the baby's haunted world and massive use of projections represent, in fact, a pathology of the infant-mother dyad. This pathological form of interaction might be resolved in the curative patient-analyst dyad, where a pa-tient who does not know how to play (to live in a "thirdness" that respects Otherness) must be taught to do so, before any other analytic issue can be addressed. For Ogden, this process is about fighting to maintain the tension and restoring the differentiation pole that is always there, however, effectively and even violently it has been denied. This must be done from within the shared experience of toxic coercion, via a subjectivity that is discovered through the analyst's ability to paradoxically think and metabolize its very absence.

The second accomplishment – The dream of the analytic third: Dreaming (Bionian) analysis into existence

Another central Bionian element that receives new meaning and new life in Ogden's theory is Bion's emphasis on dreams and his somewhat enigmatic concept of reverie. Ogden adopts the concept of reverie to explain how his proposed third subjectivity actually "works." By doing so, Ogden firmly roots his theory in established psychoanalytic ground (as a necessary elaboration of the concept) and, in retrospect, endows the Bionian term with more volume and practical utility.

For Ogden, reverie is *the* therapeutic medium. Ogden has written much on dreaming, following the Bionian notion of dreaming as the central process that transforms "raw" internal and external data into meaningful elements that are available for psychological work – capable of undergoing other transformations, perhaps in the form of more formal thinking (moving through Bion's grid). In other words, dream work, during both sleep and wakefulness, is the frontier of Bion's alpha function. Dreaming is the prototype of all thought, of the ability to experience and learn from experience and reverie is understood as a wakeful dreamlike activity, which is constantly running in the background of conscious thought (Gabbard and Ogden, 2009). It is a process used by the mother (analyst) to dream her infant's (patient's) dream for them. Ogden then departs from the main body of Bionian thought (though, perhaps, still adhering to the line of thought set forth in "Caesura") by considering this dreaming process to be a joint, co-created "dreaming entity." The dream, therefore, is not only the patient's (though he is the "privileged dreamer") nor is the container, presumably, solely the analyst's. Rather, they both partake in creating the "third," which is the container and meeting point of both their dreaming processes.

According to this assumption, it makes sense for the analyst to use the entire array of his psychosomatic experiences during a session. If these experiences are mutually created, *anything* might be useful as an "analytic object" (1994b, p. 15). This is an operational version of what "reverie" might mean, a version Bion, who always feared the concretization and premature saturation of his concepts, was reluctant to provide. Moreover, for Bion, the personality of the analyst introduces a potential for obstructing contact with O. According to Bion, the more a thought or an interpretation draws on the specific features of the analyst's personality, the more it is distant from O and bears the mark of a lie. He demanded that the analyst use intuition and come in direct contact with the chaotic turbulence of feelings; but he never explained how the analyst was supposed to distinguish the products of "intuition" (thus, of genuine contact with O) from what springs from the analyst's own particular personality (therefore condemned as a lie).

Ogden's operationalization of "reverie" solves this problem. The distinction Bion left us to sort out for ourselves is more than impractical – it is erroneous: "the task is not to tease apart the elements constituting the relationship in an effort to determine which qualities belong to each individual" (ibid, p. 4). Instead, one's "analytic radar" should be open even to what seem like trivial or embarrassingly private musings and sensations, seemingly completely unrelated to the patient and sometime even barely conscious. It is in these that the truth of the analysis lies and they are our pathway to O. To paraphrase Freud's view on dreaming, reverie, in Ogden's broad sense of the term, is the royal road to the (third) unconscious:

> The workings of analyst's mind during analytic hours in these unselfconscious 'natural' ways are highly personal, private and embarrassingly mundane aspects of life that are rarely discussed with colleagues, much less written about [...] it requires great effort to seize this aspect of the personal and the everyday from the unself-reflective area of reverie for the purpose of talking to ourselves about the way in which this aspect of experience has been transformed such that it has become a manifestation of the interplay of analytic subjects. The 'personal' [...] is never again simply what it had been prior to the creation of the intersubjective analytic third nor is it entirely different. (ibid, p. 12)

We will return later to the far-reaching consequences of the statement that no one who took part in creating an analytic field will ever fully return to their former self, "untouched" by the third. For now, it is important to note that Ogden's definition of reverie as the way in which the analytic third makes itself known enables a major technical revolution. While the roots of this revolution can be found in both Winnicott and Bion, we can now understand more fully what it means for an analyst and a patient (much like baby and mother) to "live an experience together" (Winnicott, 1945, p. 141) and how psychotherapy exists "in the overlap of two areas of playing. That of the patient and that of therapist" (1971, p. 51). This is the meaning of being immersed in reverie and, through it, fulfilling Bion's urgent injunction – "study the caesura!"

The essence of this revolution is that now the analyst's experience is also privileged as a primary analytic tool. Though the discovery of the importance of countertransference long preceded Ogden, he has taken its use as a diagnostic tool to a new level. For him, it is not only that the analyst's feelings might, or even must, to some extent be influenced by – and therefore indicative of – the patient. Rather, *everything that is experienced by the analyst during a session is a joint creation* and is, therefore, necessarily relevant and potentially trans-formative. The more subtle Winnicottian assumption that patient and analyst share a psychic field, while also maintaining their in-dependent individual existence, becomes the overt foreground in Ogden's theory. This renders attendance to the analyst's experience, in its *entirety*, a therapeutic imperative, since its co-created essence may lead (and has led Ogden) to the conclusion that no part of either party's experience is exempt from the influence of this shared, third psyche.

Finally: What does it mean to listen with one's unconscious?

Pragmatically speaking, the inclusion of everything that transpires in the analyst's psycho-soma as (at least potentially) relevant to psy-choanalytic thinking is perhaps the greatest achievement of Ogden's third. Ogden's conceptualization opened the analytic horizon and widened the scope of analytic listening to a revolutionary degree.

Though not the first to realize the importance of the analyst's experience, he was one of the first to give a real, practical and in-depth answer to the question of what it means to use the countertransference in minute-to-minute attendance in the session and how to apply this wide range of perception to analytic understanding and interpretation.

In many of his writings, Ogden fleshed out his concept of reverie through elaborate and didactic vignettes. In doing so, he (alongside other relational analysts) has released psychoanalysis from the theoretical entrapment it was placed in by the contradiction imbedded in such concepts as "containment" and "empathy." Such notions simultaneously assume both experiential knowledge of the Other and the analyst's capacity to use "discipline" to render such contact free of their impact, thus providing a reliable window into another person's soul. Ogden's solution is an elaboration of the Winnicottian one: we know the patient neither because the analyst possesses an objective method for deciphering the unconscious, nor because they can rise to the spiritual level of a "pure" receiver of another person's emotional truth. We know the patient – i.e. we have a Noetic experience of their innermost truth – because patient and analyst co-create a field of psychic overlap. It is to the dynamics of this field, rather than the patient as a separate person, that we become aware.

This awareness is a matter of discipline for Ogden as well, though of a different sort than the one described by Freud, Bion, and Kohut. Instead of trying to rise above the "personal" elements in one's unconscious attunement, Ogden states that the particular workings of these "personal" matters are the very way the unconscious connection manifests itself in the session. The discipline required here involves attendance to these formerly dismissed materials. Ogden believes such attendance to be a very difficult task. First, because of our habitual inattention to such "peripheral" thoughts and sensations – reverie by its nature is a "background" activity that is easily eclipsed by conscious thought. Second, because of the contrary – the sometimes all too obtrusive or embarrassing (sexual, narcissistic, idiosyncratic, or somatic) content of our musings. Above all, Ogden believes that practicing with the idea of the third in mind is an extremely unsettling position, because it robs us of our one true sanctuary – the privacy of our personal psychic world. It is unsettling to peer into the depths of our soul, into our most private places, and find the patient there. Moreover, for Ogden, the reverie experienced during the session is not the only indicator of the third's dynamics. The dreams we dream at night might also belong to the third. This is especially true for the patient, who, as we have seen earlier, is the "privileged" party, in the sense that her experiences are chosen by the analytic couple as their focus:

> When a patient enters analysis, he in a sense 'loses his mind' [...]
> From the initial analytic meeting onward, the analysand's personal psychological space (including his 'dream space') and the analytic place become increasingly convergent and difficult to differentiate. As a patient enters analysis, the analysand's experience of his mind, (the locus of his psychological life [...] 'the place where he lives' [...] and dreams) increasingly becomes 'located' (in a feeling sense) in the space between analyst and analysand [...] This is a 'felt place' that is by no means restricted to the analyst's consulting-room. It is a mind (more accurately, a psyche-soma) that is the creation of two yet is the mind/body of an individual [...] A dream created in the course of analysis is a dream arising in 'the analytic dream space' and might therefore be thought of as the dream of the analytic third. (1996, pp. 892–893)

The patient "loses his mind" to the joint psychic space, so that he may later regain a better one – a containing psychic space (alpha function) of his own, through the support of this joint analyst–analysand mind, this perhaps greater shared intelligence. But the analyst too, to a lesser degree, loses his mind. His dream space, though not as intensely, is likewise absorbed. While asymmetrical,[1] this absorption is sufficiently demanding for Ogden to view this "losing of one's mind" as profoundly menacing, a state that requires both analytic devotion and analytic training to withstand:

> As with most aspects of analytic technique, attention to and use of the analyst's private discourse that is seemingly unrelated to the patient runs counter to the character defenses that we have developed in the course of our lives. To attempt to loosen our dependence on these character defenses often feels like 'tearing

off a layer of skin' leaving us with a diminished stimulus barrier with which to protect the boundary between inner and outer, between receptivity and overstimulation, between sanity and insanity. (1995, p. 702)

Ogden is here stressing the threat – perhaps the same threat Ferenczi encountered when he shared his psychic space with tormented souls – and the reason why the "asymmetrical" caveat is so important. However, in doing so, he is ignoring, in my opinion, the great relief afforded by the notion of the third. It is not only the threat of insanity but also its potential cure. If nothing, not even dreams, can be considered merely "personal," if every passing bodily sensation is touched by a more encompassing entity, then these may indeed be indicative of a profound truth. It is a deep statement of faith in the power of analysis and in the analyst's ability to help. Whatever her musings and sensations, however, bizarre they may seem, the analyst is neither going crazy nor neglecting her duty. On the contrary, she is dreaming the patient into existence (Ogden, 2004, p. 858) – using their joint psyche-soma to help weave a mind and a vital existence for the patient. The appeal of this theory, from a pragmatic point of view, is great. It carries with it a profound faith in the analytic process and in the analyst herself – whose particular humanity is no longer a hindrance, but a powerful epistemic tool.

The third accomplishment – A historical presence in psychoanalysis

By now, I believe it is clear that the analytic third is more than one analyst's wild speculation. Though the choice to personify the field of psychic overlap may be controversial, this choice accentuates, as strongly as possible, an intuition that gradually ripened over a century of psychoanalytic thinking. As Ogden (1994b) argues in the beginning of his paper, this is "the present moment of the past" (p. 3) in psychoanalysis. To further support his diagnosis of psychoanalysis' moment in history, his analytic third became one of a group of theories, known as "field theories," being developed all around the globe. This group includes the field theory developed by the Italians, Ferro, and Civitarese, which, in turn, is based on the thinking of an

Uruguayan couple – the Barangers – and their theory of shared phantasy in the bi-personal field of analysis, as well as that of an American, Brown, who wrote about the intersubjective analytic field (for a brief overview of field theories see Brown, 2019). While most of these other field theories draw primarily on Bion, Ogden creatively and enrichingly integrates Winnicott's thinking, which highlights the revolutionary notion of paradox and paradoxical relation of oneness-separateness.

This is important, among other reasons, because Ogden's notion of the third stands, at least seemingly, in opposition to Winnicott's idea of the incommunicado self. Just as Ogden believes that Winnicott was playfully exaggerating when he said "there is no such thing as an infant," he seems to assume that the same holds true for Winnicott's (1963) proclamations about the incommunicado self, as that part of ourselves, the very core, that is sacredly secluded:

> At the center of each person there is an incommunicado element, and this is sacred and most worthy of preservation [...] Rape and being eaten by cannibals, these are mere bagatelles as compared with the violation of the self's core [...] for me this would be a sin against the self. (p. 187)

By proclaiming that no feeling or thought in analysis can be considered exclusively one's own, Ogden seems to be saying that this "core" communicates despite itself. However, in applying the (Winnicottian) notion of paradox to these two dramatic and polarized Winnicottian statements (see Chapter 6 for a discussion of this dialectic tension in Winnicott's text), Ogden consolidates Winnicott's achievement of demonstrating the paradoxical, "in between" nature of psychoanalysis. Psychoanalysis does not have the privilege of choosing, either theoretically or clinically, between complete separateness and complete merger. Both of these are ideals that, in the real world, can only exist as a "playful hyperbole." In even stronger terms, perhaps just as the magical appearance of the mother – the illusion of complete merger – is an illusion that babies are "allowed" to entertain, the feeling that nothing can touch one's innermost self is an illusion that the sane adult is allowed or, perhaps, required to maintain.

Nevertheless, Ogden himself seem to be making a kind of subtle choice by stressing the radical psychic unity inherent in the third; perhaps because he believes that is the hardest part to take in:

> The analysis of this aspect of the transference–countertransference requires an examination of the way we talk to ourselves [...] in a private, relatively undefended psychological state. In this state, the dialectical interplay of consciousness and unconsciousness has been altered in ways that resemble a dream state. In becoming self-conscious in this way, we are tampering with an essential inner sanctuary of privacy, and therefore with one of the cornerstones of our sanity. We are treading on sacred ground, an area of personal isolation which, to a large extent, we are communicating with subjective objects. (1994b, pp. 12–13)

Another (unconscious) reason for this stress on the pole of unity may be Ogden's adherence to the long tradition of upheld by Freud, Ferenczi, and Kohut, who proudly suggest that their theories threaten the belief in human autonomy and independence. This has led them to claim that they are dealing yet another psychoanalytic blow to human pride, one that must feel like a Copernican revolution. Though Ogden never claimed such honor for himself, he likewise sees the uncovering of this psychic unity as a great revolution. I believe Ogden (like his predecessors) is right in identifying the threat to western individualism and the danger that faces any theory (like psychoanalysis) that states that humans are never truly alone and separate, are never pristine "individuals" living in a materialistic world of "objects." Yet, in stressing the threat, these thinkers diminish the great appeal of admitting one of the inherent aspects of psychoanalysis – the freedom that inevitably follows the recognition of the limits of individuality. Now, everything that goes on "inside" the analyst is less laden with guilt and therefore more accessible and freely usable as an object of analytic play – explaining perhaps the tremendous popularity of the notion of the third.

On the one hand, Ogden's theory is a 180-degrees shift in relation to the classical Freudian position that repudiated countertransference. Ogden frees countertransference for the fullest clinical use possible, by stating that every reaction in the analyst indicates a vibration in the delicately sensitive analytic field and is thus diagnostic of its state. On the other hand, it is actually a 360 degrees shift, coming full circle to return to Freud's instructions to physicians, which require them not to replace the patient's censorship with one of their own and to give themselves completely to "unconscious memory" (1912). Ogden returns to this Freudian position, making it possible and practical by dismissing the longstanding psychoanalytic concern that paying attention to what is going on within the analyst means overlooking the analysand.

The analytic third, then, is not only an interesting integration of past contributions. It might be seen as a novel conceptualization of a very old presence in psychoanalysis, a "shadow theory" as Bollas calls it. This disavowed part of psychoanalytic consciousness materialized in the past only to be rejected through the person of Ferenczi; traveled in the most abstract form of O; or emerged as an implicit, hidden element in more conventional concepts such as transitional space and empathic matrix. Then, when the historical moment was right and by both feeling and (re)creating this moment, Ogden brought it back to light.

This presence, after being so provocatively personified in Ogden's language, can no longer be ignored. This is the third accomplishment of Ogden's conceptualization. Especially if we adopt Ogden's view of the past as being recreated by the present's interpretive gaze, it strengthens our understanding of the third as a "psychoanalytic entity, " that was there from the very beginning. It was repressed throughout most of the existence of psychoanalysis, with different thinkers giving it a more or less clandestine place in their theories. However, Ogden's generation is screaming out its name. This cry is heard in Ogden's chosen concept very much *because* the attempt to define the third's ontological status raises so many philosophical difficulties: in what way is it said to exist? how and through what medium is it connected to the two other subjectivities? In Freudian terms, this is the return of the repressed, in a form that might, for some, be most unsettling; this is the "unheimlich," psychoanalysis' own unconscious coming back.

Ogden and Buber

Let us return to Buber's thinking, which serves to bridge between the mystical and the interpersonal. The similarity between Buber's "in between" and Ogden's "analytic third" are clear, but there are some important and interesting differences, which raise questions about the universality of the phenomena described by both authors.

The "in between" space is a third reality created between two persons who share an I-Thou relation. This sharing allows them to know each other in a meaningful and unmitigated way. This mutual, in-between creation is "alive" in a dynamic and fleeting way. Still, sharing these moments is a deeply transformative experience for both participants, whose personalities are nourished and enriched. In fact, for Buber, this is where the meaning of life lies. Similarly, the analytic third is a shared space, a dynamic cocreation that transcends both participants, who are paradoxically united while remaining separate individuals. By unknown means, they become capable of Noetic contact with one another's mind, achieving a type of communication that is deeply (though asymmetrically) transformative for both patient and analyst. According to the definition I suggested, the third is thus a mystical concept, and it is similar to the Buberian notion of in-between.

Nevertheless, there are two important reservations: first, the third might, at least during certain periods in analysis, become a coercive entity (the "subjugating third"). This dynamic is, by definition, antithetical to the I-Thou relation. Like Ogden, Buber stresses separateness as a necessary pole in the paradox that facilitates moments of intimate sharing. For Ogden, however, this pole of the paradox might collapse and it is the analyst's job to reestablish paradoxical tension through reverie, by dreaming about the nature of the collapse. Another reservation is that Buber speaks of I-Thou *moments.* Just as in James' definition of the mystical experience, these are moments that sparkle and whither away "at the space of a glance" (Buber, 1963/2010, p. 76). In contrast, the analytic third is an ongoing process, a continuous form of togetherness within a shared "being" that may "live" for years on end – as long as the analysis itself goes on. Only at the end of the analytic process, do the two parties "release" each other and the patient's now more mature "matrix of mind" is once again her own.

Both these differences seem directly connected to the third being a "special type" of human relatedness, defined by the analytic setting. In psychoanalysis, by its very nature as a therapeutic process, the dyad must go through pathological forms of relationship, some of which may prevent the patient from being able to form an I-Thou connection both outside the consulting room and, for a long time, within it. Another difference which is inherent in the analytic situation is that the analyst is engaged in a special attempt – fighting, in fact – by the very definition of her job, to make contact. Buber argues that the creation of an I-Thou moment requires both will and grace. The analyst, on her part, must exert her "will" to the benefit of the patient. Is it not possible that, in these special conditions, I-Thou moments may become more frequent or prolonged? Obviously, there may also be I-It moments in therapy, where each thinks of the other as a means to an end, as an object of financial, libidinal or narcissistic gratification. Yet, in the analytic setting, especially in its total commitment to listening to *everything* that is going on, the preexisting human proclivity for intimate, unconscious contact may be maximized. In fact, the analytic situation is based on the phenomenon that Freud described with wonder – the ability of one unconscious to connect to another directly. It is a utilization and an elaboration of this – perhaps inborn – empathic ability.

In a way, Ogden's description of the third offers a theory of the possibilities of human connectedness that is more radical than Buber's. Ogden claims that everything within the analytic space (physical space, dream space) belongs to the third and is therefore an expression of an intertwined psychophysical existence. This is true even when the third is experienced as a source of estrangement, loneliness, or coercion and as an enslaving coexistence that suffocates creativity – instead of fostering it, as the I-Thou relation does. For Ogden, there is always a subcurrent of unconscious communication, even when all paths for communication (as true contact between separate beings) seem to have been extinguished. The analytic relationship is unique in making it possible for one to "sense the essence" of the Other, through the cocreated essence of the third. If it happens to be a suffocating essence, this too must be grappled with until it can be dreamt and until the space between the subjects can be reclaimed.

Curiously, Ogden himself mentions Buber in previous paper, before he fully developed the theory of the third:

(Buber [1963] uses the term 'I-Thou' to refer to the relationship between oneself as subject and the Other who is experienced as being alive as a separate subject and who recognizes oneself as a subject). A new type of intersubjective experience (a form of self-conscious subjectivity) is generated through the I-Thou dialectic, a dialectic of subjects creating one another through their recognition of one another as subjects. This conception of the space between I-as-subject and Other-as-subject represents still another way of describing the Winnicottian notion of the locus of subjectivity, a subjectivity that is always decentered from itself and always to some degree arises in the context of intersubjectivity [...] the subjectivity of the infant takes shape in the potential space between mother and infant. This space is defined by a series of paradoxes [...] of simultaneous internality and externality, paradoxes that generate a third area of experiencing [...] Winnicott's use of the notion of paradox to describe the space in which subjectivity is created represents a quiet revolution in analytic thinking in that for the first time, a dialectic conception of the intersubjective constitution of the decentered human subject is fully articulated. (1992, pp. 623–624).

In this quote, the in-between space is not mentioned by name and Ogden's stress is on the mutual recognition aspect of Buber's theory, rather than the deep, unmediated contact between subjects. Still, it is clear that Ogden not only recognizes his debt to Winnicott but also the link between Winnicottian and Buberian notions of the origin of subjectivity: both authors view subjectivity as created in the paradoxical space between self and Other. Moreover, he recognizes the "silent revolution" this caused in psychoanalysis. Nevertheless, when Ogden chooses to grant this silent revolution its full voice – that of the third as an intersubjective analytic presence – Buber is not mentioned. This omission is all the more striking because the fully developed theory of the third is much more in line with Buber's unique contribution than with Hegelian dialectics of mutual recognition, which are far from encompassing the idea of I-Thou. For Buber, unlike Hegel, this "recognition" is a result of deep and intimate familiarity with the Other's core of being, a contact between souls, which creates the in-between space or the third.

As far as the third is concerned, I believe that the I-Thou relation is more than mere historical background; it is its philosophical backbone. It gives the third its breadth and depth of context, both in terms of the history of ideas about forms of human relatedness and in terms of its disavowed (but, to my mind, evident) mystical dimension. All this is part of a revolution that is no longer silent – a revolution that rejects, at least in the context of psychoanalysis and other forms of intimate relations, the Kantian subject; that recognizes a new birthplace and living space for a full human subject: the place where subjects deeply touch and "live an experience together" (Winnicott, 1945, p. 141). Ogden has demonstrated how such an encounter takes place in the unique psychoanalytic context – both as a therapeutic process between patient and analyst and as a real dialogue between different psychoanalytic approaches.

Ogden and the mystical element

The notion of a third being, created in the space between patient and analyst through deep, almost all-encompassing mental and psychic sharing, through a shared process of dreaming that feels and creates new "truths" between them, may sound mystical even in the everyday sense of the word. Ogden's theory postulates an immaterial "being" or field, which enables a surprisingly accurate form of communication through unknown means. It is easy to picture a kind of "holy ghost" passing messages between patient and analyst. Perhaps only an author with a reputation such as Ogden's could have suggested such a notion and be taken seriously, let alone meet with such enthusiastic acceptance. It seems that most of his readers never truly contemplated the ontological reality that necessitated such an outlandish metaphor; they embraced its many clinical advantages and perhaps ignored its disconcerting implications (philosophical as well as psychological including, as Ogden himself pointed out, its threat to one's sanity).

Ogden, however, was clearly concerned about the possibility of sounding "mystical" and made sure to rule out such a reading: "in the course of the reverie just described, something had occurred *that is in no way to be considered magical or mystical*. In fact, what occurred was so ordinary, so unobtrusively mundane, as to be almost unobservable as an analytic event (1994b, p. 9; emphasis added). Ogden does not just mix together the magical and the mystical, demonstrating the usual lack of knowledge about the mystical in psychoanalytic circles. He also makes the conventional assumption that the mystical necessarily constitutes a powerful and dramatic event. Indeed, the popular notion of the mystical experience usually involves immense joy, love, awe, and sometimes fear. Still, according to James, the intensity of the experience is no indication of its mystical quality, even though their definition as deeply meaningful and potentially transformative often means that mystical experiences are associated with powerful feelings. What does Ogden mean by "ordinary and mundane?" Is he referring to the constant flow of reverie or dream-thought, before it acquires any conscious meaning? Or to the moment when the different streams of dream-thought come together to create a single moment of enlightenment, in which the analyst finally understands – deeply and experientially – the dynamics of the third and their significance?

It seems that Ogden is referring to the first option. During this phase of living within the third, before the quality of this living can be interpreted, Ogden describes the experience as vaguely disturbing and barely conscious. However, when things come together and acquire meaning – when an old object *is* viewed in a new light and becomes an analytic object, the experience is emotionally powerful and transformative:

> At this point in the hour, I began to be able to use language to describe for myself something of the experience of confronting an aspect of another person [...] A number of the themes that Mr L had been talking about now took a coherence for me that they had not held before: the themes now seemed to converge on the idea that Mr L was experiencing me and the discourse between us as bankrupt and dying. Again, these 'old' themes were now (for me) becoming new analytic objects that I was encountering freshly [...] I was unconsciously drawing on the imagery of my reveries concerning the mechanical (clock-determined) ending of the analytic hour and the closing of the garage. I view my 'choice' of imagery as a reflection of the way I was 'speaking from' the unconscious experience of the analytic third (1994b, pp. 9–10)

This quote is reminiscent of some of James' descriptions, in *The Varieties of Religious Experience*, of instances of revelation through texts (usually scripture), when a certain passage becomes a new object, is truly understood for the first time and triggers a Noetic, mystical moment. James describes similar moments involving natural objects as triggers, for example, when a person looking at a landscape experiences nature as one harmonious, meaningful whole.

Coming back to Ogden, in this excerpt, he describes his feelings of loneliness and suffocation and his longing for a personal touch. Without thoroughly understanding his feelings or their connection to the analytic session, he notices seemingly random ruminations about a letter he had received, wondering whether the envelope was part of bulk mailing or personally addressed to him; whether a message left on his answering machine contained a voice that knew him and called him by his name; and thinking about a personal errand – going to the garage. He imagined the stinking exhaust fumes and the garage door mercilessly closing before he could get in to pick up his car. Ogden tells us that, when he tried to consciously make analytic sense of these ruminations and contemplate the meaning of what happened between him and the patient, the result felt "forced" and artificial (p. 5). Then, at a certain moment, without active choice or intention, his ruminations and sensations coalesced into a coherent meaning that felt right. This description coincides with James' criterion of passivity: things suddenly "come together" unbidden. One can only be open to the experience, as Ogden's unconscious was apparently open to his patient's. Thus, the mystical moment in an analytic session is a moment in the reverie's stream of thoughts – as one oscillates between listening to the patient and attending whatever is going on in one's own psyche-soma – when things suddenly come together to make emotional sense and reignite old experiences and objects.

It is important to note that this moment is both part of the continuous accumulation of experiences in the analytic third *and* something revolutionary. It is a moment of transformation in which the protracted presence – sometimes unsettling or unpleasant and at best partially understood – beta element experiences (at different stages of mental digestion) turns into a Noetic understanding that brings insight and coherence into the state of analytic third. It is a transformative moment, that enables one to contain and think what was previously unbearable and unthinkable.

Ogden's negation of the mystical through his emphasis on the continuous aspect of the experience leads to an important observation: *in psychoanalysis, the mystical moment, though experiential and initially non-verbal is a new synthesis that bursts into consciousness as a deeply meaningful gestalt, ready to be (partially) contained in words and used in an interpretation.* In religious history, mystics simultaneously felt the mystical experience as a powerful force that strives to find articulation and holds a meaning that could be shared for the benefit of humanity and as something to which no words could ever do justice. In psychoanalysis, the analyst encounters a similar situation. The Noetic moment is experienced rather than understood; it constitutes a transformation in O, not in K. Nevertheless, it impels the analyst to find a way to give it a "good enough" approximation in words, which would serve as a truly affective interpretation. This description of a continuous, cumulative process, which culminates in a moment of enlightenment, that is ready to don a verbal form, is a new, Ogdenian contribution to the evolution of the mystical in psychoanalysis (Bar Nes, 2019).

Interestingly, despite his negation, Ogden himself seems to recognize that the mystical is not strictly understood as contrary to everyday life. Rather, along more Buberian lines, it should be seen as a true delve into that life, as being fully present in the everyday. In his introduction to Grotstein's book, *Who is the Dreamer who Dreams the Dream?*, Ogden (2000) expands on a quote from Grotstein:

"Transcendence is the mute 'Other' that lies just beyond, around, and within where we are from moment to moment. It is the core of our very Being-in-itself" (p. 301). The transcendent position involves a state of being that is not reserved for mystics who seem to float above everyday life. Transcendence is not a state of being that has left behind the concerns of everyday life experienced as paranoid-schizoid and depressive anxieties; rather, the transcendent position, as I understand it, is a psychological state in which one reaches deeply into everyday life (what other life is there?) and senses something more that saturates and enlivens one's being; it involves experiencing the pain of a beauty that is almost too much to bear. (p. xii)

Ogden is voicing the same critique Buber expressed about his "first period," in which he practiced a form of mysticism that sought to leave behind the mundane and the evils of this world. Nevertheless, at least when commenting on another author's writing – and Grotstein's text certainly highlights the prominence of the mystical, religious and mythological (ibid, p. xi) – Ogden seems to acknowledge another possibility. He "grounds" the mystical in the life of this world, describing a state of mind that involves deep connection and an almost unbearable sense of the sublime. Seemingly embracing the divine in the mundane, a "this world" mysticism, Ogden asks, perhaps with good reason, what other world, what other life is there?

Much like Freud, who attributed the discovery of the connection between transference and telepathy to others, Ogden may very well acknowledge the mystical facet of psychoanalysis, while wishing not to be affiliated with it and opting to express this acknowledgment by discussing the work of Grotstein. Is this a symptom of psychoanalysis' generations-long discomfort with its affinity to mysticism? A tendency to recognize this connection only in others, never when looking in the mirror? Ogden states that becoming aware of the third's existence and its inseparableness from our own center of being threatens our sanity. The third's mystical implications involve a continuous, "mundane" yet inherently shared life, which occasionally lights up in sublime moments of enlightenment and transformation. It sometimes entails an almost unbearable realization of the beauty of this deep and unique connection we share with the patient. Might all this also threaten the sanity of our field, overshadowing the rationality of our discourse?

It seems that Ogden is feeling something along these lines when he commends Grotestein's courage: "in the impossible task of attempting to write about the ineffable, the unknowable, the "something more," Grotstein has made significant strides where few have dared to try (or even thought to try)" (ibid, p. xiii). Ogden is, of course, right; yet he neglects to mention himself among those who "dared to try" and even succeeded – though they dared not cast a full look at where they had arrived.

The "more" and the pragmatic

Ogden is one of the most methodical authors in psychoanalytic history. His writing is not only interesting and captivating in its clarity but it is also markedly didactic. Every concept is followed by a clear definition and often compared to similar concepts; clear criteria are provided for identifying it in the clinical situation and multiple, detailed clinical vignettes are offered in order to illustrate it. To name but a few examples, Ogden (1995) claims that an experience of aliveness or deadness can be viewed as a kind of a "thermometer" that measures the state of the analysis, giving a clear (Winnicottian) criterion for measuring progress. In another paper, he (Ogden, 2004) presents his readers with an elucidating comparison between Bion's concept of containment and Winnicott's notion of holding. He further demonstrates how both concepts serve our understanding of dreaming. In *The Primitive Edge of Experience* (1989) he supplies clear, well-reasoned, and often studied guidelines for conducting the first analytic session. In some places, the argument feels almost geometrically constructed, giving the reader a fulfilling sense of symmetry. For example, in *The Matrix of the Mind*, Ogden (1986) explains how Winnicott's transitional space can collapse, manifesting in two symmetrically opposite pathologies: collapse toward the pole of imagination, resulting in psychosis; and collapse toward the pole of reality, in which one is trapped in concrete details and a meaningless existence. In addition, Ogden also points out the pathological state of dissociation between the two, which similarly results from the collapse of their dialectics.

The theory of the analytic third serves as a kind of meta-structure that elegantly brings together many other theoretical notions. For example, Ogden coins the term "interpretive action" (1994c) denoting an action that, like verbal interpretations, reflects a certain understanding about the transference-countertransference matrix that is the third. Ogden equates interpretive action with spontaneous movement emerging from the third and offers an analysis that might help distinguish it from acting-out. When possible, Ogden presents arguments that flow beautifully from each other or from a common assumption. For example, in "Reconsidering Three Aspects of Psychoanalytic Technique," Ogden (1996) shows how different elements of the analytic setting and technique should be reviewed from the perspective of the third. Technique stems neatly and logically from theoretical assumptions: if analysis is a process where patient and analyst co-create a third subjectivity and if access to this third is gained through reverie, then the use of the couch, for example, is justified because it is more conducive to quiet contemplation than sitting face to face.

Ogden gives his reader the fulfilling feeling that psychoanalytic concepts can be more than something that "sounds right." Theoretical claims can have the formal structure of a deductive argument, in which the rule leads to its particular applications and which is compellingly connected to practical clinical concerns and illustrated through Ogden's detailed and sincere vignettes. Moreover, it is hard to ignore the marked esthetic quality of Ogden's argumentation. His arguments encompass both the abstract and the particular and, in some cases, even possess some predictive power (for example, regarding how a therapeutic process would be affected by the absence of a couch; what it means if a person feels suffocated or bored in the session; how a person's life would look like if they avoided fantasy and what their biggest fear would be). In short, Ogden's writings are among the finest examples, within psychoanalysis, of James' ideal of pragmatic argumentation.

Most importantly, as mentioned before, the analytic third – the assumption that all our feelings in analysis may be relevant, that our mind, while wondering, instead of leading us astray may actually be leading us *toward* the patient – gives the analyst unprecedented freedom of thought and action within the analytic hour and unprecedented faith in the analytic process. Through the third, the Bionian epistemology of faith takes a pragmatic turn. Believing in O means believing in the emotional truth that can unfold within the analytic process – having faith in whatever arises in the shared soul that is the third. Winnicott's influence on Ogden contributes the freedom from the need to decide whose thought or feeling it is, allowing one to treat every object as an analytic object – a phenomenon in a joint field. Faith, therefore, is placed both in truth and in the therapeutic connection that discovers, creates, contains and transforms this truth.

This dual inspiration – Winnicottian and Bioanian – is powerfully demonstrated in a short paper Ogden wrote as the introduction of a collection of his major contributions published in Hebrew (including his paper about the analytic third and other closely related papers). Ogden (2010) demonstrates how certain clearly delineated ethical principles of psychoanalysis are also connected to the notion of the third. He outlines two central values that he sees as definitive of psychoanalysis: the need to act in a humane manner – from which he deduces therapeutic responsibility – and the need for truth. Those two values maintain a vital tension: it is the analyst's responsibility to find a way to access truth that does not threaten the patient's sanity; it is her job to maintain a balance, if you will, between Winnicott's holding and Bion's injunction to seek at-one-ment with O. The analyst is able to do so because of shared experience; she can "dream the patient" through her reverie on their shared experience and find a way to truth that is aimed at growth, not catastrophe. Ogden is here taking a clear stand that is not daunted by Bion's warning, that even the desire to heal can obscure the path to O. For Ogden, the analyst's job is to heal, not to strive for the truth no matter the cost. As a healer, she cannot be wholly free from memory and desire.

In the old argument regarding whether psychoanalysis is primarily a tool designed to reach the truth (either in the Bionian sense or in the more classical sense of serving as a research method) or an instrument meant to help and cure, Ogden's stand (in which, of course, he is not alone) accentuates psychoanalysis' humane mission and puts people before abstract goals. This ethic, which stresses the relevance of psychoanalysis in the field of mental health, is closely related to other pragmatic elements in Ogden's corpus and he is able to present it in the context of a singular conceptual structure – the third – that binds together a central assumption of how analysis works, a theoretical infrastructure of related concepts and a derived technique.

The downside to this impressive theoretical edifice is, of course, the fact that so much depends on the concept of the analytic third that has several vulnerabilities. One of them is strictly philosophical: if the analytic third serves to connect analyst and patient and acts as a channel through which mental and psycho-somatic elements are exchanged, what is it that connects each of them to the third? Seeing as the third is merely a description of this kind of contact, attributing this hypothesized shared field with subjectivity does not explain how information "travels" between the different parties. This calls to mind Aristotle's third person problem: Aristotle criticized Plato's theory of forms, arguing that, if connection to the form of man is what makes a man a man, one must still explain what connects a man to this form, resulting in regression *ad infinitum*. On a more modern note, postulating a "force of gravity" is a purely descriptive argument, which does not explain how masses attract each other. Before Einstein and his theory of space-time curvature, gravity remained unexplained. Changing the conceptual paradigm from a "force" of gravity to a gravitational field, whose geometry is determined by multiple masses, revolutionized physics. By analogy, the existence of a third unconscious subjectivity does not explain how two unconscious minds relate to each other. Arguing that the mind is *ab initio* (perhaps from the earliest intra-uterine existence) connected by its very nature – just as the nature of space-time is to curve in the presence of mass, in a manner that connects different bodies – still does not clarify how such influence works, but it may get us somewhat closer. Drawing from yet another science with a "field" assumption, It is like assuming an ecology of minds: while we may not fully understand it, as we do not fully fathom the complexities of biological eco-systems, the very assumption of a field, as the multilayered, multidirectional influence of multiple organisms, is helpful as a working model.

Within this frame of mind, while Ogden's claim that *everything* in the analytic field is influenced by it is a far-reaching assumption, it strikes a favorable chord with the intellectual climate of structuralism, that is keen on analyzing systems like language, ecology, etc. Patient and analyst certainly *do* create a system, perhaps even a microculture, together, so it is reasonable to view their connection as a key object of study in itself. On the other hand, Ogden himself states that each party remains both separate and connected. In keeping with the biological metaphor, it is like different organisms that share a single overarching eco-system. Is it not farfetched, therefore, to suppose that every scratch, every toothache or every idle ideation is significantly influenced or influencing the third's subjectivity? Is it not plausible to suppose that some influences are more negligible than others, like the gravitational pull of very remote stars? Pragmatically, are we not supposed to ignore certain elements if only in order to avoid being overwhelmed by needless information?

This problem is more philosophical than practical because Ogden's pragmatic nature supplies us with a useful reservation. While he refrains from addressing the problem on a theoretical level, he does advise against obsessively chasing down the meaning of every passing thought and sensation. Instead, in the spirit of Bion (and Freud), he stresses the importance of waiting, drifting on the waves of reverie, until meaning becomes evident in a spontaneous, unforced way:

> Our use of our reveries requires tolerance to the experience of being adrift. The fact that the "current" of reverie is carrying us anywhere that is of any value at all to the analytic process is usually a retrospective discovery, and is almost always unanticipated. The state of being adrift cannot be rushed to closure [...] No single reverie or a group of reveries should be overvalued by viewing the experience as a "royal road" to the leading transference-countertransference anxiety. Reveries must be allowed to accrue meaning. (1997, pp. 569–570)

In contrast, when we are inpatient, trying to force meaning onto any group of reveries, we can recognize the falsity of this formulation by its strained, intellectualized quality (ibid, ibid).

The analytic third, in short, is "alive." Its personification is useful as it points to its nature as a living, developing process that slowly accumulates meaning and (hopefully) grows. Its growth cannot be artificially rushed or intellectually prompted. Like the two other living creatures in analysis, it may linger for long periods of time in a dull, disconnected, or anxiety-laden existence. Similar to the people who cocreated it, the third is mostly unaware of itself and reluctant to feel the pain of its own existence. But sometimes, by virtue of it being a shared psyche, loneliness can be broken through and the fact of sharing become a wonderful and conscious reality, making pain bearable and even offering a clear glimpse of this magical togetherness. This does not, however, happen in every session. Indeed, in some therapeutic processes, it is very rare. But once the lives in analysis become aware of their connection, something new can happen and analytic transformation occurs.

Conclusion

The analytic third is a mysterious and "magical" cocreated psychic structure, whose magic is denied by the very author who chose to unveil this core psychoanalytic mystery. On the other hand, it is a remarkably practical concept. Pragmatically speaking, it is almost a "model theory;" its beautiful interweaving of theory and practice allows me to demonstrate how mystical elements in psychoanalysis can be understood and discussed through common pragmatic criteria that may clarify the usefulness of a theory, the pros and cons of its application and its clinical relevance. It is a curious moment in psychoanalytic history, embodying the full recognition of unconscious connection. Ogden circles back to Freud by doing what Freud could not: constructing a coherent theory that finally embraces *both* transference and countertransference and (as Bion suggested) their caesural connection. At the same time, much like Freud, Ogden denies the mystical implications of this connection, opting to express them through other authors. This duality poignantly demonstrates psychoanalysis' continuous ambivalence and painful conflict about its very roots – its core assumptions and mode of operation, its very way of being.

Note

1   Presumably, not only because of their different role, as Ogden suggests, or the analyst's more independent alpha function, but also because, while the patient has only one analyst, the analyst has many different patients with whom they share such a psychic field and are therefore less dependent.

References

Bar Nes, A. (2019). Sense and sensibility: The psychoanalytic mystic and the interpretive words. In A. Fechler (Ed.), *Feeling the Elephant: The Blind Spots of Psychoanalytic Psychotherapists* (pp. 175–216). Jerusalem: Carmel (Hebrew).

Benjamin, J. (2004). Beyond doer and done to: An intersubjective view of thirdness. *Psychoanalytic Quarterly*, *73*(1):5–46.

Benjamin, J. (2016, May 10). Professor Jessica Benjamin on intersubjectivity. Retrieved from: https://www.pesi.co.uk/Blog/2016/May/Professor-Jessica-Benjamin-on-Intersubjectivity

Brown, L.J. (2019). *Transformational Processes in Clinical Psychoanalysis*. London & New York: Routledge.

Buber, M. (1963). *The Dialogue on Man and Being*. Jerusalem: Bialik Institute. (Hebrew).

Freud, S. (1912). Recommendations to physicians practicing psychoanalysis. *SE, XII*:109–120.

Gabbard, G.O. and Ogden, T.H. (2009). On becoming a psychoanalyst. *The International Journal of Psychoanalysis*, 90(2):311–327.

Ogden, T.H. (1986). *The Matrix if the Mind: Object Relations and the Psychoanalytic Dialogue*. New York: Jason Aronson.

Ogden, T.H. (1989). *The Primitive Edge of Experience*. New York: Jason Aronson.

Ogden, T.H. (1992). The dialectically constituted/decentered subject of psychoanalysis. II. The contributions of Klein and Winnicott. *The International journal of Psycho Analysis*, 73:613–626.

Ogden, T.H. (1994a). Projective identification and the subjugating third. In *Subjects of Analysis* (pp. 97–106). London: Karnac.

Ogden, T.H. (1994b). The analytic third: Working with intersubjective clinical facts. *The International Journal of Psycho Analysis*, 75:3–19.

Ogden, T.H. (1994c). The concept of interpretive action. *Psychoanalytic Quarterly*, 63:219–245.

Ogden, T.H. (1995). Analyzing forms of aliveness and deadness of the transference – Countertransference. *The International Journal of Psycho-Analysis*, 76:695–709.

Ogden, T.H. (1996). Reconsidering three aspects of psychoanalytic technique. *The International Journal of Psycho-Analysis*, 77:883–899.

Ogden, T.H. (1997). Reverie and interpretation. *The Psychoanalytic Quarterly*, 66:567–595.

Ogden, T.H. (2000). Forward. In J.S. Grotstein, *Who is the Dreamer Who Dreams the Dream? A Study of Psychic Presences* (pp. vii–xiii). New York and London: Routledge.

Ogden, T.H. (2004). This art of psychoanalysis. *The International Journal of Psychoanalysis*, 85:857–877.

Ogden, T.H. (2010). Preface to the Hebrew Edition. In E. Berman and S. Wigoder (Eds.), *On Not Being Able to Dream: Essays 1994–2005* (pp. 7–10). Tel Aviv: Am Oved. (Hebrew).

Ogden, T.H. (2013). Thomas H. Ogden in conversation with Luca Di Donna. *Revista di psicoanalisi*, C.

Winnicott, D.W. (1945). Primitive emotional development. In *Collected Papers: Through Pediatrics to Psychoanalysis* (pp. 145–156). London: Tavistock Publications, 1975.

Winnicott, D.W. (1956). Primary maternal preoccupation. In *Collected Papers: Through Pediatrics to Psychoanalysis* (pp. 300–305). London: Tavistock Publications, 1975.

Winnicott, D.W. (1963). Communicating and not communicating: Leading to a study of some opposites. In *The Maturational Process and the Facilitating Environment* (pp. 179–192). London: Hogarth Press, 1965.`

Winnicott, D.W. (1971). *Playing and Reality*. London: Routledge.

Chapter 8

Bollas: The shadow of the divine unconscious

Many view Christopher Bollas as sharing the title of most influential living analytic writer with Ogden. It is interesting, therefore, to compare how these two central voices express, both knowingly and unknowingly, the contemporary shape of the mystical element in psychoanalysis. Unlike Ogden, Bollas makes no attempt to organize psychoanalytic knowledge under a single integrative theory. On the contrary, he seems to elude integration, even in his own texts, and, perhaps in line with his background in literature, offer a multiplicity of "free floating" concepts, a myriad of possible glances at the rainbow of the human psyche. Ezrati (2010) characterizes Bollas as a "comet": a metaphor that astutely captures his relative independence from any single definable gravitational field – despite his "travels" through the domain of the independent school and, recently, in what he himself views as his "late" period, toward a unique focus on Freud. The "comet" metaphor is also apt because Bollas seems to pierce the sky of analytic writing with an incredibly colorful, diverse, and mysterious phenomenon – which is both fundamental and infinitely elusive – the unconscious.

In both his distinct periods, Bollas' unique interpretation of unconscious processing plays a critical role in the analytic acknowledgment and understanding of the wise, communicative unconscious. Unsurprisingly, this understanding further developed the mystical element. This chapter will demonstrate that, in his "early period," Bollas used his unique language and interest in esthetics to uncover and give his own colors to certain aspects of the "mysticism of encounter" implicit in many object-relations theories. In contrast, in his

DOI: 10.4324/9781003200796-8

"late" period, Bollas shifted his focus – to my mind, in a somewhat inconsistent way – to the more classical notion of "one-person unconscious," while stressing its numinous power.

Despite this considerable disparity between his early and late periods, Bollas' interest in the mystery of the unconscious as an "intelligence of form," with an esthetic logic that is unique to each person, has never wavered. In fact, in Bollas' thinking, the wise, communicative unconscious, whose theoretical history we have been tracing, assumes its arguably rightful throne. However, the level of adoration with which Bollas' language surrounds this throne suggests a divine, unearthly being, evoking a numinous feeling, and positing psychoanalysis as a process that is, by definition, mystical – or, at the very least, mysterious. Through Bollas' lens, this process explicitly evokes Otto's *mysterium tremendum*.

The transformational object: Parent-infant relations from an esthetic perspective

As a representative of Bollas' first period, *The Shadow of the Object* is an obvious choice. This quintessential collection contains many contributions that became assimilated in psychoanalytic discourse, such as "the transformational object," "idiom," "normotic person-ality" and, perhaps above all, the concept of "the unthought known." The main thesis presented in its first chapters is that the preverbal pattern of the mother–child relationship, by interacting with the child's inborn potential, creates a unique esthetic pattern, an idiom. This idiom will characterize that child for the rest of her life: it would constitute her personality by determining the way she perceives, in-terprets, creates, and interacts with others, the way she moves and holds herself, the things she finds appealing or appalling as well as the impression she makes on others. In short, it determines her way of being, which is mostly undefinable, even unthought. It is what Bollas termed "the unthought known" – extensive unconscious "knowl-edge" of the particular way of being-together, that a particular baby shares with her mother. The mother's "esthetic logic," her particular way of caring for the baby, will be a central, though unconscious, part of who she is for the rest of her life. This is the "shadow of the object": "The mother's way of holding the infant, of responding to his gestures, of selecting objects and of perceiving the infant's internal needs constitutes her contribution to the mother-infant culture" (1987, p. 3).

At this point, Bollas claims that the main function of the mother's holding is to be a transformational object:

> Winnicott [...] terms this comprehensive mother the 'environment' mother because, for the infant, she is the total environment. To this I would add that the mother is less significant and identifiable as an object than as a process that is identified with cumulative internal and external change (ibid, ibid).

This reenvisioning of Winnicott's contribution entails an interesting nuance: not only is the mother perceived as mainly promoting a process of transformation and growth, but her way of doing so has some kind of cumulative esthetic unity, a unique form that late Bollas calls an "intelligence of form." This intelligence processes the world via nonverbal channels, drawing on a reservoir of knowledge usually inaccessible to conscious thought. Bollas distinguishes this intelligence from Freud's repressed unconscious, which constitutes only a part of the unthought known. A person's logic of form contains much more than her repressed wishes: it is a holistic structure of nonverbal knowing and being.

This is so, because the mother has not only transformed the baby from being hungry to feeling pleasantly full or from wet to dry. She facilitated integration, a growing sense of the baby's self and its nascent capacities. According to Bollas, these experiences of transformation are attended by a feeling of elation and ecstasy, of being delivered, saved, even chosen (ibid, p. 15). Thus, the transformational object also becomes the first sacred object: religious experience is born in the nursery.

Naturally, such profound experiences generate a longing for their return in adulthood, creating a specific form of object-search: a search for an object to surrender to, in the sense later described by Ghent (see chapter 2). Both Bollas and Ghent view this search as a basic human motivation, propelling the person towards a "spiritual" relationship, where one is truly enveloped by the mysterious object (Bollas, 1987) or fully known and penetrated by it (Ghent, 1990/1999). For Bollas, the mystical experience – in the sense of a communicative event, an intimate encounter involving one's entire being and an all-pervading sense of profoundly important, nonverbal knowledge – lies at the core of our existence and our object-seeking.

The sacred and the esthetic: Illusion or intimate knowledge?

Bollas (1987) is fully aware of the religious connotations he is evoking:

> I think we have failed to take notice of the phenomenon in adult life of the wide-ranging collective search for an object that is identified with the metamorphosis of the self. In many religious faiths [...] when the subject believes in the deity's actual potential to transform the total environment, he sustains the terms of the earliest object tie within a mythic structure. Such knowledge remains symbiotic (that is, it reflects the wisdom of faith) and coexists alongside other forms of knowing. (p. 5)

On the surface, Bollas' explanation of religious feeling manifests a classic object-relations view: religion inherits the longings originating in early parent–infant relations. This is similar to Freud's original claim, but with a more maternal and caring figure, in contrast with the awe-striking paternal deity. God, by this view, is likely to don the parent's form and be the object of the same wishes, fears, and fantasies as a projective, derived figure. The only difference is that Bollas also uses religious language to explain the mother–child bond, rather than just the other way around. Is this use only designed to stress the beatific (or terrific) "esthetic" trace the object leaves, her omnipresent "shadow?" If so, why does Bollas speak of "knowledge" and the "wisdom" of faith? Why is faith wise and what does it have to do with symbiotic experience? Some explanation may be offered by the following quote: "there is no delusion operating in the infant's identification of the mother with transformation of being through his symbiotic knowing; it is a fact, for she actually transforms his world" (p. 4). Here, Bollas is assuming a position that is opposite to Winnicott's characterization of the mother–infant moment of meeting as an illusion (viewed from the perspective of the infant's psychology).

Winnicott refers to the baby's magical fantasy that he created the object. Bollas chooses a different and no less compelling perspective: the child identifies a reality – the reality of the transformative object, to which it surrenders – not illusory omnipotence. It still does not know her as an object, she is still the "environment mother," but the baby has an experience-based faith in the reality of the transformational process.

Bollas does not solve the difficulty raised by the assumption that the baby recognizes (and has faith in) the transformational process that is not omnipotently controlled, while still unable to recognize the mother as separate from itself. He is keeping part of Winnicott's thinking while rejecting another, namely the view that nothing is external to the baby's omnipotence when it (unknowingly) resides in the mother–environment. This leaves Bollas' reader with the difficult challenge of determining how symbiosis can exist alongside knowledge of the transformative mother. Nevertheless, it is clear that, for Bollas, the "wisdom of faith" is knowledge drawn from experience, from an unmediated bond with the caring mother, who functions as an enveloping (symbiotic) environment. In other words, the baby's faith is based in reality.

Is Bollas implying that there the religious person's faith is similarly based in reality? There is little evidence of that. In fact, for Bollas, even objects that do not promote transformation can trigger the same mysterious and sacred feeling. Even malignant objects can engage the person in an addictive, never-ending quest to attain their dubious promise of transformation. Such, according to Bollas, is the power of commercials, promising to make us desired and popular (a longed-for transformation) if we buy some product or other. Similarly, this is why people become addicted to gambling, always expecting that the next bet will deliver the big win. Still, Bollas does not name religion as one of these obvious abuses of the sacred, transformational experience. In fact, he makes no explicit mention of his view of religion, except in the somewhat enigmatic phrase about the wisdom of faith and through the "esthetics" of his frequent use of religious terminology.

While Bollas' view on religious belief in the divine transformational object remains unclear, his use of religious vocabulary intimates a close connection between the esthetic and the mystical experience:

> It is usually on the occasion of the esthetic moment [...] that an individual feels a deep subjective rapport with an object (a painting, a poem [...] or a natural landscape) and experiences an uncanny fusion with the object, an event that re-evokes an ego state that prevailed during early psychic life. However, such occasions, meaningful as they might be, are less noteworthy as transformational accomplishments, than they are for their uncanny quality, the sense of being reminded of something never cognitively apprehended but existentially known [...] Such esthetic moments do not sponsor memories of a specific event or relationship, but evoke a psychosomatic sense of fusion that is the subject's recollection of the transformational object. This anticipation of being transformed by the object – itself an ego memory of the ontogenetic process – inspires the subject with a reverential attitude towards it, so that even though the transformation of the self will not take place on the scale it reached during early life, the adult subject tends to nominate such objects as sacred. (p. 5)

Bollas' language is designed to evoke in the reader an echo of the same sublime experience he is describing. The nuance of this description inspires thoughts of intimate, close and gentle contact, of experiences that are powerful because of their profound gentleness. It is a nonverbal experience that is felt to be transcendent to mundane life and therefore sacred. It is deeply meaningful, by definition, and Noetic – though in a unique sense: instead of revealing some new truth, it reveals a very old "ontogenetic" truth about the great transformational process of one's early and (at least consciously) forgotten infancy and the deep connection that enabled it, a connection one experienced with a (hopefully) kind force, infinitely greater than oneself – the mother.

Whether or not a current trigger is capable (or even willing) of answering the expectation for transformation, the feeling persists and may be harnessed by all kinds of social predators or even, as Bollas (1987) claims, the person's own narcissistic delusions (as in erotomania). But still, reality and hope lie behind even the most destructive behaviors motivated by the search for transformation. This hopeful search may lead to a therapeutic relationship capable of answering "the psychic prayer" for the return of the transformational object (p. 6). The analytic relationship is based on the same set of primordial expectations and might fulfill the hope for transformation, seeing as it constitutes an actual encounter with an Other wherein something new may happen, based on those old "ego memories" of a supportive environment:

> The patient is relating to the transformational object, that is, experiencing the analyst as the environment mother – a pre-verbal memory that cannot be cognized into speech that recalls the experience, but only into speech that demands its terms be met: [...] 'holding', 'provision', insistence on a kind of symbiotic or telepathic knowing, and facilitation from thought to thought or from affect to thought. (p. 11)

As noted above, Bollas seems to believe that the telepathic-symbiotic union with the mother may simultaneously coexist with a vague, though grateful, even marveling recognition of her separate function as a transformational object. This object facilities movement from thought to thought and from affect to thought by virtue of this telepathic closeness. According to early Bollas, this is how psycho-analysis works, at least with borderline patients. An object that helps contain and transform affect is part of the psyche's framework from the very beginning. This is a Bionian notion interwoven with Winnicott's concept of the environment–mother, packed together with Bollas' notion of the object's particular way of performing these fundamental roles – her "esthetics."

If we return to two of Bion's central claims – that the problem of psychoanalysis is the problem of growth and that the psyche re-quires truth to grow (a truth that is transformative and dynamic, not yesterday's truth), Bollas may provide us with a key to un-derstanding how such growth processes spark or wither. The es-thetic experience, historically linked to growth, is probably the only factor that can jumpstart the process. It does so by evoking early ego-memories that enable the patient to surrender to the holding environment provided by the analyst. On the other hand, the same implicit memories might merely evoke yesterday's out-dated truth or serve today's lies, depending on the chosen object – which may be deceitful. In turn, this choice also depends on "es-thetic" memories. People with a history of hurtful, abusive objects may feel drawn to their empty or horrifying esthetics for the rest of their lives. The negative esthetic experience (pp. 5–6) is Bollas' explanation for the baffling problem of repetition compulsion. His explanation does not derive from the death instinct, like Freud's, but suggests that it involves an abuse of the most basic life instincts, creating a propensity to be drawn to whatever gave us life in our early years, no matter how ugly a form it may have taken.

In this sense, the term esthetic is broader than the term mystical. Mystical experiences are transformative; esthetic ones are not always so, though they exert similar influence over the adoring subject through their perceived promise of change. It seems that, for Bollas, the mystical experience, as a religious kind of "object-rapport," is a subcategory of esthetic experiences. However, viewed in light of my proposed definition, many of Bollas' descriptions, even of feelings evoked by poems or landscapes, correspond to many, if not all, of the criteria for a mystical experience. The question, with which Bollas himself was also preoccupied, is whether these involve a "real" or "true" transformative Noetic experience, thus fulfilling the two most important criteria (the transmission of existentially meaningful – and thus transformative – knowledge). Similarly, this question was central to James' search for "pragmatic" markers of change in a person's way of life. In some ways, the question of whether the baby's "faith" is, as Bollas puts it, "wise" – meaning, based on reality and related to past and future growth-promoting encounters – remains open or at least context-dependent. An esthetic moment is not enough.

The epistemology of faith through the prism of the esthetic

Insufficient for constituting a mystical experience in itself, what does the term "esthetic" contribute to the evolution of the mystical element? The answer lies in the preverbal, holistic, deeply subjective and, at the same time, universally perceived nature of "form." This perceived form is, for Bollas, the deep root of faith in its various forms, a potential gateway to the Noetic moment.

Bollas sees mystical experiences as an instance of the "belief" that we must have considering our (mostly past) experience with reality:

I do not intend to write about shared beliefs [...] but rather about that occasion that a person is shaken by an experience into absolute certainty that he has been cradled by, and dwelt with the spirit of the object, a rendezvous of mute recognition that defies representation. Perhaps the most obvious example of this form of experience occurs during the moment of the unbeliever's conversion to a sacred object; in conversion to Christ, the person usually feels the sudden enclosure of the self by a sacred presence. This may be followed by a sense of being held by the object, and a recognition of some significant change in the environment's light [...] Whether this moment occurs in a Christian's conversion, a poet's reverie with his landscape a listeners rapture with a symphony [...] such experience crystallize time into a space where subject and object appear to achieve an intimate rendezvous. (p. 15)

Bollas continues, resonating classical (Jamesian) criteria for the mystical:

While such moments can subsequently be flung into hermeneu-tical explication, they are fundamentally wordless occasions, notable for the density of the subject's feeling and the fundamen-tally non-representational knowledge of being embraced by the esthetic object. (p. 16)

This is Bollas' version of one of the basic arguments in *The Varieties of Religious Experience:* when faced with a powerful, emotionally com-pelling experience, one must "believe" it. Though interpretations may vary and are context dependent, especially because the experience itself is "wordless" and manifests itself as "non-representational knowledge," one cannot doubt its reality – which is one of *intimate meeting* with the object – whatever that object is believed to be (music, a landscape, Christ, the patient's mind, one's own unconscious).

Bollas' notion of "esthetics" may add the means through which this "knowledge" is perceived. For Bollas, this ineffable experience nevertheless has "form." This evokes an association to the most compelling sensual evidence we are used to rely on – the visual order. The mystical manifests itself through some kind of perceived pattern with its own esthetic sense. This is the direct "language" of sensual data being organized, according to a certain style (idiom), into a holistic gestalt.

Unlike James, though, Bollas does not address the obvious frailty of the experience-based argument; namely, that religious or merely "sublime" esthetic experiences are not universal. Interestingly, he refers to the consensus about language, and the (pragmatic) agreement about *any* shared reality in terms of "poetic license":

> If some philosophies challenge the assumption of the verifiable "thereness" of an external object [...] it is nonetheless the case that our individual and collective sanities rest on a certain poetic license, a necessary illusion that the world we discuss is there to be experienced. (p. 15)

The poet is a "tough sell" as a truthful representative of the average person. For Bollas, however, everybody *is* a potential poet; the esthetic experience, though relatively rare, is nonetheless the foundation of being human and therefore accessible to anyone who has ever been a baby and lived with a transitional object. Of course, even if everybody is capable of an esthetic experience and even creation, the event of experiencing an esthetic moment is highly unique, personal, and private. A comparison with the psychotic experience comes to mind, although the former involves a diametrically opposite effect: transformation (real or hoped for) rather than terror and disintegration. The objects triggering the esthetic experience are also highly varied, though many might be shared – from Beethoven's 9th symphony to a new car. It is not a question of "high" versus "popular" culture but of specificity – of the singular, irreplaceable "fingerprint" of each person's early environment and, therefore, personality. For Bollas, the relation to the transformational object is a channel to the deepest, most meaningful and forever ineffable knowledge – that of the "esthetic form," the essence of self and Other. It is more than a telepathic perception of some element in the Other's thoughts or moods; the idiom imprints itself as a whole.

This is the main reward of using Bollas' concept of the esthetic: knowledge of the Other has a holistic character. Similarly, a Noetic experience constitutes nonanalytic, experiential, and essential knowledge (of the universe, of the Other) acquired in the mystical moment. Bollas writes: "the search for [...] the esthetic object is a quest for the transformational object. The transformational object seems to promise the beseeching subject an experience where self-fragmentation will be integrated through a processing form" (p. 17). The use of the word "form" directs the reader to the understanding that the caretaking/therapeutic relationship involves direct, holistic knowledge of the Other and the transformation or constitution of that Other's "form" – which is perceived as an esthetic wholeness. This is done through the caretaker's own "form" – her esthetics of being, thinking and holding. Put differently, esthetics is the language that embodies the preverbal self; it is the preverbal representation of its essence and also the means by which the presence of the sacred, transformational Other reveals itself.

Early Bollas and the mysticism of encounter

The question of whether the "ultimate transformational object" – God – is truly out there or is merely a shadow cast by the primordial mother remains open. The extent to which the reader should develop Bollas' hint that belief is "wisdom" remains unclear. It is clear, however, that for him, *belief is a kind of knowledge*, even though it may be twisted or used for pathological purposes. Like Ghent, Bollas posits belief or faith in the object as a basic, reality-based human need. He writes:

> Why does the esthetic moment evoke in us a deep conviction that we have been in rapport with the sacred object? What is the foundation of this belief? It occurs, in part, because we experience this uncanny moment as an event that is partially sponsored by the object. Further, we cannot calculate when we will have an esthetic experience. It is almost inevitably a surprise. This surprise, complemented by an experience of fusion with the object (icon, poem, musical sound, landscape, etc.), of feeling held by the object's spirit, sponsors a deep conviction that such an occasion must surely be selected for us. The object is 'the hand of fate.' (p. 16)

The subject feels that the esthetic moment is beyond their control: they did not choose it; it was done to them. Since it is an elating, wonderful, and transformative feeling, they feel chosen, selected for this most intimate, fateful embrace with the sacred object. Whatever happens does not feel like something internal or the result of projection. An "objective" Other is supposed, the encounter with whom constitutes the esthetic/mystical moment. Though the triggers of this feeling in adult life might be illusory, they are not necessarily so. The projective element that evokes echoes of the sublime is likely present because, in infancy, the object was incomprehensible as a separate whole: the experience of encountering the transformative environment precedes the actual object. In many of his texts, Bollas repeatedly stresses that being wrapped up in an environment far greater than we can fathom is the basic human condition as well as the precursor of the religious feeling. We are just like babies, who cannot grasp mother's wholeness and can only experience it through the paradoxical conjunction of profound intimacy and something utterly mysterious: true closeness, even merger, with the ultimate Other. Whether or not Bollas is hinting at the "real" existence of the ultimate Other (who, like the early mother cannot be "known" or "understood," only experienced through its presence as an environment – the world), he places religious feelings, as part of the esthetic experience, at the heart of human development. Therapy, likewise, works its "magic" through one esthetic form that processes and holds the Other as a psychosomatic whole.

This sacred encounter between one holistic form and another brings to mind Buber's I-Thou encounter. In Buber's description, the subject is, on the one hand, passive, "chosen," unable to will the esthetic moment; on the other, he chooses: reaching out, wishing and praying for the transformative object to appear. The transformative object cannot be just any object, it has a special, singular meaning to the subject. It is chosen by the subject because of the object's unique characteristics – its esthetics. As Buber would say, for the esthetic moment to happen – because it *is* an encounter – there must be both will and grace.

To conclude, the early Bollas wrote within the framework of the British middle school. The mystical element in his writing is quite similar in nature to the Winnicottian, Ogdenian, or (caesural) Bionian one. The mystical takes place in/as an encounter, which has elements of both fusion and separateness. The therapist processes and "knows" the patient through her own, unique idiom. This process takes place in a nonverbal, experiential, mostly unconscious plane of holistic-telepathic-like contact. Bollas' innovation in this intellectual climate is itself "esthetic" in nature: the esthetic and mystical qualities of the therapeutic encounter are not only told to us (like Bion told us about O), inferred (by Ogden's analysis of the meaning of O) or experienced as the vicarious meaning embedded in language and the conceptual framework (for example, in Winnicott's concepts of transitional space or maternal preoccupation and his frequent allusions to magic, as well as his "magical"/poetic style of writing). The *language*, "form," "idiom" and field of reference of Bollas' text are all strongly religious or, more accurately, mystical. Through this literary garment, he both demonstrates the meaning of an esthetic experience (by offering one to his readers) and conceals or maintains the mystery of the question of whether these words are meant to be taken as a literal indication that there is "religion" behind the religious language.

What is at stake here is not whether Bollas believes in God, but how seriously we should take the divine flavor he attaches to human encounters. Can we have faith that the esthetic encounter leads us to real knowledge of the Other – nonverbal, nonsymbolic, and transformative knowledge attained mysteriously through some kind of "deep rapport?" In other words, is Bollas speaking of a mystical encounter as the means to therapeutic change, or only asserting that the illusion of such an encounter is conducive to useful transference? Is he speaking of the usefulness of faith for the therapeutic alliance or promoting the epistemology of faith in psychoanalysis? In referring both to illusion (p. 16) and to the wisdom of faith (p. 5), he leaves this question open, perhaps even for himself. Even so, Bollas' innovation lies in the fact that he *does* offer some idea as to how we know the unknowable or experience the mystical – regardless of their ontological status. In doing so, Bollas answers certain questions about O that Bion left open.

According to Bollas, we feel the mystery of the most intimate encounter through its "form." The mystical/Noetic transformative moment manifests through the esthetics of music, landscapes, evocative texts – or the "form" of another person's character. A person's O shows itself through the entire "language" of their prelingual being.

Here, the ontological question is less poignant: in the interpersonal context, we assume the existence of a "real" Other, though their own sense of self has yet to form. Moreover, this formation is supported by our own "esthetic" experience of the Other's essence. Though Bollas does not mention Bion in the above excerpts, instead declaring himself part of a "Winnicottian" lineage of thought, it seems to me that he complements the work of Ogden in showing how O feels like. If Ogden taught us the meaning of reverie and how to work with it, Bollas shows us how we feel the "essence" of the Other through our own esthetic moment, which generates a new holistic experience of the Other's potentially transformational or transforming presence.

Bollas' late period – The divine unconscious

In his late period, Bollas declared his return to Freud's ideas. This "return," however, much like the ideas of other "Freudian" analysts, such as Klein, involves a preoccupation with and development of a very particular element of Freud's thought, at the expense of others. Bollas is aware of this and argues that the elements he chose to highlight throughout his prolific writings are the most important, the core of the Freudian revolution. The first of these is the creative unconscious, as presented in the *The Interpretation of Dreams*. This is the same communicative and creative "underground" intelligence that, inspired by Bollas, I termed "the wise unconscious" (chapter 2). The second element is Freud's technical advice to analysts (1912, 1923), namely, the patient's free association and the analyst's free-floating attention. According to Bollas (2007), when these two aspects are fully implemented, this creates a "Freudian pair" (p. 13), which he viewed as Freud's greatest contribution. Many of Bollas' books at this period revolve around the same passages from Freud, quoted from "Two Encyclopedia Articles" and "Recommendations to Physicians":

> The treatment is begun by the patient being required to put himself in the position of an attentive and dispassionate self-observer, merely to read off all the time the surface of his consciousness, and on the one hand to make a duty of the most complete honesty while on the other not to hold back any idea from communication. (Freud, 1923, p, 238; in Bollas, 2007, p. 10)

Experience soon showed that attitude which the analytic physi-
cian could most advantageously adopt was to surrender himself
to his own unconscious mental activity, in a state of *evenly
suspended attention*, to avoid so far as possible reflection and the
construction of conscious expectations, not to try to fix anything
he heard particularly in his memory, and by these means to catch
the drift of the patient's unconscious with his own unconscious.
(Freud, 1923, p. 239; in Bollas, 2007, p. 13; italics in original)

To put it in a formula: he [the analyst] must turn his own
unconscious like a receptive organ towards the transmitting
unconscious of the patient. He must adjust himself to the patient
as a telephone receiver is adjusted to the transmitting microphone. (Freud, 1912, pp. 115–116; in Bollas, 2007, p. 28)

For Bollas, if we accept the notion of the unconscious portrayed in
these two papers and *The Interpretation of Dreams* and follow
Freud's technical recommendations, we will possess both the method
and the purpose of psychoanalysis which, as we shall see, are one and
the same. For Bollas, all the theoretical developments that came after
Freud, including his own *alma mater* – the British school – are no
more than interesting footnotes to the study of the unconscious,
having little impact on the original aim or technique. Thus, any divergence from Freud's original indications is nothing short of going
disastrously astray (Bollas, 1995, 2007, 2009).

Free association and the dream-model of the mind

For Bollas, the free associations that the analyst invites the patient to
produce are more than a mere tool. He points out a constant
movement between what he terms the dissemination of associations
and their consolidation (by condensation) in a single meaningful
dreamlike moment – only to be disseminated and condensed once
again in a new way. According to Bollas (1995), the unconscious
operates through these constant heartbeats of the formation and
disruption of meaning. He infers that the "Freudian pair" functions
like a single unconscious, with one party (the patient) disseminating
associations and the Other (the analyst) listening and collecting them

into units of meaning. The movement back and forth between associations and interpretations is, for Bollas, the creative dynamic of the psyche itself.

According to Bollas, the Freudian vision of the dream process is the model of all unconscious experience:

> To dream is to be dreamed is to be part of a dreaming, which carries on endlessly in a pairing of two quite different mental processes: bringing unconscious ideas together into a dream event and breaking them up through free association. Together they reveal to a psychoanalyst certain latent unconscious themes. But, equally important, they provide evidence of the freely moving work of the unconscious, which I term "unconscious freedom." This freedom is found in the necessary opposition between the part of us that finds truth by uniting disparate ideas (i.e. "condensation") and the part of us that finds the truth by breaking up those unities. (1995, p. 3)

The somewhat enigmatic statement, "to dream is to be dreamed," is closely related to a more fundamental, as well as more provocative, statement that Bollas often makes in his late period: we are unconscious creatures. It seems that, for Bollas, we do not simply *have* an unconscious, rather, the unconscious *has us.* All that is creative, all that is meaningful or precious in human life takes place in the unconscious realm. Conducting psychoanalysis means allowing this unconscious processing, simply by setting it free: this is done by inviting free associations and listening to them with unbiased, "free-floating" attention. By producing associations and condensations only to dismantle and spread them throughout mental space and seek out new formations in their shared journey, the Freudian pair is the embodiment of unconscious freedom. Since dreaming *is* psychic being, to dream is to be dreamed or, as Ogden would say, to be dreamed into existence.

According to Bollas, there is a "fissure" (1995, p. 52) between the dreaming self and wakeful consciousness that makes the dreamer feel both connected to wakeful consciousness and as an Other. The analytic process is something of a bridge between the two:

Freud's invention of the psychoanalytic process, however, creates an intriguing confusion between the two selves. He asks the dreamer to associate freely to specific images of the dream, and as the analysand does so he unwittingly experiences the cracking up of his narrative intention and the structure of his text: in the process of talking about the dream, its latent thoughts emerge through what Freud called a process of "radiation." When the dreamer tries to get back to the dream, he is driven by countless "trains of thought" [...] The dream report, then, puts the dreamer in an intermediate space, between the dense vividness of the actual dream experience and the remote memory of the dream the following day. (ibid, ibid)

For Bollas, both in dreams and during wakefulness, especially in psychoanalysis, unconscious work continues: every text must be de-constructed in order to keep the vitality of unconscious movement: "free association is creative destruction [...] it is essential to one's personal freedom to break up lucid units of thought, lest consciousness become a form of ideational incarceration" (p. 53).

Bollas' theory of the unconscious is an expression of both his literary background and psychoanalytic erudition. He offers a synthesis of deconstructionist theories of reading – drawing on such thinkers as Barthes and Derrida, whom he calls "an intellectual cousin" (Molino, 1997) – and the Winnicottian notion that being human is about aliveness and creativity. This creativity is associated with creation: a process of self-creation through the constant pulsation of construction and destruction of meaning. Bollas offers many examples, even entire books, that convey the idea that dream dynamics – unconscious and inherently creative – are the central psychic mechanism.

Bollas' descriptions suggest a cosmological model of creation, where universes of meaning are built and destroyed through the condensation and the dispersal of matter: "such leaps are, in fact, a part of the ordinary explosive nature of free associations, rather as intensities create psychic bangs which create small but complex uni-verses of thought" (1995, p. 57). Why evoke such a powerful, grandiose metaphor? Bollas' theory about the unconscious is radical even for a *psychoanalytic* theory, which by definition affords the unconscious a central role. For Bollas, the cosmological metaphor

and the evocation of thoughts about creation, rather than just creativity, are designed to demonstrate the numinous power the unconscious has over our lives. According to Bollas, denying the idea
that we are first and foremost unconscious creatures because of the
inherent threat of internal Otherness, is pathological. The role of
psychoanalysis, on both the personal and cultural levels, is to restore
the unconscious to its central place.

This radical view has direct consequences on how we conceptualize
the analytic session. According to Bollas, neither analyst nor analysand know – in the sense of conscious understanding – what is going
on. If an analyst can answer the question of "what is happening in the
session," she is not doing her work properly. On such surprising
grounds, Bollas attacks contemporary psychoanalytic theories which
emphasize the analytic relationship, and especially the impact of the
analyst, as relational factors to be understood and interpreted:

> How might one's subjective response to the analysand be
> discovered? Setting aside the reality that an analyst – like a
> reader or a listener to music – should be so deeply lost [...] that he
> would not know how to answer this question, let's still proceed.
> [...] Neutralized by our unconscious, we simply do not have
> access to the sort of information the question seeks. Frustrating
> as this fact of our life is, if we cheat – and try to manufacture
> news from our unconscious [...] we deny ourselves and our
> patients *the fact* of living as an unconscious being. (2007, p. 79;
> italics in origin)

This passage embodies the essence of the rebellious ideas of Bollas'
second period: we are unconscious beings and psychoanalysis must be
the unknown and unknowable. Thus, his "return" is not to Freud's
libidinal metatheory, but to the Freudian method. In fact, Bollas' argumentation suggests that we have to relinquish the drive theory in
order to be able to listen impartially. Ironically, this means we must
abandon Freud's major theoretical contribution to constitute the
"Freudian pair."

Bollas' Freud seems more and more like Bion: resonating the
Bionian injunction to strip away most of what can be known in advance about the patient's psyche, and privilleging dream thought.

Through this version of Freud, Bollas offers a "pure" model of psychoanalysis that focuses almost exclusively on what he sees as free, unconscious, dreamlike functioning. In an interview (Ezrati, 2010), Bollas speaks against what he sees as the "imperialism of consciousness" and advocates returning to the "Freudian" understanding, which privileges the unconscious kind of wisdom. He does not address Freud's explicit aim of broadening the dominion of consciousness or, more precisely, of the ego. Bollas criticizes the celebration of Bion's dictum of "without memory and desire," noting that it should be credited to the Freudian technique of evenly hovering attention. But, though the "Freudian pair," as Bollas terms it, and the dream-model of the psyche are not originally Bion's, the positing of the dream-model and unconscious thought at the center of human life, *is* his doing. Freud indeed discovered the importance of the unconscious and its sometimes even coercive power, but he viewed it as a system of thought that should, in health, be subordinated to conscious thought as much as possible. Both Bion and Bollas argue the very opposite: the unconscious is both the center and the wiser part of psychic life; without it, there could be no creativity or even any other kind of thought. However, in his second period, Bollas does espouse a more classically Freudian view about the role and influence of the therapist. As I will later demonstrate, this theoretical regression creates many internal problems in his otherwise rich and fascinating texts.

The father, the mother and the eroticism of unconscious creation

In his various texts and interviews, Bollas (1995, 2007, 2009) repeatedly represents psychoanalysis, a method for deploying one's unconscious powers, as a longed-for realization of a human yearning, even a "phylogenetic search," for a human ear that is open to the language of the Other's unconscious, as a moment that humanity has been waiting for since human beings first began to dream (Bollas, 2007; Ezrati, 2010). According to Bollas, this receptive power of the unconscious was known to Freud, but repressed by him:

> Although Freud never proposed a theory of unconscious perception, his concept of the formation of a dream is impossible

without it. I refer to the unconscious that registers "psychically valuable" experiences during the day, collects them into "complexes," condenses them into the dream, and then remembers them the following day. Ironically enough, his theory of unconscious perception would seem to be unconscious! This theory [...] never entered his metapsychology. Yet, the startling one-liner in his essay "The Unconscious" (1915) – "it is very remarkable that the Ucs. of one human being can react upon that of another, without passing through the Cs" (p. 194) – can only be the return of the repressed. (2007, p. 33)

Bollas makes a compelling argument: the repressed unconscious – the primitive, instinctual part of our being – cannot be the same as the part that collects and sorts bits of information and creates new meanings in an intelligent, esthetic, even artistic manner. Moreover, it cannot be the same as the part that perceives, deciphers, and intuitively "grasps" subtle and implicit communication from the Other – the intelligence that decrypts the "electronic pulses" in Freud's telephone metaphor or, in Bollas' words, that perceives the Other's idiom through their own.

What was it that Freud repressed and why marginalize his great discovery? According to Bollas and as seen in Chapter 4, he repressed the maternal order, by focusing on the censor and on the father's prohibitions to the exclusion of the early mother-child experience: "Freud repressed knowledge of his mother, and with this repressed form of love, he was now unconscious of the mother's contribution to the self's psychic structure" (ibid, pp. 33–34). Bollas links this maternal contribution to the capability of what he terms the "receptive unconscious": "the unconscious to which Freud refers in the 1923 essay describing evenly suspended attentiveness, when the analyst catches the drift of his patient's unconscious with his own unconscious" (pp. 36–37). For Bollas, it is the maternal order, the archaic relation with the mother as environment or transformational object, from which the growing psyche inherits the capacity for this intuitive receptivity.

Bollas' claim coincides with the discussion of the oceanic experience (chapter 4), which Freud dismissed as a possible source of the power of religion and associated with "limitless narcissism" (1930, p. 72). Indeed, Freud overlooked the importance of the mother in her child's life, beyond her role as libidinal object. It was the revolution of the object-relations/British school that returned the mother from her exile in the Freudian unconscious to her place as crucially important to psychic structure. Bollas' specific contribution to this restoration views the mother (or, rather, the maternal function, which can be performed by men as well) as receptive to the baby's unconscious contents. She perceives them and "holds" them, lets them be, so to speak, or become. This is contrasted with the paternal role (which can also be performed by women) of analyzing and verbalizing, "doing" rather than "being." Given the claim that one's unconscious functioning inherits one's early relationships, it is particularly surprising that Bollas chose to assert, in his late period, that his theory is purely "Freudian" and that object-relations is but one modality among several (Bollas, 2007, 2009) through which the unconscious expresses itself – rather than a basic condition to unconscious functioning and structure.

Psychoanalysis, according to Bollas (1999, 2007), combines the maternal and the paternal orders, a combination that is embodied in the Freudian pair. The analyst's evenly hovering attention and silence facilitate free association within a dreamlike atmosphere. This function belongs to the maternal order. Nevertheless, the very need to disseminate the totality of the dream through associations, instead of clinging to its maternal "body," belongs to the paternal order, along with the analyst's interpretation, which cuts through the mother–child symbiosis. At the same time, the interpretation is a new "body" that would eventually be "cracked up" itself. All this takes place in the "intermediate space" (1995, p. 52) created, according to Bollas, by the "creative destructiveness" (ibid, p. 53) of free association – between waking life and dream life, between the maternal and paternal.

Psychoanalysis thus bridges the two orders, offering a unique opportunity, both personally and culturally, to allow free association and facilitate the encounter between the verbal and the nonverbal, the logical and illogical, condensation and the cracking up of meaning. These encounters sustain the psyche while also externalizing the "internal" structure of being "analysands" or children to our own unconscious. According to Bollas, we are held, throughout our entire lives, in the hands of a greater intelligence. This intelligence, as we have seen, is essentially creative. It is an artist and a creator of its being and interaction with the world. For example, in the introduction to *The Mystery of Things*, he writes:

> Readers of my earliest works will find a continuation and further elaboration of certain ideas, particularly the concept of human idiom, or that peculiar form of being called 'self' which seeks lived experience to realise its own particular esthetic intelligence [...] Our idiom reveals through these choices and, as Winnicott argued, through the way we make use of the objects of life. A form of desire, this choosing is the expression of any self's destiny, the aim of which is to realise one's own form of being through experience. We sense this drive to present and to represent our self as if it were an intelligent life force, and it is from this inner sense of destiny that we unconsciously create our belief in divinity. (1999, p. 3)

In this text from his late period, Bollas offers markedly non-Freudian argumentation. Not only because Freud rejected an esthetic interpretation of his ideas (Bollas, 2007), but primarily because Bollas presents a new theory of motivation that competes with Freud's. According to Bollas, we are not driven by the sexual drive but by the "desire to realize our form"; an esthetic desire that pushes us to shape the reality of our life after our own image, like God had created us in his. This drive is different from the sexual drive though it is certainly connected to it, for Bollas describes its realization as producing an acute sense of pleasure: an orgasmic-like sensation that is the deeply denied (though primary) source of pleasure in the analytic relationship. It also shares a similar result with the sex drive: reproduction, albeit spiritually rather than physically. The drive of form motivates us to create and leave our mark on the world. Freud also saw the connection between creativity and the sex drive but, for him, the former was merely a sublimation of the latter. In contrast, Bollas asserts that the need to express ourselves – through the products of our work, cultural choices, art, language, ways of loving and interacting – is the basic human motivation.

In an interview (Molino, 1997), Bollas argues that expressing ourselves, living a life that embodies our being, involves an erotic kind of pleasure. This pleasure causes what he sees as repression on the part of psychoanalysts:

> Although analysts of most schools are quick to point out how frustrating and painful the analytic process is, they shy away from describing its deep pleasure. After all, how can this pleasure be justified? [...] And as to cure? That pleasure should be a means of cure? That the free-associative process which gratifies the analysand's urges to express the self should be the essential means of transformation from pathology to well-being, that the analyst's technique should be his pleasure [...] that two people in such a place should acknowledge such a pleasure: this seems as yet an impossibility. (1995, p. 46)

Bollas ascribes the repression of this pleasure to Freud, who stressed the ascetic qualities of the analytic process and, by doing so, "uncannily" (ibid, ibid) repressed the sexual aspect of his own technique, which had been created and designed for the explicit purpose of treating repressed sexuality. Thus, according to Bollas, Freud, who discovered the communicating, creative and generative unconscious, repressed both its "spiritual" qualities (esthetic creation and direct communication) and the sexual-like gratification of its expression and thereby the erotic aspect of analytic relatedness. In conclusion, the creative and deeply passionate intelligence, whose elusiveness is the object of the psychoanalytic quest, has been ironically both discovered and overlooked by psychoanalysis.

The aim of psychoanalytic treatment: Surrender to the greater us

The notion that distinguishes the late from the early Bollas is that all we need is to entrust ourselves to this great intelligence, which far surpasses our own: the unconscious. Because our conscious minds cannot fathom its workings, what takes place in psychoanalysis remains essentially mysterious. One unconscious is communicating with and facilitating the Other. Our conscious selves are no privier to this conversation than small children are to a complex issue discussed over their heads by two intelligent adults. This simile itself is inspired by Bollas' notion that we are all children in the hands of our un-conscious. This is not a state one "grows" out of – perhaps by putting the ego where id was – but the proper state of affairs and one which, if mental health is our goal, we should stop resisting.

> Giving up narrative control to become a certain sort of subject within a process guided by the intelligence of the other may be unconsciously familiar, as the foetus has been inside the mother, the infant inside a world largely managed by the mother, and the child all the while inside the logic of family structure. The partitioning of self in the analytic process, when one gives up focalized consciousness to become part of a psychic evolution derived from more than one consciousness, is a division which each person knows, though to varying extents. (1999, p. 5)

What "sort of subject" is one expected to become through this re-linquishment? It seems that the very idea of subjectivity – as primarily dependent on conscious experiences, judgment and choices – is challenged here. We are expected to surrender to something greater than us that is not wholly understood, but believed to be vaster and wiser. Again, the religious connotations did not escape Bollas: "nor should it elude our notice that the simple self's experience of the cosmology creating work of the unconscious ego psychically sub-stantiates the conviction that we live inside a mysterious intelligence" (ibid, p. 7). The unconscious is equated to a cosmological creator: indeed, by creating the setting of dreams and dream activity, it creates the self's world and as such constitutes a creator who works in mysterious ways. The religious overtones are louder than ever. When Bollas discussed the transformational object, it was unclear whether the religious reverence with which he treated it was always an illusion. Now, it seems that Bollas claims that the unconscious is not treated with *enough* reverence and the subject's autonomy is the illusion, while the wisdom and dominance of the unconscious are the truth.

In his late period, Bollas no longer places his theoretical emphasis on the transformational qualities of the analytic relationship. The analyst is portrayed less as a transformational object and more as a *listener*. This listener is an attentive one, who attends a symphony (a favorite metaphor of Bollas [2007], because it evokes a situation where multiple threads of thought converge). Still, this listener is less of an interlocuter and more of a rapt audience member, listening to the work of a composer whose genius eclipses their understanding. Nevertheless, it is the listener's act of listening that allows the symphony to play out.

The communicative unconscious and the hidden other

In many texts from his late period, Bollas distinguishes between the repressed unconscious and his own proposed term, the receptive unconscious. The latter perceives outside information, particularly the Other's unconscious. It is this part that the analyst activates while immersed in listening. However, Bollas' exclusive focus on reception raises questions. When Bollas writes about his theory of human esthetics (the idiom), he speaks of an unconscious that, as the unthought-known, also transmits information, leaving its esthetic mark on the people with whom it interacts. This is how our inner essence radiates and our most essential truth becomes known, on some level, to others. It is the origin of the Noetic experience in human relations.

Bollas develops a notion from his early period, namely, that analyst and patient have an esthetic impact on each other. In *Cracking Up*, Bollas (1995) draws on the literary critic Holland, who argues that it is impossible to separate between the reading of a text and the text's influence on the reader's identity. Therefore, there cannot be two identical readings of the text, nor any "correct" reading. Bollas applies this notion to unconscious influence: like reader and writer, the idioms of both therapist and patient become intertwined, affecting each other in such a complex way that they are no longer separable. In *The Mystery of Things*, he writes:

> Analysands have been in the presence of the 'other [analyst] as process,' formed and transformed by the analyst's silences, perceptions, imaginings, constructions, interpretations, and vocal engagements, all reflecting an unconscious formal response to the movement of the patient's character as it uses (and shapes) the analyst. These two juxtaposed esthetics shape and know one another as moving idioms of effect. (1999, p. 10)

Seeing as the unconscious perceives information from another un-conscious, it is an unavoidable conclusion that every unconscious is also a transmitter of information about itself. There is no reason to suppose that the analyst is an exception, merely receiving information without exerting his own unconscious influence on the other. Thus, why not call it the "communicating unconscious?" The primary reason might be Bollas' change of heart regarding the centrality of the analytic relation, by which he seems to abandon this object-relations milestone in favor of the numinous – and arguably solitary – unconscious.

The apparent tension between these two positions is found, for example, in the first chapter of *The Mystery of Things*, from which the above quote was taken. In the very same chapter, Bollas asserts that:

> We may further wonder if the creation of neutrality bears the curious truth of the impossibility of transferring the self analytic experience to the self-other relation. Turning to contemporary interest in the field of the interpersonal, we would have to find a place for neutrality as a representation of an essential feature of all human relations: that the other is beyond hearing and knowing – speakable to, but impossible to hear from. Neutrality is, then, an indispensable part of the psychoanalysis. Too interpersonal a relation, one that socialized neutrality and displaced it, would refuse this truth. (1999, p. 13)

Bollas returns to the classical ideal of neutrality, explicitly contrasting it with the contemporary relational approach. Moreover, his notion of "neutrality" even diminishes Freud's classical and universally in-fluential notion of transference. Freud profoundly believed that the self can be transferred to the analytic "self-Other relation." In fact, Freud saw this as the central way of working-through unconscious difficulties. In this context, Freudian neutrality was aimed at keeping countertransference in check rather than minimizing the importance of the analytic relationship. For Bollas, however, neutrality is a de-mand to acknowledge the patient's utter Otherness – the Other as the essentially unknowable.

Another example may be found in *The Freudian Moment*, where Bollas returns to Freud's original argument for neutrality: neutrality allows the patient to free associate without their flow being interrupted by the analyst's materials. As mentioned by Bonaminio (in Bollas, 2007), Bollas' critics confront him with the clinical finding that free association is not a method that fits everyone: some patients are too sick to generate free associations; others may be deeply hurt by a "neutral" stance, as Bollas himself passionately argues in *The Shadow of the Object*. Bonaminio claims that, when it comes to treating personality disorders, free association is an ideal that is hard to realize, even an illusory ideal. Bollas replies that he had always worked with all his patients in this same way! (Molino, 1997, p. 16) This is a surprising statement, not only in light of his early position, but in light of his current definition of pathology as a restriction of unconscious freedom, manifest in free associations (Bollas, 1995, 1999, 2007). Bollas further argues that everyone is capable of free association and that it is usually the analyst herself who stands in their way. This occurs whenever analysts hold any pre-existing agenda, such as the importance of analytic relation, and offer interpretations in this light (2007, p. 17). Again, he returns to the topic of mystery: analysts focus on object-relations, language (as Lacanians do), or any other pre-existing theory as an unconscious defense against the indescribable and unfathomable mystery of the unconscious. "The result is a tragic one: the analyst *intervenes* and incarcerates the analysand's unconscious thinking long enough to throw things off. Then both patient and analyst are in a state of resistance to unconscious communication" (2007, p. 19; italics in origin).

This quote points once again to the central claim about unconscious communication. Is it a one-way street, then? If the patient's and analyst's idioms process each other – as suggested by the very definition of "idiom" – how can true neutrality exist? Is Bollas guilty of the same accusation he lay at Freud's door – of being both the discoverer and the repressor of the very same idea? As one of the most important analytic thinkers elucidating the "fingerprints" left by one's personality on those with whom one interacts, has Bollas repressed the therapist's esthetic mark? Is he trying to flee the (perhaps self-cast) "shadow of the object?"

Conceptualization in crisis: Together or apart?

The role of the therapist becomes increasingly vague in Bollas' later texts. On the one hand, he writes in *The Mystery of Things* that the patient constructs himself using two materials: his own movement through language and his unknown voyage in "the material of the analyst's passing ideas" (1999, p. 11). This notion coincides with his claim that the analyst allows himself to be affected and shaped anew by the patient's esthetic pattern, potentially echoing the Winnicottian notion of object-usage. On the other hand, it is difficult to reconcile this notion with the following quote from the very same chapter:

> The silence of the analyst, a particular form of listening, privileging the word as the means of the subject's movement [...] it is a movement that operates regardless of what the analyst thinks or feels. [...] Free association, for example, is independent of a relation to the analyst even when it alludes to it, and even though it exists only meaningfully within proximity to the attentive other. [...] Important features of psychoanalysis are beyond the interpersonal [...] Rudely inconsiderate of feelings, personal relations, and theaters of the mind, the symbolic function of language simply speaks regardless. It does not care about the countertransference. (ibid, pp. 13–14)

Even if we set aside the problematic assertion that the relational aspect can be isolated from symbolic functioning, especially when the latter relates to it specifically, we are left with the question of how the patient can "create himself" (p. 11) using materials derived from his "movement" through the analyst's ideas and feelings, if this unconscious movement (or, at least, its verbal facet) is completely independent of the analyst's personality and countertransference and lies beyond the interpersonal? Moreover, if this is true, how can the analyst possibly impede a movement that does not depend on him?

Tensions of this kind are abundant in Bollas' late period, to the extent of becoming veritable contradictions. In their discussion of Bollas' contribution to the understanding of intersubjectivity, Gerhardt and Sweetnam (2001) note some of these tensions, especially concerning the analyst's influence. As they aptly describe it:

"Bollas's hauntingly idiomatic presence, which his reader becomes quite drawn in by, is never adequately theorized in terms of its influence on the patient" (p. 51). At other times, these tensions seem to achieve some measure of integration or synthesis that may later be disrupted again. In this sense, Bollas' writing illustrates his ideas about the construction and destruction of meaning.

In Bollas' texts, the theoretical conception of relations seems to flicker, inconsistently shifting between all-important and inconsequential, somehow separate from other mental functions and potentially disruptive to unconscious freedom.[1] In contrast, Bollas celebrates the independent unconscious:

> It allows us to see how a patient is at work all by himself or herself [...] most analysands ask either explicit or implicit questions in sessions. It is as if there is an epistemophilic drive that poses unconscious questions and works out unconscious answers. Indeed, almost invariably when a patient asks an explicit question, the very next topic answers the question. One can point this out to the analysand and in this way rather introduce them to their own unconscious. (2007, p. 18)

Bollas (2009) dedicates an entire book, *The Infinite Question*, to this claim, viewing the unconscious as almost entirely self-sufficient, needing only a sounding board, at most. The analyst can only (consciously) introduce a patient to their own unconscious powers. Contrary to the leading notion in contemporary psychoanalysis, the truth that emerges in analytic sessions is not mutually constructed. Nor is it something that, like Winnicott believed, is both created and found. According to the above passage and similar arguments Bollas makes, the truth is found in the very workings of the unconscious: the unconscious creates its own problems, raises questions about them and works out the answers for itself. Truth and healing, just like pathology itself, is a derivative of unconscious functioning.

In conclusion, Bollas presents two theoretical positions that are difficult to reconcile. One posits the unconscious as almost self-sufficient, needing perhaps only the environment-mother to support its free play of meaning. The other views the unconscious as a communicative system, one that needs to communicate itself and be transformed in its relation to the listening Other. Because the idiom realizes itself through its movement in other objects who possess their own esthetic integrity, it is inevitably influenced by their characteristics.

These two portrayals, however, are not entirely mutually exclusive. Communicating and not communicating, in Winnicott's theory for example, are not contradictions but different states, evolving from and depending on each other. Similarly, conscious and unconscious thinking are not opposites one must choose from; rather, the role of psychoanalysis is to make their interaction and mutual enrichment more flexible. Bollas (1996, 1999) sometimes makes a similar point, vehemently criticizing the "cannibalistic," "matricidal," and "patricidal" (1996, p. 19) tendency of post-Freudian psychoanalytic schools to appropriate one element ("self," "name of the father," etc.) as their exclusive domain, while diminishing the importance of all other psychic elements. For him, the main split is between "maternal" receptive functions and "paternal" interpretive functions. Through the demand to choose between mother and father, secondary and primary mental processes, conscious and unconscious, preoedipal relations and sexuality, these sparring schools rob the patient of her right to both parental functions, which are equally necessary for mental structuring. Furthermore, this demand compromises the integrity of the oedipal structure, which relies on relations between different approaches and perspectives (or the "authorships" [Bollas, 1996] of the maternal, the paternal, and the dreaming baby).

Nevertheless, in some of his late texts, Bollas seems to argue for the overwhelming precedence of unconscious over conscious thought and of free association over any other access point to the unconscious. He prioritizes the analyst's maternal receptive function, which facilities the all-powerful unconscious and allows the patient to associate in the analyst's quiet, unobtrusive presence, over the more interactive analytic functions of mutual play and interpretation – especially the interpretation of elements of the analytic relationship. It is of these elements, in contrast to other unconscious facets, that the Bollesian analyst should be particularly oblivious.

Bollas offers an abundance of new concepts, perhaps as a symptom of this theoretic tension or as a result of the inherent mysteriousness of his subject matter. Paradoxically, although Bollas explores the unknown, he has quite a lot to say about it, much like the mystic who feels compelled to speak of the ineffable. The next two sections of the chapter will present some of these paradoxical Bollasian concepts to further exemplify and analyze this tension and its influence on the evolution of the mystical in Bollas' theory.

The separate sense

In a chapter of this name in *Cracking Up*, Bollas (1995) discusses a sense that some call intuition, presenting an example in which he knew the exact word (among several similar options) that would finish a patient's sentence. He wonders how this is possible:

> Magic? Not if we see this type of forgetting, on the part of the first person, and remembering on the part of the second, as a subtle elisionary act that enhances unconscious communication. And not if, in psychoanalysis, we recognize the intelligence behind the patient's continuous creation of such elisionary moments. (1995, p. 30)

According to Bollas, the unconscious deliberately creates these elisions or spaces, inviting the Other to fill them. This is an invitation for communication, for completion by the Other. Most of this communication (of which "word-forgetting" is just an example) happens on the nonverbal plane, where an unconscious dialogue of mutual attunement and sometimes misattunement is constantly taking place as the analyst slowly learns the patient's unconscious "language" and becomes more receptive. This attunement feels magical while being an inherent part of our social coexistence, though one we rarely question and are often unaware of: "in some respects it is an ordinary form of the uncanny, of one person speaking the Other's mind and the recipient not having to ask 'how did you know' [...] because this is assumed to be an ordinary part of relational knowing" (ibid, pp. 31–32).

In psychoanalysis, however, there is something that goes beyond such common relational knowing: "psychoanalysis offers two people the opportunity to collaborate in a deeply unconscious way, creating profound caesurae that 'find' the contents of the unconscious" (ibid, p. 32). This reference to caesurae directly evokes Bion's ideas and

Bollas indeed links this patient-analyst caesura to Bion's notion of intuition. The caesura refers to the tension between unconscious unity and separateness, explaining both the mutual attunement and mis-attunement of patient and analyst. Here, Bollas is not only resonating Bionian notions of psychic overlap but his own early period as well.

Bollas hypothesizes the establishment of a psychosomatic matrix of unconscious ideas and bodily sensations, pre-conscious ideas and "music metaphors" (p. 39) that is specific to each patient and allows unconscious attunement to them. This "separate sense" – separate for each patient – is the elaborate internal echo that stirs in the analyst in response to each patient's "intelligence of form." This sense is de-veloped "as the patient takes the analyst through a process that de-rives *entirely* from the patient's esthetic in being" (p. 37; italics added). In contrast to Ogden's psychosomatic third, Bollas does not indicate that this matrix is shared. Rather, he seems to be suggesting that the analyst develops an internal system of perception for each particular analysand, a system that is altogether unaffected by the analyst's own "esthetic logic" – her own way of processing other people's idioms and their relation to hers. This is indeed a state of pure intuition being attuned to nonpersonal truth, as advised by Bion, but it is difficult to reconcile with Bollas' other claims about the communicative essence of the unconscious, which is emanating its being through its own esthetics and understanding others through its own logic of form.

As mentioned, Bollas states that this "separate sense" is a part of human social capability, a universal potential which psychoanalysis utilizes (p. 37). Outside of psychoanalysis, the situation is mutual and, in some places, Bollas acknowledges that this mutuality exists in psychoanalysis too:

> The separate sense – that skill that derives from unconscious ability and unconscious communication – comes in large part from the exercise of the style of self and the idiom of each other's in-forming of one another. This in-forming is pleasing. Free association, when both participants are engaged in a mutually informative exchange, is a specific pleasure of psychoanalysis as it exercises the esthetic functions of both patient and ana-lyst. (p. 45)

If the patient also perceives the analyst's esthetics and not only vise-versa, how can we suppose that the processing done in the session remains unaffected by the analyst's form of being? How can such mutual moment-to-moment processing not lead to mutual esthetic creation, arising, perhaps, from a joint esthetic matrix? And if so, how can one minimize the profound importance of the analytic relationship? Calling this faculty for profound connection the "separate sense" is both highly paradoxical and, much like "the receptive unconscious," only takes into account one side of the story. The unconscious both communicates and receives; the "separate" sense, while potentially involving a different constellation for each patient, is hardly a "separate" function, but rather a dialogical one.

Numinous transference

The concept of Numinous transference, presented in *The Mystery of Things*, likewise exemplifies the textual tension between the late Bollas and those aspects of his early period that he could not discard. This somewhat vague concept is related to what Bollas sees as the patient's epistemophilic drive to know things as they are and, in particular, to know the analyst for what she really is: her life, biography and opinions as the logic informing the therapeutic situation. Comparing it to the search for the white whale in *Moby Dick*, Bollas claims that this drive to know "the real" is potentially destructive for the analytic alliance. Bollas defines it as "a reversal of [Bionian] negative capability: a willful insistence of evidence for belief" (1999, p. 10) and even seems to view it as sinful:

> The analysand who challenges the working alliance may express an noumenal transference as he challenges illusions in order to see the real: the real analyst, the real intelligence assumed to be there somewhere guiding the movement of the analysis. Analysis of the destructive, paranoid and primal scene derivatives may not suffice, as the extent to which this action characterizes the destruction of any working alliance necessitates a recognition of what the analysand actually seeks (ibid, ibid).

Bollas does not directly specify what the analysand seeks, but his language points to an "ultimate" sin against the analytic alliance, deeper then destructiveness or the wish to participate in the primal scene. The patient demonstrates "willful insistence" to know and receive proof instead of believing. But what are they supposed to believe? Drawing on Bollas' late period, it seems that the answer is the power of the unconscious and the analytic process that gives it space and time to work. In the next quote, the biblical and mythological associations grow even stronger: "do analysands break the alliance to ask who really runs this show? The fact that no one may, that it just is, and that we just are, may drive many to disprove the processive cure of analysis, by aiming to see through the person of the analyst" (ibid, ibid).

"No one may" is a strong assertion that echoes mythological warnings against revealing things that must remain hidden – like the apple in the Garden of Eden or the dangers of Pandora's box. "It just is" is reminiscent of the biblical "I am what I am": no one may see the face of God or utter his name; no one may or even can look beyond the curtain. Like with religion, the patient is asked to take the "processive cure" of analysis on faith.

This prohibition against knowing the "real" Other is contrasted with Bollas' saying that the patient *does* know the analyst as a process, through their mutual esthetic influence. Even though only the patient free associates, the analyst is not wholly neutral: she can be known through her esthetic "form."

> Unconscious to unconscious, a noumenal-noumenal encounter, a meeting of two immaterial logics engaging one another. To this inner logic guiding us we have always used our highest signifier; it is from this experience that we construct a theory of God from which we originate. And the intelligence inside us – internally guiding us – seems to connect with a similar 'soul to soul' meeting in the other. It is a paradoxical meeting. So deep, and yet so impossible to describe. (ibid, ibid)

In this dramatic paragraph, Bollas appears to be in full agreement with the thesis of this book, that the mystical encounter with God is intimately connected – psychologically, if not ontologically –

with the "soul-to-soul" meeting in analysis. It is important to notice that here, this numinous experience is a result of an encounter. Just like Buber theorized, the I-Thou meeting is similar whether it is with "another soul" or with the "ultimate Thou"; it is a meeting with the Other's very essence or, in Bollas' terms, with the Other's esthetic form, their unthought but deeply known unconscious intelligence.

It is curious that Bollas strips this encounter, that for him must take place through esthetic mediums of style ("intelligence of form"), of its corporeal elements. In contrast with Bollas' other references to "form" as a psychosomatic gestalt, this meeting is depicted as an encounter between two "immaterial logics." This sounds like a dualistic spirituality, based on an assumed "mind-matter" split. Indeed, in the "Abrahamic" religions, God must be above the mere carnal; it is essentially unknown, never fully grasped or understood. For Bollas, the unconscious is similarly sacred.

Nevertheless, Bollas states that we may hope for a "soul-to-soul" meeting, for the fullest intimacy with the Other. Indeed, mystical encounters are believed to be moments of intimacy with God. If so, why is the desire to know the Other is so sinful and why should it be impossible? We can only conclude that what Bollas objects to, with such religious-like horror, is the desire for *conscious understanding*. It is possible, sometimes even unavoidable, for one unconscious to know another. One unconscious can even be invited to penetrate the Other through intentionally left gaps. But, for Bollas, to wish to understand, to think we are in control of any of this, is not only impossible or pathological but sacrilegious.

To communicate or not communicate: The collapse of the Winnicottian paradox

The conclusion that the ultimate sin, for Bollas, is the desire for conscious knowledge of the unconscious, is based on his repeated statement that whatever happens in psychoanalysis happens on the level of unconscious communication, very little of which can be accessed consciously. Moreover, if an analyst tries to create a story line, he would be cheating the patient out of her true life as an unconscious being (Molino, 1997).

Still, it is curious that the barrier to knowledge is that much greater when it comes to the therapeutic relationship, where what Bollas calls "sequential logic" reveals itself in free associations. His book, *The Infinite Question*, is dedicated to demonstrating the intelligence behind the sequence of associations, using extensive clinical examples. In this context, Bollas does not seem to shy away from reconstructing a conscious sequential narrative. In fact, the uncovering of this hidden "story" is the core of every example. Though Bollas does stress that this understanding is partial and occasionally after the fact, he does not view it as "cheating." Rather, he demonstrates how analysts should intervene on the basis of such insight into the unconscious sequence. This seems to contradict his assertion that the analyst should be so absorbed, lost in in the session, as not to be able to describe what is going on (Molino, 1997).

When Bollas (Molino, 1997) criticizes object-relations notions, most of his examples of what can be known about relations in analysis refer to conscious attempts to affect the analyst's feelings or crude unconscious manipulations. He uses the word "theater." The more subtle nuances of the unthought known described in *The Shadow of the Object* are nowhere to be found in this description. It is almost as if Bollas makes a distinction between unconscious *communication*, which is the core of his theory in both periods, and unconscious *relations*, which he views as largely overstressed by object-relations theories.

According to Gerhardt and Sweetnam (2001), Bollas condemns the interpretation of the relational element because the truly deep (unconscious) layers of analytic relations and mutuality are unknowable. While I agree with their claim, I view the word relational as much more meaningful than some "theater" with pre-written lines. Moreover, seeing as the relational inevitably involves unconscious communication, this view does not explain why other elements of unconscious analytic communication can be interpreted and brought to consciousness or how this restriction on what can be fruitfully verbalized in analysis is reconciled with the aim of setting the unconscious – its relational element included – free.

Paradoxically, designating the relational element as "unknown" only stresses its importance, accentuating the deep mystery of human relationships at the unconscious level and their numinous, mystical quality. They are the "holy of the holies," something Bollas feels we can say nothing about, more ineffable than the great mystery of the unconscious. I believe the isolation of the relational element is not only due to our tendency to be more blind to our own influence as therapists; this could have been stated quite plainly and straightforwardly. Moreover, this difficulty does not obviate the analytic task of integration and understanding. Rather, it seems to stem from some deep ambivalence, perhaps surrounding Bollas' middle-school heritage.

However, the late Bollas (1999) stays (consciously) loyal to one Winnicottian concept: the sanctity of the inner core which, for Bollas, is the unconscious. Yet, Winnicott highlights the maintaining of paradoxes, including the paradox of communication (see chapter 6), that can only be real when coming from the sacred, incommunicado core. For Bollas, the paradox seems to collapse into a split, with object-relations on the one hand and the unconscious reception of the patient's communication on the other. For him, a psychoanalytic theory that focuses on relations might "desecrate" this sacred core by pretending to know the unknowable and allowing the analyst's self to intrude into the mysterious unconscious. Indeed, it seems that the crux of his crusade against object-relations and relational theories is his protest against what he sees as an attempt to negate the great mystery of the unconscious.

At the same time, his late period sharpens even further the intuition that psychoanalysis is an encounter, in which both parties transmit and receive unconscious messages, that the esthetics of the analyst is important to working out that of the patient's – that erotism cannot exist without a partner (except as a fruitless auto-erotic act). This means that the Other is crucially important – and not just the internal Other. Influenced by his concern that fully integrating this understanding will amount to betraying the mystery, Bollas offers a caricature of object-relations theory: the patient puts on a "theater" show, often because of the analyst's own intrusions on his process of association. The analyst suffers from the "paranoid delusion" that all the patient's associations are related to him, a situation that he "interprets," thereby inducing more allusions to himself and reinforcing this vicious circle. This undermines unconscious freedom (Molino, 1997), which is the central analytic value of Bollas' second period and inseparable from "The Mystery of Things."

Indeed, in the book bearing this name, Bollas concludes a chapter about the therapeutic alliance with the following words:

> Is psychoanalysis a dialogue? A conversation? An intersubjective occasion? Is it one body psychology or a two body psychology? [...] There are dialogues. It can be interpersonal. In some respects it is also even intersubjective [...] Transference always occurs as does countertransference and they are rather enamoured of one another. [...] it is all those things, but in the end, none of them. It is the site of mystery that will not vanish through the appropriative aims of categorical nomination. (1999, p. 14)

Pragmatic thinking about the late Bollas' mysticism

In my opinion, some of the abovementioned textual tensions could have been avoided if Bollas had balanced his original and beautiful concepts with the Winnicottian heritage of the importance of paradox to psychic life and theory. If he had placed greater emphasis on con-scious–unconscious dialogue (the importance of which Bollas *does* acknowledge, though less often and less emphatically than that of unconscious life), on the inherent tension between the irreducible mystery of the (internal and external) Other and the intimacy and occasionally even merger with that Other – then his "numinous" view of the unconscious, a powerful reminder as to the mystery of our being, would have been a more complete thesis. This, of course, is a paradox. Indeed, it is almost impossible to write about the ineffable without encountering paradoxes and contradictions and my own text must have similar blind spots. Still, I believe that being aware of the inevitability of paradox helps avoid the danger of feeling compelled to "choose" between poles – as Bollas, Freud and, to some degree, Bion did. As mentioned, Bollas himself voiced a similar criticism of psychoanalytic schools who choose between parental functions.

Given all this, why choose one element – free association – and elevate it beyond any other psychoanalytic accomplishment, either theoretical or technical? For Bollas, associative freedom is the quintessential expression of the true self in a session (Molino, 1997) and the freeing of the patient's associative capability is the essence of the psychoanalytic cure.

In *The Infinite Question*, Bollas shows how the patient asks a question and then also provides an answer. But if the answer is there, who poses the problem? An easy answer would be the conscious system. Yet, what is the meaning of psychopathology when the cure is already potentially "known," merely waiting for unconscious processing to be freed? An unavoidable conclusion would be that the unconscious is not one thing and not just in the sense of having different categories of expression, the object relation modaluty being merley one of them (Bollas, 2009). Bollas' description suggests that there is an "ignorant" agency that asks the question or presents the problem and an "intelligent" one that is capable of working out an answer. Indeed, Bollas never denied the repressd unconscious. But how does the "wise unconscious" interact with it to produce a cure? For the object-relations theory, this is hardly a theoretical problem, for it already presupposes the existence of multiple internal "struc-tures" or relational patterns, that are internalized throughout life and engaged in a complex system of connections, dissociations, and conflicts. According to this outlook, the unconscious is indeed the origin of pathology and the establishment of new (analytic) connec-tions that process this complex matrix and offer new organizations would be the source of cure. The analytic relationship is at the heart of the process, not because the analyst wishes to intrude his self (though such an unconscious wish may exist in analysts of all schools), but because the cure is believed to be where the injury occurred: in a human relationship.

In abandoning the centrality of the relational assumption, by portraying it as yet another unconscious "category," (Bollas, 2009) Bollas undermines this etiology of psychopathology and makes it more dificult to account for the analyst's role, which is narrowed to a listener to the unconscious – which, if allowed expression through free association, would likely "do the trick" itself. If this is the case, why do people need years in analysis? This line of thinking suggests that as soon as the patient has achieved the ability to free associate and has internalized the "Freudian pair" as the psyche's internal method, analysis is no longer needed. Moreover, why is a human listener needed? Why, as Bollas dramatically states, is having someone listen to our unconscious a fulfillment of phylogenetic yearning? Is it not because only a human listener can, in Bollas' own language, provide the uniqueness of their idiom? Because only a human encounter allows our "intelligence of form" to be processed by the Other and the destiny of our idiom to play out?

Bollas' commitment to the ultimate mystery of the Other and his just criticism of agenda-oriented analysts led him to the same pragmatic difficulty Bion encountered, for similar reasons: both view the unconscious and, therefore, psychoanalysis as a total mystery and hold that any attempt to peek behind the veil is not only futile, but constitutes a sin or a lie, a distorting defensive maneuver. Instead of such attempts, Bollas offers technical advice that is almost identical to Freud's: encouraging free association. To what aim? The aim is identical to the means: free association… Unconscious freedom begets more unconscious freedom. While this is certainly a persuasive argument, if there are no other criteria for analytic usefulness, it renders psychoanalysis a closed circle of associations for associations' sake, feeding upon itself, impenetrable to any criticism, an opaque process that cannot be consciously understood, even by the people doing it. Unlike Bion, however, Bollas *does* speak of curing as the aim of psychoanalysis. Moreover, he offers another criterion besides free association – one which may be seen as its day-to-day counterpart: creative living. Bollas demonstrates that pathology is repetitive: an imprisoned unconscious manifests itself in things like compulsions or sado-masochistic relationships. An ill person is predictable, rigid and repetitive, while a healthy one is creative and capable of enjoying the realization of their idiom in the world. Moreover, Bollas (1999, 2007) views pathology as a pattern one can easily become aware of and verbalize; in contrast, the unconscious of the healthy individual is mysterious. This means that being unique and, to some degree, unexpected, to be free and to feel alive, to deeply enjoy one's engagement with the world – one's erotism of form – is psychic health. These criteria are similar to Winnicott's indicators: aliveness and the ability to play.

Here, again, we come up against a contradiction: the ability to play (according to Winnicott) and the movement of the idiom through life (according to Bollas) both rely on encounters: idiom with idiom, form with form. The Winnicottian criterion is far from solipsistic: it is firmly rooted in one's interaction with the world and there is always an Other (see chapter 6). Life cannot exist exclusively as dream-life, as Bollas (1999,

2007; Ezrati, 2010) sometimes portrays it. The idiom expresses itself through its creations, which require conscious effort (concentration, logical thought, information gathering, etc.) as well as dream-like creativity, as Bollas (1999, 2006) acknowledges at other times. This is true of every achievement – in love, art, technology, and science. Without these interactions and encounters between conscious and unconscious, self, and Other, the idiom would not have been able to express itself. Moreover, too much "freedom" would imprison a person in a psychotic state.

All these tensions notwithstanding, Bollas' theories with their esthetics – manifest in both his evocative concepts and writing style – remained deeply appealing in his late period as well as the first. His language reflects the numinous power he wishes to convey. Like Bion, Bollas recognizes the limitations of conceptualizing the unconscious as a mere "theater" of internalized figures. This theater, just like Freud's repressed sexuality, is far from enough to plumb the depths of the unconscious. Its ability to communicate – and create – primarily its own dream, character and destiny, is evidence of a great, mysterious intelligence that cannot be fully grasped, let alone defined. Bollas showed psychoanalysis its blind spot – which is, ironically, its own discovery – the communicative, wise unconscious.

Unlike Bion, whose writing Bollas describes as difficult and uninspiring, though still something he feels compelled to learn (Molino, 1997), Bollas' own writing, his "idiom" is a powerful tool that faithfully shows the mysterious world of which it speaks. Yet, to my mind, Bollas' worship of his rediscovered unconscious sometimes leads him to exhibit a radical "monotheism," whereby he views the psychoanalytic "God" – who reveals itself in the analytic situation without showing his face – as a self-sufficient creator. He does not need a covenant with the Hebrews, incarnation in human flesh or any other close partnership with the corporeal world. The unconscious hardly even needs the therapist, except as a passive medium that allows it to reveal itself to itself.

Bollas backs away from the "mysticism of encounter" that characterized his early period and embraces a less coherent mix of this mysticism and a more classical, "religious" mysticism, reminiscent of divine revelations. Much like the cases quoted by James, the divine unconscious reveals itself to (the conscious) man, who is unable to understand the revelation or really speak about it. Instead, *it* speaks *through him*, by way of free associations, and transforms his life. The therapist, herself but a medium, allows the patient to become a more effective medium to that internal, almost wholly alien being that is nevertheless his true self. Like in Bion's texts, we encounter an old platonic idea: the person's true essence is transcendent to his conscious self.

Concluding philosophical reflections on late Bollas

In his late period, Bollas creates a kind of hybrid humanistic-romantic vision (certainly an antienlightenment one), where man reigns and psychoanalysis is the embodiment of his being and the pinnacle of his historical accomplishments. However, man is not celebrated as a rational creature but portrayed as a dynamic whole-ness, a developing esthetic gestalt that is mysterious even to itself. Though it is not a dark vision of humanity, like that put forward by Freud, it still expropriates man's essence from himself, albeit in a different manner: man is not in control of himself not because he is an animal, but because he is the host of a mysterious divinity to which he should surrender himself and never presume to understand.

Through a pragmatic lens, which entails the criteria of agency and the ability to effect change, which James deems most important for a theory to be accepted by its hearer's "sentiment of rationality," Bollas' theory gives man – and his creation, the analytic process – almost infinite power on the one hand, while rendering him completely powerless on the other. Human beings, according to James, long to take part in creation, to know that they have an impact and that their concepts play a part in shaping reality. Bollas portrays human beings as possessing a great power, but one that is veiled and mysterious, while the knowledge we do "posses" is most likely an illusion.

The unconscious, especially in Bollas' later period, is an erotic being that enjoys its own creative acts. Is it, however, an auto-erotic being? Is the analyst there only as clay, waiting for the sculptor, or is she a partner, though a passive one (see Bollas' [1996, 1999] discussion of the abandoned "motherly" principle in analysis)? It seems that, in his late period, Bollas returns to the one God, who breathes life into man, abandoning what he came to view as a "pagan" worldview: object-relations and the Buberian/Winnicottian encounter – creation originating in twoness. And yet, the tension remains, craving a new, perhaps impossible synthesis. More importantly, the feeling of awe and wonder increases: the Freudian pair is simultaneously a real, fertile pair and a vital externalization of the internal division between the self as an object and the self as a subject; the self that experiences and the interpreter, the giver of meaning – the spirit of God hovering above the primordial waters.

I believe that this sense of mystery is the great contribution of Bollas' late period. Its contradictions may be inherent: a great mystery like the unconscious cannot simply allow integrated, seamless conceptualization. Bollas introduces Otto's *mysterium tremendum* to our lives as therapists, while also bringing forward the "charming" moment of the divine experience. Bollas is both charmed and awed by the phenomenon of the unconscious and he reminds us to feel the same.

As an illustration, I would like to share a personal experience. In contemplating my position on the late Bollas' contribution to the evolution of the mystical element, I thought about the *mysterium tremendum*, but that did not feel descriptive enough. After a while, I became aware of music "playing" in my head, as a background for my thoughts: Albinoni's Adagio. This realization led to a kind of an enlightenment: to me, this musical piece always felt to manifest the sublime in sound. Moreover, I realized that the developing musical theme feels to me like a revelation, like the dawn as it progresses and takes dominion over the night sky. I then realized – or, more accurately, felt – why Bollas is so meaningful to my work as a therapist, in spite of the contradictions I find in his late work. This revelation was related to Ezrati's (2010) description of Bollas as a comet. Like Albinoni's music, Bollas' late writings evoke more than explain; they cultivate the feeling of awe and wonder that are sometimes sorely missing in an experienced therapist's consulting room. Like the majestic night sky, they evoke the feeling of the great "Otherness" of the universe and our own smallness. At the same time, we feel deeply connected to this majesty, as an intimate part of it, and that feeling moves us. These different aspects cannot be reconciled; they just are.

Note

1 Naturally, some relational patterns or moments are indeed disruptive of emotional freedom, like in the case of an intrusive mother. It is a different thing entirely to argue that the essential independence of the unconscious is hampered by all except a neutral listener.

References

Bollas, C. (1987). *The Shadow of the Object*. New York: Columbia University Press.

Bollas, C. (1995). *Cracking Up*. London: Routledge.

Bollas, C. (1999). *The Mystery of Things*. London & New York: Routledge.

Bollas, C. (1996). Figures and their functions: On the oedipal structure of a psychoanalysis. *Psychoanalytic Quarterly*, *65*:1–20.

Bollas, C. (2006). Perceptive identification. *Psychoanalytic Review*, *93*(5):713–717.

Bollas, C. (2007). *The Freudian Moment*. London: Karnac.

Bollas, C. (2009). *The Infinite Question*. London: Routledge.

Ezrati, O. (2010, April 5). The dream underlying all dreams. *Haaretz*. Retrieved from http://www.haaretz.com/israel-news/the-dream-underlying-all-dreams-1.283926

Freud, S. (1912). Recommendations to physicians practicing psycho-analysis. *SE, XII*, 109–120.

Freud, S. (1923). Two encyclopedia articles. *SE, XVIII*, 233–260.

Freud, S. (1930). Civilization and its discontents. *SE, XXI*, 57–146.

Gerhardt, J. and Sweetnam, A. (2001). The intersubjective turn in psychoanalysis. *Psychoanalytic Dialogues*, *11*(1):43–92.

Ghent, E. (1999). Masochism, submission and surrender: Masochism as perversion of surrender. In S.A. Mitchell and L. Aron (Eds.), *Relational Psychoanalysis: The Emergence of a Tradition* (pp. 211–242). New York and London: The Analytic Press. (Original work published 1990).

Molino, A. (1997). *Freely Associated*. New York: Free Association Books.

Chapter 9

Eigen: Faith and turbulence – The psychoanalytic mystic

Little analysis is required in order to uncover the mystical element in Michael Eigen's prolific writings. Eigen himself explicitly proclaims its presence, viewing himself as a part of a "budding culture of psychoanalytic mystics, more of whom may be coming out of the closet" (Mitchell and Aron, 1999, p. 1). This is a modest statement, for Eigen is one of the main driving forces of this "budding culture." Moreover, as one of the prominent voices in contemporary psychoanalysis, he may have greatly facilitated the choice of other authors to "come out of the closet" – the present book included.

In his interview with Eigen, Molino (1997) offers the following description:

> All your writing is imbued with a deeply charged sense of religiosity, of mystery and wonder. There is throughout the evident sensibility of the mystic. You speak of Bion as a mystic; you often cite Buber's *I and Thou* and speak of the co-union and communication, not only of self and other, but of self and God [...] This kind of language, this kind of revelation [...] is courageous on the part of an analyst. (p. 107)

Eigen is indeed courageous; he willingly shares his deep, idiosyncratic religiosity and mystical experiences with his readers. Therefore, I am spared the burden of proving the presence of the mystical element as far as his writings are concerned. Instead, this chapter examines how an explicit (Eigenian) mystical element looks like and how it affects psychoanalysis. I will argue that, in some ways, Eigen completes and brings to fruition the process by which the mystical element in

DOI: 10.4324/9781003200796-9

psychanalysis made its appearance, became suppressed and found various modes of immersion and transformation, as traced throughout this book. This achievement is due, among other things, to the fact that Eigen is a true and committed practitioner of the analytic (originally, ancient Greek) directive: "know thyself." He is not ashamed of owning his mystical part (as well as his aggressive and sexual parts), both as a person and as an analyst or theoretician. Secondly, he contributes to the meta-theoretical work of shedding new light on the long unsettled and unsettling question about the epistemological foundation of psychoanalysis and especially "mystical psychoanalysis." As the discussion will demonstrate, Eigen is not only a successor of the British object-relations school but, knowingly or unknowingly, his views on psychoanalysis and the question of knowledge in general echo the American pragmatic tradition. It is only fitting, then, that the chapter devoted to Eigen should be the closing chapter of this book, completing its circle.

After analyzing some of Eigen's contributions, his various mystical concepts and mystically-oriented theorizing – his notion of psychosis, destructiveness, the ideal and the human face – this chapter will present a threefold analysis of Eigen's notion of mysticism. Furthermore, it will be argued that Eigen's conceptualization of the mystical experience is underpinned by his belief in a mystical ontology of a pluralistic yet unified reality. A meta-theoretical analysis of Eigen's epistemology of faith and how it is counterbalanced by a pragmatic approach follows, pointing out that, while Eigen explicitly strives for a balance between the mystical and the pragmatic, his informal style clearly tilts to the first. While his evocative style offers a deeply emotional, almost first-hand experience of the mystical, this may hinder the understanding, acceptance and assimilation of the mystical in psychoanalytic culture. As this chapter shows, Eigen promotes a vital rebirth of the mystical element as a paradoxical experience in a paradoxical psyche. Yet, by assuming an extremely pluralistic, almost all-inclusive stance towards the theorization of experience (especially mystical experience), he occasionally lapses into some of the epistemological traps he himself warns against.

Basic assumptions

Like Ogden and Bollas, Eigen is deeply influenced by Bion and Winnicott. He names them, alongside Lacan, as his main sources of analytic inspiration and his many books are dedicated to a re-envisioning of some of their key ideas. A central issue Eigen (1998) often discusses is the limits of containment:

> What is in stake is whether an individual (or group) can take its own capacity for experiencing. To what extent its emotional life and mental life in general, too much for us? How much of ourselves can we take and allow to develop? Can we do so in life giving ways? How do we relate to our destructive tendencies? How best we make room for ourselves? Are we creatures destined to always have low tolerance for ourselves, or can tolerance for ourselves and each other truly grow? (pp. 73–74)

These questions resurface in various forms in all of his texts. It can be argued that Eigen's chief concern is the quest of fully encountering human experience, including its mystical facets. Eigen follows in Bion's footsteps by viewing the central mission of individual life and the broader task of human civilization as one and the same: developing openness and tolerance to experience, without escaping its paradoxical nature or "choosing sides" (Eigen, 1993a, 1993b, 1998, 2004, 2012). Following Winnicott, Eigen sees human experience as inherently paradoxical and this idea becomes a pillar of his theory, deeply affecting his notion of the mystical.

The mystical experience is a field that particularly interests Eigen, both as a unique experience or, more accurately, a unique range of experience, and as a basic characteristic of being. Like James, Eigen treats mystical experience (or any other experience) as an unavoidable epistemological anchor and even celebrates it as an expression of psychic richness. Loyal to his values, Eigen does not choose which experiences are "valid" or better correspond to "reality," suggesting instead that we should examine the relations between experiences rather than "side with" one of them. Health is about the personality's ability to give every experience its proper "voice," with reference to what is perceived as the "outside" – empirical reality. This perpetual balancing act is what Eigen (1998, p. 57) calls Winnicott's "democratic self." The key role of experience in Eigen's thinking and his reverential treatment of experiencing can be seen as a psychoanalytic version of James' radical empiricism, where human experience is "the pillar of (the real as well as the perceived) universe."

Self and other

For Eigen, the self is dynamic. It moves between different, even contradictory positions, experiences and ways of being and, above all, between the poles of self and Other. One of Eigen's central claims, based on his reading of Winnicott, is that self and Other were always there, as the eternal coordinates that define psychic space throughout our lifetime. He thereby resembles Ogden (1994), who views Winnicott's statement – "there is no such thing as an infant" as "playfully hyperbolic" (p. 4). Though self and Other constantly change in relation to each other, especially at different developmental moments, they are always present: not only from the perspective of "external" reality, but also as the prerequisite poles of experience. The elimination of one of these poles amounts to a pathological defense mechanism or a theoretical fiction, such as psychoanalytic notions of early mother-baby unity. According to Eigen, while such fictions accentuate an important facet of experience, they should not be taken literally:

> The notion of a wholly undifferentiated state was not found to be useful as a clinical concept. In actual clinical experience areas of union and distinction are always found together. Pure union and pure distinction are abstract concepts which do not characterize living experience. [...] It seems fairer to say that a basic ambiguity – a simultaneity of areas of distinctness and union – represents an essential structure of human subjectivity, whatever developmental level. If one tries to push beyond these poles, the sense of self must disappear: to be undifferentiated and exist is not possible. (1993a, p. 57)

This quote is one of the most decisive passages in Eigen's writings. As will be elaborated later, Eigen tends towards theoretical pluralism and sometimes refrains from such clear-cut assertions. Still, on this topic, his opinion is unequivocal: the distinctness-union tension is the psyche's basic structure and the psyche must bear this tension, moving between its poles, for as long as we live. Like Ogden, Eigen believes that the collapse of this movement creates pathology. In its extreme form, it leads to psychosis wherein the self ceases to exist.

According to Eigen, the notion of a nurturing unity, from which the self is said to emerge, is only meaningful if some kind of self – one that enjoys this enveloping protection and feels the support of the nurturing Other – has existed all along. In the beginning, the sense of self is perhaps vague and more dependent on the support of the Other – an Other equally amorphous and diffuse, whose contours alternatively emerge from and become submerged in a primordial, mostly un-differentiated experience. The presence of this Other was nonetheless felt as an essential precondition to any experience, especially mystical ones: "for many mystics, the difference between self and God is what makes union possible" (1998, p. 36).

Psychosis

Eigen's understanding of psychosis stems directly from his distinction-union assumption. His book, *The Psychotic Core*, presents a theore-tical framework by which the human personality dwells in these deli-cate self-other and mind-body tensions. Eigen then draws several original conclusions that are particularly relevant to the understanding of Eigenian mysticism. The first is that psychosis is a result of the failure to manage these tensions and the ensuing collapse to either side of the paradox: the psychotic person cannot bear living inside their body and therefore disperses into infinite particles that are lost in space; alternative, they cannot bear living beyond bodily concerns, so that their selfhood contracts and collapses into specific body parts (typically the reproductive or excretory orifices); the psychotic may feel merged with others or lead a schizoid life, in which no one is real but themselves. Though the other pole is always there in the background, the psychotic cannot bear this reality and must "choose sides." By intensifying or nullifying one part of experience, the psychotic destroys the possibility to form meaning, which requires more than one di-mension. The dire consequence is the destruction of the psyche itself.

While many proponents of the "middle school" would agree with the first claim, the second claim – though based on the first – is an extremely rebellious notion, namely, that mental health depends on a balance between the material and the immaterial – the spiritual. One must experience herself both as an organism and as a being that transcends its body. Eigen is here drawing on the relatively forgotten Paul Fedren (1926, in Eigen, 1993a), Freud's contemporary who believed that the "mental ego feeling is the first to be experienced by the child; ego feeling related to the body and to perception conveyed through the body come only gradually" (ibid, p. 143).

Eigen explains that, according to Federn's reasoning, since the feeling of self may expand or contract so as to include or exclude the body, it cannot be considered a mere derivative of the latter.

> If Federn's formulations are taken seriously, therapeutic work should help the individual interact with and build a creative tolerance for his dual sense of boundlessness-limits or cosmic and practical I-feeling. One task is to allow the larger and the smaller "I" to adapt to one another, to give each its due. Each has a story to tell, a life to live, and much to contribute. (1993a, p. 146)

According to Federn, the psychotic person is one who never entered their own body. The complementary view offered by Eigen is that a person who lives solely in their body – identifying with it completely – is also ill. In most of psychoanalytic thought, the first rift is from the mother's body. For Federn, who was influenced by gnostic thought, the soul must be lured into the body and the first rift thus takes place before leaving the womb:

> Our experience would not be what it is without a double sense of materiality – immateriality. It is part of what gives our experience its resonance, depth and elusiveness. We move in and out of ourselves as if we were air, yet we also meet with resistance. Our thoughts are at once clouds and stones. Our flesh melts but our muscles hold their ground. We are one two, three, infinity… Our mysterious I feeling spreads through earth and heaven. For Freud it comes from the body. For Federn, it moves towards the body. Where is its point of origin? We grow and fade in the mystery of doubleness. (1993b, p. 147)

And further:

> The mystery of doubleness is nowhere more intensely encoun-
> tered than in our sense of self and other. We feel both connected
> with, yet separate from ourselves and others. In mystical
> communion (co-union) the self feels wholly in union, yet distinct
> at the same time. At deep levels of our being, we feel part of
> others, and others part of us, yet we also maintain areas of
> difference. We may swing back and forth, now emphasizing the
> dimension of union, now that of difference whereas the two
> belong together and make each other possible. Take away
> either, and the self would disappear. (ibid, ibid)

These quotes are a faithful example of both the style and spirit of
Eigen's writings. His poetic ability is evident and fits well with his
contents, which repeatedly stress the tensions and paradoxes of human
existence. These tensions are also found in every theoretical claim, as
Eigen regularly presents both poles and shows how not to choose sides
– even within the same sentence. The poetic genre is perhaps the best
container for such a message: We are both rock and cloud.

The Eigenian mystical moment is the unity that shines, paradoxically, against the background of irreducible Otherness or vise-
versa. Among other forms of experience, the fully sentient self is
capable of having mystical experiences – which may demonstrate the
paradoxes of our existence better than any other type. This view is, of
course, closely related to that of Buber, who stresses the paradox of
preservation and the growth of the individual personality in the
blissful and fleeting moments of the I-Thou encounter. Indeed, Eigen
often mentions Buber, though without really exploring theoretically
the interface between their thinking, relies on his favorite Buberian
quote: "all real living is meeting."

In one way or another, psychosis refuses meeting. The psychic and
the bodily, the physical and spiritual, are each other's constituting
Others. While fundamentally different, they constitute a unity: the living
human organism. Becoming detached or split-off from one's body is a
known and often-discussed pathology in psychoanalysis, but its counterpart, being split-off from one's spirit is ironically unmentioned. This
idea was presented more palatably by Ogden, who spoke of the collapse

towards the pole of reality as negating imaginative life and, therefore, the psyche. Eigen takes this idea a step further by addressing the rejection of the spiritual and immaterial, not only the psychic.

This is more than semantics. Both Ogden and Eigen believe that the tension between the internal and external worlds constitutes psychic life and both explore the place where these worlds meet. Both believe that being human means living with the moment-to-moment struggle to reconcile them. However, Eigen is the one who unreservedly declares that one pole is not more "real" then the other. It is not just that we should protect fantasy life and illusion from being wiped out by the demands of "reality" and ensure their mutual enrichment. We are dealing with a spiritual, immaterial reality with ontological "rights" that are equal to those of its material counterpart and that makes similar demands on our "internal" world. For Eigen, giving up our "spiritual" self is a psychotic act, tantamount to sacrificing a critical aspect of reality.

It seems that Eigen is highlighting Winnicott's view of man as a paradoxical creature, while pulling on a hidden thread concerning psychic paradoxes to offer a wider understanding of reality. Human beings are creatures of both an "earthly" and "spiritual" nature, both material and immaterial, living out an inherently paradoxical existence. This nuance may not seem that foreign in a relational context, but it is nevertheless revolutionary: the mystical is not only a possibility within the wide range of human experience, but part of our being, our developmental journey and the formation of our personality.

Eigen's third claim about psychosis, from which the book derives its title, is that we all have a psychotic core. We all are afraid of some reality (inner or outer, corporeal or spiritual) and we all, to some degree, reject parts of it, refusing certain meetings. Eigen emphatically rejects the early psychoanalytic view that psychosis is unanalyzable, showing how Freud and especially object-relations theorists based their theories of the personality on the understanding of the psychotic part. Even Freud, who believed psychosis could not be treated analytically, established a connection between the psychotic and non-psychotic personality in the form of dream-life. Moreover, says Eigen, Freud's structural theory describes psychic structures designed to handle psychosis, instincts and overwhelming guilt, alongside the painful need to accept reality as it is.

Still, Eigenian "reality" is wider than most analysts are willing to admit. This difference stems from a wider cultural choice, which makes one type of "psychotic" pay a much heavier price than "normal" people who, in his view, are just as sick:

> One marvels, however at the precision and thoroughness of the accomplishment. With the surefootedness of a phobic cat, this psychotic subject steers clear of all signs of the ineffable, often employing a bizarre version of "common sense" as an allay. Meanwhile, his brothers on the other side of the coin wave to him from the wings of the world that threatens to blast them beyond space. We are all projects between these extremes, and the extremes as well. (ibid, ibid)

It is curious how a phobic animal was used at the dawn of psycho-analysis to illustrate the results of repressing the reality of sexuality (Freud's "Little Hans") and is now being used to illustrate the disavowal of the spiritual. In both cases, the individual suffers from the illness of their society – a society that represses some part of being human. Undoubtedly, the "normal psychotics" have made the more sensible choice in what Eigen sees as a psychotic culture.

Evil and the ideal: God and the devil in culture and the human psyche

For Eigen, the numinous is a part of our lives: we live among true good and evil, both of which have a share in our soul, but neither can be reduced to psychoanalytic explanations. Eigen devoted much of his work to understanding the relation of the human psyche to these forces. The next three subsections discuss the way Eigen grappled with these historically religious ideas, giving them a "psychoanalytic flavor" as well as transforming the essence of psychoanalysis by introducing it to God and the Devil.

Destruction

In *The Psychotic Core*, Eigen (1993b) writes:

> To discuss issues of human aggression solely in practical, realistic terms is to miss the mystical, cosmic underpinning of affects. We

are destined to fail in our management of ourselves as long as we downplay one or the other term of experience. It is as mad to disregard the numinous in daily affairs as it is to turn away from the pressing requirements of social-political-economic factors. (p. 211)

This bold claim, made in the context of a psychoanalytic text about psychosis, signifies a new era in psychoanalytic thought. It fully accepts destruction as an omnipresent force, without attempting to explain it away in terms of defense mechanisms or blind instincts, which are neither "good" nor "evil" in themselves. Instead of supposing, like other analytic authors, that God and the Devil are but split-off and projected parts of our own human nature, Eigen sees them as essential facets of reality – of human reality, but with a clear hint of something beyond. Eigen makes the refreshing (and logical) claim that knowing about splitting does not necessarily "explain away" God or the Devil. However, acknowledging the reality of the diabolical does not mean going back to exorcisms and resorting to blaming demons. Rather, Eigen suggests a deeper sense of responsibility: acknowledging what is beyond us as part of our life-long journey to live with what we cannot dominate, eliminate or explain away. It may be said that his "religious" battle against evil requires a deep psychoanalytic understanding.

Eigen maintains that human destructiveness grows more powerful through our attempts to get rid of it. This, in itself, is a well-known Kleinian notion: "evil" is projected onto another object, which then perceived as an external prosecutor, inspiring more fear. But Eigen takes this a few steps further, not only in suggesting the autonomous ontological structure of good and evil, but in maintaining that materialistic culture attempts to deny not only the numinous, but psychic life itself. The psyche's immateriality is a threat to materialistic values. In the resulting attempt to kill the psychic or the immaterial, everything that is emotionally intense, spiritual, idiosyncratic or even painful (let alone violent) is cast aside and given little chance for proper containment and growth. Technocratic culture thus blocks our ability to become fully aware of the evil within us, precluding our ability to process it and mitigate its influence.

Eigen demonstrates what he means by this attempt to "kill" the psychic by discussing different approaches to mental illness. According to Eigen, the psychiatric drug industry shuts down experience. In doing so, it allows many psychotic individuals to function, at the price of blocking their potential to transform and evolve their experience. This practice stems from a materialistic ideology that reduces the human to a byproduct of chemical reactions, a manipulable effect. Even inside the "psychological" establishment, Eigen (Eigen and Govrin, 2007) sees forces that portray the human personality as a programmable machine comprised of impulses and reactions. These forces, in collusion with insurance companies, are waging war against psychoanalysis. For Eigen, the goal of psychoanalysis is to facilitate *openness to experience*, to allow experience to unfold over time, to take its "place" and be "heard" in the psyche. This is the only way for it to create dialogue with other experiences and to evolve. According to Eigen, attacks against psychoanalysis result from an inability to do just that: they constitute a defense against the overwhelming fear of the numinous and the ineffable in human experience, which psychoanalysis deals with. He explains that "you *have* to reduce complexity, nuance and fullness [...] to fit what your techniques allow you to talk about [...] a next step is devaluing experience the machine can't pick up [...] a further step is saying such experiences don't really exist" (Eigen and Govrin, 2007, p. 14).

Eigen states that he is not opposed to scientific study or the accumulation of knowledge, avowing that the scientific value of doubt is essential. What he decries is the opposite: the lack of doubt, the inability for modesty, the "psychotic" mind that does not recognize its own limitations and presumes to dismiss what it cannot explain. Eigen often warns against the delusion of omniscience, which he views as the psychotic, even sociopathic facet of culture. Coupled with the human proclivity for destructiveness and reinforced by modern technology, this pseudo-omniscience is an apocalyptic threat (Eigen, 1993b; Molino, 1997; Eigen and Govrin, 2007). Without recognizing the real evil within us, we stand little chance against it.

The face

Another of Eigen's original contributions concerns ideal experience and a novel appreciation of the centrality of the human face. As in the case of destruction, Eigen argues that the experience of the divine and the sublime should be respected in itself and not treated as a derivative of something else. Just as divinity should not be reduced to humanity, humanity should not be reduced to its animalistic, bodily facet. He protests the reducing of the mother (or Otherness in general) to "the breast," offering instead a more holistic representative of the human Other: the face. Eigen reviews the history of analytic writing about the face, and contrasts it with the works of the philosopher Levinas:

> Levinas... has developed one of the most extended accounts of the experience of human face that has been written. He associates the birth of the human personality with a positive experience of the face. For Levinas the human face gives rise to a sense of the infinite in relation to which one can become inexhaustibly real. In his phenomenological philosophy the experience of the other's face carries with it a sense of goodness that becomes the tonic chord or home base of the human self. (1993a, p. 55)

Eigen had to "import" the centrality of the human face from philosophy. In his view, psychoanalysis never acknowledged its significance, although some analytic authors did discuss the face, from what Eigen views as a more limited perspective. Spitz (1965, in Eigen, 1993a) described the infant's preference for the human face and his first smile in evolutionary terms: a survival mechanism, designed to elicit caring behavior from adults. For Eigen, Spitz missed the point entirely: the baby's first smile on encountering a human face, on recognizing, perhaps for the first time, the sense of selfhood and Otherness conveyed therein, is a reaction of pure joy. It cannot be reduced to manipulative behavior or animal signaling. While these two explanations are by no means mutually exclusive, Eigen is right in indicating that psychoanalytic writing neglected the idea of the face as a signifier of a whole relationship and cast the (m)other as a means to an end – feeder, soother and sexual object. This Other-as-means is then symbolized by (or reduced to) various organs, like the breast or the eyes (as the function of mirroring). Bollas (2007) noticed the same lacuna, addressing it through the concept of the integral object. Eigen's formulation, which preceded Bollas' by two years, argued that the integrity of the human Other, its wholeness and uniqueness, are conveyed by the human face.

Lacan wrote extensively about the face, which he saw as an aspect of the imaginary. For him, the face led one to temptation and obscured true self-knowledge. Eigen agrees that the face might be an instrument of temptation, but it is also so much more. He draws on Winnicott's mention of the glimmer of recognition in the mother's eyes, through which the baby forms his selfhood. Expanding on this notion, he writes:

> In general, of all body areas the human face is most centrally expressive of human personality and exerts its prominence as an organizing principle in the field of meaning. It acts as a reference point by which all other body areas may acquire deeper personal significance […] Normally, body-oriented lines of association, such as the breast-face-ass equation may be more or less present, but are situated within a more encompassing perspective in which the face has primacy. This is in distinct contrast with most animal life, wherein perception is preeminently organized around securing physical sustenance. (1993a, p. 56)

Here, Eigen indirectly criticizes his colleagues for their "animalistic" view of humanity. More directly, he claims that psychoanalysis has chosen to focus on the tactile instead of the visual route: the former derives from skin-to-skin contact and is represented by the breast; the latter. requiring a certain distance and a recognition of Otherness, is represented by the face. While we obviously need both routes to function in an integrative way, it is the face, not the breast, that the baby smiles upon meeting.

On a deeper level, Eigen criticizes what he sees as a basic failing in many psychoanalytic approaches: the lack of a holistic view. Why should we favor the tactile over the visual, unity over difference? Why, as Eigen asks time and time again in his writings, must we always "take sides," stressing one aspect of human experience while diminishing and silencing the other? In contrast to this theoretical tendency, Eigen depicts the face as a holistic gestalt, comprised of various parts that have meaning as a pattern. In heralding the face, *because* it is the mark of Otherness (as mediating the creation of selfhood), Eigen moves beyond Winnicott and Kohut, both of whom highlighted the importance of mother's gaze. For Eigen, the face is more than mirroring eyes; it is the signifier of another person's being *in itself* (not as a means or a function): the mother is important as an Other with her own unique face.

The face, therefore, is an important part of Eigen's developmental worldview. Eigen's baby does not live in a symbiotic enmeshment from which it should somehow "hatch." It lives in a pulsating field, checkered with areas of unity and distinctness, enjoying its complete dependence and merger with the protective mother while also experiencing the joy of discovering her welcome Otherness from the very beginning. The face – signifying this Otherness, while also reflecting the baby's own selfhood – unites these interdependent developmental needs.

But the face is significant for another reason as well: as the organizing focal point of both self and Other and their relation, it is also the signifier of the numinous. Eigen wishes to convey to his readers a notion of the face as evoking the feeling of the infinite, while, at the same time, constituting a home for the self. He claims that some patients experience the therapist's face as such a numinous/intimate gateway to transformation:

> I see you, but not just you. I am experiencing a more real, perfect version of you, a glowing-light you, inexpressibly radiant and fluid. I can go in and through you yet feel more myself than ever. It is as if I entered and passed through a highly charged yet resistanceless medium and feel newly conscious and restored. (1993a, pp. 58–59)

Eigen explains that, for the patient, the therapist's face conveys, through its material existence, the sense of the transcendent. The therapist is a medium, mediating the material and immaterial spheres of being and embodying the experience of self-transformation with the help of the Other. The therapist's face signifies an Other whose concrete humanity and the experience of transcending it allows the ineffable to become, if only for a moment, "a distinguishable mental object" (ibid, p. 59). In Freudian terms, Eigen sees the face as the meeting place of the "heimlich" and "unheimlich," offering a new understanding of the role of the therapist. This role is to introduce the patient not only to human Otherness and, thereby, to his own self, but also to the numinous facet of life. This is achieved by demonstrating its continuous existence with the psychic "home," embodied in the face of a loving Otherness. This embodiment turns the eerie "unheimlich" experience into a "heimlich" feeling of being deeply connected to the wholly (holy) Other.

The ideal

In *The Psychotic Core*, Eigen rises a question that had never been seriously considered: why do children create monsters in their imagination? Where does the perfect goodness attributed to God come from? Why is mother either a beautiful angel or an awful witch – why not simply a kind or disappointing mother? The answer was traditionally given in terms of defense: Freud's paternal God is the projection of fear, adoration and the need for protection; the Kleinian baby's turbulent experiences are the result of splitting, taking its perception of good and bad to extremes. Eigen, however, demands that we notice our need to form ideals as a phenomenon with an intrinsic quality. He calls it an "ability" – which is diametrically opposed to seeing it as derived from defensive activity.

According to Eigen, the notion that, at some point, the real mother emerges from the "shell" of her idealized figure and that this same idealization can later be applied to other figures shows that the relationship with the "real" mother cannot be the origins of this ideal experience (ibid, p. 102). This argument is flawed because the fact that idealness persist beyond the mother does not contradict the Kleinian argument that idealness stems from splitting mechanisms that isolate and thus intensify her good and bad aspects – mechanisms that are equally applicable to other objects. Simply put, everything can feel powerful and all-encompassing when taken out of context and only a mature mentality can think contextually. But Kleinians were the ones who argued that these splits are a result of an extremely powerful, innate way of experiencing, which they attribute to the drives. Rejecting this conceptualization as reductionistic thinking, Eigen asks the question anew: why are we built this way?

In Freudian dramas the ideal imago variously saturates one's own body, ego, mother, father, and on to a wide range of possibilities (e.g. feces, feet, science, nation, God). A goal of analysis is to unmask the hidden god sense displaced or mixed up in some mundane reality [...] In work at the deepest levels of character it is necessary to search out and clarify the subject's relation to his power source with its ideal penumbra (or core) and chart how the subject maintains and gives away power in complex ways. [...] In the course of therapy it is possible to help the individual become aware of the play of "divine-demonic" ideal images in his life. By [...] making *the ideal imago, as such,* the object of one's attention, one may acquire a greater capacity to enter fruitful communion with it. In optimal instances one does not only become free from it but through it. One draws on a power that previously seemed enslaving. (ibid, p. 103; italics in origin)

Eigen makes a revolutionary claim: instead of the established psy-choanalytic approach of unmasking the false god as a projection of (sometimes perverse) desire, Eigen looks for the real God even in the most perverse objects (feet, feces). In *Psychoanalysis and Kabbalah*, Eigen (2012) offers his understanding of ideas from Lurianic Kabbalah: human beings are tasked with extracting the "fallen" sparks of divine presence even in the most obscure or evil places of this world. Experiencing the ideal is, therefore, not some "manu-facturing defect" of the psyche; on the contrary, striving for it is a human mission.

Moreover, Eigen believes, like Ghent after him, that in pathology the capacity to create an ideal imago has been corrupted. Instead of having a healthy relationship with their "power center," the person perverts it by giving their sense of power to another person (for ex-ample, in sado-masochistic constellations) or even to a fetish-object. The ideal therapeutic outcome is not only to liberate oneself from the idol, but to reestablish an authentic relationship with the real God. The individual can then use the ideal imago as a source of power to set themselves free. Therefore, Eigen sees the ideal experience as an autonomous phenomenon of great developmental importance. Though its developmental aim may be obstructed and perverted, just like libidinal development, and though these two courses of development are entangled throughout the emergence of object relations, the libidinal and the ideal are seen as independent phenomena whose interplay is necessary for healthy creativity.

For Eigen, following Winnicott, creativity is the foundation of mental life. The sense of self-integrity and authenticity depends on experiencing the self as creative and the Other as separate, yet deeply connected. This Other is an object of longing and the one to whom the creative act is addressed: they are the most important and most intimate audience. According to Eigen,

> This basic ambiguity of human life [being one with yet distinct from the other] was carried forward by the ego ideal which in its dual capacity acts as a subjective object mirroring one's own creative urges while it simultaneously reflects the endlessly inspiring Other, the intended object pole of all authentic, creative strivings. (ibid, p. 74)

The ideal experience, then, is the living center of the personality, in whose orbit the self is created. Like James (1890/1950), Eigen suggests that we may find God (the ultimate Other) by looking at the very core of our self. This idea is different from Kohut's ideal selfobject or the theory of internalization, because it is not a relationship with single object or a derivative of past relationships. Rather, like the Winnicottian transitional object, this inner God is neither a figment of one's imagination, nor an external reality that is unaffected by one's inner world. One's relation to the ideal, divine or demonic, is part of the human make-up, like instincts, biological functions and the ability to love and hate. God is as real as the body or the psyche. The important question is what kind of a relationship do we have with the ideal image: an enslaving relationship, like that of religious fanatics or the masochist who imagines he has found God in the person who hurts him? An imaginary relationship, in which one commits the sin of omniscience by "knowing" what God wants, maintaining a delusion that blocks any authentic acceptance of the ineffable?

> Ideal experience is a basic human capacity and emerges spontaneously in the course of human development [...] To explain the

felt sense of infinite perfection or an intimation of immaterial boundlessness solely in terms of their material occasions (mother, breast, father, penis, etc.) seems at best careless; it assumes what it needs to understand. (p. 74)

Eigen warns us against idolatry, including that of psychoanalytic reductionism. Yet he believes that the real God is out there as well as in here – in the most intimate core of our being.

The mystical

What, then, is Eigenian mysticism? Contrary to what could be expected from a theoretician who talks openly of the mystical, this is not an easy question to answer. Until now, discussions of Eigen's theory mostly dealt with his early books, where the mystical dimension (most notably in terms of the ideal experience and the union-separateness tension) constituted an organic part of his theory of development, psychopathology and self-structure. However, Eigen has also written explicitly about faith and the mystical experience, rather than simply discussing traditional psychoanalytic topics with a mystical "twist." Even in texts such as *The Psychoanalytic Mystic* and his books on Kabbalah, where the mystical is the main subject, it still remains undefined. In the beginning of *The Psychoanalytic Mystic*, Eigen (1998) avows that he cannot offer such a definition:

> I have not defined mystical feeling because I am unable to. My hope is, if I speak around it, or from it, well enough, something of value will be communicated to the reader and myself. Discussions of mystical awareness tend to undo themselves because of the paradoxical nature of the experience involved. (p. 31)

True to his word, Eigen does not offer a definition of the mystical, but he does present many valuable observations. One of these key insights concerns the paradoxical nature of the mystical experience, which serves Eigen to explain why discussions of this term tend to "undo themselves." But, even if the mystical *experience* is paradoxical, discussions of its traces and reflections in psychoanalytic theory *need not* undo themselves and may even yield important introspective and meta-theoretical results. In my view, his references to the mystical *can* be theoretically analyzed, yielding both definitions and different categories of the mystical.

I suggest that Eigen refers to the term "mystical" on three different levels of meaning: as a certain quality of experience, a structural element of the personality and a position of faith. This division branches still further: on the experiential level, Eigen speaks of different kinds of mystical experiences and different kinds of mystics. On the structural level, he discusses development and examines health and pathology in both the personality and the mystical experience. Finally, in discussing the position of faith, Eigen offers an extremely important and rich discussion of the epistemological footing of psychoanalysis, its ethics and its very essence. The following subsection explore these different dimensions, keeping in mind that this division is merely methodological and that these different levels are intertwined. While their separation may go against the grain of Eigen's position, I see it as necessary for facilitating the meeting of the ineffable and the conceptual, the mystical and the pragmatical – hopefully without compromising either one too much.

Faith – The mystical as a position

This discussion of the position of faith is mostly grounded in Eigen's (1981) well-known paper, "The Area of Faith in Winnicott, Lacan and Bion," but the same profound understandings inform his other writings as well. Eigen considers "faith" as both a starting point and a developmental achievement: it is the ideal position of the healthy personality and, in turn, its emergence is based on beneficial experiences. It is the necessary and sometimes sufficient condition for the mystical experience. Faith, in other words is a pivotal concept, from which the three abovementioned levels emanate.

This paper is important both because of its content and because of its historical context as the opening paper of Mitchell and Aron's collection of key contributions to the emergence of the relational tradition. Furthermore, according to Eigen, Winnicott's widow, Clair, sent him a letter expressing her appreciation of the fact that someone had finally understood her late husband's notion of "the use of the object" – a paper that was poorly received in Winnicott's lifetime – and offered a reading of it that Winnicott would have approved of (Eigen, 1999, p. 36). This statement supports the claim that Eigen's perspective is one of the theoretical peaks inspired by the Winnicottian revolution and that his interpretation is critical in illuminating the least understood and under-appreciated parts of Winnicott's paradigm shift.

Unlike his treatment of the "mystical," Eigen defines "faith" at the very beginning of this paper: "by the area of faith I mean to point to a way of experiencing which is undertaken with one's whole being, all out, 'with all one's heart, with all one's soul, and with all one's might'" (Eigen, 1981, p. 413). Faith, in short, is very similar to the concept of surrender later offered by Ghent (1990/1999), who indeed quotes Eigen. But what should one have faith in or surrender to? According to Eigen, Winnicott, Lacan and Bion all dealt with inevitable, even constitutional experiences of gaps: for Lacan, it was the gap between the real and the symbolic; for Bion, it was the ever elusive O; for Winnicott, it was the inherent paradoxicality of psychic existence. Moreover, for Winnicott (in Eigen's reading), the gap between self and Other – paradoxically co-existing alongside self-other continuity – is the infrastructure of human existence (with the famous true-self / false-self gap as its pathological manifestation). All three authors sought the path to authentic life, to what they saw as a fully human existence and Eigen argues that they have found it in the position of faith.

In his in-depth discussion, Eigen shows how all three thinkers view faith and trust as prerequisites for psychic development:

> For them, I believe, the vicissitudes of faith mark the central point around which psychic turmoil and conflict gather. In the hands of these authors, further, the area of faith tends to become a founding principle for the possibility of a fully human consciousness, an intrinsic condition of self-other awareness as such. (ibid, ibid)

Faith is thus deeply connected to the central human task of constructing a self capable of relating to Otherness, whether as the actual human Other (primarily in Winnicott's thinking), the Other within us or the unconscious (primarily in Lacan's thinking) or the most abstract Other – ineffable, Godlike truth (in Bion's thinking). For all three, the main issue is openness to "real" experiences of gap, Otherness, paradox: the challenge of accepting such experiences for what they are. In my understanding of Eigen, such acceptance of inherent absence *is* faith; possibly because it requires knowledge of/ faith in its opposite: fullness and being.

For Eigen, it seems that experience, especially powerful experiences that tax our capacity for containment, always bear the mark of Otherness. The constant and everyday need to deal with emotional experience is a paradoxical challenge. It means constantly coping with the Otherness within us while also recognizing the intimately familiar "outside" ourselves, in the actual Other. When facing Otherness, one may react defensively, by pushing it away or denying it; or one may choose authentic life and genuinely try to encounter this Otherness. Like Bion's striving for O, Eigen portrays this attempt as an endless voyage, because one cannot and should not live without defenses. Full openness to the truth is an ideal that is never fully reached. This means that a position of faith is something one continuously aspires to achieve. In contrast, a life that neglects this striving is a pathological life, that falls short of full human potential.

This potential, as we have seen, is creativity in the Winnicottian sense which, for Eigen, is made possible by the presence of the ideal:

> These authors attempt to differentiate the positive and negative aspects of ideal experiencing without reducing one to the other [...] If one reads these authors carefully one discovers that *the primary object of creative experiencing is not mother or father but the unknowable ground of creativeness as such.* [...] Maternal or paternal object relations may subserve or thwart this experiencing but must not be simply identified with it. (1993a, p. 135; italics in origin)

In Eigen's reading of his favorite authors, the ideal is part of the reality to which one must be open and which must be balanced against other aspects of reality, if one wishes to live an authentic and creative life. Negating any aspect of reality, let alone a central one like the ideal experience, is a lie in the Bionian sense. As such, it cannot be considered a psychoanalytic position, which must be one of faith in *the truth*. Self-deceit is un-Freudian regardless of Freud's personal opinions about the spiritual.

The most comprehensive definition Eigen gives for the concept of faith is that the position of faith requires tolerance to the unknown, the unknowable, the infinite:

> The vicissitudes of faith involve the struggle not only to know but in some way be one's true self, to take up the journey with all that one is and may become, and to encounter through oneself the ground of one's being. This is undertaken with the knowledge that we are mediate beings, that certainty is beyond certain reach, but that anything short of this attempt portends disaster and self-crippling. The undertaking itself involves one in continuous re-creation. (ibid, p. 127)

Living a life of faith is an ongoing struggle to create oneself and realize one's life, while accepting the humbling caveat of our human limitations and knowing that some aspects of ourselves and (especially) the Other will forever remain unknown. This humility is a necessary condition of one's openness to experience, which is the essence of faith. It means knowing that we do not know, that we are lacking and therefore strive to keep expanding our contact with reality. This call for humility, however, is not meant to diminish man's status in creation. On the contrary, being in contact with lacks, gaps and paradoxes necessitates a profound trust in the creativeness of the self and the intrinsic value that its creations (particularly the self as a creation) hold for oneself and for humanity.

Faith and catastrophe

Eigen creatively combines Winnicottian and Bionian thinking, not only conceptually, but also in terms of "mood." Eigen has adopted the Bionian notion of truth as forever eluding understanding, let alone representation. Moreover, this truth is terrible: the full truth is inevitably "too much" for the frail human thinking apparatus. Nevertheless, Eigen also embraces Winnicott's optimism about truth, trust in the human ability to balance and create transitional space between self and world and view of human beings as fundamentally creative. Eigen discusses the difference between Bion, who "pessimistically" stressed the catastrophic impact of truth, and Winnicott, who, despite acknowledging the catastrophic ("Fear of Breakdown"), saw the encounter with Otherness as a primarily joyful moment, a discovery of love. For Winnicott, a true encounter is necessarily creative and, therefore, deeply optimistic. Though Bion also saw the striving for truth as a precondition for creativity and even thinking, he considered this striving terribly painful, even a menace to one's sanity. Eigen uses the bleak Bionian view to demonstrate that Freud was deeply mistaken in seeing faith as a product of illusion, comforting the feeble or the foolish. On the contrary, faith is the willingness, even the demand, to accept the truth, no matter how terrible. Yet, this openness to encounter truth inevitably contains the seed of optimism:

> What is crucial is *how one relates to* whatever one may be relating to. In Bion's view, the basic analytic attitude or way of relating is to keep aiming towards O. If, for example, one's emotional reality or truth is despair, what is most important is not *that* one may be in despair, but one's attitude *toward* one's despair. Through one's basic attentiveness one's despair can declare itself and tell its story. One enters profound dialogue with it. If one stays with this process, an evolution even in the quality of despair may begin to be perceived, since despair itself is never uniform. (ibid, p. 133; italics in origin)

This beautiful passage conveys Eigen's chief theoretical belief and technical advice as well as his vision for humanity: the whole person is one who is open to the whole of experience; one who listens to the many voices they encounter in inner and outer reality. This openness, rooted in the position of faith, potentially leads to personal and social evolution. For Eigen, that is the main role of psychoanalysis, both on the personal and universal scale. Somewhat like Bollas, Eigen declares that "the essential freedom analysis brings is the analytic attitude itself, the liberation of the capacity to focus on O" (ibid, ibid). This liberation, however, is not only of one's unconscious thinking, as Bollas stressed, but of all kinds of experiences and their nuanced interrelatedness. It is about the ability to listen, rather than what one hears, and this polyphonic reality is a recurrent theme in Eigen's writing. Eigen's faith is a deep commitment to give every experience and every person their due attention and, therefore, their chance to evolve and participate in human creativity. It is, in fact, a faith in the sanctity of the self and the Other, with their manifold facets.

Faith and the mystical

In *The Psychoanalytic Mystic*, the word "mystical" replaces the centrality of the word "faith," though Eigen sometimes treats these two concepts as interchangeable:

> The modern and post modern mind is permanently critical ironical, skeptical. Hopefully, this saves us from gullibility [...] Bion's work can hardly be called gullible. Yet mystical tendencies persist, and intertwined with critical thinking. In Bion's work, mysticism and criticism feed each other. One cannot choose between faith and irony since both are real capacities. The rule in psychoanalysis is the openness to the play of voices. (1998, p. 34)

In this quote, Eigen seem to view Bion's concepts of the mystical and of faith as synonymous: mysticism and criticism are equated with faith and irony. At the end of the passage, he again states that openness to many voices is the "rule of psychoanalysis." As we have seen, this openness is the essence of faith and, through the extrapolation suggested by this passage, one could argue that faith equals openness equals a mystical tendency.

Nevertheless, there is also evidence that faith is a wider concept. If faith equals openness, then it is tantamount to the ability to contain mystical experience alongside critical thinking, without having to choose between the two. Confusingly, faith is both the opposite of skepticism *and* the ability to contain both it and itself. Maybe this confusion is inevitable and not only the result of Eigen's informal style. Eigen is not the only thinker who failed to clearly delineate the difference between faith and mysticism. Barnard (1997) showed that, in James' texts, it is hard to distinguish his definition of faith from his view of mysticism. This suggests that the two concepts are intimately connected. Furthermore, Eigen illustrates this connection when discussing several key analytic concepts that he considers as mystical:

> Winnicott, Milner and Bion share a conviction that an originary, naked self is the true subject of experience. Internalization processes are necessary [...] but something originary shines through [...] Winnicott's incommunicado self, transitional experiencing and object usage, Bion's faith in O, Ps-D rhythm, being over knowing, Milner's pregnant emptiness and I yet not I moment; all point to and grow out of moments of real living, in which fresh possibilities of experience uplift the self. (1998, p. 34)

Here, Eigen speaks of the mystical experience as "moments of real living" that involve the "shining through" of the real self. This true personality core, though it refers to each self's essential and unique quality, is not static. Rather, it makes itself known in moments of intense living: in Bion's Ps-D oscillation and his movement towards O; in Milner's pregnant emptiness and the movement between moments of I and not-I. Since Eigen defines faith as openness to such movements of experience, with their tensions and paradoxes, we can see that the position of faith is what allows mystical experiences to occur and evolve. It is Faith that permits contact with the "naked self." At the same time, it seems that this very state of open "listening" to experience is, *in itself*, part of the range of experience Eigen labels "mystical." The distinction between "structure" (the personality's ability to tolerate openness) and "content" (having a particular mystical experience) becomes blurred, even non-existent. As Eigen illustrates again and again (for example, 1993a) openness begets more openness; the ability to withstand paradox, to tolerate experiences, is fueled by its own success. A successful encounter with experience deepens one's trust in one's ability to contain, transform and survive even destructive moments. In other words, it strengthens one's faith. Put differently still, it contributes to the resilience of the alpha-function.

For Bion and Eigen, faith and the ability to think are one and the same. But some faith, *enough* faith had to be there to begin with, to allow one's initial encounters with experience. It is like the paradigmatic moment portrayed by Winnicott, in which the baby takes a leap of faith into the hands of the real object, that had survived its destructiveness. As Eigen (1981) argues, this is a moment that creates faith, but also requires it. It is a circle with no clear beginning since, for Eigen, self and Other were always there, becoming increasingly delineated as time passes and faith grows.

This paradigmatic moment is also a mystical moment – a moment of "real living," of the "naked self" putting itself out there to meet another, of the great joy of discovering that the Other is there to "catch" it. In this moment, reality is (re)claimed as real and nourishing, though sometimes painful; faith is (re)established and self and Other are (re)created. These moments are both the result and the precondition of experiencing. This is especially true for mystical experiences which, by their very nature, (re)create the self–other matrix of interpretation and boundaries.

Faith is a state rather than a structure; openness is both a potential and a specific state of being. In more Winnicottian terms, one may be developmentally capable of transitional experiences, without dwelling in intermediate space at a given moment. On the other hand, one does not just simply "enter" transitional space at will; something happens, an encounter occurs. Eigen's position of faith is similar: we are open *to* something that comes to meet us. Openness and meeting, faith and mystical experiences, become difficult to distinguish.

Varieties of mysticism

Eigen (1998) begins his discussion of the mystical with Freud's reference to the oceanic experience. In Eigen's opinion, the fact that this is the first reference to mysticism in psychoanalysis is unfortunate, because it represents a less mature version or type of mysticism. It seems that, for Eigen, this choice may resemble the attempt to present the notion of "literature" by choosing dime-store novels as its representatives. But Eigen also draws a broader conclusion from Freud's treatment of mysticism. Eigen shows that, for Freud, the ego undergoes a mystical experience when it senses the Otherness within itself (the id) or experiences a sense of union with the Otherness of the outside world. The oceanic experience is clearly a form of the latter. In both cases, however, the ego discovers something meaningful and new about itself and its boundaries: these become either sharper or vaguer and the ego either expands or contracts. Eigen embraces these Freudian notions, using them to support his intuition that the mystical experience, its dramatic potential notwithstanding, is part (perhaps the pinnacle) of the most central and ongoing developmental challenge: the structuring the self in the matrix of its relation to Otherness.

> Freud plays with dimensions of inner-outer, bigger-smaller: what is inside and outside I feeling. That the boundaries of I feeling shrink and expand suggests that mystical states vary, partly as a function of what the I imagined was included or excluded within it. A sense of numinosity or mystical charge can fall more on self or other, depending on a host of variables, including disposition, mood, developmental phase, and situational factors. (1998, p. 31)

A central characteristic of the mystical experience is the numinous feeling: an encounter with an object that gives rise to a feeling of the deeply meaningful, mysterious or even divine. While Eigen argues that the objects that inspire such feelings vary according to several psychological factors, his phrasing does not clarify the ontological underpinnings of this experience. The person has encountered something that deeply affected them; but could that something simply be a part of themselves? According to the "ego-boundary theory" that Eigen presents in Freud's name, such an encounter may very well occur with one's own id. It does not have to be a bad experience; it can even be uplifting, but mood is no evidence of having encountered something transcendent. Far from pointing exclusively towards the divine, Eigen bluntly declares that an oceanic feeling may arise during a fetishistic sexual act with a stocking or with feces, even during the act of murder (ibid, p. 30). Sometimes, however, the mystical experience entails a more mature encounter:

> Mystical moments also involve a sense of movement *between* dimensions of experience and between self and other. A heightened sense of impact may characterize subject to subject meeting. In light of this Buber wrote "All real living is meeting" [...] the self that enters an I-Thou relation is not the same as in an I-It relation. Oceanic fusion, absorption or oneness would not do justice to the

drama of self-other meeting and intersection that Buber points to. For one thing, the mystical moment may involve enormous upheaval, turbulence, overthrowing and reworking of self. A new meeting may change one's picture of what self and other can be. (p. 31)

For Eigen, then, mystical moments are moments of movement, where the self undergoes transformation and is exposed to different forms of being and new ways of situating itself vis-à-vis the Other. Yet, as suggested by his examples of fetishistic use, Eigen believes that some mystics use mystical experience for defensive purposes, as a means of fleeing other forms of existence. Paradoxically, some mystical experiences might be utilized to avoid real meeting and real living.

Here, we re-encounter the Buberian distinction between "this-world mysticism" and a sedated state that keeps one in a blissful detachment from other aspects of life. It is for good reason that Eigen "falls in love" with Buber's declaration that "all real living is meeting." Like anyone else, mystics may have their safe zones and their rigidity, but it is quite clear that Eigen views the Buberian I-Thou meeting as the most evolved form of mysticism. He thus speaks of a very "human" form of mysticism – the psychoanalytic mystic. In fact, Eigen is the only analyst discussed in this book who fully adopts the Buberian ideal about the human encounter as an ideal for the psychoanalytic session and an aim to which analytic processes should strive, by allowing the patient to partake in this full form of living.

The Psychoanalytic Mystic is full of examples of what may be called "pathological mysticism" or less evolved, non I-Thou mysticism. For example, Eigen describes a young patient named Dolores, who "became dependent on mystical feeling to offset dread of disintegration" (p. 112). Dolores is described as a "body mystic," who dives into intense sensations and lives "in timeless time, a world in which experience of moment was real, a world of the realness of experience as such, especially the sensation-feeling side of things" (p. 113). Eigen emphasizes that this was a "real" mystical experience, not merely a defense mechanism, and that it saved her life. At the same time, however, all this intensity rendered her life quite limited: Dolores could never plan or see beyond the moment; material considerations were irrelevant to her and she lived in poverty, turning her back on people who did not share her worldview. She was unable to consider the addictive side of her mysticism and saw it only as a liberation. In contrast, Eigen describes two other patients who subscribed to the opposite "brand" (p. 112) of mysticism, a Buddhist search for emptiness that counterpointed Dolores' basking in fullness. These two men led rather schizoid lives, unable to form intimate connections because they could not respect the Other's feelings, see the Other as a full subject or find meaning in anything but the sought-after feeling of emptiness associated with their own personal space.

Eigen finds both forms of mysticism appealing: he practices meditation and is attracted to Buddhistic ideas; but he also appreciates "body mysticism" (Molino, 1997). He maintains that pathology in mystical experiencing does not necessarily lie in a specific "brand" of mysticism, whether it is a mysticism of "fullness" or "emptiness," (though he is particularly suspicious of the oceanic experience, which is a type of the former). What is pathological is the lack of movement between mystical forms. The healthy personality moves between different experiential dimensions: fullness and emptiness, the "incommunicado" zone, where one can be alone, rest, allow self-rehabilitation, and an area of full, intense living, where one is wholly engaged with external objects. Furthermore, mature mysticism is about more than just having the experience, it is about learning from experience in the Bionian sense, and allowing oneself to be transformed by it. This is why Eigen takes issue with the oceanic experience. What happens in a Buberian I-Thou moment is not necessarily harmonious; the impact of an encounter with the true essence of the Other may be more of a shocking jolt than a blissful embrace. To initiate growth, one must sometimes tolerate even the catastrophic.

In this view, mysticism is not one thing but a wide range of deeply meaningful experiences that rearranges the self's boundaries and its place in the world. These experiences can be more or less growth-promoting, depending on their "variety" but above all on one's openness and tolerance to the mystical experience in general. The effect of the mystical moment, then, depends on psychic flexibility or, in other words, faith. At the same time, fully assuming a position of faith may be considered a mystical moment in itself, for one's faith is necessarily *in* something or "towards" something, as an open-heartedness to whatever may come.

The phenomenology of the mystical and the three levels: Is everyone a mystic?

If a disposition to the mystical is tantamount to psychic flexibility and openness to experience, does this mean everyone is a potential mystic? According to Eigen (1998), not all lives contain a mystical element: some people do not seek, do not find and perhaps do not need the experience of the numinous. Here, he refers to the mystical as an experience, rather than a personality structure or position (thought this categorization, as mentioned, is not his own). One of his case studies illustrates the blurring of the boundary between these two levels. Eigen describes a patient named max, a financial genius with a disrupted emotional life who lives without any awareness of the terrors that shaped him. In therapy, he finally encounters these parts of himself and experiences his first dream as an adult (p. 132). Max seems to be deprived not only of certain experiences, but also of the very capacity to experience and dream. Why does Eigen describe this patient in his book about mysticism? If the mystical ability is likened to musical or mathematical talent, then its absence may deny life of some of its richness, but is not truly debilitating. However, if the mystical is not just a particular kind of experience, if it is related to the very *capacity for experience*, then Eigen is making an implicit yet very provocative claim: *every person who leads a psychic life, because of its paradoxical nature, carries within them a mystical dimension.*

Indeed, the present analysis of Eigen's recurring references to the mystical as a capacity for movement, openness, dialogue and tolerance for paradox, has led to the conclusion that he equates the mystical with both the ability to participate in or create potential space and Bion's alpha-function. Chapter 6 explored a similar complexity in Winnicott's writing: potential space can facilitate a mystical experience, but its own transitory existence has a certain intrinsic magical quality, regardless of its present contents. As Clair Winnicott wrote, Eigen understood something that had been overlooked in Winnicott's texts. I believe it was, among other things, the undercurrent of sacred feeling that runs through them. The person who respects life, who respects experience and its transitional quality, who tolerates their essentially unknowable "place" in the electrically charged self-other field, leads a truly religious life, in the deepest sense of the word. This is a sacred way of living because it reveres life.

But the difficulties remain: even if the division between the mystical as an ability and an experience is valid, one must still inquire about the psychological and even ontological meaning of perceiving the process of personality growth and the ability to negotiate self-boundaries as mystical. Another question concerns Eigen's view of the possibility of a healthy mental life that is devoid of mystical experiences. His proposed developmental axis moves towards greater openness to experience, a continuously widening perceptive and potential attunement to more and more pieces of reality. Given that Eigen sees the numinous as an immanent part of reality, can one achieve true growth without ever encountering it? Moreover, does this mean that Eigen, despite arguing in favor of pluralism and tolerance, despite presenting the mystical as counterbalanced by the legitimate claims of rationality and even materialism, is not so tolerant towards non-mystical individuals? Does he see them as "living in denial?" Is he implying that whoever opens their heart and mind to truth, to reality, will inevitably encounter the mystical?

Eigen seems to believe that, whether we are aware of it or not, transitional and paradoxical experience is the "stuff" we are made of. But can one be ignorant of this aspect of human nature and the nature of reality and still be considered in sound mental health? Can one be sufficiently open to all other experiences except the mystical? Perhaps, for Eigen would surely claim that openness or faith are not a matter of "all or nothing." Still, is Eigen's reasoning not suggesting that ignoring such an important part of reality may amount to some kind of developmental arrest? In more direct terms, will anyone who truly surrenders to the paradoxical movement of life meet the living God?

Paradoxical monism

As a partial answer to these questions, I wish to review a concept Eigen proposed in *The Psychoanalytic Mystic*: "paradoxical monism." While this concept remains somewhat undefined, like that of the mystical,

Eigen uses it to stress the pluralistic aspect of experience and warn against exclusively identifying the numinous reality underlying mystical experiences with either unity ("we are all one") or multiplicity. Just as mystical experiences themselves differ, ranging from deep awe to powerful joy, numinous reality is complex and at least as multifaceted as the human psyche. He writes:

> I do not find a problem in moving between more anonymous and personal moments, and their various amalgams. To say New York city exists, doesn't mean Chicago doesn't, although many New Yorkers cannot imagine real living goes on elsewhere. (1998, p. 38)

On a less witty and more seriously religious note, he adds:

> In Hebrew, one can turn various nouns or verbs into names of God [...] There is a plural as well as singular name of God, apparently referring to the many in one and one in many [...] I love the part of Judaism that speaks of the living God, a God of life. St. Paul confessed it dreadful to fall into the hands of the living God, but it is more dreadful not to. (ibid, ibid)

On the one hand, the "living God" is like life itself: it cannot be faithfully described as one thing, it is not static and therefore not "whole," in the medieval sense. Much like the more tangible aspects of reality, numinous reality is a complex picture of many-in-one and one-in-many. Eigen resorts to astrophysics to support his claim, stating that the universe is not homogenous: differences in the concentration of matter following the big bang created the galaxies, the stars and life as we know it as islands of matter surrounded by an inconceivably immense void. Paradoxically, these differences also allow for connection, as gravitational influences can only exist between two celestial bodies that do not collapse into one. This is true for both stars and human beings: "without tensions and inhomogeneities, there would be no shared processes" (ibid, p. 40). On the other hand, these metaphors have limited power, for God is also different from anything we know. Meeting God exposes one to a shattering experience of Otherness, for which nothing can prepare us: "it is dreadful to fall into the hands of a living God."

Paradoxical monism is thus the paradoxical reality of unity of the many and multiplicity of the one. It is paradoxical because neither facet can be considered more fundamental than the other. Elaborating Eigen's cosmological metaphor, before the big bang, everything was in a state of singularity, of infinite timeless and spaceless density. Yet, viewing the universe as a unity overlooks its inconceivable vastness and diversity and the complex relations between its various parts. When it was only "one," there could be no universe, let alone life. Both viewpoints are valid and neither is true; a "living God" does not succumb to any delimiting description. Eigen's paradoxical monism resembles the arguments James makes in *A Pluralistic Universe*, against restricting our conceptions of the transcendent to thin, pale concepts that fall so short of the variety, complexity and richness found in (human) nature. This complexity is no less "real" than its uniting elements and its supposed all-embracing unity. Still, both thinkers, perhaps because of their Judeo-Christian background, share the monotheistic intuition that this pluralistic reality exists alongside profound kinds of connectedness, some of which we recognize (like the ecological co-dependency or the original singularity that preceded the big Bang) and some we know little or nothing about (James, 1907/1987b). Fundamentally, these connecting qualities may reflect some all-embracing unity like the "world soul" (James, 1909/1987a) or Buber's "eternal Thou" – the origin of all I-Thou attachments.

Though this discussion may seem strictly "philosophical," it affects our notions of therapeutic work, as illustrated through another of Eigen's concepts: "impact." Eigen discusses the impact one personality has on another, especially in analysis, as a deep, sometimes shattering touch. He envisions it along Bionian lines as an "electric storm" that erupts when two personalities meet or, perhaps more accurately, collide (Eigen, 1993a, 1993b; Eigen and Govrin, 2007). Such profound impact is possible because of the reality of paradoxical monism: we are united enough with the patient to achieve deep influence, separate enough for its impact to be meaningful (we are neither talking to ourselves nor to a narcissistic extension) and, sadly, far enough to be able to miss each other. According to Eigen, we enter a highly charged and meaningful matrix of psychic overlap and distance with the patient, which generates a sacred feeling:

> In therapy we use mutual impacts of self-other (therapist-patient) to help constitute psyches more capable of working with the impact that therapy generates. If therapist and patient can't respond creatively and usefully to impacts they have on each other, it is unlikely they will do much better with portions of life outside therapy. In therapy we give ourselves time to catch up with each other, to catch up with ourselves. we give ourselves time to give life a chance [...] Therapy is a holy business for me and was so from my first session [...] There is nothing we can't come through together, no hell, no death, if only we give each other time. (1998, pp. 41–42)

Paradoxical monism is the ontological reality behind the power of psychotherapy. It is how the therapeutic couple is able to come through every hell, every death. The openness to the reality of the paradoxical unity-separateness of their two psyches, the willingness to encounter the horror and deadness or aliveness and extreme joy that may ensue from the different facets and compositions of this paradoxical tension are, for Eigen, a mystical act.

The therapeutic couple commits, as an act of faith, to give time and place to every experience that emerges, to whatever is created in the encounter. They commit to processing the impact each of them has on the other, to recognizing and working with whatever destructive or creative consequences this may have. Hopefully, such devoted listening and faithful willingness to meet whatever comes will tip the scales toward growth and change that which, outside the sanctity of analytic encounter, might have a destructive, even catastrophic impact. No other human institution affords such an opportunity, which is why psychoanalysis is such an important, sacred business. Therefore, as Bion implied, the analyst must be *a mystic*. She is charged with the task of making a place for her own and another person's soul – and for their mutual impact. This provides some answers to the question of whether one could fully realize one's human potential without perceiving the mystical. It seems that, for Eigen, the real answer is no. For him, as well as for Bion, the "psychoanalytic function" of openness to experience, as a position of faith, is an ideal for every human personality, an ideal whose ultimate manifestation is the figure of the analyst/mystic.

The striving for truth and authentic encounter enables the therapeutic couple to traverse hell together. This "together" is what makes such extreme and dangerous acts of faith possible. Therapy, then, is the earthly embodiment of the psalmist's words: "though I walk through the valley of the shadow of death, I will fear no evil; for thou art with me." It is particularly important that, like the psalmist, Eigen does not suggest that evil goes away; it is there, though much less feared when encountered together. He also says that therapy is a holy *business.* Meaning, it does not stop being a business. Materialistic reality does not change, but this does not stop therapy from being holy, either. The mystical act lies in accepting and truly living the paradox: falling in the hands of the living God.

Poetic writing and theory

Eigen is unique in perceiving both the ability to contain complexity and the capacity for intense experiences as essential poles in the dialectic of the mystical and, more generally, of the movement that sustains life. He embraces the Bionian notion of Ps↔D movement and, through his writings, allows us to experience the importance of the Ps part. It is not just something to be tolerated until we achieve integration; rather, it is what gives life its taste, what quenches one's soul. Unlike the Freudian–Kleinian position (at least as Eigen sees it), maturity should not dim experience, even if contextualization might somewhat attenuate its flame. Eigen speaks loudly, even louder than Winnicott, in praise of life's more intense colors.

The problem is that "life" or "psychic life" is like an ocean whose edges are hard to see. Likewise, Eigen's notion of the "mystical" is an immensely vast territory with blurred boundaries. It is difficult to distinguish between the mystical element and other types of experience. Eigen's alternating reference to the mystical as an aspect of the psyche, a type of experience, a position of readiness and an essential structural psychic matrix hinders the attempt to outline a systematic theory of the mystical in psychoanalysis. Eigen is also provocatively honest about his avoidance of definitions and seems to believe that it is not only necessitated by his "mystical" subject matter but is also a merit in itself. Thus, instead of defining the mystical, Eigen offers a phenomenology of the mystical (Eigen and Govrin, 2007) using poetic language, which he finds particularly suitable to psychoanalysis.

But he also has another side, which calls for balance. Eigen (1998) describes two opposite characters: the "everything-at-once or all now individual," who cannot bear the limitations of representation and views any limit or representation as blasphemy, and the fanatic of the reductionist medical model, who embodies the opposite extreme. The psychoanalyst, of course, cannot afford to be either.

The analyst, as well as psychoanalysis as a discipline, should serve as a model of growth through an unending quest for greater knowledge and understanding, while respecting the mystery of reality and one's human limits. Eigen draws a parallel between what takes place in analysis and what happens in the theoretical sphere:

> The analyst models the realization that only uncertain growth is possible. When he tries to communicate with his colleagues, he must struggle to find models for his experience that are not too general or too concrete, not too inclusive or exclusive. A parallel struggle goes on to find intuitive models or images to communicate with patients. Myths of destruction or creation encode processes that go on in a session. Which image is valuable when? What lens, at whatever distance, provides most mileage at a given time? (ibid, p. 67)

We must ask ourselves what would be the most *useful* representation at any given moment? What myth is most helpful? This is a pragmatic and Wittgensteinian view of language as a tool, whose usefulness is context-dependent. Language is not a perfect mirror of reality, since reality is infinitely complex. Nevertheless, the generative power of language is charged with the sacred task of finding words for the soul. These words should serve as a properly focused lens, neither too general and abstract nor too concrete. According to James' criteria for the sentiment of rationality, a good theory should be as faithful as possible to both experience and the need for abstractions, for its "job" is to provide the tools to handle this experience.

Does Eigen meet this pragmatic criterion, which he himself formulates so well in the psychoanalytic context? Govrin (Eigen and Govrin, 2007) points out certain differences between Eigen's more "poetic" books (such as *Ecstasy*, *Rage*, *The Sensitive Self*, *Emotional Storm*) and his more "structured" texts. Eigen replies that the poetic can be found in everything he writes: "form and structure vary in my books, but the poetic thread runs through them. Poetry as a mode of cognition [...] but more than that, a mediator of emotive reality, a creator of expressive reality, part of the evolution of experiential capacity" (p. 59). Eigen's "kind" of psychoanalysis springs, in part, from a poetic impulse (p. 59) and, moreover, he also views his main influences – Bion and Winnicott – as poets of sorts. I believe these comments indicate the kind of place Eigen wishes to occupy in psychoanalytic history: less of a theoretical thinker, and more of a psychoanalytic poet, who profoundly touches experience down to its very bottom and up to its highest peak, opening and cultivating the mystical sensitivity of the therapists who read him, helping them be at-one-with, yet separate from their patients. He sees himself – justifiably, in my opinion – as part of the evolution of psychoanalysis, of its quest to expand its own experiential ability and, through it, that of humanity. Eigen tells both Molino (1997) and Govrin (Eigen and Govrin, 2007) how thankful and moved he was by the hundreds of letters he received from people with whom he had established such intimate, growth-promoting contact.

As one of those people, this chapter, despite its more critical parts, is my way to partake in this gratitude. My first encounter with Eigen's writings was through his paper on "The area of Faith," which helped shape my personal view of psychoanalysis, and was one of the moments that led me to write this book. My second meeting with his texts was even more dramatic: it was with the more poetic *The Sensitive Self*. I was an intern at the time and had just begun my own first (meaningful) therapy as a patient. Reading Eigen's book was uplifting. Though I cannot remember its main ideas (a common problem, I believe, with such "poetic" texts) and though I never re-read that particular book or "analyzed" it, for fear of ruining my initial experience of being moved to my very core, I felt that it deeply resonated with my therapeutic process. Though my own therapist's character seemed to me very different from how I imagined Eigen, I felt that the both of them were treating me, making deeper sense together, giving a new, richer and more reverential meaning to psychoanalytic psychotherapy. In fact, it was the closest I ever got to having a mystical experience by reading a text.

Govrin shares his own experience of Eigen – derived both from reading his texts and meeting him in person. In their interview, he repeatedly tries to elicit structured concepts, definitions or an organized theory from Eigen, but this makes Eigen withdraw and increases the distance between them. Only when Govrin learns to listen to Eigen the way Eigen wanted to be listened to, does something happen. Govrin comes to experience Eigen's transformative power, rather than comprehend his worldview intellectually:

> But as I started meeting Eigen I soon came to realize that talking to him, like reading him, is a transformative experience. If you want to "understand" a therapeutic method, which is embedded in an integrated and structured world view, Michael Eigen is the last psychoanalyst you would think to interview. (ibid, p. xiii)

Despite the importance of poetics – the kind of transformation Govrin and I experienced could not have happened without it – the relative absence of structure might be highly problematic. Govrin summarizes both the virtues and shortcomings of this style with an apt metaphor:

> Borges imagined an empire in which the art of Cartography had gained such perfection that a map was exactly the same size as the area it depicted. Michael Eigen's attempt to mirror experience from inside, to practice a peculiar form of correspondence to experience (in contrast to correspondence to reality), runs the risk of reaching a similar condition. His words do not represent, stand for, or analyze from a distance, but rather authentically convey many living moments. (p. x)

Govrin feels that, with all its emotional power, Eigen's "non-academic" style challenges his communicative channel with his readers/hearers (ibid, xiii). To my mind, Govrin accurately pinpoints the problem facing

Eigen's reader and, more importantly, the problems inherent in his "impact" on the psychoanalytic world. Eigen draws a map that is almost as large as the terrain itself; is it a useful model or only an assortment of evocative pictures – all "art" and no "science?"

The epistemology of faith and pragmatism in Eigen's writings

Eigen expanded psychoanalysis' area of faith. Moreover, he showed psychoanalysis that it *had* one. He claimed that faith is a central premise for any psychoanalytic work and for human growth in general. He showed, both theoretically and through his style, how such psychoanalytic faith should be practiced, offering his readers what James (1890/1950) calls "knowledge of acquaintance" and not only "knowledge about." Eigen creates opportunities for intimate encounters, personal experiences of the "impact" of the Other. We feel Eigen's impact, meet those who impacted and inspired him and become more open to encountering our patients. Yet, also like James, he maintains that both kinds of knowledge are crucial; that we, as therapists, must struggle to represent our experience of that impact as truthfully as possible.

In many ways, Eigen is the embodiment of the well-balanced thinker, who recognizes the unique epistemic status of psychoanalysis – requiring what I termed "pragmatic epistemology of faith." (see chapter 3). The *epistemology of faith* is an epistemic and emotional position towards reality that involves deep trust in the Other and/or the shared process. This trust facilitates openness to the I-Thou encounter as a mystical, Noetic moment in psychotherapy, in which one truly knows the Other and promotes their growth. On the pragmatic side, he adheres to the latter while taking care to secure an anchoring grasp on external reality. He addresses the need to keep the dialogue between "subjective" and "objective," maintaining the precarious, transitional tension between them. According to Eigen, we should keep communicating, searching time and again for a useful language for the soul: a fundamentally pragmatic approach. Furthermore, this approach – in which knowledge springs directly from a reservoir of deeply trusted emotional contact, to which the therapist commits her full attention – is an ethical, almost religious approach to psychotherapy. But it is also an epistemological one. For Eigen, knowing someone is a result of truly encountering them:

> The infinite aspects of time and meaning of every session always give analyst and patient a way out. They may never have to pass through the eye of the same needle. They can always find ways of being somewhere else, of pointing elsewhere, of failing to meet. Even when they want to meet, it is always possible to miss each other. Nevertheless, multiplicity and uncertainty do not completely obliterate impact. Meeting flows from impact [...] The sense of impact is the raw datum analyst and patient have to work with. (1998, p. 67)

Psychoanalytic mysticism is anything but delusional omniscience. It acknowledges that reality is infinitely complex and not-knowing or missing each other is inevitable. Yet, when an I-Thou encounter does occur, in that state of grace enabled by the position of faith, a Noetic element is present, constituting what "real" knowledge we do possess. Every knowledge stems from encounter, all knowledge worth having is the result of mutual impact. It is a "knowledge of acquaintance," raw data that awaits further working-through and representation. This "raw" data must be "cooked" for the benefit of both the particular patient who must digest it and the psychoanalytic community that needs theoretical tools. As a poet, Eigen does not always "fully cook" his concepts. But no one, perhaps, can present the textures, smells and colors of the "raw data" of psychoanalytic experience, can paint so powerful and lively a portrait of it, as this "psychoanalytic mystic."

Eigen and the sentiment of rationality

As we have seen, Eigen does not so much analyze the word mystical as much as sets it free, in the poetic beauty and relative lawlessness of his texts, to tell its own story. In that, he clearly leans towards the detail-oriented rather than abstract tendency in James' formalization of what feels "rational." Though Eigen *does* offer new and, to my mind, extremely important theoretical innovations (the psychotic core, the area of faith, paradoxical monism, the ideal, impact), he seldom seeks to integrate them into a systematic and structured theory.

Another central criterion for the sentiment of rationality is the ability to make predictions. Though any psychoanalytic theory, especially such a "mystical" one, is hard pressed to offer these, Eigen does provide, in my opinion, some key ideas that help navigate the turbulence of a psychoanalytic session. Unlike Bion, Eigen supports his concept of faith with numerous clinical examples and even offers specific technical advice, that I cannot do justice to here. His claim that both unity and separateness are omnipresent axes that are constantly co-creating psychic reality – what he calls the "distinction-union structure" (ibid, p. 35) – certainly helps direct the analyst's interventions. For example, the therapist should not encourage "full" regression to a supposedly undifferentiated state, nor expect his patient to "grow" and become more "adaptive" – an approach that Eigen would probably deem anti-psychoanalytic. Eigen's theory makes it clear that full merger or complete autonomy are impossibilities and that striving to achieve either might lead to one of the two kinds of psychoses he described. Moreover, as a general technical position, since mutual impact is the core of psychoanalytic work, an Eigenian analyst would probably tend to embrace a relational approach, in which such impact is a basic assumption. Such an analyst would look for the aspects of the unique life created by this mutual impact and attempt to both live and represent it.

Though those are not exactly predictive tools, they are orienting guidelines for being in a session. This brings us to what James deemed his most important criterion for the sentiment of rationality: a theory's ability to encourage agency, a feeling of meaningful involvement or, in Eigenian terms, impact. In the Eigenian world of mystical encounters, where everyone remains separate while having the potential to deeply touch each other, the unique individuality of both participants is critical. Paradoxically, precisely because the therapist is *not* omniscient, she has the potential for truly "knowing" the patient and achieving transformative impact.

Surprisingly, this more egalitarian position enables both the analyst and analysis to wield great power, even on a numinous level. The analyst's unique personality, her openness to multifaceted, multilayered contact with her patient and her ability to make time and place for processing this impact are the factors that promote personality growth or even post-catastrophe rebirth. One should keep in mind that even the analyst's face, as both the unified gestalt of her unique being and a portal to the ideal, may trigger a transformative mystical experience. Truly being there – in the session – facing the patient (with one's unique face) and encountering everything that comes up – truly works. Unlike Ogden, Eigen does not think that every passing sensation in a session informs the analytic process. Therapist and patient might move in opposite directions and miss each other. The feelings of the therapist are critical, but they are far from being a magic mirror. And yet, both parties *know*, because they feel it with all their being and all their might, whenever and wherever true contact occurs.

Eigen paints a Janus-faced psyche that reflects a Janus-faced universe. Reality is both destructive and creative, pluralistic and unified. We are all mystics capable of embracing this paradox and we all have a psychotic core, for this precariously held tension crumbles time and again, taking us with it. Some of us feel the need to constantly choose sides and thus become ill; sometimes, society itself becomes ill. The human task of gazing at the numinous and surviving is almost impossible, yet it is our "job" as humans and especially as analysts.

Whereas Ogden fleshes out our hidden unity with (alongside our separateness from) our patients and gives us the tools to work with it, Eigen imbues us with its numinous power, showing us that not only man, but human connection as well, was made in God's image (indeed, in that part of the creation story in Genesis, God suddenly speaks in the plural: "let us make man in our image"). Like Bollas, Eigen recognizes the great mystery of Otherness, but for him the deepest intimacy is no less real. Meeting God, meeting oneself or, in other words, engaging in a mystical/psychoanalytic encounter means living on reality's troubling seams, on its fringes. But, in such encounters, instead of falling into the abyss, the fabric of reality is recreated, healed.

With Eigen, the therapist is once again simply a fallible person: in his version of the psychic overlap paradigm, the "third" area, where psyches meet, does not grant us complete access to Otherness; the unconscious is not numinously knowledgeable as it is for Bollas. And yet, it is in this very humanity that divinity lies. Mystical contact carries the divine spark of creativity, self and even world-making.

Conclusion – The fate of the messianic idea

Eigen is a paradoxical thinker in a paradoxical time. He is a well-known and well-liked author, who is also a strange bird, even in these pluralistic times, much of whose thinking is perceived as either an avant-garde performance or erratic musings. This leaves open the option of considering his notion of the mystical element as yet another personal quirk, not to be taken literally.

Phillips (1993) sees Eigen as positioned at a crucial historical cross-road, "between the prefoliation of fringe therapies and an increasingly militant psychoanalytic orthodoxy" (p. xiv). I would add that he is also situated at a historically curious time, which sees the coexistence of the orthodox rejection of the mystical *and* an over-pluralistic, "everything goes" approach that welcomes almost everything, without setting systematic criteria or seriously examining mystical ideas. In Philips' opinion, Eigen may be showing us how to write in continuity with the idolized figures who created psychoanalysis, while remaining truly original; how to adore without submitting. One might wonder whether Eigen himself should be considered one of these founding figures, an author who introduced a new psychoanalytic revolution beyond those of Winnicott and Bion. Is he such a new genius, the herald of a messianic idea, challenging the psychoanalytic establishment to either transform itself or turn away from the truth and reject the messiah? On the back cover of *The Psychoanalytic Mystic*, Philips argues that:

> At a time when contemporary psychoanalysis asks us, with insufficient irony, to choose between sexuality and relationships, Michael Eigen [...] adds the third term that might make the debate intelligible again. It is mysticism – not exactly sexuality, not quite aggression – which is the unacceptable in psychoanalysis. It is the mystic – as both external and internal object – that is the true critic of psychoanalysis.

For both Philips and myself, Eigen represents continuity as well as revolution. He engages in standard, cumulative "science" (being a Bionian and a Winnicottian) *and* represents the beginning of a paradigm shift (Kuhn, 1962) by offering a new integration of these two thinkers through his creative mysticism of separateness and union. This conceptualization is a new idea about the working mechanism and the deep meaning of psychoanalysis – both its "how" and its "why."

The mystic is an external and internal object (the Otherness inside and outside of us) that undermines psychoanalysis' view of itself. Eigen is both a "real" figure, presenting theories that have their own substantial value, and a critic – representing a subversive outlook on well-established psychoanalytic thought. Indeed, it seems that, until now, the mystical challenge, similarly posed by the writings of the canonical figures of psychoanalysis – Freud, Winnicott and Bion – remains unassimilated and far from worked-through by the psychoanalytic community. The mystical has not been taken seriously enough and not just because of the psychoanalytic community's lack of openness or lack of "irony," when it asks us to choose between different poles of experience, as Philips so aptly put it. An equally valid reason is that mystics like Eigen have not provided a sufficiently structured theory, leaving this task to the "establishment."

However, arguing that a different style could have achieved more in terms of the status of the mystical element – regarding either the politics of psychoanalytic ideas or its theoretical understanding among psychoanalysts – is mere speculation. It stands to reason that in other aspects, those of intimately introducing the mystical and making it an emotionally meaningful concept, a more systematic style would have achieved less. Yet, there is little doubt in my mind that the greatest contemporary champion of the mystical element, leaves quite a bit of work to his readers in terms of processing his vision. To sum up this vision, I prefer Eigen's own words:

> The need to learn more about the intricate comminglings of the sense of self, the Infinite, social, and materialistic realties invites reasoned vision and hard work. [...] We cannot afford a naïve approach to either the mystical or the practical sides of life. Neither is going to go away. (1993b, p. 212)

This book had been an attempt to process this vision: to couple mysticism and pragmatism, to give words to that which refused to go away and resurfaced time and again, in many different psychoanalytic concepts, to offer a unifying theoretical structure for these manifestations and promote greater self-awareness of our basic assumptions as psychoanalytic therapists. To claim that we must make room for the psychoanalytic need for applicable theories while respecting the mystery of psychoanalysis which, despite all this effort – never went away.

References

Barnard, G.W. (1997). *Exploring Unseen Worlds: William James and the Philosophy of Mysticism*. Albany, NY: State University of New York Press.

Bollas, C. (2007). *The Freudian Moment*. London: Karnac.

Eigen, M. (1981). The area of faith in Winnicott, Lacan and Bion. *International Journal of Psycho-Analysis*, 62:413–433.

Eigen, M. (1993a). In A. Phillips (Ed.), *The Electrified Tightrope*. Northvale, New Jersey: Jason Aronson Inc.

Eigen, M. (1993b). *The Psychotic Core*. New York: Karnac.

Eigen, M. (1998). *The Psychoanalytic Mystic*. London & New York: Free Association Books.

Eigen, M. (1999). Afterward. In S.A. Mitchell and L. Aron (Eds.), *Relational Psychoanalysis: The Emergence of a Tradition* (pp. 36–37). New York & London: The Analytic Press.

Eigen, M. (2012). *Kabbalah and Psychoanalysis*. London: Karnac.

Eigen, M. and Govrin, A. (2007). *Conversations with Michael Eigen*. London: Karnac Books.

Ghent, E. (1999). Masochism, submission and surrender: Masochism as perversion of surrender. In S.A. Mitchell and L. Aron (Eds.), *Relational Psychoanalysis: The Emergence of a Tradition* (pp. 211–242). New York and London: The Analytic Press. (Original work published 1990).

James, W. (1950). *The Principles of Psychology*. New York: Dover. (Original work published 1890).

James, W. (1987a). A pluralistic universe. In Bruce Kuklick (Ed.), *William James Writings 1902–1910* (pp. 627–819). New York: The Library of America. (Original work Published 1909).

James, W. (1987b). Pragmatism. In Bruce Kuklick (Ed.), *William James Writings 1902–1910* (pp. 481–624). New York: The Library of America. (Original work Published 1907).

Kuhn, T. (1962). *The Structure of Scientific Revolutions*. Chicago: The University of Chicago Press.

Mitchell, S.A. and Aron, L. (1999). Editors' Introduction. In *Relational Psychoanalysis: The Emergence of a Tradition* (pp. 1–2). New York & London: The Analytic Press.

Molino, A. (1997). Michael Eigen. In Antony Molino (Ed.), *Freely Associated* (pp. 93–126). London & New York: Free Association Books.

Ogden, T.H. (1994). The analytic third: Working with intersubjective clinical facts. *The International Journal of Psycho Analysis*, 75:3–19.

Phillips, A. (1993) Introduction. In Adam Philips (Ed.), *The Electrified Tightrope* (pp. xiii–xvi). Northvale, New Jersey: Jason Aronson Inc.

Conclusion

This long voyage has exposed different views of the mystical in psychoanalysis – from an "oceanic" merger to a full I–Thou connection. It has traced different attitudes towards it – from fear and dissociative splitting, through various forms of disregard/repression and the "return of the repressed," to full recognition (Bion) and even provocative celebration (Eigen). Now that the journey has come to an end, one wonders what can be said to unite all these facets of the mystical? What is the mystical in psychoanalysis and why is it important for us to recognize it?

The mystical in psychoanalysis is the mystery that is paradoxically inherent in intimate human encounter. It is the mystery of unity and separateness (involving, as we have seen, vastly different mixtures of the two), which is the transformative power of psychoanalysis. The numinous feeling of transformation and rebirth through connection to an other who is also deeply intimate. It is knowing something about someone else with every fiber of your being, yet also knowing that they *are* someone else and thus unreachable in their otherness. In the context of the analyst's position, it means holding the paradox of simultaneously trusting your intuition and being able to doubt your interpretation of it.[1]

The *psychic overlap paradigm* suggested in this book argues that we have areas of overlap and areas of separateness. However, it might sometimes be very difficult to distinguish true intuition from the products of our hopes, fears and desires – even more so, because these are always touched by those of the other. As Ogden stated, everything is influenced by the third, yet everyone is also an individual, both

DOI: 10.4324/9781003200796-102

physically and psychologically. In fact, the third relies on autonomous individuals for its creation (save perhaps for its subjecting form, which does not produce growth-promoting contact). In the Bionian sense, it means that there might be truth even in what is mostly a "lie" and vice-versa.

Despite being inherently confusing, this overlap is our most powerful tool. I believe that this is how therapy works. Another paradox is that everyone knows this, but it nevertheless remains unacknowledged as a basic assumption. Theoretical or clinical discussions of this overlap (Ogden's, for example) seldom acknowledge its mystical overtones. I believe that this potential mystical foundation is why the psychic overlap paradigm has remained an unacknowledged assumption for so long.

A vast majority of analysts would agree that the existence of the unconscious is the fundamental assumptions of any psychoanalytic theory. This usually entails the further assumption that the unconscious communicates and is unconsciously understood. Still, the recognition of bi-lateral *unconscious communication* (let alone unconscious overlap) as basic working assumption of psychoanalysis has lagged behind. Likewise, many contemporary psychoanalytic therapists would agree that psychoanalysis is a transformative encounter and may accept Winnicott's statement that its power springs from therapist and patient "living an experience together." However, this is not the same as acknowledging that – underlying our technique and practice and at the very core of our theory – is the assumption that we are not truly separate from our patients, that this is how we sometimes "know" things that were never said, through our famous psychoanalytic "intuition."

By tracing the footsteps of the theoreticians who shed light on this phenomenon, from Freud to Ogden and Eigen, I hope to contribute to psychoanalysis' quest for self-knowledge. I believe that fully recognizing our hidden assumptions will further crystalize both our theory and practice. As I tried to demonstrate throughout this book, what we tell ourselves about how we know things and about how transformation occurs – in short, our beliefs about the "active ingredient" in psychoanalysis – have a profound impact on our freedom of thought and action. They change the way we listen to the patient and to ourselves, the degree to which we trust our feelings, our awareness of our limitations and how we create or read theory.

This brings us to the second question this book addresses: what is the epistemological status of psychoanalysis? Again, to some extent, everyone knows the answer. I believe it is impossible to work analytically without what I term *the epistemology of faith*: trusting the mutual process, what comes up in the encounter, as a primary source of both information and growth; "knowing" things by experiencing them, by "becoming O." On the other hand, a responsible therapist must be pragmatic. She does not rely on her feeling alone but remains grounded in the context of the overt "text" of the patient's words and gestures and in visible results: actual changes in the patient's lived experience and in the quality of the analytic relationship (such as greater freedom of association or playfulness).

Here, again, we encounter a paradox. Although everyone "knows" this, it is still hard to communicate it to the "outside" world, which time and again puts psychoanalysis on the spot by posing a question that has long-since become an internal persecutory object: is psychoanalysis a science or part of the humanities? It feels as if refusing to "choose sides" amounts to condemning psychoanalysis to the worst fate of all – being a pseudo-science. As Klein argued, feelings of persecution are assuaged by integration, by knowing that both sides are part of us. I believe that, by acknowledging that our "knowledge" draws on faith and intuition as well as pragmatic criteria, the science versus hermeneutics debate would stop being so tormenting. Moreover, it might become an enriching dialectic tension in psychoanalytic thought. Making our unconscious assumptions conscious may help us further rethink and develop our meta-theory, whereas abjected, hidden assumptions, have a smaller chance of evolving.

To my mind, fully embracing Winnicott's paradox – that we should never ask the baby whether its special object is a discovery or a creation – means applying it to psychoanalysis as well. Not because it is an "infant" discipline, but because its "object" will forever live in the twilight zone – discovered (originating in the patient) but also (jointly) created in the special form of encounter instituted by Freud. The only way of owning this *transitional epistemology* to the outside, in non psychoanalytic circles, entails the introspective understanding that this is what we do: we deal with "magic," with the mystical force of the human encounter, with immaterial experiences. Nevertheless, we are constantly redefining this magic, developing adequate tools and interpretations for working with it – all of which should be pragmatically justified and satisfy our sentiment of rationality. Once again paraphrasing Eigen, neither the practical nor the mystical side of life is going away; it is up to us to construct a new vision that allows us to work with both.

Note

1 I dealt more extensively with the subject of intuition and doubt elsewhere; see Bar Nes (2019a, 2019b).

References

Bar Nes, A. (2019a). Sense and sensibility: The psychoanalytic mystic and the interpretive words. In A. Fechler (Ed.), *Feeling the Elephant: The Blind Spots of Psychoanalytic Psychotherapists* (pp. 175–216). Jerusalem: Carmel. [Hebrew]

Bar Nes, A. (2019b, June 20–23). On imagining one's patient: Between the imaginary and the intuitive [Conference presentation]. 2019 IARPP conference, Tel Aviv, Israel.

Index

Printed in the United States
by Baker & Taylor Publisher Services